FUNDAMENTALS OF CASE MANAGEMENT PRACTICE

Skills for the Human Services

Third Edition

Nancy Summers
Harrisburg Area Community College

Australia • Brazil • Japan • Korea • Mexico • Singapore • Spain • United Kingdom • United States

BROOKS/COLE
CENGAGE Learning

Fundamentals of Case Management Practice, Skills for the Human Services, Third edition
Nancy Summers

Acquisitions Editor: Seth Dobrin

Assistant Editor: Christina Ganim

Editorial Assistant: Ashley Cronin

Technology Project Manager: Andrew Keay

Marketing Manager: Karin Sandberg

Marketing Coordinator: Ting Jian Yap

Marketing Communications Manager: Shemika Britt

Project Manager, Editorial Production: Rita Jaramillo

Creative Director: Rob Hugel

Art Directors: Vernon Boes, Caryl Gorska

Print Buyer: Rebecca Cross

Text Permissions Editor: Mollika Basu

Production Service: Matrix Productions

Copy Editor: Kay Mikel

Cover Designer: The Resource Agency

Cover Image: Getty Images

Compositor: Integra

© 2009, 2006 Brooks/Cole, Cengage Learning

ALL RIGHTS RESERVED. No part of this work covered by the copyright herein may be reproduced, transmitted, stored or used in any form or by any means graphic, electronic, or mechanical, including but not limited to photocopying, recording, scanning, digitizing, taping, Web distribution, information networks, or information storage and retrieval systems, except as permitted under Section 107 or 108 of the 1976 United States Copyright Act, without the prior written permission of the publisher.

> For product information and technology assistance, contact us at
> **Cengage Learning Customer & Sales Support, 1-800-354-9706**
>
> For permission to use material from this text or product, submit all requests online at **cengage.com/permissions**.
> Further permissions questions can be e-mailed to **permissionrequest@cengage.com**.

Library of Congress Control Number: 2007937455

Student Edition:

ISBN-13: 978-0-495-50147-3

ISBN-10: 0-495-50147-6

Brooks/Cole
10 Davis Drive
Belmont, CA 94002-3098
USA

Cengage Learning is a leading provider of customized learning solutions with office locations around the globe, including Singapore, the United Kingdom, Australia, Mexico, Brazil, and Japan. Locate your local office at **international.cengage.com/region**.

Cengage Learning products are represented in Canada by Nelson Education, Ltd.

For your course and learning solutions, visit **academic.cengage.com**.

Purchase any of our products at your local college store or at our preferred online store **www.ichapters.com**.

Printed in the United States of America
1 2 3 4 5 6 7 12 11 10 09 08

*To my parents, whose humor and wisdom about people and relationships
formed the foundation for my work with others*

Contents

Preface   xii

Section 1 Foundations for Best Practice in Case Management

Chapter 1   Ethics and Other Professional Responsibilities for Human Service Workers   1

Introduction   1
Dual Relationships   2
Value Conflicts   5
Clients' Rights   9
Privileged Communication   18
Diagnostic Labeling   21
Involuntary Commitment   22
Ethical Responsibility   23
Stealing from Clients   26
Competence   27
Responsibility to Your Colleagues and the Profession   28
Professional Responsibility   30
Summary   31
Exercises: Ethics   31
Exercises: Ethically, What Went Wrong?   34
Exercise: Decide on the Best Course of Action   38

Chapter 2   Case Management: Definition and Responsibilities   39

Introduction   39
A History of Case Management   40
Why Case Management?   40
What Is an Individualized Plan?   41
Assessment   42
Planning   44
Linking   48
Monitoring   49
Service Coordination   49
Levels of Case Management   52
Separating Case Management from Therapy   55

Case Management in Provider Agencies   56
Managed Care and Case Management   57
Underlying Principles: Hope and Self-Determination   58
Generic Case Management   62
Summary   63
Exercises: Case Management   63
Exercises: Decide on the Best Course of Action   67

Chapter 3   Applying the Ecological Model: A Theoretical Foundation for Human Services   69

Introduction   69
Seeking a Balanced View of the Client   70
The Three Levels   72
Looking at What the Person Brings   72
Looking at What the Context Brings   73
Developmental Transitions   74
Developing the Interventions   75
Working with the Generalist Approach   76
Larger Interventions   77
Summary   77
Exercise: Looking at Florence's Problem on Three Levels   77
Exercises: Designing Three Levels of Intervention   79

Section 2   Useful Clarifications and Attitudes

Chapter 4   Cultural Competence   83

Introduction   83
Where Are the Differences?   84
Strangers   86
Anxiety and Uncertainty   87
Thoughtless Versus Thoughtful Communication   89
Dimensions of Culture   92
Obstacles to Understanding   98
Competence   100
Summary   102
Exercises: Testing Your Cultural Competence   102

Chapter 5   Attitudes and Boundaries   105

Introduction   105
Understanding Attitudes   105
Basic Helping Attitudes   106
Reality   109
How Clients Are Discouraged   109
Understanding Boundaries   112
Seeing Yourself and the Client as Completely Separate Individuals   112
Erecting Detrimental Boundaries   113
Transference and Countertransference   114
Summary   115
Exercises: Demonstrating Warmth, Genuineness, and Empathy   116
Exercises: Recognizing the Difference—Encouragement or Discouragement   120
Exercises: Blurred Boundaries   120

Chapter 6   Clarifying Who Owns the Problem   123

     Introduction   123
     If the Client Owns the Problem   124
     If You Own the Problem   127
     If You Both Own the Problem   127
     Summary   128
     Exercises: Who Owns the Problem?   129
     Exercises: Making the Strategic Decision   131

Section 3   *Effective Communication*

Chapter 7   Identifying Good Responses and Poor Responses   135

     Introduction   135
     Twelve Roadblocks to Communication   136
     Useful Responses   140
     Summary   148
     Exercises: Identifying Roadblocks   148

Chapter 8   Listening and Responding   151

     Introduction   151
     Defining Reflective Listening   152
     Responding to Feelings   152
     Responding to Content   156
     Positive Reasons for Reflective Listening   158
     Points to Remember   158
     Summary   160
     Exercise: How Many Feelings Can You Name?   160
     Exercises: Finding the Right Feeling   160
     Exercises: Reflective Listening   161

Chapter 9   Asking Questions   167

     Introduction   167
     When Questions Are Important   168
     Closed Questions   168
     Open Questions   168
     Questions that Make the Client Feel Uncomfortable   170
     A Formula for Asking Open Questions   171
     Summary   173
     Exercises: What Is Wrong with These Questions?   174
     Exercises: Which Question Is Better?   176
     Exercises: Opening Closed Questions   176
     Exercises: Try Asking Questions   179

Chapter 10   Bringing Up Difficult Issues   181

     Introduction   181
     When to Use Confrontation   182
     The I-Message in Confrontation   183
     The Rules for Confrontation   184
     Asking Permission to Share Ideas   188
     Confronting Collaterals   189
     On Not Becoming Overbearing   189
     Summary   191

Exercises: What Is Wrong Here?   191
Exercises: Expressing Your Concern   193
Exercises: Expressing a Stronger Message   195

Chapter 11   Addressing and Disarming Anger   197

Introduction   197
Common Reasons for Anger   197
Why Disarming Anger Is Important   198
Avoiding the Number-One Mistake   199
Erroneous Expectations for Perfect Communication   200
The Four-Step Process   201
What You Do Not Want to Do   203
Look for Useful Information   205
Managing an Angry Outburst   205
Summary   206
Exercises: Initial Responses to Anger   206
Exercises: Practicing Disarming   207

Chapter 12   The Effective Combination of Skills   209

Introduction   209
Combining Skills and Attitudes   210
Communication Skills That Facilitate Change   211
Trapping the Client   216
From Adversarial to Collaborative   217
Case Manager Traps   219
Summary   222

Chapter 13   Putting It All Together   223

Introduction   223
Exercises: Putting It All Together   223

Section 4   *Meeting Clients and Assessing Their Strengths and Needs*

Chapter 14   Documenting Initial Inquiries   231

Introduction   231
Guidelines for Filling Out Forms   232
Steps for Filling Out the New Referral or Inquiry Form   232
Steps for Preparing the Verification of Appointment Form   236
Summary   237
Exercise: Intake of a Middle-Aged Adult   238
Exercise: Intake of a Child   238
Exercise: Intake of an Infirm, Older Person   238

Chapter 15   The First Interview   241

Introduction   241
Your Role   241
The Client's Understanding   242
Preparing for the First Interview   242
Your Office   243
Meeting the Client   244
Taking Notes   245
Collecting the Information   245

Asking for More Clarification   245
What Information to Collect   246
Client Expectations   246
Social Histories and Forms   247
Wrapping Up   247
The Client Leaves   248
Summary   248

Chapter 16   Social Histories and Assessment Forms   249

Introduction   249
What Is a Social History?   250
Layout of the Social History   250
How to Ask What You Need to Know   251
Capturing the Details   257
Who Took the Social History   258
Social Histories in Other Settings   258
Writing Brief Social Histories   262
Using an Assessment Form   266
Taking Social Histories on a Computer   267
The Next Step   267
Summary   268
Exercises: Practice with Social Histories   268
Exercises: Assessment of a Middle-Aged Adult   269
Exercises: Assessment of a Child   269
Exercises: Assessment of an Infirm, Older Person   270
Exercise: Creating a File   271

Chapter 17   Using the DSM   273

Introduction   273
Background Information   275
Using the DSM   278
Making the Code   284
Summary   286
Exercises: Using the *DSM*   287

Chapter 18   The Mental Status Examination   291

Introduction   291
What to Observe   292
How to Observe   292
Documenting Your Observations   292
Mental Status Examination Outline   293
Summary   309
Exercises: Using the MSE Vocabulary   310

Chapter 19   Receiving and Releasing Information   313

Introduction   313
Sending for Information   313
If You Release Information   313
Directions for Using Release Forms   314
Examples of the Release Forms   316
When the Client Wants You to Release Information   317
When the Material Is Received   318
Summary   319
Exercise: Send for Information Related to a Middle-Aged Adult   319

Exercise: Send for Information Related to a Child   319
Exercise: Send for Information Related to a Frail, Older Person   319
Exercise: Maintaining Your Charts   319

Chapter 20   Facilitating a Meaningful Change and Recovery   321

Introduction   321
How People Do Not Change or Recover   322
What Is Change?   322
What Is Recovery?   323
Physical Health Is Part of Wellness   324
Self-Determination   324
Relationships that Support Recovery   324
Encouragement as Part of Recovery   326
Stages of Change   330
A Case History   331
Ambivalence and Reluctance   333
Rolling with Resistance   333
Summary   334
Exercises: Helping People Change   335

Section 5   Developing a Plan with the Client

Chapter 21   Developing a Service Plan at the Case Management Unit   337

Introduction   337
Involving the Client and the Family   338
Using the Assessment   339
Creating the Treatment or Service Plan   340
How to Identify the Client's Strengths   341
Individualized Planning   342
Sample Goal Plan   343
Summary   346
Exercises: Broad Goal Planning   346

Chapter 22   Preparing for a Service Planning Conference or Disposition Planning Meeting   349

Introduction   349
What You Will Need to Bring to the Meeting   350
Goals for the Meeting   350
Preparing to Present Your Case   351
Making the Presentation   352
Collaboration   354
Follow-Up to Meeting   354
Summary   355
Exercises: Planning   355

Chapter 23   Making the Referral and Assembling the Record   357

Introduction   357
Determining Dates   358
Sample Referral Notification Form   359
The Face Sheet   359
Summary   362
Exercises: Assembling the Record   363

Chapter 24 Documentation and Recording   365
- Introduction 365
- Writing Contact Notes 366
- Labeling the Contact 367
- Documenting Service Monitoring 367
- Documentation: The Finishing Touches 368
- Government Requirements 371
- Do Not Be Judgmental 372
- Distinguish Between Facts and Impressions 372
- Give a Balanced Picture of Your Client 373
- Provide Evidence of Agreement 373
- Making Changes to the Plan 373
- Summary 374
- Exercises: Recording Your Meeting with the Client 374
- Exercises: Recording Client Contacts 375
- Exercises: Using Government Guidelines to Correct Errors 380
- Exercises: Spotting Recording Errors 381

Section 6 Monitoring Services and Following the Client

Chapter 25 Monitoring the Services or Treatment   383
- Introduction 383
- What Is Monitoring? 384
- Purpose of Monitoring 384
- Collaboration 386
- Leave the Office 386
- Responding to a Crisis 387
- Follow-Up 388
- Summary 388

Chapter 26 Developing Goals and Objectives at the Provider Agency   391
- Introduction 391
- Client Participation/Collaboration 392
- Expect Positive Outcomes 392
- Writing the Goals 393
- Objectives 394
- Combining Goals and Treatment Objectives 394
- Finishing Touches 396
- Summary 398
- Exercises: Developing Goals and Objectives 400

Chapter 27 Terminating the Case   407
- Introduction 407
- A Successful Termination 408
- The Discharge Summary 410
- Summary 413
- Exercises: Termination of a Middle-Aged Adult 413
- Exercises: Termination of a Child 414
- Exercises: Termination of a Frail, Older Person 414

Chapter 28 Taking Care of Yourself   415
- Introduction 415
- See Yourself as an Effective Tool 415

    While Attempting to Understand Others, Don't Fail to Understand
        Yourself   416
    Consistently Underestimating Clients Wears Workers Out   417
    Develop Healthy Relationships Away from the Agency   420
    Develop Other Stimulating and Rewarding Interests   421
    Summary   421

Appendix A   Wildwood Case Management Unit Forms   423

    Arrangement of the Client's Chart   423
    Face Sheet   424
    New Referral or Inquiry   425
    Verification of Appointment   426
    Request/Release of Information   427
    Release of HIV/AIDS–Related Information   428
    Intake Assessment Form   429
    Peer Support Services Referral Form   436
    Peer Support Mutual Agreements Plan/Outcome Report and Renewal   437
    Planning Conference Notes   441
    Treatment or Goal Plan   442
    Referral Notification Form   444
    Contact Notes   445
    Contact Notes: Children's Case Management Services   446
    Discharge Summary   447

Appendix B   Work Samples   449

    Examples of Progress Notes or Contact Notes   449
    Dating Your Forms   451
    Sample Cases with Service Plans   453

Appendix C   Grading the Final Files   455

References   458

Index   460

Preface

In a small nonprofit agency handling cases of domestic violence, a woman answers the phone. She assesses the caller's concerns, accurately notes the caller's ambivalence on the inquiry record, and readily connects the caller to the person most able to assist.

Down the street a young man acting as a case aide in a mental health center handles calls from clients assigned to the case managers. He competently notes the callers' mental status, and he asks the questions he knows will give him information that doctors and therapists will need later as they work with these callers. His notes are clear and useful.

How long did it take these two people to acquire these skills? Did they acquire this ability well after being hired in a social service agency, or did they arrive with a clear degree of competence?

Purpose

For me and for students, the issue has been how we can teach the skills that will promote their walking from the classroom into the social service setting with confidence. How can we be assured that students, often steeped in sound theoretical knowledge, will be able to fill out an inquiry form or make a referral effectively?

In addition, it is important to equip students with the vocabulary and methods used by more advanced professionals in the human service field. Although entry-level individuals would not usually give a *DSM* diagnosis, it is useful for individuals entering the field to be knowledgeable about what such a diagnosis is and what is meant by an Axis I or Axis II diagnosis. In this way, conversations among professionals will not be misunderstood.

Today individuals with a sparse education or with recent college degrees are finding themselves thrust immediately into roles for which they have had little formal training. It is important, therefore, to find a method for teaching the actual human service experience at the entry level. *Fundamentals of Case Management*

Practice: Skills for the Human Services, third edition, seeks to provide that experience in a thorough, step-by-step process that leads the reader from intake through monitoring to termination.

New in the Third Edition

New material has been added to this third edition to bring the textbook up to date. Added to this edition:

- Additional ethical considerations
- Expanded information on the recovery model
- Information on self-determination and how to apply it
- How to write impressions and recommendations
- How to write brief social histories
- A new chapter on the change process
- A new chapter on burnout and stress
- In the appendix, new forms for using peer support
- In the appendix, examples of contact notes
- In the appendix, case examples and service plans
- In the appendix, directions for dating forms
- In the appendix, checklist for grading final files

In addition, a number of items specifically requested by our reviewers were added to the textbook.

Fundamentals for Practice with High Risk Populations (Summers, 2002) has been published as an adjunct to this text, giving students information and scenarios on populations in which they are interested or with whom they intend to work. Chapters cover topics such as case management with children and their families, survivors of rape and violence, older people, issues with drug and alcohol dependence, and mental illness and mental retardation. Each chapter is replete with information about specific populations, and provides exercises and intake forms. This textbook also contains a set of forms that can be copied (see the Appendix). These forms, taken from actual social service settings, give the reader an opportunity to practice accuracy and skill in handling social service forms and records and in organizing information.

If you do not wish to cover all of the populations discussed in the text on high-risk populations and instead want to focus on specific populations, you can order individual chapters from *Fundamentals for Practice with High Risk Populations* (Summers, 2002). Please visit http://www.textchoice2.com to view chapters online and to build your custom text. You can pick chapters about specific populations and create individualized booklets that you can bundle with this text. If you would like more information about custom options, please contact your local customer service representative. You can locate your representative by using our rep finder at http://custom.cengage.com.

Format

For each chapter in the workbook, basic information is laid out, followed in most chapters by many exercises that prompt the reader to handle real issues and practice real skills. As readers progress through the text, they gradually assemble files on specific cases. Students can create and monitor believable fictional clients using one of the high-risk populations discussed in *Fundamentals for Practice with High Risk Populations* (Summers, 2002). Classroom discussions about these cases and the best disposition for each of them are not unlike the discussions that occur every day in a variety of social service settings.

Organization of the Textbook

The organization of the textbook follows a logical progression, beginning with the most basic foundation for good practice, moving to what is in the student's mind about other people, followed by what the student will say to others. The second half of the book follows a similar process, beginning with the clients' first contacts and their assessment and planning through all the case management procedures to termination.

In Section 1, "Foundations for Best Practice in Case Management," readers are introduced to important foundation pieces for this field. Ethics and ethical issues, the reasons for case management, and the importance of the ecological model in assessment and planning give readers an introduction to professional basics.

In Section 2, "Useful Clarification and Attitudes," readers are invited to examine what in their thinking will impede effective helping in the social service setting. Beginning with issues of cultural diversity and moving to the role of personal attitudes and boundaries, this section concludes with information and exercises related to determining who owns the problem. Each chapter in this section contains exercises encouraging readers to examine realistically their own attitudes and judgments.

Section 3, "Effective Communication," begins by introducing the reader to good and poor responses, with exercises that help students see the consequences of poor communication. Chapters on listening and responding, asking questions, bringing up difficult issues, responding to emotions, confronting problematic behavior, and disarming anger are included. The section ends with a chapter on the effective application of what students have just learned and exercises designed to have students practice all the communication skills in order to smooth out the communication and allow it to become natural and responsive.

In Section 4, "Meeting Clients and Assessing Their Strengths and Needs," readers begin to take inquiries for services. Forms are provided that ask for basic information, teaching the student what is important to find out in that first call. This section also includes a chapter on preparing for the first interview, helping the reader become sensitive to issues that clients might have at a first meeting. A chapter on social histories and assessment forms teaches students how to use these to assemble relevant information. Introductions to the *DSM* and to the mental status examination allow the reader to become familiar with the vocabulary and the information most important to other professionals in the human service field. Students are encouraged to begin noting how a person seems to them at the time of contact. The chapters and classroom discussions will help students pin down what is important to note. In this section, readers also practice completing release of information forms for the clients they have developed in the classroom setting, mastering which records are useful and which are not. A new chapter on planning for meaningful change rounds out this section.

Section 5, "Developing a Plan with the Client," allows readers to further develop a plan for those clients for whom they have created phone inquiries. Here, individually or in planning teams, according to the instructor's process, students develop realistic plans for their clients. A chapter is included instructing students on how to prepare for and participate in team planning. In the final chapters, students refer cases to providers of services and learn about documentation and recording.

Section 6, "Monitoring Services and Following the Client," is the final section, and it begins with a chapter on monitoring services and treatment. Students switch to the role of a worker in the agency of a provider of service and take the general goals given them by case managers and develop specific goals and objectives to be accomplished within stipulated time lines. In this section, readers also learn the importance of monitoring cases from a case management perspective, how to terminate the case, and the importance of self-care by the worker to avoid burnout. Numerous documentation exercises provide opportunities for students to begin writing professional notes and keeping good records.

To the Students

It is always a challenge to know what skills and information you will need on the first day of your first job. Even when you are already working in the field and managing many of the tasks well, you often do not know for certain why agencies choose to do things one way as opposed to another. This textbook seeks to empower you to be able to function competently and to know why you are proceeding or should be proceeding with clients in a particular way.

In *Fundamentals of Case Management Practice*, you will follow a specific series of steps, beginning with what you are thinking and how to think ethically in client–worker relationships, continuing through your communication with clients, and ending with your putting together hypothetical case files and managing those hypothetical cases.

Throughout the course you will find yourself in discussions with others about possible treatment or service plans or the dynamics of a person's situation. Use these discussions to learn more about collaboration and to increase your ability to participate in the same sort of discussions in the agency where you will work.

Many students have taken this textbook to work with them and have found it both useful and realistic. Students have contributed their experiences on the job to make this textbook replicate as nearly as possible the issues and concerns you will encounter in your work with other people.

Further, in developing your hypothetical clients, you may want to refer to *Fundamentals for Practice with High Risk Populations* (Summers, 2002). In that textbook, six populations commonly served by social services, such as those with domestic violence, substance abuse, or mental health issues, are detailed so that you will be very familiar with their issues and likely problems. It is also possible to purchase individual chapters from that textbook on the population or populations that interest you. Each chapter will give you information on common problems, diagnoses, medications, treatments, and other considerations such as legal issues or common medical problems each specific population often experiences. See the instructions on how to order specific chapters in the earlier section of this Preface titled "New in the Third Edition."

To the Instructor: Suggestions for Using This Text

This text can be used to take students step by step through the case management process outside of the often harried and pressured atmosphere of a real social service agency. When the student is ultimately confronted with the actual situation, the routine and expectations will not be new. Chapters are broken down into each step in the process. Students progress according to their skill levels, finally creating cases and caseloads with you acting as the supervisor, much as a supervisor would act in an actual agency. Without the urgency, you will have time to let students look up information, discuss possible diagnoses, and develop sound interventions under your guidance. For example, exercises on the *DSM* and on the mental status examination have a number of possible answers. Your discussion with your students, similar to the discussions that take place in agencies about these possibilities, is more important than the actual answers that are chosen.

Most chapters include exercises to help students practice their skills. Often several versions of the same exercise are provided. It is useful to students to begin in small groups to address the issues posed in the exercises. Their discussions and the ideas and concerns they bring back to the larger class are consistent with discussions held in social service agencies. Later, versions of the exercises can be used as tests, or you can go back to them at a later time to make sure students continue to practice their skills.

It is extremely useful for students to apply the skills described in this book to specific populations. To do this, you can use this book in conjunction with my other book, *Fundamentals for Practice with High Risk Populations* (Summers, 2002). After students have read the chapters on the specific populations you have assigned or on those that are most interesting to them, they can create a fictional "typical" client that they can then walk though all the exercises from intake to termination. Case notes would reflect the common problems encountered by the population, and intake would describe a common reason for seeking services among people in this population. This gives students a good beginning look at how cases come in and unfold while clients are receiving services.

Details on six high-risk populations are provided in *Fundamentals for Practice with High Risk Populations* (Summers, 2002). A detailed chapter on children and their families gives students information on how to include others involved in the child's life and how to coordinate all the various entities with whom the family interacts. Another chapter focuses on domestic violence and rape, including how these issues affect children.

A third chapter looks at substance abuse and includes the common social and medical issues that arise for this population. This chapter also includes the common challenges this population presents to case managers and gives tips for how to handle these. Mental health and mental retardation each are featured in chapters, giving common problems and issues, diagnoses, and treatments. Finally, there is a chapter focusing on aging that includes both medical and social issues for this population. All the chapters include an assessment form for that population and give the most typical diagnoses and medications used with each population. Where a population has special considerations the student should know, these are included as well. For example, in the chapter dealing with issues most likely to affect women, there is a discussion of how women's programs and agencies differ in their approach to clients from other social service agencies. To order specific chapters related to specific populations, see instructions in the earlier section of this Preface titled "New in the Third Edition."

Benefits and Advantages

This material has been used in my own classroom for 20 years and has been updated to meet current social service trends. Students have commented that using this text is like walking from the classroom into the social service setting with very little lost time in learning the actual process. Instructors teaching the practicum course have used the word *empowered* when describing what this text has done to give students confidence and skill in their first encounter with a social service position.

Three positive features of this textbook make it especially useful in preparing students to work in this field:

1. The text gives very basic information a person needs to handle each of the tasks described. Theoretical information can be found in many other places, and thus the concentration and focus are on what is important to note, think about, document, and pass on in each step of the human service process.
2. Numerous exercises create very real situations for students to consider and handle. These exercises are based on real experiences taken from my 23 years of practice in human services and from the experiences of many others who graciously contributed to this book. Doing the exercises and participating in the classroom discussions that follow will expose students to an extremely broad range of possible circumstances and difficulties in the field.
3. The book contains forms that give students an opportunity to practice compiling information at various times throughout the management of the case. These forms can be copied and used to create files on clients developed by the students. Using each form a number of times gives students practice in preparation for real clients in real social service settings.

These features, when taken together, create a nearly realistic social service setting in the classroom, giving the instructor many opportunities to strengthen student skills and sensitivity.

In addition, *Fundamentals for Practice with High Risk Populations* (Summers, 2002) supports students with applicable details and considerable information on various at-risk populations. This textbook acts as a reference so that the hypothetical clients students develop are real with entirely likely problems. Students can use the material found in this supplemental textbook to develop realistic clients, create useful service plans, and make appropriate referrals.

Acknowledgments

I would like to thank the staff at the Dauphin County Case Management Unit for their time and enthusiasm for this book. Many times they dropped what they were doing to give me information or advice on how an actual case management unit is being run under new federal guidelines. In particular I want to acknowledge the help of Mathew Kopechny, Executive Director; Gregory McCutcheon, Mental Health Services Director; Dan Sausman, Mental Retardation Services Director; and Michael Beck, Administrative Case Management Supervisor. I am grateful for the time and useful examples Michelle Beahm, Adult Resource Coordinator, and Kathleen Stence, Adult Blended Case Manager, gave. In addition, numerous case managers took time to talk over the things they felt were important to include based on their very real experiences. Those people include Krista Field, Adult Resource Coordinator; John Synoraski, Children's Intensive Case Manager; Chanel Smith, Child and Adolescent Resource Coordinator; and Rachel Young, Miranda McGrew, Liz Daly, Kari Harding, and Karen Kraft, all case managers in the field of developmental disabilities. I am grateful for the time Eric Elliot, Certified Peer Specialist, took to explain the realistic use of peer support. At the Dauphin County Executive Commission on Drugs, Alcohol and Tobacco, I want to thank John Sponeybarger for his help in formulating realistic plans and services. I am grateful to Ruby Porr for her ideas based on her work as a service provider and to Ruby Porr, Aimee Bollinger Smith, Karen Polite, and Barbara Miller who use this textbook and had suggestions for additions to the text.

I would like to thank Christopher D. Carrol MSc., Ken Thompson, M.D., and Paolo Delvecchio, of the substance Abuse and Mental Health Services Administration in the Department of Health and Human Services. I want to thank my husband, Martin Yespy, for his unfailing support of these textbooks and the useful material and information he brought from the field of crisis intervention.

I would also like to thank the reviewers of this textbook for their helpful comments: Misti W. Silver, Maryland Community College; Margaret Credle-Thomas, Urban College of Boston; Sheri Goik-Kurn, Baker College, Muskegon; and Mary Jo Blazek, University of Maine at Augusta.

Chapter 1

Ethics and Other Professional Responsibilities for Human Service Workers

Introduction

Ethical principles are the foundation of good human service practice. In fact, workers who do not practice within ethical parameters cannot be called professional. True professionals understand their ethical obligations and seek guidance when they do not. Each social welfare profession, from psychologists to social workers to human service workers, develops a set of ethical principles appropriate to the practice. Most professions monitor the behavior of their members with regard to these principles, singling out those who violate ethics codes for disciplinary measures.

Ethical principles are generally created in order to protect clients of the profession from exploitation In the work we do, there is considerable opportunity to exploit vulnerable people because the clients who seek our help are dependent upon us for the aid they need. Any violation of their trust on our part will only compound the clients' problems. Ethical principles provide guidelines to protect clients from exploitation. However, when professionals practice within the parameters of ethical principles, the public can feel confident that their interests will be respected and protected. Thus, ethical principles inform the decisions we make that affect clients, and they provide guidance in choosing the approaches we take with clients.

In this chapter we will look at some ethical guidelines common to all the helping professions. Failure to know and follow these guidelines in your future practice can result in dismissal from an agency or, worse yet, in a civil suit brought against you for a violation of the ethical code wherein the violation caused damage to the client. Although violations of ethical principles may have negative consequences for you and your career, they are always extremely destructive for the client, who is already vulnerable.

Dual Relationships

A dual relationship occurs when you and a client to whom you are giving services have more than one relationship. You may be a client's case manager as well as her cousin, her boyfriend, or her customer at her beauty salon. Or you may be a client's case manager and also his employer for your yard work, his Sunday school teacher, or his Little League coach. In other words, a dual relationship occurs when you are in two different relationships with a client, one related to your position as the person's case manager and the other unrelated to that role.

The first rule is to avoid all dual relationships. Your practice gives you a position of power. Clients look up to you as someone who can provide real assistance. Furthermore, you might be the one who will determine when a client can return to work, or you may be the person who reports a client's attendance in your program—attendance that keeps that client out of jail. It is possible that you could exploit or give the appearance of exploiting this power. In addition, there is enormous potential for a conflict of interest.

Suppose, for example, that your supervisor tells you on Thursday afternoon that you have been chosen to represent the agency at a big dinner being given to honor a county official at the Hilton Hotel on Saturday night. This gives you little time to prepare. You need to get your hair cut and styled. You call your client, who is a hair stylist, and prevail on him to work you in at the last moment. Your client does you a favor and sees that you get a good appointment. You are very grateful, go to the wonderful dinner, and think little more about it.

Several months later your client calls you. He has a need for a prescription refill from his psychiatrist. It is Friday afternoon, and the psychiatrist will not be back in the agency until the following Wednesday. The client feels you should be able to do this favor for him because of the favor he performed for you. He does not have time to see the psychiatrist regularly, he tells you. When you refuse to call in a prescription for him without the doctor's prior knowledge, he cannot understand why you are being "so rigid." He indicates that he thought the two of you were friends who helped each other out when needed.

Whatever you do in this situation, you will lose. If you call in the prescription, you will have violated an agency rule that a client must be seen at regular intervals by his psychiatrist before medications can be refilled. This could cost you your position or result in a disciplinary action. On top of that, you could start down a very slippery slope with this client. He may come to expect special favors from you and offer you special, very tempting favors related to his business in return. On the other hand, if you do not call in the prescription, you have alienated a client who needs the services of your agency. You have created a barrier to his feeling comfortable with you and getting the help he needs in the future. The client is harmed. A relationship that was or could have been useful to him in resolving problems is now something else. The opportunity for real progress is diluted with issues of friendship and favoritism.

From a shortsighted point of view, you and a client may see the convenience of exchanging favors as trivial and unrelated to the therapeutic relationship. In the long run, however, when scenarios such as the one just described occur, the relationship can never return to a professional one; and if in the future your client is in acute need, you may no longer be able to provide the professional intervention needed.

In some very small, rural communities, it is not possible to avoid dual relationships entirely. In those situations, after doing all that you can to make other arrangements, you must talk with the client about the possible problems that could arise and how each of you must avoid these problems together. The client then has the choice to continue the relationship, find other arrangements, or discontinue services altogether.

Although gift giving by clients does not pose a dual relationship, clients who bring gifts for you do pose a particular conflict of interest. It is usually best to avoid accepting gifts and keep the relationship professional. Often, though not always, gifts are the client's way of manipulating the situation. "I'll give you this item and you accept it. Next time you owe me something" or "I gave you this lovely thing. I am such a nice person. Even you think so or you would not have taken my gift. How can you then refuse to give me what I want?" Clients need to learn to express their desires clearly rather than by using gifts.

Gifts are not always manipulative, however. For example, a case manager working in a fuel assistance program worked closely with a family. The husband was injured when an automobile he was working on at a garage slipped on the lift. Unable to work, the family's meager resources began to dry up. The wife managed to find work in a greenhouse, but as winter approached, she was laid off and the expenses, particularly for fuel, increased. The couple had two children, both in elementary school, and they struggled to clothe and feed them as the wife sought another job.

The case manager saw this family through their difficulties by getting them welfare checks, seeing that the husband enrolled in the community college for courses in high-tech auto repair while his injuries healed, and finding school clothes for the children. The husband did well in school that winter and set a good example for his children, who seemed to do better in school than they had the previous year. The wife returned to the greenhouse in the spring and found that not only was she needed as a manager, but there was also a strong possibility she would have a year-round position there.

Elated by how well things were going and how much better the future looked, the couple came to see the case manager one day in the early summer and brought her a pot of black-eyed Susans from the greenhouse. "We just wanted you to have these for all you have done for our family," the husband said, smiling expansively. The husband and wife looked pleased and happy. Obviously the couple was proud to now be in the position to able to give something too. It was important to them not to see themselves as the recipients of handouts all the time, but to be able to also give something to someone who had been helpful.

Refusing a gift in such circumstances can be interpreted as rejection. If the worker had said, "Oh, I can't accept that. You'll have to give it to someone else," the client might have heard a different message: "You are the client and I am the benevolent worker. I help you, but you can never get to the position where you could possibly do anything for me. I don't need anything you could give me; but you, on the other hand, are a poor soul in need of my help."

If your agency has a policy against your personally accepting gifts, try to find a way to accept a gift of this sort on behalf of the agency. In this case, the worker planted the flowers in a planter near the door of the agency. This was a better solution than outright rejection of the gift.

The rule is to be very careful about accepting gifts from clients. Whenever a client offers a gift, make a note in the client's record of the offer as well as whether the gift was accepted or rejected and why.

Sexual or Romantic Relationships

Individuals who come to human service workers as clients often feel isolated, discouraged, and misunderstood. The relationship they form with a respectful, concerned worker may make them feel understood and appreciated for the first time. This relationship may be so comforting that clients attempt to turn it into something more permanent, more personally meaningful.

It is not uncommon for clients to fall in love with their workers in what we call "transference." In a sense, such clients transfer to the workers the attributes they are seeking in another person. They may assume the love and affection they are seeking will be forthcoming from their workers because the workers have been so kind and helpful. These clients fall in love with their workers because of an erroneous perception: They see concern and encouragement as gestures of love and affection—as an invitation to create more than a professional relationship.

Countertransference also can occur. It is not unusual for workers who are harried and overworked, and possibly coping with difficulties in their personal lives, to find the willing ear of a client very supportive. Clients are often attractive, sensitive people who can convey warmth and support when case managers are most vulnerable.

Take, for example, Kent, a case manager. Kent's wife left in the middle of a Tuesday morning, and Kent was to be at work that afternoon at 3:00. Though he fought hard to dissuade her from going, she left. For the rest of the day before work, Kent tried to get some money from their joint account, tried to find out where his wife was going, and tried to make some decisions. He arrived at work feeling exhausted and bitterly betrayed.

That evening, Kent made a home visit to Lucy's house. Lucy had first come to the agency with extreme depression, but she was doing so well now that Kent was considering terminating these follow-up visits. Lucy, an artist, greeted Kent warmly. She had put on a pot of tea and made some banana bread for his visit. Gratefully Kent sank down on her sofa. Instead of asking Lucy how things were going for her, whether she had enough medication, and whether she had any medication questions, Kent found himself talking about his upsetting day.

In response to Lucy's first remark, "You don't look very well tonight, Mr. Paulman," Kent heard himself pour out the day's events; then he went on to talk at length about how his marriage had unraveled. He felt comforted by Lucy's interest in him as she listened intently. Here was a person who appeared to respect him as a professional and as a person. Here was a woman willing to listen to his problems. Here was a warm retreat from the job and the problems of the day where Kent could feel safe and supported.

Kent never intended for a real relationship to develop between Lucy and himself. In fact, as he left that night, he told himself that he might have crossed a dangerous line and that he should avoid further contact of this sort with Lucy. Nevertheless, based on that evening, Lucy called; and because Kent was lonely, his life was uncertain, and he was filled with anger and bitterness about his situation, he continued to see Lucy, finding in her a warm, supportive person, someone who could reassure him by her presence that he was attractive and interesting.

The relationship moved from his visiting in her home after work to his staying overnight at her house to his moving in his belongings and beginning to live there. They went out on dates. The furtiveness of these activities only made the relationship seem more romantic and important. Finally, a supervisor discovered the relationship, and Kent lost his job. After 3 years, he and Lucy have separated, and Kent is not working in the human service field anymore because he violated such an essential ethic. Instead, he sells appliances in a local store. Lucy became depressed when the relationship ended and has entered treatment again.

The person responsible for maintaining a professional relationship regardless of personal feelings is the case manager. Regardless of how you feel about your client or how the client apparently feels about you, you are the responsible party. You will be penalized if the relationship crosses from professional to intimate. It is always assumed that the client is the vulnerable party.

Figure 1.1 lists some warning signs that indicate when a worker or client might be moving away from a professional relationship and toward a personal one. Make certain you are familiar with these signs.

PLEASE NOTE!

It is a violation of all ethical codes, and in most states against the law, to engage in a sexual or romantic relationship with a client. This is *clearly* exploitation. It is never tolerated. You must be aware that, although attractions can occur between clients and those who provide service, acting on those attractions is entirely unethical in professional practice, and illegal in most states as well.

Value Conflicts

Generally, the client's values and your values have little to do with why the client is seeking services from you. Sometimes, however, religious, moral, and political values play a pivotal role in the problems clients bring to agencies. It is rare for case managers to get deeply involved in such primary problems, but it can happen.

FIGURE 1.1

Warning signs the worker–client relationship may become too personal

Warning Signs from the Client

- The client shows overt sexual interest in the worker either through conduct or verbally.
- The client describes dreams that are increasingly sexual in which the worker is prominently involved.
- The client is excessively interested in the worker's private life.
- The client inquires about the worker's relationship with his or her spouse and children.
- The client attempts to give the worker romantic gifts. (Be careful about accepting gifts from a client. Note every such offer in the record, along with whether the gift was accepted or rejected and why.)
- The client wants to see the worker outside the office in places such as restaurants or movie theaters.
- The client gives the worker romantic poetry or brings in romantic articles and books.
- The client dresses in seductive attire.
- The client interprets the worker's statements of concern for the client to mean the worker has a romantic interest in the client.
- The client repeatedly hugs and touches the worker.
- The client indicates a desire to be special to the worker.

Warning Signs from the Worker

- The client is prominent in the worker's dreams.
- The worker looks forward to seeing the client, more so than other clients.
- The worker begins to see the client as more understanding than others in the worker's life.
- The worker inquires about the client's sexual life and fantasies when these are not relevant to case management.
- The worker is more interested in this client's attire than in the attire of other clients.
- The worker is more concerned with his own attire on days when he will see the client.
- The worker begins to see the client as a person without issues or problems or minimizes these so that the client seems more acceptable as a partner or friend.
- The worker takes many innocuous actions the client might interpret to mean the worker has a special interest in him or her.

Source: Based on a list created by attorney O. Brandt Caudill (1996). Used with permission.

First, you can be prepared by consciously knowing yourself and your feelings about certain value-laden issues. Then, if a conflict of values occurs between you and a client, you should be able to tell the client that the conflict exists and may interfere with services. You can begin to inventory some of your own attitudes and strong feelings by completing the self-assessment exercise in Figure 1.2.

FIGURE 1.2
Self-assessment exercise

Self-Assessment Exercise: Possible Values Conflicts When Helping Others

Look at each description of a person or group of people, and assign a number to each.

1 Give the description a 1 if you think you could work with the person or group.
2 Give the description a 2 if you think you could work with the person or group, but would find it uncomfortable or difficult.
3 Give the description a 3 if you could not work with the person at all.

_____ 1. A woman who wants you to help her feel comfortable with her decision to have an abortion
_____ 2. A man who frequently brings up his fundamentalist religious beliefs
_____ 3. A homosexual couple who want help in improving their relationship and resolving their interpersonal conflicts
_____ 4. An interracial couple seeking premarital counseling
_____ 5. A man from Iran who strongly opposes the equality of women and talks about women working in denigrating tones
_____ 6. A man who has for years been getting more welfare than he is entitled to receive by using certain tricks he developed to beat the system
_____ 7. A man and woman who say they want to improve their marriage, but the man will not end his affair with a second woman
_____ 8. A white couple seeking help for behavior problems with their adopted son, who is African American
_____ 9. A man who makes it clear he often disciplines his children by using corporal punishment
_____ 10. A person who refuses to discuss feelings and says that all that matters are facts and logic
_____ 11. A woman who has chosen prostitution as a way to support herself and her children
_____ 12. A gay man dying of AIDS who comes in with his lover to resolve conflicts around how he contracted the disease
_____ 13. A man seeking help to curb his extreme abuse of his wife
_____ 14. A woman who sexually molested her son
_____ 15. A lesbian couple seeking to adopt a child
_____ 16. A woman dying of breast cancer who wants to take her own life
_____ 17. A person who relies heavily on cocaine to get through the day
_____ 18. A couple who are openly anti-Semitic
_____ 19. A vocal member of the Ku Klux Klan
_____ 20. An orthodox Muslim who cannot always see you because his appointments often interfere with his times of prayer

Second, if a severe conflict of values exists, you might need to make arrangements to transfer the client to another case manager. You would not do this because of a simple value conflict, but you should try to make such a transfer if you find you can no longer be objective, you are extremely uncomfortable with the client because of her or his values, or you feel compelled to counteract the client's values by imposing your own.

For example, a human service worker who did not personally believe in birth control (including tubal ligation) was a case manager for individuals with developmental disabilities. When a young couple on her caseload decided to marry, she became actively involved in discouraging them from the idea, particularly when she learned that the woman planned to have a tubal ligation so that they would not have children. The families of the two individuals supported the marriage. The clients were high functioning, each client had a job, and each had the support of other community agencies.

In the months before the wedding, the case manager did not attempt to transfer the cases to another case manager. Instead, she harangued the couple about the sins of birth control and of marriage without children, and about the unwise decision to marry at all, given their "mental impairment." The families complained to the agency, asking that she stop pressuring these vulnerable individuals. Twice the supervisor disciplined the worker. When the worker persisted—visiting the couple's minister who would perform the ceremony, the supervisor where the man worked, and the woman's parents—she was fired from her position.

The worker's behavior was harmful to the clients. For those two people, who had always relied on a case manager who had seemed to be wise, the worker introduced uncertainty and fear. Her constant negative warnings damaged their fragile self-confidence and self-esteem. For them, what should have been a happy decision, supported by family and friends, became a decision fraught with anxiety. Family and friends had to work long and hard to restore their confidence in their original decision.

This is an example of the worst possible way to handle a values conflict. In this situation, the worker attempted to impose her own point of view, her own personal values, on the clients. She denied them the right to choose for themselves and interfered in what was largely a personal and family issue unrelated to case management.

Avoiding Value Conflicts

Following are some rules for avoiding value conflicts and ensuring that your clients get professional service:

1. Be respectful of attitudes and lifestyles that differ from your own.
2. Never practice prejudice toward minorities, those with disabilities, or those differing in sexual preference.
3. Always give your best service to your client, even when you disagree with the person.
4. Never attempt to change the client's values to coincide with your own.

Using Values to Motivate Clients

When clients come in seeking assistance, they are usually hoping to make things better in their lives than the way they are right now. In the course of your time with them, it is important to explore the values that caused them to seek help. Find out what goals clients have for themselves if their situations were better, and what values those goals reflect. Here we are looking at the things that people value for themselves: being a good parent, living an independent life, living free of the symptoms of schizophrenia, or being free of addiction to cocaine. The client is envisioning something up ahead that involves a goal or value dear to that person.

You often learn about clients' values when you ask them where they would like to be in 5 years. What you hear when they answer will point to what they hold important for themselves and those around them. When people are having trouble making changes that will move them toward their personal goals and visions, it is helpful for the worker to know what the clients' values are and to look at the clients' situations with those values on the table.

Clients' Rights

Anyone who gives service in one of the helping professions must be familiar with the rights of the client and make a particular effort to see that clients understand they have rights when they seek help. Often clients mistakenly assume that they have few or no rights when they come in for services. In addition, professionals may fail to inform clients of their rights because it is easier to work with individuals who are vulnerable, dependent, and uninformed. This, of course, sets up a situation in which it is easy to exploit the client. The purpose of educating clients about their rights is to allow them the opportunity to become active participants in their care and partners in decisions that affect them.

Most agencies prepare client rights handbooks for clients to keep as a reference. A hospital for the mentally ill would include the right to be released from the hospital as soon as care and treatment in that setting are no longer required. Some agencies inform clients that they have the right to participate in the development and review of their treatment plan. Clients generally have the right to participate in major decisions affecting their care and treatment. Most clients who are involuntarily committed to an inpatient setting have the right to refuse treatment to the extent permitted by laws in that state or the right not to be transferred to another facility without clear explanations regarding the need for the transfer. Inpatient units stipulate it is the client's right not to be subjected to harsh or unusual treatment. The hospital may also spell out the fact that the client may keep and use personal possessions, or the client must be informed about why something is being removed. In most settings, clients have the right to handle personal affairs and to practice the religion of their choice.

In outpatient settings, clients have the right to a flexible and responsive treatment plan, the right to expect an individualized plan of service, and the right to make suggestions and express concerns. Often there is a procedure clients can follow if they are dissatisfied with the worker assigned to them or the service plan laid out by the agency.

The following sections discuss some important rights that belong to clients.

Informed Consent

A client receiving services always has the right to consent to these services or withdraw from them. In making this decision, the client must be informed enough to make a wise decision. When the client is informed and consents to treatment, we call that *informed consent*. Making certain that a client can give informed consent begins with the intake, during which the agency policies are explained and choices of treatment or services are outlined. This level of information should continue throughout the entire relationship between the client and the agency until termination. This means that clients informed about treatment or services can make their own decisions with regard to the services.

The following list contains items that should be addressed when relevant to the client's services. The client has the right to be informed about:

1. Any side effects, adverse effects, or negative consequences that could occur as a result of treatment, medications, or procedures.
2. Any risks that might occur if the client elects not to follow through with treatment or services.
3. What is being offered to the client, including what the treatment is, what will be included, and any potential risks and benefits.
4. Any alternate procedures that are available.

Some of the people with whom we work have a limited capacity to understand all the details of service and treatment. It is our task to find an appropriate balance between too much and too little information and to make our information clear and easy to understand.

Informed consent consists of the following three parts, or criteria. All must be present in order to say that the client gave informed consent.

1. *Capacity*. The client has the ability or capacity to make clear, competent decisions in his or her own behalf.
2. *Comprehension of information*. The client clearly understands what is being told to him or her. To make sure that this is so, give your information carefully and always check to be sure the client understands what you have told him or her.
3. *Voluntariness*. The client gives his or her consent freely with no coercion or pressure from the agency or the professional offering the service.

Currently laws and courts are recognizing more and more often the client's right to self-determination. When we fail to tell our clients the information they need in order to give informed consent, we run the risk of being found negligent, particularly if the treatment or service involved was unusual.

Confidentiality

Confidentiality is both an ethical principle and a legal right. It is the most basic right of any client, either in treatment or receiving services, to know that what the client is sharing in your office will remain confidential. It is important to protect clients by not disclosing their personal situations without the clients having authorized such a disclosure. Today, under new laws discussed in the text that follows, agencies have very specific guidelines for protecting confidentiality.

Release of Information Form

Not many years ago a person seeking services, particularly from a public agency, signed a blanket permission statement allowing information to be shared with others as the agency and the worker saw fit. Today, release of information forms must state specifically to whom the information is being released and must be time limited (good for 3 months, 1 year, and so on). Do not use forms that are not specific in this manner. New regulations now stipulate what is permissible on a release of information form.

Release of Information Regarding HIV/AIDS

In most states, release of information forms for releasing information regarding a client's HIV/AIDS status must specifically state that you may release information regarding the client's HIV status. All references to HIV/AIDS must be deleted from the record unless the client signs a separate form that specifically states that you have permission to release this information. If you are asked to release information about a person who is HIV+ and the client signs a release form, the law in most states specifies that it is not good enough to simply remind the client that his case contains references to his HIV status and get his verbal permission to release the information anyway. You also must have his written permission. If the client has not given you written permission, you must delete all references to HIV/AIDS, including the fact that he may have been tested and the test was negative.

If your state does not have such a law, you are still responsible for protecting your client and must be alert to the possible harm such a release might cause the client. In such a situation, it is wise to involve the client in a discussion about the release of this sort of information or, if the client is unable to participate in such a discussion, to take steps to protect the client from undue bias.

In some instances, workers have informally notified their friends and acquaintances in other agencies of a client's HIV+ status, thinking they were doing these people a favor. In fact, this behavior is entirely unethical and can lull other workers into believing they know who is and who is not HIV+. We can never actually know this for certain because of the length of time it takes for the disease to register positive on a blood test. A person can be positive early in the illness and still have negative blood tests. For this reason, workers should use universal precautions with every client when those precautions are called for. Workers who fail to use universal precautions on the false assumption that they know the client is not HIV+ place themselves at undue risk.

ASSIGNMENT

Find out what the laws are in your state for releasing information about a client that contains references to the client's HIV status.

Collegial Sharing

Out of respect for clients, you should ask clients for permission before sharing information with colleagues from whom you are getting opinions or supervision, unless the case is going to be discussed in the normal course of supervisory meetings with a regular supervisor. Likewise, you cannot share information with student interns without making certain the students have signed agreements to observe strict confidentiality while acting as part of the agency. Suppose you are working in an agency and have been asked to give a student a view of what you do. To illustrate what you have told the student, you show her several case files. She reads the cases and discovers that one of them is the boyfriend of her cousin. What she reads in the file is alarming to her, and she decides her cousin should not be dating the client. She leaves the agency and begins to share information with the cousin, causing considerable conflict among family members and anguish to the cousin, who knew part of the story but not all of it. This kind of sharing of information is unacceptable, and most agencies do not allow students or volunteers to read anything before they have signed a pledge to honor the confidentiality of the clients.

Guarding Confidentiality on the Phone and in Other Conversations

Other situations also provide opportunities for violating confidentiality. For instance, a person receiving services from your agency may also be receiving services from a local physician. Suppose someone calls, claiming to be the physician's nurse and needing to know at once what medications the client is taking. She may really be the physician's nurse, or she may be a person posing as the nurse in order to determine that the client is using your services and the level of his problem. Even if she is the nurse, the client may wish to keep his physician uninformed about the involvement with your agency. All agencies have procedures for such situations in the event of a real emergency. You, however, must never openly and automatically acknowledge that a client is being seen in your agency, no matter how important and official the other person seems to be. In the case of a seeming emergency, refer the call to your supervisor unless you know the emergency workers or emergency room personnel well enough to recognize their voices.

When a request for information is presented in a situation that is not an emergency, here is how you might handle the request:

YOU: Hello.

CALLER: Hi. This is Ann Taylor. I'm a counselor at Harrisburg Middle School, and I'm calling about Jimmy Smith. Did he and his mother keep their appointment with you today?

YOU: I'm sorry, I can't help you with that. Would you have Mrs. Smith sign a release of information form stating what it is you need to know, and if Jimmy Smith is known to us, we can send you that information.

Another way to violate confidentiality is to talk about your cases with your friends and relatives, leaving out the names. Others may be able to piece together the identity of the person you are talking about based on other information they possess. In this way, they may discover far more about the client than the client ever intended them to know.

Minors and the Infirm

Take special care to protect the confidentiality of minors and the infirm (individuals who are frail, sick, and are unable to fully participate in decisions about their care). Not all systems respect confidentiality to the degree that we in the helping professions are committed to doing it.

In one children's case management unit, parents were routinely urged to sign blanket release of information forms. When the school requested information on a child being seen, all the information was sent to the school. It was stamped in red letters with the word *confidential*, and it was sent to the school psychologist. Nevertheless, school clerical personnel assisted in typing and filing information for the psychologist and generally read the information sent by the case management unit. Having no training in confidentiality, these clerical people talked among themselves about students, sharing personal information they had learned. Many times they passed on to teachers tidbits of what amounted to gossip. This information shared outside the professional context and without professional understanding jeopardized the progress of the children and the relationship of their parents with the school personnel. As these children moved through the school system, the gossip followed them. Always be very careful about what information you release. Remember that information given about a child can follow that child all through school, prejudicing responses to that child.

In another case, a woman with a developmental disability got a job at the police department as a cleaning woman. She was told that she needed to bring in her "records from mental health" so the police could know why she went there. She arrived at the case management unit, pleased about the job and ready to give all her records away. The case manager talked to her about the wisdom of retaining most of the information as confidential. In the end, a short statement was released, with the client's permission, giving only the most general information about her relationship with the mental health/mental retardation case management unit. It is important to remember that older people or individuals who do not have the capacity to protect themselves can be easily led to sign releases regarding information that might best be kept confidential. The responsibility belongs to you to protect your clients from unnecessary intrusions into their personal information.

Minimum Necessary Rule

Before releasing information, ask yourself whether you are about to release more information than is needed for this other business or organization to accomplish its work with the client. For example, Melissa was a case manager who knew a worker in a remedial education program where one of her clients, Jill, was attending. Although the program needed to know why Jill was referred and what goal the referral was intended to accomplish, they did not need to know that Jill was arrested once for a DUI and that Jill's father was in prison for murdering a neighbor. When dealing with other organizations not engaged in treatment, release only what that organization needs to work effectively with the client. If the client authorizes you in writing to disclose more, only then would you do so.

When You Can Break Confidentiality

The law in all states does make exceptions. The following are circumstances that allow you to break confidentiality:

1. When you must warn and protect others from possible harmful actions by the client. For instance, you or your agency must warn another party if your client is intent on harming that other party. In addition, you should notify the police.
2. When the client needs professional services. For instance, if the client has taken an overdose of medication and is in the emergency room (ER), the ER staff may call, needing to know what prescriptions the client was taking in order to give the proper antidote.
3. When you must protect clients from harming themselves. An example might be people who are threatening to take an overdose of their medications with the intention of committing suicide or people who appear so depressed or desperate that they are talking about ending their lives.
4. When you are attempting to obtain payment for services and the payment has not been made. Your agency would refer a client for nonpayment only after reasonable attempts had been made to remind the client of this obligation and only if the client had made no effort to arrange even minimal payment.
5. When obtaining a professional consultation from your supervisor regarding how best to proceed with a case in the course of normal supervision.

Privacy

Privacy is very much related to confidentiality. Siegel (1979) calls it "the freedom of individuals to choose for themselves the time and the circumstances under which and the extent to which their beliefs, behaviors, and opinions are to be shared." Stadler (1990) calls it "the right of persons to choose what others may know about them and under what circumstances." Privacy is invaded or altered under some circumstances, and clients need to be informed of those circumstances. The point you should stress with your clients is the fact that third-party payers will have access to diagnoses and, in some cases, to actual records or summaries of records. The agency must provide this access in order to be paid for the services it has rendered. Many clients are unaware of this fact or unaware of the extent of the information being shared. They should have this situation explained to them. This allows clients to make an informed decision about whether to pay for services themselves and not involve the insurance company.

Health Insurance Portability and Accountability Act

The federal Health Insurance Portability and Accountability Act (HIPAA) was passed in 1996 in part to ensure that people did not lose medical coverage when they changed jobs. Title II of the act contains the security and privacy mandates. These contain stringent rules for protecting a client's health information, and most social service agencies must adhere to these rules. Where state laws are more stringent than this federal act, the state laws take precedence. Failure to follow the guidelines set forth in HIPAA can result in fines from $100 to $250,000 and from 1 to 10 years in prison for those individuals and institutions with the ultimate responsibility for safeguarding patient privacy.

The new rules apply to case management and to care coordination and cover not only formal records but also personal notes and billing information. When you begin work at your agency, they will see that you are informed of their policies and procedures under this act.

Disclosure

Under the new rules, "disclosure" is defined as occurring when health information is released, transferred, or divulged outside the agency. This includes allowing access to patient files to others not working for the agency. The material in question is often referred to as protected health information, or PHI.

Agency Requirements

In order to comply with HIPAA, every agency must have the following:

1. A statement of the agency's privacy and confidentiality procedures, particularly as it relates to releasing patient information. This statement must be given to every client of the agency. It is considered a notice clarifying how health information will be used and stipulating the client's privacy rights. This is a public document and can be posted in waiting rooms and on websites.
2. A form that clients sign and return to the agency indicating that they have received the statement on confidentiality policies.
3. A privacy officer who is familiar with HIPAA requirements and can oversee implementation within the agency and resolve privacy issues as they arise.
4. A set of safeguards to protect client records.

The privacy concerns addressed by HIPAA were raised because of the increasing demand by insurance companies, employers, and others for detailed information on clients and patients, often in excess of what was necessary to process claims.

Security and Privacy

Security in the act refers to procedures to protect health information from inappropriate access by others. These procedures usually include controls on who has physical access to the records, security of work areas and record storage areas, and destruction of duplicate or obsolete files. Electronic security measures are also instituted, such as changing passwords and encryption.

Privacy refers to the client's right to keep specific information private and includes the agency's release of information policies and the rights of the individual in this matter.

Oral Communications

The law states that agencies are to make "reasonable efforts" to safeguard clients' information. This extends to oral communications. Taking precautions to protect oral communications means:

- Not discussing a client's personal health information where others can hear
- Avoiding situations with clients where there is no privacy, particularly privacy from other clients
- Lowering your voice when discussing clients with others in the agency

Release of Information Form

Under HIPAA, the form signed by the client or a legal representative of the client must adhere to the following:

- The entire form must be in plain, understandable language, and it must be signed and dated.
- There must be a description of the information to be used.
- The form must name the recipients of this information.
- Those who will disclose the information, such as the agency or a therapist, must be named on the form.
- The form must have an expiration date.
- There must be a statement describing the purpose of releasing the information.
- There must be instructions telling the client how to revoke the form.
- A statement must be included to indicate that the information may not be as protected once it is released.
- If the agency will receive money for the information (for example, payment from an insurance company), this must be stated on the form.
- The form must make clear clients' rights to a copy of the authorization they have signed.

It is assumed that reasonable steps will be taken to release only the minimum information necessary to support the purpose of the release. When the purpose is continued care of the client or when the client requests that more information be released, it is expected that more information will be released. Any request for the entire client record, however, needs detailed justification.

Individually Identifiable Health Information

Individually identifiable health information includes demographic information (such as age, gender, income, or race) and other information that identifies the individual or could reasonably be thought to identify the individual. Information that relates to an individual's past, present, or future condition is also included in this category.

Clients have the right to ask that their information be restricted. They may indicate, again in writing, that information is not to be shared with family or friends. These requests are generally honored except in medical emergencies. In addition, clients may ask, in writing, that mail from the agency not be sent to their home address or that calls from the agency not be made to their home telephone, and the agency must honor these requests.

A client may ask, in writing, for a written list of how their PHI was disclosed. The request can extend as far back as 6 years. Note that clients can specifically request how information is to be shared or restricted, but must always do so in writing. A client not able to write such a request may need the help of a case manager.

Accessing the File

Under the new HIPAA guidelines, clients now have a right to:

1. Read their files
2. Make copies of their records
3. Make corrections or additions to their files, as long as the changes are accurate

As noted earlier, such requests must be presented in writing to the agency and must be accommodated within a specific time period. Clients who are going to amend their files must state the reason for amending the record in the written request. Client representatives, such as guardians, have the same access and rights as do clients. There may be times when the client will need the help of the case manager to formulate that request.

The rights discussed here are guaranteed under federal law; thus, it is illegal to discourage or threaten clients when they make these requests. Currently there is evidence that clients who have read their charts and received clear information are less likely to sue for malpractice or create other legal problems. It is not a good idea, however, to just hand someone a chart and provide no explanations for technical information that may be written there. This potentially creates misunderstanding. If at all possible, sit with the client and carefully review the important points in the chart. Answer questions and explain what has been written so the client understands what is written and does not draw erroneous conclusions or conclusions that could lead the client to believe there is an adversarial relationship described in the chart.

Self-Determination

Educating clients and informing clients about their rights are both done so that clients can exercise the right to self-determination. Paramount to any relationship between professionals and their clientele is the right to self-determination. Clients have the right to do research about their diagnosis or problem and to question the treatment plan or make suggestions. Clients have the right to withdraw from treatments and services they find are not helpful. Clients have the right to decide when and for how long they will use services (unless their involvement with the agency is based on an involuntary court commitment). Clients have the right to choose their own goals.

Often this presents a problem for a worker who feels compelled to look after the best interests of the client. One of the hardest lessons you will ever learn is how to let clients make mistakes and learn from those mistakes. You can make suggestions and express concerns, but ultimately clients have the right to determine what they will do. You may feel strongly, for example, that one of your clients is not ready to walk away from the agency; and you may feel certain that the client's doing so prematurely will result in further problems with alcohol. In fact, your client leaves treatment against your advice and eventually does end up with another DUI charge. Although your worst fears and predictions came true, you cannot know for sure that the work with you and the new charge were not important learning opportunities. In other words, clients have the right to test the waters, so to speak, and to learn that they are not as ready as they thought they were.

Increasingly, however, self-determination means more than this. More and more funding sources and governments, as we shall see in the next chapter, are asking case managers to go beyond simply arranging for services in collaboration with the client. They are asking case managers to encourage clients to articulate what their vision of a healthy, productive future would look like. As people do better on medications and remain in their communities, how they function in those communities—how they contribute, feel secure, and pursue their own interests—becomes more important. Self-determination now takes on the future beyond the social and emotional problems that were the original reason for seeking help. Now clients are being energized by their case managers to explore and create a better tomorrow of their own making.

Privileged Communication

Clients and workers alike talk about privileged communication without truly knowing what it is. First of all, it is a *legal concept*. It protects the right of a client to withhold information in a *court proceeding*. It is a right that belongs to the client. It does not belong to the worker or the agency.

All states have a law that stipulates what communication between a client and professional shall be considered privileged in order to protect the client from the disclosure of confidential information during a court proceeding. These laws designate who is to be considered a professional. You may recall a recent case in which a man who committed a murder confessed this murder in an Alcoholics Anonymous (AA) group. He tried to invoke the right of privileged communication, but the courts denied it because the state law did not specifically name AA as a group protected by this statute.

Only clients can invoke privileged communication in order to protect themselves. Professionals and agencies cannot use it to protect themselves. If the client waives the right to privileged communication, the professional or agency has no grounds to withhold information. Clients waive this right if they sue your agency or if they use their condition as a defense in a legal proceeding.

When You Can Give Information

At certain times, you can provide information about clients in a court proceeding. In some situations, you are required to do so.

Legal Proceedings

In a legal proceeding, you may give information about clients under the following conditions:

1. You are acting in a court-appointed capacity, such as that of guardian or payee.
2. You or your agency is sued for malpractice.
3. The court mandates that you turn over certain information.
4. The client uses a mental condition as a defense or as a claim in a civil action.

Protecting Clients and Others from Harm

Other situations in which you can give information about clients relate to your responsibility to protect clients and those connected with clients from harm. These situations are:

1. When you believe the client intends to commit suicide
2. When a child under 16 years old is believed to be the victim of a crime such as sexual or physical abuse or sexual exploitation
3. When you determine the client needs to be hospitalized for a mental condition
4. When the client has told you of his intention to commit a crime, harm another person, or harm himself

Intention to Harm Another. On October 27, 1969, Prosenjit Poddar killed Tatiana Tarasoff and set in motion court proceedings that brought about changes in the way confidentiality is viewed. That October, Poddar was a patient of Dr. Lawrence Moore at Cowell Memorial Hospital at the University of California, Berkeley. Moore, a psychologist, was told by Poddar of his intention to kill Tatiana Tarasoff. Moore contacted campus police, who briefly detained Poddar but released him when he appeared to the police to be rational. Apparently, Dr. Powelson, Moore's supervisor, directed that no further action be taken to detain Poddar. No one warned Tatiana Tarasoff of the danger she faced, and as a result she lost her life.

The Tarasoffs brought charges against the professionals in this case for failure to warn the victim of the impending danger. When the California Supreme Court eventually heard the case, the court ruled that

> [T]herapists cannot escape liability merely because Tatiana herself was not their patient. When a therapist determines...that his patient presents a serious danger of violence to another, he incurs an obligation to use reasonable care to protect the intended victim against such danger. (*Tarasoff v. Regents of the University of California*, 1976)

The steps the court included were warning the intended victim, warning others who would apprise the intended victim of the danger, and warning the police. The court went on to state:

> We recognize the public interest in supporting effective treatment of mental illness and in protecting the rights of patients to privacy, and the consequent public importance of safeguarding the confidential character of psychotherapeutic communication. Against this interest, however, we must weigh the public interest in safety from violent assault.

The opinion closed with the following:

> We conclude that the public policy favoring protection of the confidential character of patient-psychotherapist communication must yield to the extent to which disclosure is essential to avert danger to others. The protective privilege ends where the public peril begins.

This case established a "duty to protect" for individuals who treat patients who appear to present an imminent danger to an identifiable person or persons. The ruling appears to apply mainly to therapists, but here the waters are muddy. Human service professionals in all states have taken the position that if such circumstances were to occur in the course of their work, the courts would find them negligent if they had not exercised the precautions laid out in the *Tarasoff* case. Most states now have statutory or binding case law that establishes the duty to warn, but some do not. Regardless, you must assume that the courts would find you or your agency negligent if you failed to take the precautions outlined in the *Tarasoff* ruling. It is unlikely that you would be excused from liability because you are a case manager, and not a therapist.

Rarely would you make the decision to warn alone. If you believe a client poses an imminent danger to another identifiable person or persons, you must take the matter up at once with your supervisor. If your supervisor is not available for consultation and you believe you cannot wait, notify the police.

In a step down unit for the mentally ill, a man living there left one evening. No one knew where he was going, and when he didn't come home that late evening, the staff became alarmed. He had been talking about going back to the farm where he grew up to "evict those people who put us out." In fact, the family had sold the farm, and the people living there were the owners. At this point the worker determined that the family at the farm should be warned. The supervisor, unfamiliar with the law, resisted, even though she would have ultimately been responsible had something happened. Later the worker ran into the director of the agency and asked her opinion. Immediately the director told the worker to contact the people at the farm and let the police in that jurisdiction know he might come to the farm. In fact the man did show up and talked about the need for the owners to move out. He did not pose a threat, but the fact that he might have done so was important to consider. In this case the police returned him to the step down unit where his behavior was discussed with him. This supervisor's lack of understanding about the law could have caused problems for the client, the people living at the farm, and the agency.

ASSIGNMENT

Find out what laws exist, if any, in your state regarding your duty to warn. If there are no laws on the books, what is common legal opinion regarding the duty to warn?

Mandated Reporting

All states have laws requiring professionals to report the abuse and neglect of children. In some states, laws require human service workers to report elder abuse. The definition of child abuse and elder abuse varies from state to state. Professionals who must report abuse and neglect under the law are called "mandated reporters." The laws in each state stipulate who is a mandated reporter; variations exist among the states in regard to which professionals are considered mandated to report.

Even in states where there is no mandate to report elder abuse, there may be protective services for the elderly to which you can report suspected abuse of an older person. You have an ethical responsibility not to ignore abuse of this type, regardless of the law. It is your responsibility to protect clients, particularly individuals who cannot protect themselves.

ASSIGNMENT

Find out your state's definition of child abuse. Learn which professionals in your state are considered mandated reporters of child abuse. What are the laws in your state regarding elder abuse?

Diagnostic Labeling

Agencies that rely on a diagnosis in order to be paid for service by a third-party payer (such as an insurance company, Medicare, or Medicaid) need to inform clients of that fact. Clients rarely understand that labels are used in this way, and most clients do not know what the labels are or what they mean. They are rarely clear about the fact that the information will be passed on to their insurance companies. Clients need to know this, so they can then decide whether to continue to receive services from the agency.

Some clients may elect to leave the agency or to pay for the services themselves, without involving their insurance companies, as a means of ensuring their privacy. Unless they are informed, they will not know they have these choices.

Another point about diagnosing clients is that practitioners use the categories of illness to know which treatment to use and how to develop the most effective treatment plan. Much research has been done to link the best treatments with each of the diagnostic categories. Clients will appreciate the need for a diagnostic label if they understand this. What may appear to clients as simple respect, kindness, good communication, or personal support on the part of their therapists may actually be the use of well-developed treatment modes.

Involuntary Commitment

Generally, an involuntary commitment occurs to a facility that specializes in inpatient mental health care. It could be a unit in a general hospital in the community where the clients live, a private psychiatric hospital, or, in some cases, a partial hospitalization program where clients receive treatment during that portion of the day they are most at risk.

Patients have a right to expect the least restrictive form of treatment. If they need hospitalization but not a locked ward, they should not be locked up 24 hours a day. If they can get the care they need in a partial hospitalization program, they should not have to go into the hospital. In talking about the movement to deinstitutionalize mental patients, Bednar, Bednar, Lambert, and Waite (1991) wrote, "[T]reatment should be no more harsh, hazardous, or intrusive than necessary to achieve therapeutic aims and to protect clients and others from physical harm."

The courts take seriously their responsibility to commit individuals in need of psychiatric care who are unable to obtain it because of a current severe impairment. In making the commitment, the courts make it clear that the purpose is treatment, and not punishment for behavior. For that reason, court commitment proceedings are often less formal and more pleasant than criminal proceedings. Students may observe these proceedings if they choose, as the proceedings are public. If you are involved in a commitment procedure, be sure to document all the steps you take in order to protect yourself from liability.

The criteria for committing someone against her will are as follows:

1. The person poses a danger to self or to others, *and possibly one or more of the following*:
2. The person has a severe mental illness or a mental illness that is currently acute.
3. The person is unable to function in occupational, social, or personal areas. The impairment is severe enough that the person cannot provide adequate self-care.
4. The person has refused to sign a voluntary commitment for treatment, so that an involuntary commitment is the last resort; or the person is incapable of signing such a commitment or of choosing appropriate treatment.

5. The person can be treated once committed; that is, known treatments and medications can relieve the acute condition the person is experiencing at present.
6. The commitment adheres to the criteria of the least restrictive treatment setting.

ASSIGNMENT

Find out what the commitment laws are in your state. Look at the various types of voluntary and involuntary commitments. Find out under what circumstances the client can leave a facility when voluntarily committed. Find out what constitutes due process in your state for those being committed involuntarily.

Ethical Responsibility

Responsibility for the client's welfare while the client is in your program is yours. The client views you as an authority. No matter how inexperienced you feel, when clients work with you, they will see you as the person with all the answers. For this reason, you will have considerable influence over what your clients decide to do. It is important to keep their needs at the forefront of your planning and delivery of services.

Burdening Clients with Your Problems

Sometimes people in human services use clients to meet their own needs. You could, for instance, burden the client with your own problems. You might say things like "Oh, that happened to me too" or "Wait until you hear what happened to me!" You might have had a bad day and want to talk to someone about it, and so you tell your client all about it, as Kent did with his client Lucy.

Meeting Your Needs

Do not ask the client to do something that meets your needs or is not in the best interest of your client. Because of the influence you have with this person, it is easy to influence a client to do something that is beneficial to you. You might get the client involved with a friend of yours who sells insurance, or you might ask the client to go on television with you or to do an interview about the client's condition for the paper. There might be some payoff for you, but because the client could have considerable difficulty saying no to you, it is imperative that you never place your client in this situation. Often the media wants to interview a person with schizophrenia or a recovering alcoholic. Inform members of the media that they will have to locate their own interviewees.

Insisting on Your Solutions

You may have a need to look efficient, innovative, or particularly therapeutic, and so you might try to give your clients solutions to their problems. You may have had a similar problem at one time and feel there is only one good way to resolve it—the way you used to resolve it, a way your clients can use without experiencing the hard knocks you took figuring it out. You might be tempted to lecture, to discuss your situation and how it compares with theirs, or to warn your clients. None of these actions will help your clients to grow by finding their own solutions.

Another way you can make clients do what you want them to do is to treat clients rudely if they fail to use your solutions or to move quickly enough toward a solution. Being rude is not the same thing as being firm. You can set limits, but it is inappropriate to treat clients brusquely for not improving or for not taking what you suggest as healthy measures.

Exploiting Dependency

Clients are naturally vulnerable. They come to you at a time in their lives when they are hurt, upset, and disorganized—a time when it is easy to come to rely on another person. You are in a position to exploit this vulnerability by maintaining the client in a dependent position long after such dependency is useful for the client. For example, you might enjoy having clients call you about the details and decisions of their lives. It might make you feel important or needed. You might encourage them to lean on you for assistance in matters they could manage themselves. Be very careful not to allow this sort of relationship to develop.

In one support group run by a psychiatric nurse, individuals gathered once a week to discuss their problems. Most of the participants were also depressed. A student, Grace, from the local college joined the group and was an active participant for about 2 years. During that time, the nurse who led the group often went out to lunch with Grace and was extremely encouraging. It appeared in retrospect that the nurse had developed dual relationships with a number of group participants, eating with them, inviting them to her house, and going to plays and concerts with them. The nurse explained that this was her way of supporting her clients.

Grace completed her associate's degree and her bachelor's degree before she was accepted at a graduate school in another state. She told the group and the nurse in charge that she was no longer depressed and that she felt she was ready to move on now. She shared her good news about her acceptance to graduate school. Instead of showing pleasure and encouragement, the nurse became angry. She told Grace that she was trying to deny her need for the group and for the nurse. She ridiculed Grace's acceptance to graduate school, telling Grace she was not ready for such a large step and would surely fail. When Grace continued with her plans, the nurse stopped speaking to Grace and encouraged others to stop speaking to Grace as well. This is an example of a group leader, a worker, who could not tolerate the fact that her clients would not always need her. The group was meeting her needs, which she was clearly putting before the needs of her clients.

Protecting a Client's Self-Esteem

We can all agree that denigration of clients, whether through verbal or physical abuse, is unethical, and in some cases illegal. You may believe that you are highly unlikely to encounter such behavior except in extremely unusual cases. Nevertheless, it is wise for you to understand that some workers are tempted to treat clients this way. There are four reasons this is likely to happen.

Unpleasant People. Just as in any other walk of life, there are people in social services who are not pleasant people. They are unpleasant in many different aspects of their lives, and they are insensitive to the toll it takes on others, particularly clients who are uncertain of their self-worth.

Need for Power. There are workers whose own sense of self-worth seems uncertain to them. They choose fields where they will have a degree of power over others. In this way they seek to elevate themselves at the expense of people they can clearly believe are poor souls. These individuals make life difficult for clients simply because they can, because they have the power to do so.

For example, one student reported that while she was on a fieldwork assignment, she and the staff and clients were all having soft drinks together. A client approached the worker in charge and timidly asked if he could have more ice for his drink. The worker responded with, "No, you don't need any more ice. If your drink is warm, it is because you are so slow drinking it. Go back and join the others and drink up." After the client turned and walked away, the worker leaned over and helped himself to ice for his drink, laughing as if this was a joke.

Lack of Support for Workers. Social service workers who lack support from their supervisors or administration often lean together for support. They tend to develop a we–them attitude with regard to the clients, feeling the need to do whatever they must to support each other and hold clients apart. In one unit adolescents were housed together after committing offenses. The least experienced staff came on in the evening, and that is when the teens would challenge the authority of the staff. Calls for help and requests for information and training on how to better handle the evening shift were ignored by the administration. Left alone with little support or knowledge, the staff resorted to coercion, often physical coercion, to manage the disruptive situation. In the end the staff were blamed for using excessive force, but the lack of support and interest in these workers by supervisors and the administration contributed significantly to the way these adolescents were treated.

Isolated with Unpredictable Behaviors. Workers in group homes, partial programs, or evening residential programs often are left alone without support when clients are exhibiting unpredictable behavior. Fear and a need to control the behavior and the situation can lead workers to use verbal, and even physical, abuse. For instance, two workers, one a student in a fieldwork placement and the other out of social work school only a year, were in a group home for the mentally ill. One evening when one of their clients clearly became manic, the student made a number of calls to supervisors. Supervisors responded irritably. It was their time off, they complained; the workers would have to figure it out for themselves. That's what they were being paid to do. A subsequent request to call in the crisis team was similarly denied. The two students spent the evening and all night with a client who was increasingly out of control with no supervision or support. Agencies who do not provide good support for less skilled workers are open to having workers band together against the clients in self-defense.

One problem new workers can encounter is finding themselves working for the first time in a place where they question the treatment of clients. If this happens to you, those in charge may tell you that this is the "real world" and that what you learned in school is impractical and does not apply. In these situations, the new workers clearly have entered situations that developed among the other workers long ago. Workers who encounter such abusive situations have a choice of either reporting the abuse or looking for work in a place where clients are treated ethically, but they do not have a choice about their own behavior.

Ethically you are charged with the care of the client. That includes the client's feelings of worth. Ethically your behavior toward clients should help enhance their view of themselves as worthy. Behaviors on the part of social service workers that subtract from a client's sense of self-worth are entirely unethical.

Stealing from Clients

It goes without saying that it is illegal and certainly unethical to take money or things belonging to patients. We have looked closely at how patients lose their privacy. Gossip, giving information to strangers without a release form signed by the client, and releasing more information than is needed are all ways that patients can lose their privacy or lose control of their information when they are being served by social service personnel. As previously noted, HIPAA laws outline the right to privacy and the protection of clients' health information. However, workers can steal from clients in other ways without even thinking about it. When you enter other people's lives and those people are not in a position to protect themselves, they are just as vulnerable as you are when you allow service or repair people into your home when you are not there to protect it.

There are two ways workers steal from clients. Both of these are theft and are entirely unethical:

1. Workers can steal a person's privacy.
2. Workers can steal a person's esteem and sense of worth.

Consider how clients can be robbed of their self-esteem and self-worth. Vulnerable and unsure of themselves, perhaps feeling awkward and dismayed over needing to ask for help, clients come for assistance with precious little self-confidence and self-esteem What they do have is needed for support in their struggle to regain their health or recover from bad habits. Workers have an opportunity at this point to reassure and encourage or to steal clients' sense of self-esteem. It happens when clients are denigrated, spoken to rudely or brusquely, called names, ignored when they are present, made fun of, treated cruelly, shamed, and ridiculed or forced to perform actions they are incapable at the time of performing.

Let's look at some examples. Kimberly had a long-standing battle with schizophrenia. When her mother was diagnosed as terminally ill, she called a crisis hotline to talk about this pending loss. The day her mother died she called again and the worker replied, "Didn't we discuss this before?" When Kimberly said they had "but my mother died today," the worker went on, "well, do you have anything else to talk about because if you don't you are wasting my time."

Peter had been sober for 2 months when he began to drink again. He felt bad about it and fearful that he would go on a binge, so he sought out the worker at the detox unit assigned to him. When the worker finally took him into his office, he said to Peter, "So you couldn't stay off the bottle! What a loser. I guess you know that by now."

In an after school program for teens with behavior problems, Curt was telling his worker that he could not return to school until he had completed the program. "I have no time for you. Grow up and complete it," said the worker, and with that she walked out of the room. For the rest of the afternoon and evening she refused to acknowledge Curt, invite him to eat with the others, or respond when he approached her. She would look past him or turn to another client.

I am sure that as you read about these incidents you felt these were egregious examples of workers mistreating clients or patients, but in many settings rude and often unkind communication is used frequently, either because workers feel harried or because they see this as a way of motivating clients. For the truly professional worker, it means that you will decide consciously that you will never knowingly subtract from clients any sense of self-worth or self-esteem. If you can make this promise to yourself, you will be conscious of how even your most casual remarks can either steal something of value or enhance the health of the people you help.

Competence

A significant characteristic of professionals is their ability to clearly know their limitations. Ethical professionals do not try to do work for which they have not been trained. Recognizing the limits of one's training and experience is very important. This means that you will be aware of areas where you could use some help or direction and that you will seek assistance when you need assistance. You will ask those who have more experience or education to assist you rather than attempting to do work for which you are not qualified.

In addition, seek additional training throughout your career. Most certification and licensing programs require that individuals obtain further training on a yearly basis. Even if you are not part of such a program, you have an ethical responsibility to increase your skills, knowledge, and understanding of the field in which you work.

Responsibility to Your Colleagues and the Profession

We all have an ethical responsibility to protect our clients. Sometimes our clients need to be protected from those who are charged with their care. Nearly every professional code of ethics contains statements supporting the ethical responsibility of the professional to take action when a colleague is no longer able to function effectively or is openly violating ethical guidelines.

Impaired Workers

A social service worker is considered impaired when he or she is no longer functioning effectively due to substance abuse, mental illness, or personal problems. In such cases, impaired workers are so consumed with their problems that they are no longer able to focus on the needs of clients. In other words, they are distracted, focused on things other than their professional responsibilities, and often neglectful to the point of endangering clients.

If Someone with Whom You Work Becomes Impaired

If you find yourself in a situation where a coworker appears to be impaired and therefore unable to be effective, you have an ethical obligation to take action. Generally the first action to take is to talk privately with the person who seems to be having problems. Point out your concerns and listen to any explanations you receive. Explore ways to help the person resolve the problems.

Usually agencies have established procedures for handling concerns about colleagues who are thought to be impaired. Sometimes, if the person holds a professional license, the licensing board is notified so it can take appropriate steps to curtail the individual's opportunity to practice until the personal problems are resolved.

In one outpatient unit where clients received medications, it became obvious that one of the RNs was taking some medication for herself. At first the staff was not sure how to handle this. The RN was the supervisor. She did the pill count, but the workers noticed that clients ran out of medications sooner than expected with numerous seemingly reasonable explanations. The staff was torn between wanting to let someone know and fearing that they could be wrong. Finally, in a staff meeting one member remarked that she was concerned that the clients were so often out of medication and she wanted to better understand how that happened so the agency could take steps to correct it. When the RN became defensive and refused to participate in the discussion, the staff went with their concerns to the administration.

If you have concerns about how to proceed, it is useful to discuss your concerns with a senior professional. Here you may be able to clarify whether and to what extent clients are endangered by the behavior you have observed, and how the behavior indicates that your colleague is impaired.

If You Become Impaired

Ethically you have a responsibility to refrain from activities that may lead to your own impairment. Should you become impaired for whatever reason, you have a further ethical responsibility to resolve your problems if they will interfere with your ability to practice. Practicing with clients if your physical, mental, or emotional problems will interfere to the detriment of the clients is unethical. It is important to have good self-awareness and be alert to the possibility that personal problems are interfering and having a negative impact in your work with clients. If this is the case, you have an ethical responsibility to seek help and to limit or cease your work with clients until your own problems are resolved.

Roy had had a drinking problem off and on all his adult life. He managed to hide it well enough to function in college and in his work as a case manager for many years. When his wife left, however, he began to drink more and missed work more consistently. A coworker noticed the problem and talked to Roy about getting help, but Roy brushed him off. Soon after, Roy began seeing one of the clients who also had a drinking problem and had come to the center for both her depression and her alcoholism. Roy kept this relationship secret, and the couple drank in bars that other case managers would not frequent. On night Roy and his girlfriend got into a fight at the bar where they had gone after dinner. The bartender asked them to leave; the fight moved to the street, Roy beat his girlfriend, and the police were called. Only when Roy ended up in jail, his career and marriage in a shambles, and his addiction out of control did he sober up enough to agree he needed help. Roy served his time, was terminated from his position as a case manager, and began outpatient treatment for his addiction. He is currently working as a night watchman for a furniture store.

It is often difficult to admit that we have problems, particularly when we work in a field where clients expect us to have healthy answers to their issues. Nevertheless, problems are part of life, but they always present opportunities for growth. Denying our own problems is not healthy and further impairs our ability to be useful social service workers in the future. Address your own problems as they occur as part of a lifelong pursuit of health and wisdom.

Ethical Violations

This chapter has put forward some of the common ethical standards and issues you will encounter, but it is not entirely comprehensive. You may encounter situations in which you have questions about what is ethical and what is not. Consult your code of ethics and talk to senior professionals about your concerns. Not all situations present clear-cut ethical options.

Sometimes you may have a colleague who is seemingly violating an ethical principle. A discussion with your colleague about your concerns is often the first step you might take, describing what you have observed and your concerns about your observations. If no satisfactory resolution results, you must then express your concerns to senior professionals or the administration in order to end the unethical behavior. Your agency will likely have a procedure for reporting unethical behavior; if so, that procedure should be followed.

Professional Responsibility

Finally, remember that you represent an agency and that it is your responsibility to establish a relationship with your client that is befitting of the agency. This will affect your relationship with the client in two ways.

First, know the parameters of your agency and operate within them. If you work for an agency that gives out food and fuel to the poor, do not attempt to do mental health counseling. If you are a case manager in a drug and alcohol unit, do not attempt to arrange foster care for one of your client's children except through the agency designated to handle that. If you work in a shelter for battered women, do not try to do drug rehabilitation. When a client needs services that fall outside the particular focus of your agency, make a referral to another agency that can best handle the problem.

The second way your relationship with the client is affected is related to dual relationships. Remain professional. Limit your contact to the focus of your agency and to the focus of that particular client's problems. Do not invite people home to dinner, take them home with you for the night, or become socially involved with them because you feel sorry for them.

Perhaps you are in the ER giving assistance to a woman who has been raped in her home. You are working for a rape crisis center. It is late. The woman you are interviewing is terrified of going home. You call crisis intervention to arrange for temporary lodging, but they are currently out of the office on a call and will have to "get back to you." The woman has tried unsuccessfully to reach two family members but has reached only their answering machines. Finally, in desperation, you take the woman home with you. You would rather do this than sit in the ER all night because you have to be at a meeting in the morning. The woman is educated and seems very pleasant and refined. She goes home with you, spends the night at your house, and returns with you to the agency in the morning, where they help her obtain temporary housing and see that she gets safely to work.

Two months later you begin to receive calls from the woman, who seems to want a friendship with you. She has found your number in the phone book. Soon after this, you receive a call in the middle of the night. It is the same client. She has had a fight with her boyfriend, and now she wants to stay with you. You tell her she cannot do that, and she becomes hysterical. In the next several weeks, she appears at your house several times, asking to stay with you. Always there is some reason she cannot stay where she is currently living. She knows your phone number, so she calls frequently. You have to be very firm in order to set limits; sometimes it is hard to do.

This story about a worker taking someone home is not all that unusual; it does happen. Rarely, however, is a person who is hurting and vulnerable able to reestablish a professional relationship with such a worker, complete with boundaries and limits, once the worker has extended this kind of friendship or kindness.

Summary

This chapter is particularly important because it involves your ethical obligation to the client and outlines some legal concepts you must follow to protect your client and yourself. The primary issue is always the welfare of the client. That must come before all other considerations. When we choose this line of work, we deliberately choose to work with vulnerable people who cannot be expected to protect themselves or to know their rights. It becomes our responsibility to see that clients are well protected and are treated or given service under the highest ethical standards.

Common codes of ethics, including the *Code of Ethics* of the National Association of Social Workers (NASW) and the *Ethical Standards of Human Service Professionals*, can be found in *Codes of Ethics for the Helping Professions* (Brooks/Cole, 2004).

Now that you are thoroughly familiar with your ethical and legal responsibilities, it is time to turn to case management as a basic area of practice in which ethical behavior is expected and informs your decisions.

◆ Exercises: Ethics

Instructions: The hypothetical practice situations that follow are designed to stimulate thinking and discussion on the issue of confidentiality. Each situation is followed by a multiple-choice list of possible responses you might make. Choose the response that you consider the best. Others may choose a different answer. Discuss with your fellow students the different possibilities and what might present the best outcome for the client.

1. Paula is a 17-year-old client in the daytime partial hospitalization program. Her mother phoned and requested to know Paula's psychiatric diagnosis so that she could inform the family's physician who is treating Paula for diabetes. You should:

    a. Advise the mother of the diagnosis and the name of the psychiatrist who made the diagnosis.
    b. Call the family physician directly and advise him of the diagnosis.

c. Ask Paula to sign a release of information form giving consent for the physician and/or the mother to be advised of her diagnosis.
  d. Refuse to release the information at all.

2. A client requests a copy of his current treatment plan. You should:
   a. Have the client put the request in writing and discuss the issue with the treatment team.
   b. Make a copy of the current treatment plan and give it to the client.
   c. Discuss the treatment plan and give it to the client.
   d. Refer the client to the attending psychiatric physician.

3. A 13-year-old client requests that his school counselor be sent a copy of his initial interview and discharge summary. The client signs a release of information form, documenting his written consent for the information to be transmitted. You should:
   a. Forward the material to the school counselor.
   b. Give the information to the client who can deliver it to the school counselor.
   c. Have the medical records department forward the information to the school counselor.
   d. Refuse to release the information until a parent cosigns the release of information form.

4. Mary Smith is a depressed elderly woman who was admitted to Polyclinic Hospital due to severe back pain. She was advised she might need surgery to correct the problem. You are her case manager at the Office of Aging, and she calls to say she is considering suicide. The constant back pain has made her feel like "just giving up." Mary is currently at home, awaiting a surgery date. You know Mary has a supply of pain pills, and she says she wants to take all the pills. You feel there is a substantial risk that Mary might follow through on her threat. You should:
   a. Contact the Polyclinic orthopedic staff who are currently seeing Mary in the outpatient clinic.
   b. Maintain frequent contact with Mary, but respect her wishes to keep her suicide plans confidential.
   c. After discussing with Mary what you are about to do, contact crisis intervention.
   d. Advise the city police department of Mary's suicide plans.

5. Bill Jones is a client who has been in alcohol treatment programs at your facility. He is currently depressed about his pending divorce and present marital separation. He has signed a release of information form for you to share information with his priest, who is counseling Bill about his religious conflicts regarding the divorce. A man calls you claiming to be Bill's priest

and requesting information on Bill's current state of mind. You have never actually spoken with Bill's priest, and you think this might actually be Bill's wife's attorney calling. You should:

a. Give no information on the phone until you have verified the identity of the caller.
b. Refer the caller to Bill.
c. Insist upon meeting with the priest in person.
d. Refuse to share any information with the caller.
e. Get the person's number and call him back.

6. Patty is completing a student internship for her associate's degree in the therapeutic activities program. She asks to review the medical records of the clients who were just in her projects group. You are supervising Patty. You should:

a. Advise Patty that the records are confidential and may not be inspected by students.
b. Make certain that Patty is well trained in the policies and procedures relating to confidential information, and only then allow her access to the medical records.
c. Permit Patty free access to the records because she is like part of the staff.
d. Obtain written consent from each client for Patty to review the records.

7. Jerry was a client who improved and was discharged 2 years ago. You receive a call from the National Can Company. The caller explains that Jerry has applied for a job and that the company would like to hire him. Jerry told them he was in treatment 2 years ago and was discharged after showing considerable improvement. The company wishes to confirm the fact that Jerry did indeed complete the program as he claims. You should:

a. Be very careful not to reveal whether Jerry was ever in treatment until a signed release form is received.
b. Confirm that Jerry completed his treatment but make no comment on progress or condition at discharge.
c. Explain, on the phone, that Jerry did successfully complete treatment and request that the company forward a release of information form to you in the next mail.
d. Make no comment and hang up quickly.

8. Clark is currently enrolled in treatment, and you are his case manager. He asks you if he may read his medical record. You should:

a. Ask Clark to put the request in writing, and assist Clark in completing the written request if he seems to have limited skills in reading and writing.
b. Present Clark's request to Clark's treatment team.

c. If the treatment team concludes that it will not harm Clark to review his record, allow Clark to read it in the presence of a therapist (after deleting information from sources that asked to remain anonymous).

d. Decide with the treatment team who will assist Clark in reading and understanding his record. Then follow through by allowing Clark to review his record with that person.

◆ Exercises: Ethically, What Went Wrong?

Instructions: The following hypothetical practice situations are designed to help you apply what you have learned in this chapter. For each situation, decide what was done in the situation that was unethical.

1. Jennifer had a long day and was trying to get out of the office before 5:00 p.m. She had one more client to see. Dr. Adams had asked Jennifer to give the client, a young man recently diagnosed with schizophrenia, a prescription for a new medication. Jennifer had her coat on when she handed the prescription to the client in the waiting room. The client wanted to know what the medication was and why his prescription was being changed. "Will there be any side effects?" he asked Jennifer. She replied hurriedly, "Oh, no. Dr. Adams says just take this until he sees you next time."

2. Carl is uncomfortable around gay men. A client of his is gay and has just broken up with his lover. This client, a 42-year-old man who had been in a long-term relationship, is devastated and is in tears in Carl's office. Because the client has suffered from severe depression in the past, Carl is attempting to have him evaluated by the therapist this afternoon. In the meantime, the client is weeping and threatening to take his life. Carl is particularly uncomfortable with this man's tears and believes this is all a drama. Carl says, "Oh, c'mon now. Let's get a grip. You can't sit in here all afternoon carrying on. Here. Take some tissue and go out in the waiting room until Dr. Paul can see you."

3. Elizabeth visited in the home of an elderly man and got him to sign a release of information form so she could process an application to the county nursing home. In the man's records were references to the fact that many years ago as a teenager he was convicted of shooting a man in a bar fight, a crime for which he served 2 years in prison. She knows the people at the home will be titillated over this little tidbit of information, especially her friend

Rhoda, who does the intakes. Even though she knows this is not part of the home's evaluation, that the client has led an exemplary life since that time, and that the nursing home staff might take it out of context, she releases the information anyway, based on her client's signature on the release form. She and Rhoda have a good laugh about it the next day.

4. Jim is doing an intake with a man who claims he is depressed. He tells Jim that ever since his wife left he has had trouble concentrating and waking up in the morning. He talks about how lonely it is at home, how much he misses his children, how he is tempted to drink in the evenings, and how little he has to look forward to. Jim nods. He understands. "Yes, my wife left last month too," Jim tells the man. "I know just what you mean. I get to feeling like, well, like there isn't as much meaning. I never knew the kids were so important to me, but I guess they were. On Saturdays I used to do things with my son and I still get him every other weekend, but it's not quite the same thing, is it?" "No," the man responds, "I was thinking..." Jim interrupts the man to say, "Well, I do a lot of thinking too. I think about what I could have done differently and if it was my fault. Don't you think these women would see that it's hard, too hard I think, to raise kids alone?" The conversation continues in this vein until the end of the interview.

5. Carmen is supposed to see her small caseload of persistently mentally ill individuals at least twice a week. Lately with school and her mother's death, she has not really seen her clients that often. She has checked in with them on the phone, but she also has used time when she was out seeing clients to do errands at the library and to empty her mother's home. Now one of her clients is in court after committing a crime. The client and the lawyer agree that the client might be able to use his mental health status as a reason for committing the crime, and they ask to introduce the case record as evidence in the court proceedings. Fearing that it will be discovered how little supervision and attention she has given her client, and knowing that ultimately she could be blamed for the fact that her client committed the crime while under her somewhat irresponsible care, Carmen invokes the concept of privileged communication to avoid having to give the file to the court.

6. Ted is in a clinic with his elderly client for a routine blood workup, which they do every other month. He notices the client is bruised on the face and arms. For a while he makes small talk with her, and then he asks her about the bruises. She is somewhat evasive but indicates, "They weren't the result of no fall!" Without explicitly blaming her daughter and son-in-law, with whom she lives, she makes it quite clear that the bruises are not the result of an accident. After the blood test, during which neither the doctor, who sees her briefly, nor the technician make any mention of the bruises, Ted takes his client home. He toys with the idea of reporting the bruises to protective services at the county Office of Aging but decides not to. He bases his decision on the fact that the law does not specifically require him to do so, that it would be hard and take a lot of time to have to place this client in another living arrangement, and that the daughter seems like a very nice person whom Ted does not feel like stirring up over an uncomfortable situation.

7. Kitty has a whole list of things to do today and doubts she can get it all done. She hates the way there are always things left to do at the end of the day. It just seems that no matter how hard she works, something new comes up that she cannot complete. One of her clients has told her on the phone that she wants to sign a release of information form for her lawyer. Kitty has the form ready for the time when this client will be coming in at the end of the week. Today a man calls and says he is the client's lawyer and he needs just two dates to help him file a brief with the court on the client's behalf. Kitty gives him the two dates and hurries to the next thing on her list.

8. Jorge is mad at lunch in the staff room this noon. He spent one morning taking a meticulous social history from a new client. The client, a man in his 20s, was pleasant and helpful. He seemed to genuinely want the assistance of the agency and to like Jorge. Two more interviews followed to set up services, and the client signed a release of information form for Jorge to meet with the client's physician. Jorge cannot understand why the client never mentioned the fact that he is HIV+. This Jorge found out in the conference with the client's physician some weeks later. "How do these clients think I am going to help them if they don't tell the whole story?" Jorge fumed. "They come in here and want my help and then withhold information from

me. They leave me in the dark. I don't know what's going on, and then they think I'm going to be able to help them."

9. A new worker, Jill, is working at a large residential facility for the mentally ill and has been assigned four clients for whom she is to develop goals and objectives to help these clients move forward to greater independence. She meets with the first two clients and then confides to a worker who has been there longer that she had trouble understanding what the clients wanted to work on. The worker tells Jill, "Just make up the plans. These people are a waste of time. They won't ever get any better. Look at that one. This is his fourth trip through here. No one ever made a difference with a plan, and you won't either. Just put something down to satisfy the insurance company, and come in here with us. There is a good movie on TV tonight, and the staff is going to put the clients to bed early and get together in the patient lounge to watch it."

10. Beatrice, who has suffered from schizophrenia for most of her life, has been placed in a long-term residential facility. One night the worker decides to take the clients to a movie. The clients all get in the van to go to the movies, and the worker waits to leave until everyone has a seat and has fastened their seat belts. Beatrice finds a seat but complains that the seat belt does not fit, that she cannot fasten it around herself. The worker replies, "Well, if you didn't eat so much, you wouldn't be so fat. You always pig out at the table, and this is what you get. I guess you're too fat to go to the movies tonight, Beatrice. Guess you'll have to just stay home."

11. Pedro noticed that his colleague, Antoine, was using clients' spending money to make small purchases for himself. Each client in the group home was given a specific amount of spending money every month, and it was kept in the client's envelope. When money was spent from the envelope, a receipt was to be left in the envelope showing where the money went. Antoine was taking money for small purchases for himself—lunch, movie tickets, a gold chain. He was placing the receipts for these purchases in the clients' envelopes. It was not possible for administration, when doing an audit of all the clients' accounts at the end of the month, to determine from the receipt who actually benefited

from the expenditure. Pedro thought about telling the administration but felt it was likely that Antoine would deny the allegations, and this would ruin their working relationship. Therefore, Pedro did nothing.

12. Marcella began to drink in the evenings after work when her husband left her for another woman. As the months went by, the divorce became increasingly acrimonious. There were accusations, attempts to take Marcella's money, and attempts to deprive her of custody of the children. The children began to exhibit problems, and there were financial problems as well. Drinking in the evenings expanded to a drink with lunch and later to a drink and then several drinks in midafternoon. In time, Marcella could not face the day without alcohol when she first got up. She continued to report for work where she was the sole worker on the day shift in a small residential setting with four clients. Marcella began to ignore the clients. It started with naps in the afternoon, which left the clients unsupervised. Later Marcella found it too hard to fix dinner for her clients and began to allow them to eat junk food for dinner. As the situation deteriorated, Marcella became more and more mired in self-pity, anger at her ex-husband, and alcohol abuse. She continued to work at the group home.

◆ Exercise: Decide on the Best Course of Action

Instructions: Sit with a small group of other students and decide how you will handle this situation. There are many areas both ethically and legally that are not clear, so the discussion you have with your colleagues is much like a discussion you might have in a real agency. There are no "correct answers."

You have been working with a client who is HIV+ and is a regular user of heroin. He needs both medical and substance abuse treatment. However, he is inconsistent about coming for regular treatment and medical care. You suspect he is not taking medications prescribed for him. In addition, he is sexually active with several women. He has asked that you not contact him at his home where he lives with one of his girlfriends. He has stipulated that no family members may have any information about him. You think that if you could commit him to a substance abuse treatment facility he will be out of circulation sexually and he will receive the treatments he needs to save his life. You do not know where he is but know his girlfriend probably does. Can you do this? What ethical and legal principles are at play here? What do you decide to do or not do?

Chapter 2

Case Management: Definition and Responsibilities

Introduction

Case management is one of the primary places in human service systems where the whole person is taken into account. Unlike specific services, case management does not focus on just one problem but rather on the many issues, strengths, and concerns a client brings.

For example, an elderly person may be referred to Help Ministries for a voucher for fuel oil because it has been unusually cold and the elderly person has been unable to pay for the additional oil needed to warm his home adequately. In this case, Help Ministries is concerned with his fuel oil need and the warmth he will need to stay in his home during the winter. That is their only concern with regard to this client.

The case manager, on the other hand, is concerned with the client's need for fuel oil, with his desire to move into public housing for the elderly in the spring, with what resources he has among his children, with his recent slurred speech indicating a possible stroke, and with his need for meals-on-wheels. The case manager is aware that there is a neighbor who can look in on her client daily, that the client has ties to a church, and that he receives Social Security, but little other income. She knows he has a sense of humor, goes to bingo once a month, and should be fitted for a cane.

Case management is a process for assessing the client's total situation and addressing the needs and problems found in that assessment. As a part of this process, the client's strengths and interests are used to improve the overall situation wherever possible. The primary purpose for case management is to improve the quality of life for the client. This might mean more comfortable or safer living arrangements, or it might require psychiatric care or medication for diabetes. Another major purpose of this activity is to prevent problems from growing worse and costing more to remedy in the future. In the situation of the elderly man just described, we find that the meals-on-wheels program will deliver a certain standard of good nutrition, preventing malnutrition and costly medical bills in the future. By getting the man a cane, we may be preventing falls that would shorten his life and cost much more in medical bills to repair his injuries. If we enlist the neighbor to look in on our client every day, we have provided a link between the client and his neighborhood. In addition, the neighbor can alert us to small problems that require our attention.

A History of Case Management

In the late 1800s a formal attempt was made to organize the delivery of services to people in need. The Charity Organization Society took control of this approach, making the collecting of information and the delivery of services more systematic. In the course of its work, the society developed casework as a useful method for tracking needs, progress, and changes in each case. As people had more needs and problems beyond poverty, the need to coordinate these services became important to prevent duplication. Casework also was employed as a means of tracking and using scarce resources to the best advantage. In the 1960s the process of deinstitutionalization meant that individuals once housed in institutions were now placed in communities where they needed considerable support to live more independent lives; as a result, casework became ever more important for a larger number of people.

In the 1980s the term *caseworker* evolved into the term *case manager*, and these managers took on greater responsibility for managing resources, finding innovative supports, and coordinating services. Agencies began to use case management as a procedure to assess needs, to find ways to meet those needs, and to follow clients as they used those services. In addition to keeping an eye on how scare resources were spent, case managers were charged with taking a more holistic approach to their clients, looking at all their needs rather than addressing only those that brought the person in for assistance. As part of this charge came the directive to develop individualized plans, plans constructed specifically for the client and not a cookie-cutter approach to supplying services.

Today case managers are seen as a significant service in almost all social service settings and are viewed as the most important way to prevent relapse, track clients' needs, and support progress toward good health.

Why Case Management?

Case management serves two purposes. First, it is a method for determining an individualized service plan for each client and monitoring that plan to be sure it is effective. Second, it is a process used to ensure that the money being spent for the client's services is being spent wisely and in the most efficient manner.

The money you oversee in client care may be public money, such as the money that comes from the state to a county to administer mental health services or substance abuse treatment. It may be money that is provided by insurance companies for services to a policyholder. It may be money provided directly to an agency from either of these sources for the care of a client. The agency uses case managers to make certain the most effective use is made of the money. It is, therefore, the case manager who determines what is needed and how to prevent needs and problems from escalating. It is the case manager who, in collaboration with the client, determines what services should be authorized with the existing money. It is the case manager who then follows the client and the client's services and treatment to keep the plan on track.

Case management is more than looking out for another entity's money. It is also the most efficient way to make certain a client receives the most individualized plan for service and treatment possible. To ensure that this will be done, case management responsibilities have been broken into four basic categories of service: assessment, planning, linking, and monitoring. Let's look at those categories in the order in which they are usually accomplished when working with a person.

What Is an Individualized Plan?

After you have worked with clients to determine where the problems are and what areas need attention, you will also know about the supports and other resources clients have in the community and among their family members and friends. You will know what they do well and what interests them most. Each client will be different.

As you go about designing the plan with the person, you will place in that plan elements that take advantage of the client's strengths and supports. In addition, you will address those problems most outstanding or immediate for that client. Each person has a different set of strengths, life circumstances, immediate problems, and personal goals. No two clients view their situations in exactly the same way, so no two plans will be exactly alike. Each plan will be developed specifically for that individual client.

At one time, a small program for homeless women employed a part-time case manager for the children. Homeless women were given 2 years' residence in apartments belonging to the program to work hard on getting an education, training, and a stable source of income. Many of them were distracted from this by concerns about their children. Still others had little time to think about what their children needed as they went about restructuring their lives. The county mental health/mental retardation program gave the shelter a small stipend to hire a children's case manager. The shelter hired a young woman who had just graduated from college. This seemed like an ideal choice. She was energetic, related well to the children, and was genuinely concerned about each of them. In the next year, the program monitor from the county noticed two things. First, there seemed to be very little material on the children in any records. No individual plans could be found, and no assessments on each child appeared to have been done. Second, the children were all following much the same plan. All the girls attended gymnastics; all the boys were enrolled in Little League. On certain weekends, all the children went to the zoo or to the circus.

After receiving repeated requests for individualized plans for each child and some guidance about how to create them, the case manager quit. She said, on departing, that she did not have time to sit and write up records, that the children had been "having fun," and that the county was unreasonable. The county became more involved in hiring the second case manager, and this person was well aware of the importance of individualized planning.

In the first 6 months, two children began to get orthodontic work done, one received a scholarship to a private school, four boys went to Little League, one took violin lessons, and a third joined the swim team at the YMCA. Most of the younger children went to the circus and to the zoo. Most of the older children went on a bus trip to Washington, D.C., and half of them went to two symphony orchestra performances that winter. No child's plan was the same as that of another child. Each child's needs had been documented and addressed in some way, and each child's strengths and interests were brought into play as the plans were developed.

In developing these plans, the case manager called all her contacts in the community. She asked two dentists to donate their time. She prevailed upon the symphony to give her the tickets for two performances. She went to a private school and talked to them about this particularly gifted child until a plan for financing the child's education was worked out. She found a violin teacher and asked for 15 free lessons as a gift to the shelter. In churches and synagogues, she got people enthused about helping the children whose mothers were working so hard to put a stable life together for their families. She looked at scout troops, church youth groups, and organized sports for possible answers to the children's needs. In any number of cases, the plan simply involved the case manager helping an older child choose from among school activities and arranging transportation.

This is what is meant by individualized planning. When it is done well and done creatively, your clients can grow and thrive.

Assessment

The first case management task is assessment. This is an initial assessment, meant to be comprehensive and thorough. Therefore, it covers many different aspects of the person's life in an attempt to develop an accurate profile of the client and the client's problem.

There are several kinds of assessments. In some cases you will be asked to do a social history (see Chapter 16). Here you ask a series of questions, and as the person answers, you construct a written narrative. Social histories usually have a number of elements that you are to assess, and each is given a subheading within the narrative. For example, current medical condition, living arrangements, relationships, and work experience are all important. In another kind of assessment, you may be given an intake assessment form that lists all the questions you are to ask and gives you a place to note the answer. Each of these assessment procedures attempts to be comprehensive. Each seeks to assemble a considerable amount of material about the client and the client's problem.

The first thing the case manager does is assess the initial or presenting problem. Why did this person come into the agency, and what is the person asking for? Here case managers look at the extent to which problems have interfered with clients' abilities to function and care for themselves. Does this problem interfere with work or with relationships? It is especially important to note the background of the problem, how long it has gone on, and how it started. In addition, the reasons the client is seeking help now are important.

Case managers include an opinion about what possible problems might arise for this client in the future and what plan might be put into effect with the person to prevent these problems. Your opinions about potential future problems are formed as you listen to clients describe their situations. Will the client be likely to be around people who encourage him to drink? Does she have a medical problem that needs attention because it exacerbates her depression?

A discussion of the problem uncovers the person's needs. Case managers look at the overall situation and consider what the client needs to bring stability and resolution to the client's life and problem. Are there needs that can be addressed that will relieve the problem, or at least alleviate it to some extent?

In every assessment with a client, you will begin to learn what strengths the person has that you and the client may draw upon to resolve the current problem. Does your client have an advanced degree, a particularly supportive family, a number of friends and other supports, a particular skill? An assessment should never be just about the person's problems, but should also include the strengths the person brings to the problems and the strengths you see in the person's environment.

As you take the information from the client, you are also evaluating the person's ability to think clearly and to understand options, and the person's general mood. Chapter 18 discusses in more detail something called the "mental status examination." This is not a series of questions but rather your astute observations of the client during the interview.

At the end of your assessment document, you will be asked to express your assessment and recommendations. Here you will summarize briefly the problem and the client's ability to handle the problem, noting the person's strengths and needs. Then you will give your own recommendations for service or treatment. Recommendations are generally worked out with the client as you learn what it is the person is seeking and share with that person what you have to offer.

To summarize, in an assessment you are exploring and evaluating the following:

1. The initial problem and the background to that problem
2. The person's current situation
3. The person's background in areas such as education, relationships, work history, legal history
4. What the person needs to make life more stable and to resolve the current problem
5. The strengths, including both those the person brings to the problem and those in the person's environment, that would be useful in resolving the situation
6. Observations about how well the person functions cognitively and any seeming mental problems you have noted
7. Recommendations for a service or treatment plan for the person

A good assessment is the foundation for the development of an individual plan for service or treatment. It delineates the provision of essential services and provides for individualized treatment.

Planning

After the assessment, you will be expected to develop an initial plan with the client that is comprehensive and addresses all the issues raised in your assessment. This plan should show incremental steps toward improvement and expected outcomes. As a case manager, you cannot plan well with your client unless you are thoroughly aware of the services, social activities, and resources in your community.

Formal Agencies

Every community has social service agencies that serve specific needs. The best case managers seem to know all the good places to send clients for the services those clients need. Some communities and counties have more services than others, but in most locations agencies are serving children and their families, older adults, individuals with substance abuse problems, individuals on probation, women, and individuals with mental illness or mental retardation. Generally case managers need to learn about other services as well, and these numbers and information about the services should be readily available to you when you practice. You will want to gradually develop contacts in these places so that your referrals are smooth and problems are quickly handled.

Begin by knowing what formal agencies are out there to help with a particular issue. For instance, if your client has a mental health problem, you might refer him to an agency that specializes in mental health treatment. The staff at that agency is familiar with medications, diagnoses, and treatment alternatives for mental health problems. Another client may be elderly and in need of protective services because you suspect she is being physically abused by her family. You would refer her to a specific agency that offers protective services to older people. A third client may have intermittent problems with substance abuse and need services from an office where there is an intensive outpatient treatment program in the evenings.

Generic Resources

Good planning is not limited to formal agencies, however. Learn about resources that are available for common problems we all have. Not every problem a person with a developmental disability has will need to be treated by agencies set up exclusively for individuals with developmental disabilities. For example, a woman with mild mental retardation, grieving the death of her mother, was welcomed into a grief support group at the local church and given much support. In another example, a child with academic problems in school was referred to the free tutoring at a local church. An older person who needs more social contacts might be referred to a senior center where many older people go for social and recreational opportunities. In the previous examples, the older person suffering abuse may also need the services of your local district attorney, and the person with a substance abuse issue might need medical care from a general practitioner and a public defender for pending charges of disorderly conduct. These are all services anyone can use.

Other Established Community Resources

Another resource often overlooked are support groups and educational seminars. For example, you may have referred the family of a child you are working with to formal family therapy sessions. In addition, you would look at support groups where parents dealing with these specific problems can get together to support each other. Further, you might find a workshop on parenting skills that would greatly benefit this family, and you would tell them about the workshop and strongly encourage them to attend. A client on probation might benefit from a workshop for job readiness or a support group for ex-offenders attempting to make significant life changes.

Peer Support

A relatively recent trend is to use peer support wherein a former client who is doing well is hired by an agency to support others on the road to recovery and life changes. It might be individuals who were able to turn their lives around after a period in juvenile detention and now are supporting others coming out of juvenile detention to do the same thing. It might be someone who has had a mental illness and is now helping others who are recovering from their own mental illness. And, of course, in substance abuse AA has always used that model of one person in AA helping another. The idea is based on the fact that not all professionals know what it is like to experience some problems firsthand. The peer support person is able to say he has been there and can show the client how to resolve the issues with firsthand practical information.

Individuals whose functioning is impaired might benefit from a peer support person who can help them function better educationally, socially, or vocationally and may even become involved in helping them with issues of self-care. Much like case management, the peer support person ascertains that the client will accept peer support and then works with the client to set realistic and meaningful goals the two can approach together. Good peer support helps clients formulate the small action steps needed to move toward the goals the two have identified together, and the peer support person can be there with advice and ideas if the action step doesn't work very well. As a case manager, use peer support when a person needs more sustained time than you can give and the support will significantly help the person move toward recovery.

Informal Resources and Folk Support Systems

You also need to be aware of social activities your clients might enjoy that would keep them involved in their communities. Perhaps one likes to work on models and could become a member of the model railroaders club. Perhaps another genuinely likes people and enjoys being with them. This person might do well as a member of the Jaycees.

Clients do better living in a community in which they have healthy folk support systems. A folk support system refers to the kinds of supports most of us have in our communities such as Lions Club, a church, or volunteering on specific community projects. All of us need to feel we are a part of the place where we live, but many people do not have the skills to interact with others and find useful activities on their own. As a case manager, it is your responsibility to integrate your client into the community if this is a need. Find social clubs, churches, and groups that pursue similar interests, and help your client make contact with those people. The more contacts your client has and the more useful activities your client engages in, the more support the community can give.

A particularly touching example of the use of informal supports occurred in a small town in which the firehouse was located just around the corner from a group home for five older men with mental health problems. They had been institutionalized for most of their lives, spent years on medication, and had the common long-term side effects that can develop. One of the men, Nick, wanted to be a fireman, so the case manager connected this man to the fire company. The men at the firehouse made Nick a part of their everyday routine. Nick helped roll hoses, swept floors, and took his meals with the men. Nick was included in meetings and made decisions about the dinner menu. He became such a part of the fire company that when he died suddenly of cardiac complications the men were deeply saddened. As a tribute to Nick on the day of his funeral, the procession from the funeral home to the cemetery was led by a number of fire trucks, beginning with the trucks from Nick's home station and including some from neighboring communities. This was an excellent example of using folk supports to give a person a valued place in the community and a sense of doing something worthwhile.

Case managers often fail to use these valuable informal resources for several reasons. They may feel that their client cannot handle being with ordinary people in ordinary settings. This is often based on the case manager's attitude about the client's disability and is often quite erroneous. Having clients in small numbers in social activities or organizations that give them an opportunity to practice strengths is an invaluable experience for everyone concerned. Another reason a case manager might be reluctant to place a client in a community social group might stem from the case manager's perception that people in such groups do not want to be bothered with people who have disabilities. In some cases, this assessment is correct, but in others it is quite the opposite. Many organizations are set up to provide service and perceive this as an opportunity to grow and serve the community.

Doing your homework pays off. You cannot rely on suppositions and speculations. Know what is available in your community and have places in mind that would serve your clients as the need arises. Meet people and talk to them about what you would like to have available for your clients. Gradually you will develop a list of people and places that welcome your clients and provide the specific experiences and support you are seeking. Your task is to have many resources you can use at your fingertips when developing plans for your clients and to continually be developing new ones in your community.

Continued Planning

In continued planning, as you follow the case, you will take into account changes the client may face. An example will illustrate this kind of planning, which you may be called upon to provide. Mary Beth has a mild developmental disability and was assigned to you when she left a state-run institution for individuals with mental retardation. When you did the intake planning, you determined that she would do better initially in a sheltered living arrangement for about a year. Because the goal is for her to move to an apartment of her own at the end of the year, your planning should start well in advance of this move. This planning makes the transition easier for her and for you. There are no shocks and sudden surprises that might necessitate her need for hospitalization or a regression back to greater dependence on the agency.

You might begin by setting up services and activities with Mary Beth that involve her in her community. Mary Beth told you when you first talked to her of her interest in singing. The people at the institution said she loved music and sang well, although she could not read music. At the time Mary Beth came out of the institution, you could not find a good place for her to use her musical interests, but you noted this as a strength and kept your eyes open for an appropriate link. Now you have found a choir director at a small church who is willing to have Mary Beth sing with her choir. The church has numerous activities, and there are members who see to it that Mary Beth is included. In this way, you begin to prepare her for a move to more independent living. You seek and find a place for her to live not too far from the church, and you work with interested members to ensure that Mary Beth will have their continued help with transportation and inclusion in church activities.

You may think it best that Mary Beth has other social ties to her community as well. There is the Aurora Club, created by professionals just for people with mental illness and developmental disabilities. This club is a place to go and meet others; and the club takes trips, goes bowling, and goes out to dinner together. You could refer her there; however, you might decide that Mary Beth's mild disability does not warrant her being limited to social activities only for individuals with mental retardation. Instead, you might develop a relationship with a local women's club, getting them to take Mary Beth as a member.

As Mary Beth makes an adjustment to being outside the institution, you look for a job placement. You make a referral to Goodwill, where she is able to develop her social skills, and soon she is hired by a local Wal-Mart as a greeter.

By the time Mary Beth moves into an apartment of her own, she has gained new confidence and many friends who connect her to the community. Her success is due in large measure to both your wise initial plan and your modifications of the plan as Mary Beth grew more independent.

Linking

Once the plan is drawn up, the case manager links (or transfers or refers) the client to the service or persons who will carry out the plan. Linking a client to a specific service requires care and skill on your part. You need to know the best service that will meet the individual issues and needs of your client.

Linking your client to a social service agency that provides a specific service—such as day treatment, drug rehabilitation, or groups for victims of violent crime—will require a written referral. You will state why you are making the referral, indicating the problem for which the referral is being made and the goal that you expect as a result of your client's contact with the agency. The referral will also indicate the amount of time you estimate it will take for the agency to reach this goal. The time limit is very important. It keeps treatment from becoming endless and unstructured. With a goal and a set amount of time in which to attain that goal, both the agency and the client are more likely to make the most of their time together.

Sometimes clients can take advantage of services on their own. You might tell a client about the Aurora Club, for example, and the next week he may take a bus there and begin going to the club regularly, participating in activities and social events. At other times, you may have clients who are unable to take the first step and who will need you to accompany them or to arrange transportation for them.

In a formal social service agency, personnel at that agency will be able to support your clients in their programs and implement the goals and work on the issues you and your clients have identified as important. Some agencies with very fine programs or specialized services are small, which may require you to give more support to your client. For example, at New Start, a staff of three focuses on second-stage groups for victims of rape and domestic violence, and much of the work is done by volunteers. The success rate is excellent, and clients report a high degree of satisfaction with the agency. However, the small staff is not equipped to handle other problems that might develop while your client is in their group. If you refer a client to a group at New Start and your client has landlord problems between group sessions, the staff at New Start may not be aware of it in time to prevent an eviction notice. Even if they become aware of the notice, they will need to refer the client to you to resolve the matter because of the limited staff time available to clients. On the other hand, at Riverview, a day-treatment program, nurses are aware of medication problems, social workers monitor progress toward goals, and staff can work to prevent eviction of a client, if that appears imminent.

On occasion you may find a service for your client at an agency that does not seem interested in serving her. Perhaps they are reluctant because your client has been ill recently or because the agency is not interested in her type of problem. The agency may accept the client into service with them to fill all their slots and draw down payment for services, but in reality they may give poor or no services. In such instances, linking becomes advocacy as you advocate for your client or on behalf of your client. In a situation like this, advocacy means you will attempt to seek the best services for your client, and you will insist that your client be treated fairly and with respect.

Monitoring

After the plan has been made and implemented (meaning the referrals indicated in your plan have been accomplished), it becomes your responsibility to monitor the services given to your client. When a formal agency is holding a planning or treatment conference about one of your clients, you should be invited to attend. You should also receive written reports about your client's progress and about the services given to him or her. If you do not receive reports at specified intervals from the agency, you need to contact them yourself on a regular basis.

Talking with another agency about the service they are giving your client is done for two reasons:

1. To be certain that the treatment or service you authorized for this client is in fact the treatment or service that is being given
2. To keep track of your client's progress toward the goals you developed with the client, and to be aware of times when modifications and revisions in either the goals or the plan need to take place

Less formal groups or institutions that are part of your plan should get a call or visit from you occasionally to monitor how the plan is working. Suppose that the neighbor offers to take your client, Bill, to church with her family every Sunday. In August, the family goes away for a month and does not make arrangements with anyone else to take him to church. He begins to feel lonely, and one day he goes to another church closer to his apartment. There he is extremely friendly to everyone, which seems to bother the minister and several members of the church. They decide he is "inappropriate" and call crisis intervention, which gets tied up going to the church and sorting out what happened. All of this could have been avoided if you had been able to have regular contact with the family who took your client to church. In that case, you would have known of the vacation and could have requested that they find a substitute or could have found a substitute yourself.

Figure 2.1 outlines the knowledge base and skills needed for case management and offers some useful guidelines for you to follow in practicing case management.

Service Coordination

Service coordination refers to working with other agencies or systems in a client's life. Many of your clients will be involved in other programs and systems, and each of these programs or systems may have a different plan for the client. Each of these plans may be headed more or less toward the same broad general goal, but their specifics for each client are different. Often the major and most significant role for the case manager is

FIGURE 2.1

Knowledge Base, Skills, and Guidelines for Case Management

Knowledge Base for Case Management

In order to do case management, you need knowledge of the following:

1. *Individual and family dynamics* (which you find in courses such as Human Development, Introduction to Psychology, Marriage and the Family, and Abnormal Psychology)
2. The relationship between and among social, psychological, physiological, and economic factors (as found in the *ecological model*, a theoretical basis for evaluating a person's situation and needs)
3. The *focus and policies of your agency*
4. *State and federal laws and regulations* that affect your agency's delivery of service
5. The vast array of *community services and resources* where you practice

Skills You Need to Be an Effective Case Manager

To be an effective case manager, you need the ability to:

1. *Work effectively with people* to promote their growth
2. *Work with people* of various professions, paraprofessionals, the public, and clients and their families
3. *Identify what your client needs*
4. *Keep accurate and well-organized records*
5. *Allow the client to take leadership* in planning services
6. *Develop creative resources* within your community to meet client needs

Guidelines for Case Management

Here are some useful guidelines for you to follow in practicing case management:

1. *Plan ahead.* Plan before there is a crisis. Develop a plan that will prevent crises based upon what you learned about your clients in the assessment and what you can foresee happening in their situations if the issues are not addressed. Alleviate crisis-provoking situations before the crises occur.
2. *Be accountable* to your client and to the community. Do what you say you will do. Do it *promptly*. And carefully *document* what you have done.
3. *Be optimistic* about your client. Expect improvement and some degree of independence, and that is what you are most likely to get. Reinforce success, and never miss an opportunity to give positive feedback. Set up situations in which your client is likely to succeed rather than situations that are complex and tricky.
4. *Involve your clients* in all phases of planning. Let your clients decide what issues and problems in their lives take priority. Get their opinions and feedback about services and about their plans.
5. *Go where your clients are.* Do not stay shut up in your office. Go out and see where your clients are interacting with others, and teach your clients new skills in the field where they will need them.

(continued)

FIGURE 2.1 *(continued)*

6. *Promote independence.* Show pride in the independence your clients demonstrate regardless of how small it is. Model independence, encourage independence, and teach as often as it takes the skills to maintain independence.
7. *Develop a large number of resources* and know how to find good ones for your clients. Know what formal agencies exist in your community and their focus. Look for and develop good folk support systems on which you can rely. As you move about the community, look for new resources you can add to your list.

to bring representatives of these different systems together, forming a team that collaborates with one another in supporting the client's goal.

This is not as easy as it sounds. Communities and counties have numerous services, such as the school and other educational systems, mental health and the mental retardation systems, the criminal justice system, a substance abuse system, and health care systems. These organizations often operate as though they are the only program with which the client is involved. Case managers who attempt to get everyone to work together are sometimes not welcome, and the program may be closed to outside input and collaboration with other agencies. However, coordinating the different services can enhance clients' movement toward their goals. When coordination is not possible, clients' goals can be impeded tremendously.

For example, Norita was a student at a community college and also a mother on welfare with one child. Because of her mental health problems in the past, her case manager at the mental health unit had facilitated Norita's receiving welfare to support herself while in school, and the case manager had worked with Norita to get her into school where she was an excellent student. Then the welfare worker insisted that Norita drop out of school and take a job readiness course as all single mothers on welfare were required to do. This demand came in the middle of a semester, and time and money would have been wasted if Norita was forced to drop out of school. The case manager worked with both the school and the welfare office to form a team working to support Norita in her movement toward financial independence.

At first the welfare worker was not happy about working with the case manager. She was curt and unpleasant and stipulated that the rules for remaining on welfare meant that Norita would have to drop out of school and take a 7-week job readiness course. The case manager made an appointment to meet and brought an academic counselor from the college to the meeting. In this face-to-face context, the welfare worker began to soften and see advantages to Norita's current plan. Norita was only one semester away from graduation after she completed the current semester. The college counselor stated that the counseling department was available to help with resumes and job searches. In fact, it was likely that Norita would be hired from her internship as she was going into a field with a high demand for workers.

Gradually a team was formed, and collaboration around helping Norita become independent took place. In the end each party felt the outcome was beneficial to its system. This last element is crucial when coordinating with other agencies and systems. To support the overall plan, each party has to feel that what is being agreed to will have a satisfactory outcome for the system he or she represents. In this case both the welfare worker and the case manager met the goal for Norita to become independent and self-supporting. In addition, the case manager avoided duplication of services. If the college was showing Norita how to get a job and the welfare system was as well, there would have been duplication of services. What could have been competing systems and ill will became, instead, complementary services integrated around a specific goal and working together on Norita's behalf.

You will not always be coordinating with other social services agencies. In one instance Meredith's client, Phillip, believed he was employed by the Fresh 'N Save grocery store near his home. This was a delusion Phillip had held consistently for over a year. Phillip had gone to the store on numerous occasions, rearranging things on the shelves, helping shoppers with their bags and carts, and generally impeding some of the daily tasks at the store. On a number of occasions Phillip was arrested for defiant trespass, and often he was escorted off the property by the local police. In one instance he was given a short jail sentence, but 6 hours after his release from jail he was back at the Fresh 'N Save. The case manager pulled together a team of people who previously had been working on their own to try to solve this problem. Present at the first meeting was the probation officer, the county mental health representative, a person from the police department, and the manager of the Fresh 'N Save. The question before the team was: "What resources do we need to resolve this problem and move Phillip to more constructive activities?"

Everyone on the team recognized that there was no treatment in the jail for Phillip, so the team looked at what other resources would be needed. It was agreed Phillip needed some level of supervision. A commitment to a partial hospitalization program would be obtained. Phillip would go there 5 days a week. In addition, supervised housing was arranged for Phillip. In this way, someone would know where Phillip was or should be at all times. The police and the store manager agreed to call the partial hospitalization program or the supervised housing unit if Phillip returned to the store. The case manager agreed to work with Phillip and staff in the partial hospitalization unit to seek other goals Phillip might have for himself. The county mental health representative agreed that the crisis intervention team would intervene when necessary if the case manager was off on a weekend or in the evenings. In this way individuals representing a number of different places went from feeling frustrated and exasperated to leaving with a plan and some assurance that Phillip would get the assistance he truly needed.

Levels of Case Management

Some agencies have several levels of case management, and clients receive a level of case management commensurate with their need and ability to function. In this text, we look at three levels of case management: administrative, resource coordination, and intensive. In addition, "targeted" or "blended case management" is discussed. In some agencies, these categories may have other names or there may be more than three levels of case management. The following sections provide examples of how case management services might be organized.

> **ASSIGNMENT**
>
> Begin now to put together a resource book listing agencies and what they do, support groups, and places where educational seminars and workshops are held for the general public. Collect them from the community where you expect to practice, and keep the latest copy of social services agencies found in most telephone books.

Administrative Case Management

This level of case management is assigned to high-functioning individuals who need very little assistance navigating the system. On occasion they might need a prescription refilled, an emergency appointment, or a return to outpatient substance abuse treatment, but for the most part they are capable of handling these details themselves. These clients are placed in a pool with other clients who require little service or follow-up beyond the original referral. For the most part, the clients function independently, using well the services to which they were referred. When something does come up for a client in this caseload, an available caseworker handles it. This means that a client on this caseload does not always see the same case manager.

Resource Coordination

This next level of case management is reserved for individuals who have some trouble handling the details of their treatment or plan. They usually need help and may have more involved or chronic difficulties that require more assistance. They do not, however, pose a risk to themselves or to others. In addition, with good support, they are unlikely to experience repeated hospitalizations or other crises. Here caseloads are larger, and clients are often in need of services and assistance on issues such as housing, medication, and therapy, but generally the clients do well with the services offered. A person going through a particularly difficult time might be moved up to intensive case management and then return to resource coordination after the stressful circumstances have been addressed.

Intensive Case Management

Individuals receiving intensive case management require considerable supervision and assistance in order to remain in the community and in circumstances that do not exacerbate their problems. Generally, the caseloads of intensive case managers are smaller, allowing for more individual attention. Clients in the caseload would be those at high risk for repeated emergencies and hospitalization or at risk of deteriorating to the point that they pose a danger to themselves or others. Intensive case management is usually available 24 hours a day and requires intense involvement to ensure that the person has a support network available and is not in high-risk situations, such as running out of medications or living in a housing situation likely to trigger stress and relapse.

Targeted or Blended Case Management

Some agencies are moving toward a type of case management called targeted or, in some cases, blended case management. This is a different way of delivering case management services. Instead of dividing clients according to their level of need, clients of varying needs are given to a case manager who carries a smaller caseload as a result. In this method the person has the same case manager through stable times and times of crisis, so that there is good continuity of care and rapport that might support that client when things become unstable.

Margery, a 36-year-old single mother of one child, a daughter, was stable and in school when she was transferred to a blended case management caseload. She had needed little contact with the agency in the past year, and the contact she did have was mainly for medication checks and prescription refills. In March the man she had been dating and talking about marrying was killed in a single-car accident. In the car with him at the time was another woman, who survived the accident and insisted she was actually the man's girlfriend. Margery was devastated. She began to skip classes, jeopardizing her place in the career program she had chosen. She took her medication erratically and gradually became in need of emergency care. Her case manager was a person she had known for some time, and it was her case manager who came at once to the emergency room when Margery was brought in by family members.

Liz, her case manager, was shocked at the changes in Margery. Margery was haggard, thin, and unkempt. She looked past Liz and said little. Liz made certain there were arrangements for Margery's daughter with family members and stayed in the emergency room until a bed was found for the patient on the psychiatric unit. During Margery's 6-day stay, Liz visited often and worked with Margery to make contact with the school and brought her daughter in for a visit after school two afternoons. When they talked, Liz worked on some of the supports Margery would need to return home. Of paramount importance was that Margery stay on her medication and call Liz when she felt distressed about something.

Gradually, with the 9 weeks of counseling arranged by Liz and a return to school the next semester, Liz saw positive changes in Margery. Her home became cleaner and brighter and so did Margery's appearance, indicating that she was taking an interest in herself and her surroundings. Liz arranged her schedule to be at Margery's graduation and continued to have contact with her client regarding renewal of prescriptions and regular contact just to see how Margery was doing.

This is an example of blended case management in which one case manager provides services to the same client regardless of the level of need at any particular time.

When Liz needed an emergency intervention, she had a case manager at her side with whom she was familiar, someone she knew and trusted. Figure 2.2 illustrates the case management process.

Separating Case Management from Therapy

Case management is not therapy. Often beginning case managers believe that they are to do therapy; that is, that they are to provide weekly talking sessions in which deep-seated conflicts and concerns are exposed and resolved. That is not the purpose of case management, and, indeed, most case managers are not prepared to handle this type of work.

In the course of case management with a client, you may uncover deep-seated problems and issues. These become the basis of a piece of the plan developed to resolve these issues. The client is referred to a person or agency that can do that work expertly. As the case manager, you may be the one your clients call when they are having a crisis and their therapist is unavailable. Good listening skills and helping

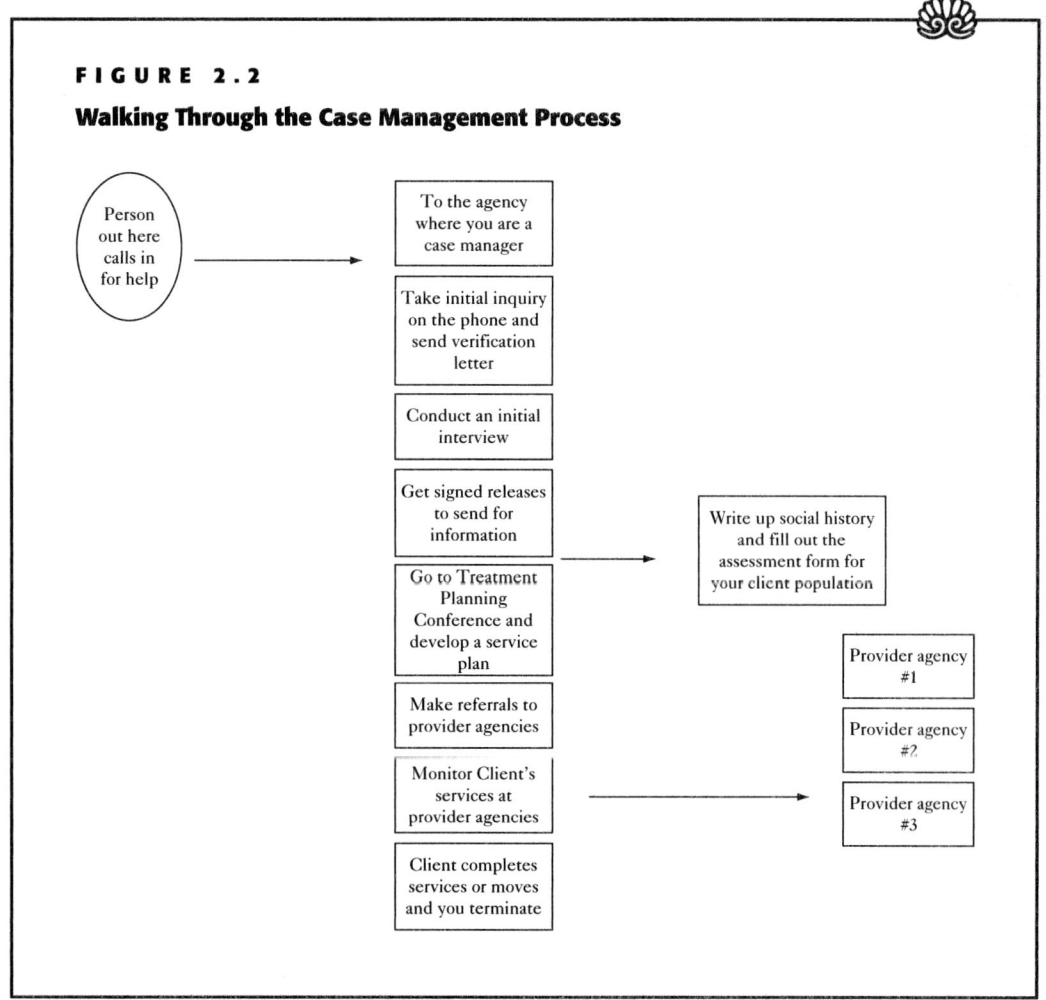

FIGURE 2.2

Walking Through the Case Management Process

such clients develop a way to handle things until they are seen in therapy is the case manager's role. It is not your role to intervene with a therapy session.

Finally, you will find plenty of other problems that do call for innovative interventions on your part. Learning to be independent, adopting useful and appropriate work habits, practicing good interpersonal skills, and behaving appropriately are all areas that you may address with your client in the course of case management. Although the client may be referred to a specific agency for exactly those skills and that information, you should support that intervention in your contacts with the person.

Many clients do not require therapy. Perhaps they have had considerable therapy in the past and are not able to benefit from it now or were never able to benefit from it. Perhaps their interpersonal problems are more a result of the chemical imbalance they suffer than psychological dynamics. For instance, research shows that individuals who are depressed or suffer from a bipolar disorder do well when they receive both medication and therapy. Many, however, have had considerable therapy in the past and are now maintained on effective medications. Other clients may have developmental disabilities and only need skills to attain as much independence as they are capable of handling. Some clients might have suffered a crisis such as rape or domestic violence and need a plan that focuses on protection and independence. Others may be out of fuel and need a plan that resolves the problem of a cold home with small children in it.

What case managers do is therapeutic in the sense that it benefits the client. Conducting clinical therapy, however—where a person comes in about long-standing emotional problems or pervasive affective disorders—takes years of study and training and should never be attempted by a person not specifically trained to conduct therapy.

Case Management in Provider Agencies

A provider agency is an agency that "provides" specific services to clients. A case manager might refer clients to such an agency for a specific service. There are positions in provider agencies, however, that are sometimes titled "case manager."

Case managers in provider agencies have oversight responsibility for the service or treatment given by the provider agency to the client. These case managers generally make sure the reason for the referral from the general case management unit is actually addressed, and they communicate with the client's general case manager on progress, goals for the client, and any changes that may need to be made in the service or treatment plan. Because the client is being seen regularly at the provider agency, the case manager there may also handle some of the personal issues and problems that arise for the client while in the care of this provider agency.

When Jennine came to the Wildwood Case Management Unit, she was suffering from depression and was not able to go to work. After she and the case manager discussed her mood and a social history was developed, Jennine agreed to go to a partial hospitalization program at Marshall River Center where her medications could be monitored, she would be attending groups, and she would get a lunch every day. Her husband agreed to the plan, feeling that this would prevent Jennine from sleeping all day and going without lunch. Jennine, her husband, and the case manager decided on the goal together. That goal was to alleviate Jennine's depression. They further decided together on the best place for Jennine to go to meet this goal.

At Marshall River, Jennine had a case manager who set up groups and activities to meet the goal. This was important because the Wildwood Case Management Unit generally authorizes payment for the service given the client and expects that the goals for the client's recovery will be addressed in return.

The goal for Jennine was to alleviate her depression. Jennine and her general case manager decided this was a top priority for her. The case manager at the provider agency addressed this goal by instituting a regular lunch and two healthy snack breaks, physical exercise, and group discussions on ways to handle or relieve depression. During that time, the case manager set appointments so that Jennine saw the psychiatrist twice a week for medication checks and adjustments.

During the 4 weeks Jennine was in the care of the Marshall River Center, her husband lost his job. This threw her into a panic and exacerbated her depression. The case manager was in touch with the Wildwood Case Management Center about these developments, and there was agreement that Jennine would need 2 more weeks at Marshall River. In this case, the Marshall River case manager saw Jennine daily to talk to her about her husband's job search and how Jennine was viewing the loss of his job.

In this textbook, you will learn how to do general case management with clients in which you work to address many of the problematic aspects of their lives. For example, if Jennine and her husband further stated that part of Jennine's depression came from her inability to discipline her 8-year-old son, the general case manager might have made a separate referral to parent education classes. Once you understand how general case management is done, you will be able to take on case management responsibilities in agencies that provide services and treatment to clients.

Managed Care and Case Management

Managed care is a phrase you will hear often when you go to work. Managed care is a financial system developed to contain the soaring costs of health care. It works like this: A managed care organization (MCO) receives a pool of money, allocated on the basis of a specific number of patients or clients who will be served by this MCO. The MCO hires case managers who oversee the care given in order to prevent the costs of caring for these patients or clients from running over the amount allotted. An MCO can be either a private insurance company or a company that handles public money.

In situations where the insurance covers medical and physical problems, the case manager is generally a nurse who has specific training in the managed care field. In MCOs set up to deal with behavioral health issues, a variety of social service professionals may be employed and trained as case managers.

You are most likely to deal with an MCO when working with clients with developmental disabilities, those with substance abuse problems, and individuals who have mental health problems. Because managed care is an economic system to control costs, you may find yourself at odds with the decisions of the MCO case manager. For example, you may be required to receive permission from the MCO case manager before you can implement a service or treatment plan. This is called a preauthorization. You may have a client sitting in your office who seems clearly suicidal to you, but the MCO case manager is denying hospitalization and suggesting partial hospitalization instead. There is little room for individual variations or innovative treatment plans in managed care where an MCO is paying for the services because MCOs generally have a cookbook approach to various health problems. There are specific protocols or decision trees to help case managers decide what treatment or services are appropriate, and these protocols do not take into account individual differences in clients' personalities and circumstances.

Figure 2.3 explains some recent trends in case management in managed care organizations.

Underlying Principles: Hope and Self-Determination

The thrust today is toward case management activities that promote both hope and self-determination. Increasingly, beginning at the federal level and moving down to state and local requirements, case managers are being given a mandate to conduct case management services in such a way that hope and self-determination are prominent features of their work.

FIGURE 2.3

Recent Trends in Managed Care Case Management

1. Some MCOs want to make the MCO case managers the only case managers for clients. These MCO case managers see the clients directly, make home and site visits, and manage the case as a general case manager might do. In most instances, these case managers are trained social service professionals and would be likely to follow the steps outlined in this book for case management while keeping a strict eye on the financial bottom line.
2. In some places MCOs are paying for the contact case managers have with their clients. In this way the agency draws down funds for case management services while providing considerable support to clients. In other words, the more contact given to clients the more the agency is paid and the better service the client receives. This appears to keep individuals in a more stable situation and acts as prevention for crises.
3. Individuals with chronic mental illness or substance abuse problems do not live as long as the general population. These people are less likely to seek help, to be able to use the help that is given, and may have had long-term substance abuse or long-term use of psychotropic medications. Case managers are being urged to integrate the physical needs and the substance abuse or mental health needs of their clients to facilitate a longer and healthier life span.

At the U.S. Department of Health and Human Services, the *Child and Adolescent Service System Program* (CASSP) promotes these concepts. They expect case management to be "child-centered and family focused." This means that case managers need to have a respectful focus on each child as an individual and need to include the child's family as a partner in planning for the child. The CASSP emphasizes community-based services that keep children at home, or at least in their own community. Further, the CASSP expectation is that case managers will respect and be competent when dealing with diverse cultures.

Recovery is a model put forth by the U.S. Department of Health and Human Services and the office of the Substance Abuse and Mental Health Services Administration (SAMHSA). They are changing the view of mental illness and substance abuse from one of gradual deterioration or a lifetime of chronic illness to one of recovery and a productive life. Spurred by the self-reports of people who have recovered from their addictions, mental illness, or emotional problems and went on to live productive lives, this model is being applied to mental health and other fields. Professionals who did research on how individuals recover concluded that it is possible to recover and lead a normal life *provided the services are in place that will cause outcomes beneficial to this process*.

In this model, case management is extremely important because the research showed that many times people did not recover because they either did not have access to services that would promote their recovery or these services were improperly coordinated. Now the movement is toward services that are diverse enough to meet clients' needs, well coordinated, and easily accessible. Clients' personal visions for their lives and respect for clients' self-determination are always foremost in planning, reclaiming the role of "healthy person" rather than "sick person." When appropriate, the client's family is included.

The *recovery* mission is respectful because it seeks to give clients more self-determination or empowerment and improved role functioning. This is done through a set of identified services combined to result in the stated desired outcomes clients have articulated for themselves, such as improved role functioning, self-development, services that support recovery, and symptom relief. In this model, relapse is seen as similar to relapse in any other illness (for example, diabetes or diverticulitis). Most of the time, the client will be healthy and functioning. See Figure 2.4 for an outline of the 10 fundamental components of recovery.

Also coming from SAMHSA is the *resiliency model* for children, again based on research. The findings showed that at-risk children often "bounce back" when they have someone in their lives who makes it clear that they are important regardless of the past; with this kind of support, many at-risk children go on to live healthier lives. A children's case manager certainly should be conveying this important sentiment, but the case manager can also find those people in a child's life who will do this as well: family members, teachers, youth counselors or workers, or neighbors.

The *resiliency model* adopts a positive view (the glass is half full) of the child's life and circumstances, actively seeking strengths on which to build. The belief is that children, like all people, have a "self-righting mechanism" that will help them bounce back from problems using their own power and ideas. The case manager facilitates this self-righting by naming the child's strengths and teaching the child to

FIGURE 2.4

Ten Fundamental Components of Recovery

Self-Directed Consumers lead, control, exercise choice over, and determine their own path of recovery by optimizing autonomy, independence, and control of resources to achieve a self-determined life. By definition, the recovery process must be self-directed by the individual, who defines his or her own life goals and designs a unique path towards those goals.

Empowerment Consumers have the authority to choose from a range of options and to participate in all decisions—including the allocation of resources—that will affect their lives and are educated and supported in so doing. They have the ability to join with other consumers to collectively and effectively speak for themselves about their needs, wants, desires, and aspirations. Through empowerment, an individual gains control of his or her own destiny and influences the organizational and societal structures in his or her life.

Non-Linear Recovery is not a step-by-step process but one based on continual growth, occasional setbacks, and learning from experience. Recovery begins with an initial stage of awareness on which a person recognizes that positive change is possible. This awareness enables the consumer to move on to fully engage in the work of recovery.

Individualized and Person Centered There are multiple pathways to recovery based on an individual's unique strengths and resiliencies as well as his or her needs, preferences, experiences (including past trauma), and cultural background in all of its diverse representations. Individuals also identify recovery as being an ongoing journey and an end result as well as an overall paradigm for achieving wellness and optimal health.

Holistic Recovery encompasses an individual's whole life, including, mind, body, spirit, and community. Recovery embraces all aspects of life, including housing, employment, education, mental health and health care treatment and services, complementary and naturalistic services (such as recreational services, libraries, museums, etc.), addictions treatment, spirituality, creativity, social networks, community participation, and family supports as determined by the person. Families, providers, organizations, systems, communities, and society play a crucial role in creating and maintaining meaningful opportunities for consumer access to these supports.

Strengths-based Recovery focuses on valuing and building on the multiple capacities, resiliencies, talents, coping abilities, and inherent worth of individuals. By building on these strengths, consumers leave stymied life roles behind and engage in new life roles (e.g., partner, caregiver, friend, student, employee). The process of recovery moves forward through interaction with others in supportive, trust-based relationships.

(continued)

FIGURE 2.4 *(continued)*

Peer Support/Mutual Support Including sharing of experiential knowledge and skills and social learning—plays an invaluable role in recovery. Consumers encourage and engage other consumers in recovery and provide each other with a sense of belonging, supportive relationships, valued roles, and community.

Responsibility Consumers have a personal responsibility for their own self-care and journeys to recovery. Taking steps toward their goals may require great courage. Consumers must strive to understand and give meaning to their experiences and identify coping strategies and healing processes to promote their own wellness.

Respect Community, systems, and societal acceptance and appreciation of consumers—including protecting their rights and eliminating discrimination and stigma—are crucial in achieving recovery. Self-acceptance and regaining belief in one's self are particularly vital. Respect ensures the inclusion and full participation of consumers in all aspects of their lives.

Hope Recovery provides the essential and motivating message of a better future—that people can and do overcome the barriers and obstacles that confront them. Hope is internalized; but can be fostered by peers, families, friends, providers, and others. Hope is the catalyst of the recovery process.

Source: U.S. Department of Health and Human Services, Substance Abuse and Mental Health Services Administration, Center for Mental Health Services, *Consensus Statement Defines Mental Health Recovery*, March/April 2006, Vol. 14, Number 2.

---

acknowledge them. In addition, case management either provides or coordinates others who provide the following: opportunities for the child to participate in meaningful activities, including those that help others; communicating high standards for the child and equally high expectations; providing consistent support and care; increasing prosocial bonding; setting clear behavioral boundaries and consistently observing these; and teaching life skills for success. Combined successfully, these factors allow a child to bounce back successfully.

Further research has shown that the inclusion of several activities not commonly considered when planning formal services is extremely important. A good children's case manager will develop contacts for these activities. First is reading practice so that at-risk children become competent readers. This is extremely important to later cognitive functioning, success in school, and other endeavors. Another activity involves opportunities for children to give something to others, to be helpful, to be in a situation where they exercise concern for others.

Finally, the *resiliency model* seeks case managers who are culturally competent, respectful of diverse religions, and able to respect and include the children's families.

In another move in this direction, director Elizabeth J. Clark of the National Association of Social Workers (NASW) testified before the President's New Freedom Commission on Mental Health in July 2002. She stated that as a profession, the NASW has made a commitment to mental health care that is driven first by the client and the client's family rather than by the preferences of the professional or the limits of the formal service system. She called for more accessibility to services, early mental health screening, and a national campaign to reduce the stigma of mental illness.

In the field of developmental disabilities, the concept is called *self-determination* or, in some places, is referred to as *Everyday Lives*. The emphasis is on clients' personal choices for the life that is most meaningful to them. Case managers look for services and activities that validate those choices and collaborate with the family to consider how best to spend money allocated for the care of a person with severe mental retardation. Rather than the case manager deciding what the client needs, the family is able to request what would be most helpful to them. Some families might ask to use the money for a ramp and a remodeled bathroom to accommodate a wheelchair. Another family might request special speech or physical therapy. What is important is that the case manager takes an active role in helping clients and their families conceive of a hopeful future and looks with them at the supports that could be accessed to make that happen.

From these efforts, you can see that case management is moving rapidly away from coordination of existing formal services for individuals who are seen as chronically handicapped and therefore unable to lead productive, rewarding lives. Instead, in all fields of service, whether mentioned here or not, the emphasis is on respect for the wishes and the vision of the client and undertaking activities that will achieve it.

For case managers, it now becomes imperative to know what your client wants, not just in terms of services, but also in terms of a productive, useful life. It involves careful listening and encouraging people to dream and hope. It entails respect for the client, the client's family, and the diversity of human experience. Funding sources are building into their reviews a surveillance of the capacity of case management to support these aspirations not only with standard formal services and, in some cases, medication, but also with the use of community resources and folk supports to assist the client toward a healthy, productive life.

Generic Case Management

The skills you learn to perform here can be used in any social service setting in which clients' needs and situations are evaluated, addressed, and monitored. Every agency does things in its own way, uses different forms, and often has a specific focus, but the tasks of case management are the same. Once you have learned how take a social history, make a referral, and document contacts, you will be able to take that knowledge to any agency and quickly adapt to that agency's methods and way of doing things.

Summary

Case management is not therapy, but it requires a set of skills that is nonetheless therapeutic to clients and to their well-being. The practice of case management requires an ability to listen to clients and accurately assess their problems, offer a range of diverse and innovative interventions, and follow their progress toward the goals they have set for themselves.

New models coming from the federal government and professional organizations stress the importance of giving clients ample opportunity to plan for the kind of future they wish to have for themselves. These models have introduced the concept of recovery from the problems and issues that occur throughout the course of life and recovery from mental illness as well. With a belief in the capacity of people to move beyond illness or current difficulties, case managers plan with their clients for more than just immediate treatment and service needs.

In the long run, it is the case manager who takes the long-term view of the client. In addition, it is the case manager who develops a comprehensive picture of the client, identifying the specific interventions that each particular client will need.

◆ Exercises: Case Management

Instructions: In each of the following situations, develop a tentative plan for the client. List the various services you believe each client needs initially. Include in your plan for each client both formal and informal services, and where appropriate, use generic services and agencies. Suggest other services the client might use later once the case is stabilized. Think about how you can involve others close to the client and how you will involve the client in planning.

1. You are called by the daughter of an elderly woman who lives alone. The daughter lives in another city and is concerned because her mother does not drive and has seemed unhappy and listless on the phone. The daughter expresses concern that her mother seems lonely and is perhaps depressed. The daughter does not know her mother's neighbors and calls you instead at the Office of Aging. She has told her mother she is going to call your agency for help, and the mother had no objection to that.

2. A man with a developmental disability lives alone with his widowed mother. She has fallen and broken her hip and will be at the rehabilitation hospital for about 6 weeks. He cannot stay alone. He has a job at Goodwill Industries. County transportation takes him there every morning at 8:30 and brings him home at 5:00 p.m.

3. A woman and her two children are waiting to receive their welfare check. They came to your state from another to escape an abusive husband and father. The woman is frail and appears sick. They have no place to go and have not eaten in several days. The children smell as if they need a bath and are listless.

4. A mother of two preteens has brought her son in for services. The woman is a widow. She confides that she has been having trouble controlling the boy, who is the oldest, and that the girl is disgusted with her brother's behavior and does not want to be involved in helping him. Lately the boy has become involved with teens his age and older. They have been drinking and coming home when they feel like it. The mother allowed them to smoke pot in the garage in hopes that she could keep the boy at home, but now she feels that backfired. The boy makes it clear that he thinks coming for help is ridiculous and says the one thing he will not do is give up his friends.

5. A man has been referred by his family physician for help. The man seems extremely inebriated. His wife brings him in and says she is worried that he may go into delirium tremens if he withdraws from alcohol too quickly. His family physician did not see him but sent the couple straight to your office.

6. A father brings in his 14-year-old daughter who is running the streets, refusing to listen, and failing in school. He is at his wits' end, saying he must work and cannot be home when the girl returns from school. Her mother died 4 years ago, and the trouble started when the daughter was about 12. The father feels that he and his daughter have a difficult time communicating with one another.

7. A police officer asks you to come to the home of an older man he has been concerned about for several weeks now. The man is delighted to see you and tells you that he is having pains in his legs and is unable to walk. During your visit, he asks you to get things for him that are nearby, but obviously it is too painful for him to get up. He says he does not go to the kitchen often to prepare meals, but the police officer has stopped by several times with sandwiches, and Mrs. Jones from up the street, an old friend of the man's late wife, has brought a casserole on occasion. He is adamant that he wants to stay in his home as long as he can.

8. A woman comes in complaining of depression. She says it started when her husband left with a younger woman and she has not been "right since." She reports having difficulty falling asleep and complains of no appetite. She says she has missed more than 3 weeks of work since he left last month. There are no children, but she tells you she has neglected the dog and cannot remember if she fed him last night or not. She appears listless and very sad, weeping off and on during the interview.

9. A man in his 60s comes in on the recommendation of his doctor. He had a back injury some years ago and was placed on codeine at the time. After the back injury, other things went wrong. The plant where he worked closed down and his mother died. He found himself feeling very alone and uncertain about finances. "It was then that I started to drink too," he tells you. When you ask what he means by "too," he says his doctor believes he has become addicted to codeine. "I don't know," he says. "I've gotten to the point that I can't get through a day without a lot of help."

10. A mother brings her 12-year-old son in because they are "not getting along." She reports that he does not listen and comes and goes as he pleases. His homework has fallen off and his grades have slipped, but he is still doing well in math and likes his math teacher. The boy's father was killed in a railroad accident 2 years ago. The mother tells you that the boy and his father enjoyed a close and warm relationship and that she has felt her influence on him slipping away since the accident.

11. A woman comes to your agency on a referral by the courts after she was arrested for selling various prescription medications on the street. She tells you she currently has some amphetamines, Xanax, and a popular addictive pain medication in her bag. The court is ordering her to show within the next week that she has enrolled in a program that will get her help with her own addiction to some of the medications she sells. "I have regular customers," she tells you. "And they are going to crap when I stop coming around." Asked where she gets her medications, she smiles mysteriously and says, "The police are looking into that—you don't need to." She denies she is addicted to anything, but court records, including an evaluation by a psychologist, which she has brought with her, indicate that she is addicted to several different medications.

12. A woman who was recently placed in the community after 3 years in a state mental hospital is having trouble adjusting to the living arrangement made for her by the hospital. She is not going out and does not participate in any activities. She is friendly when you talk to her and seems glad to have your company, but she does not seem to know how to take care of the details of everyday living. She has a roommate who is more competent and independent. The two get along well.

13. A woman with two small children is referred to you because she recently lost her apartment. She has a meager income from a part-time job as a clerk in a convenience store and was unable to pay the rent and take care of other bills. She seems unaware that she might be eligible for financial assistance. She is not sure where her children's father is at the moment. All her belongings are packed in five bulging garbage bags. She and her children seem malnourished and thin.

14. A man comes in who was referred by his job for possible crack use. The man admits he uses crack, but rarely and certainly not to the extent that it would interfere with his work! He will be given 4 weeks off if he enrolls in a legitimate program for detoxification. He seems reluctant and torn. Eventually he agrees to work with you on a plan.

◆ Exercises: Decide on the Best Course of Action

Instructions: Sit with a small group of other students and decide how you will handle this situation. There are many areas both ethically and legally that are not clear, so the discussion you have with your colleagues is much like a discussion you might have in a real agency. There are no "correct answers."

You are the case manager for a man who has only recently had a first manic episode. He had submitted to treatment, responded well, and returned to work. However, he is currently experiencing another episode, and this one seems more severe. He is not sleeping or eating, is sending cryptic messages on the Internet, and believes everything he reads there is directed at him. He believes the government is "monitoring" him and that he has an important job lined up with a record company in New York. You have determined that he is not leaving his house and that he is preoccupied with what is happening on message boards and chat rooms on the Internet. You have checked in with him several times by phone. Each time he assures you that he is fine and does not need help.

What is the best course of action? Do you risk seeking an involuntary commitment, knowing that he seems just well enough to convince the emergency room physician he is not in need of hospitalization? Will this alienate him and make it impossible for you to work with him? Do you wait for things to get worse? If so, is there a chance he may leave the house and get into trouble? What might happen if you wait it out?

Chapter 3

Applying the Ecological Model: A Theoretical Foundation for Human Services

Introduction

In working with other people, human service professionals apply the ecological model to develop a broad understanding of each individual client who comes before them. This model, sometimes referred to as person-in-situation or person-in-environment model, looks at the individual client in the client's context.

You are well aware of how distorted communication can become when a statement is quoted out of context. It is possible to skew impressions and deliberately create misunderstandings by quoting only a portion of what someone has said and not the entire conversation. For instance, when Matt's teacher questioned him in class about his homework assignment, he said he was not sure if he could help people with a certain disability. He went on to explain that at one time it was thought that he had that particular disability, and he had worked very hard to prove that he was not disabled and to overcome people's initial impressions of him. Now he found himself feeling uncomfortable with people who suffered from that disability. He also explained that he expected his course of study to help him overcome the problem and that he was very aware that his reactions might be inappropriate.

Later Anne, who was in class that day, confided to Aisha and Alice that she did not feel Matt should be allowed to continue with his studies. Surprised, Aisha asked Anne why she felt that way. "Oh, because he said in class the other day that he feels uncomfortable around certain disabled people. I mean, if you can't work with disabled people, you need to find something else to do." Aisha and Alice quickly agreed.

Anne's description of what Matt had said was distorted because Matt's comments were repeated outside the context in which they were said. That kind of distortion takes place when we look at individuals out of context. In your work, every person you will see functions in a context, an environment. You cannot adequately understand that person without also being able to understand the context in which that person functions and interacts.

It is very tempting to overlook context. Many of us fall into the trap of thinking that A causes B: "Juan is irresponsible, so he lost his job." If we eliminate A, B will cease to be a problem. If we make Juan more responsible, he will not lose any more jobs. Or "Jill is too demanding, so her husband left her." If we teach Jill better interpersonal skills, she will have better relationships. Although helping Juan to become more job-ready and helping Jill to communicate better may very well be a positive part of your plan for them, this kind of understanding of their problems and assigning of solutions largely ignores the context in which these problems arose. It also makes it much easier to see the individuals as being responsible or to blame for the problems they have brought to your attention. When we blame others, we nearly always feel less empathy with their difficulties, and we are less inclined to be truly useful in the human service sense.

Seeking a Balanced View of the Client

All individuals constantly interact with any number of systems in their environments. All individuals bring to those interactions unique characteristics. Unless the human service worker has a balanced view of both the client and the client's context, important information and constructive opportunities are lost. In the cases of Ralph and Eduardo, we can see how important this is.

Ralph went to prison because of some youthful gang activity. While he was there, he took advantage of every opportunity to change. He went to church regularly, developed a personal relationship with a minister who came to the prison often, and obtained his high school diploma. Ralph was a warm, humorous person who attracted many friends. His outgoing personality attracted people to him who ultimately encouraged him and gave him support. During his time in prison, his mother wrote to him often, pleading with him to change his ways. Ralph felt bad about the trouble he had caused his mother, particularly in view of the fact that she had raised him after his father left home, and he saw her letters as a reason to do better. When he left prison, he enrolled in college courses and attached himself to the church, where he was warmly welcomed.

Eduardo was in the same prison also because of youthful gang activities. He was quiet and retiring and did not attract the attention and support that Ralph had secured for himself. Eduardo attempted to get his high school diploma while in prison, but he had trouble asking for help when he needed it and eventually abandoned the project in frustration. Preferring not to join groups, he did not go to church or any other group activity that promoted independence and responsibility. Because Eduardo spoke so little and rarely smiled, he was often misunderstood and thought of as being hostile. In fact, he felt shy and awkward around other people. Eduardo's mother wrote to him regularly, and she too pleaded with him to do better and "turn his life around," but Eduardo tended to see these letters as nagging and to blame his mother for the fact that his father left when he was very young. He rarely answered her mail. When Eduardo left prison, he moved back with his old friends and resumed his former criminal activities.

This illustration demonstrates how individual characteristics play a role in the outcome for the client. Part of developing a balanced understanding of the client is being able to see what the client brings to the situation and how that interacts with the larger context of the client's life. Ralph brought a personality that attracted others to assist him. He brought a good relationship with his mother and a motivation to do things more constructively. Eduardo brought a more retiring personality, one that was less attractive to others and often misunderstood. Eduardo's interpersonal skills were not as developed as Ralph's. The individual characteristics of Eduardo and Ralph affected the outcome of their prison time.

Now we will look at Eduardo and Ralph differently. For our purposes, let us suppose that Ralph and Eduardo are both warm, humorous people. Both make friends easily and enjoy the company of other people. Each of them is sent to prison for youthful gang activities, but the context is different. Eduardo goes to a recently built prison upstate that focuses on rehabilitation. There he is provided with high school and college classes as well as religious and self-improvement activities. He is able to take advantage of many different programs to further his goals. A supportive counselor meets with him on a weekly basis and works with him to create a good set of goals and implement them. The location of the prison has another advantage. Eduardo is now closer to his father, who lives only a few miles from the prison. His father begins to visit, offering his support and a place for Eduardo to live when his sentence is completed. Eduardo leaves the prison on a solid footing and continues his work toward a college degree.

Ralph, on the other hand, is sent to an ordinary prison where the counseling staff is overwhelmed. His counselor sees Ralph's potential but has difficulty enrolling Ralph in high school courses because they are crowded. During the time Ralph is at the prison, the education staff experiences a number of turnovers and layoffs. Ralph never can get into the program and stick with it. He rarely sees his counselor because of the number of inmates with whom the counselor must work. No family member comes to visit Ralph, partly because he has been sent so far from where they live, and partly because they blame him for his incarceration and have lost interest in him. Ralph's mother, sick with severe chronic asthma, rarely writes. Ralph attends church services at the prison regularly, but the prison does not allow inmates to meet with the pastors before or after services because of a strict schedule. The pastors who have formed relationships with some inmates visit irregularly at other times. When Ralph leaves the prison, he has not completed his high school diploma. He moves near some people he knew in prison, and soon he takes up the criminal activities in which he participated before his incarceration.

Here it is the context that is different. Eduardo finds himself in a supportive context: a counselor who focuses on his goals and sees that these are implemented, plenty of self-improvement opportunities, a warm relationship with his father, and a prison committed to education. Ralph, however, finds himself confronted with indifference, lack of supportive programs and activities, an overwhelmed counselor, and a family too distant to give encouragement.

The interaction never ceases. The individual makes choices, but the environment prompts those choices. The individual responds to the outcome of those choices, and the environment reacts or adapts to that response. This interaction begins at birth. A fussy baby with calm, patient parents will start life differently from a fussy baby with overworked, anxious parents. An infant with severe disabilities will receive a good start with a large, loving family who devote their time and energy to getting her the best medical and rehabilitative care. An infant with severe disabilities may arrive in another family where everyone tries their best to give the infant a good start; nevertheless, the disabilities prove overwhelming to the caretakers, there is no cure, and family members find that any semblance of a normal home life or time with other siblings is severely curtailed. The first baby is raised at home; the second one is placed in a good institution.

In human services, the trained eye will look for and see a balanced view of clients and their contexts when assessing individuals' needs. Just as important is the human service worker's understanding of how person and context interact to produce certain outcomes for the client.

The Three Levels

Client and context have been defined as having three levels:

1. *Micro level*, where the focus is on the client's personality, motivation, affect, and other personal attributes
2. *Meso level*, where the focus is on the context immediately surrounding the client (family, church group, close friends, and work group)
3. *Macro level*, where the focus is on the larger society's characteristics and the way the client experiences these or the way these are brought to bear on the client's situation (institutions and organizations such as the political system, social stratification, the educational system, and the economy)

Human service workers are expected to be aware of all three levels when assessing a client's situation and to be able to intervene on all three levels when such intervention is appropriate.

Looking at What the Person Brings

When you do an assessment to open a case or do follow-up planning, a number of individual characteristics will impinge on the problems and the eventual outcome. These micro-level characteristics can be divided into two broad categories:

Biological Characteristics	Psychological Characteristics
Neurological development	Early shaping experiences
Reflexes	Perception
Genetic makeup	Personality
Degenerative processes	Affect
Illness (chronic, terminal, or temporary)	Cognition
Physical health	Nurturance
Nutrition	Life transitions/position in the life cycle
	Motivation

This general outline gives you a starting point for understanding what your client has brought to the situation.

Clients have had different early life experiences, are composed of different genetic configurations, and possess different personalities and perceptions. Each of these differences interacts with the external circumstances of the client's situation to promote self-fulfillment and well-being, to block those goals, or, quite possibly, to have no effect at all.

This topic is discussed in greater detail in Chapter 16 on assessment; this discussion puts forth the framework you will follow in assessing the individual's contribution to the situation.

Looking at What the Context Brings

Clients function in contexts that are personal to them and in a larger context, which is the larger society. These contexts can be divided into two broad categories:

Personal Context (sometimes referred to as the mezzo or meso level)	Social Context (sometimes referred to as the macro level)
Family	The larger culture of the society
Work group	The larger organization of the church or workplace
Social groups	
Family culture	The larger community
Family values	Government
Family structure	Economy
Religious group	Social stratification
Social class	Prejudice and discrimination
Role status, conflict, and strain	Political system

It is important to obtain information about the contexts in which clients grew up and in which they are now functioning. The reason for the client's problems may lie in the context rather than with the client.

When you learn about the context, you learn more about what motivates your clients, the environmental cues they receive to behave or make decisions the way they do, and what early circumstances shaped their way of responding to their community and their situation. Clients come from different social contexts. Clients grew up in different households with different parents and different levels of nutrition and encouragement. Clients have different ways of looking at things and explaining them. The economy may have favored their work or begun to dispense with it. The political system may have awarded your client's subgroup's power or disenfranchised that group in some way. Your client may have experienced prejudice, an indifferent medical system, or a poor educational system. On the other hand, this person may have grown up in a wealthy suburb, attended private schools, and received the best medical care money could purchase.

Developmental Transitions

The ecological model is also concerned with normal life changes, often referred to as *transitions*. These changes are called transitions because they are events that move a person from one phase of life to another, requiring the person to make adjustments or to adapt in some way to new circumstances. Many of these events are simply part of the normal development that all people experience from birth to death. These transitions are often expected, and for some transitions there is preparation.

Some people do not cope as well with the changes brought by transitions as others do. Perhaps they have more going on in their lives than they feel they can handle. Perhaps the events have changed their lives dramatically in ways that are viewed as negative. Many of the people we see in the human service field are going through, or have recently experienced, one or more transitions. Here is a list of some of the transitions that people experience:

Starting kindergarten or first grade	Starting a new job
Going to high school	Getting married
Going out on the first date	Buying a first home
Leaving home for the first time	Experiencing ill health
Losing one's job	Losing a spouse through death
Experiencing a disaster	Divorce
A large mortgage or other debt	Losing some physical capacity
Considerable financial losses	Considerable financial gains
Children leaving home	Children marrying
Birth of grandchild	Death of a child

And there are many more. Although every single one of these events probably will not happen to one person, we can expect that most people in the course of a long life will experience many of the transitions on this list.

It is important to know about the common life stages a person passes through and to recognize where your clients are in their life stages and transitions. Transition problems are common to so many people that self-help and support groups that do not entail treatment by a mental health professional are often available that provide support from others who have been through the same transition.

Sometimes, however, a person may find the changes overwhelming, completely negative, or intolerable. These people may need professional help to handle these changes and adjustments.

Developing the Interventions

You have looked carefully at your clients' issues and problems. You have come to understand the ways in which your clients have responded to their context and the way the context has contributed to your clients' motivations and decisions. As a case manager, your role is to design a plan with each client that will address the areas of need. Human service workers can and do intervene on several levels.

Many clients of the social welfare system appear to be individuals who have encountered inadequate support in their context. One or more of the institutions that we believe should support the individual in our society has failed these people or has been unable to supply what was necessary to avoid problems. Institutions such as education, medicine, the economy, politics, and the family may have let this person down in some way.

When this occurs, our society looks to the social welfare system to supply what is needed, to address the unfortunate gaps in a person's life, and to apply interventions that will prevent a worsening of the problems. Your task as case manager is to look at the client and the client's context, to gather the facts about each of these, and to understand how context and person interact to the detriment or the well-being of the client.

With this information, a plan is developed with the person that addresses maladaptive interactions between the individual and the environment and that notes those parts of the environment that are positive and useful. The interventions you design or choose should be two-pronged: personal interventions that strengthen the person to handle the environment, and environmental interventions that change the context to accommodate the person. Here are some examples of the types of interventions that can be incorporated into individual plans:

Interventions to Strengthen the Person	Interventions to Strengthen the Environment
1. AA for substance abuse	Family education to support sobriety
2. Parent skills training for the parents of a child they abused	Temporary removal from home to foster care
Group therapy for abused child	Foster home parents given information on creating supportive foster home environment
3. Job training for the person with a developmental disability	Work with the employer to provide a supportive work environment
4. Interpersonal skills training for the adolescent in minor trouble	Use the child's interests to develop more constructive in-school activities
	Bring father into the picture in a positive way
	Family therapy with the mother

5. Medication for the person with schizophrenia
Regular appointments with the psychiatrist

Place in a supportive living environment in the community
Develop constructive connections with the local church
Two family sessions to reinvolve the family in the person's life

These are fairly routine interventions in a person's problems to ameliorate a negative or destructive situation or to enhance the person's self-fulfillment. The point is, however, that a service plan formed without the understanding that interventions take place in two distinct areas could be quite hapless and without focus. When doing a service plan, the human service worker makes certain that both areas have been addressed with appropriate interventions wherever possible and that the interventions are documented in the record.

Working with the Generalist Approach

The ability to recognize and address issues on all three levels is generally referred to as the "generalist approach." Aware that problems occur between the designated client—be that a family, an individual, or a group—and the client's environment, it is important to see the interaction between the two and to look for ways to intervene on all the relevant levels on behalf of your client. As noted previously, clients are affected by the environment they occupy, and the environment is affected by the clients' response. For example, look at how Ralph affected the people around him, their response to him and his response in return. Contrast that with Eduardo's environment and the response he received as a result of his interactions with his environment. The client affects the environment and the environment affects the client in a never-ending interaction that can have positive and empowering results for the client, or just the opposite.

When case managers look at how people and systems on each of the three levels affect the client's problems, the case manager has correctly made a multilevel assessment. This assessment should lead case managers to develop interventions that will enhance both the identified client and the client's environment. The generalist approach has as its goal the better functioning and increased competence of all parties. By looking at the whole picture instead of just a piece of the picture comprising only the identified client, the case manager has laid the foundation for making solid and long-lasting change possible.

ASSIGNMENT

Talk to a human service professional in your community about what that person sees as an unmet need in the community. What one service would the professional like to see developed? What specific need would that service meet? What client population would that project address? How could the clients who need this service be mobilized to work in their own behalf?

Larger Interventions

It is assumed that the human service worker is not limited to just helping individuals. Your work as a human service professional places you in a unique position to be able to speak to the problems affecting large numbers of people. This happens in two ways.

In the course of your work, you will encounter many who have been damaged by abuse or discrimination. You will see groups of people harmed by poor school systems, a lack of medical care, or scant supervision. Ethically we have an obligation to speak to the needs of those with less advantage in our society. Having seen the damage firsthand, we are better able to speak to conditions that need to be remedied in our larger society and to keep statistics and information on the extent of the problem for use in persuading lawmakers and others in power to take action.

You will also see areas of service that have been neglected or that require development. Perhaps there is a need for more supported living arrangements for those with mental illness in the community. It may be that mothers returning to work from welfare lack the means to dress appropriately for the job, need day care for their young children, or require transportation to get to job interviews. Who better than the human service professional to bring to the attention of those who develop programs the areas of service that are lacking in your immediate community? You and others can bring to light the unique needs of your community and help to develop much-needed services.

Summary

In this chapter we have looked at a method for assessing your clients in three different dimensions. This method, often referred to as the ecological model, looks at the attributes clients bring to their problems, as well as the contributing factors in clients' immediate environments and in the larger societies in which they live and function. Using this model prevents us from blaming only the clients for the problems in their lives. In addition to recognizing all the factors that make up clients' problems, this model also allows us to recognize the broader need for interventions and to develop interventions that address issues on all three levels.

Using the ecological model, you can now produce effective remedies to the problems and the social issues brought to you in the course of your work. In this way, you serve your clients and your society in meaningful and useful ways.

◆ **Exercise: Looking at Florence's Problem on Three Levels**

Instructions: Look at Florence's problem as she presented it to the case manager. Decide which parts of her problem are on the micro level, which parts are on the mezzo level, and which parts are on the macro level.

Florence came in to see a case manager in an agency that addresses child abuse and neglect. Recently her daughter, Crystal, was removed from the home because of complaints by neighbors that she was abusing the child. An investigation of the situation by child-care workers indicated the abuse was severe. The discipline she was administering was discipline she had experienced and witnessed as a child from her own parents and her aunts and uncles who lived on farms near her family. Florence related that she was the oldest daughter, third in line of nine children, of a farm family of 12 people. Her parents worked hard from sun up until long after dark. Much of the housework was done by Florence and her aunt, who lived with them. Her mother was ill, often in her room in bed. Florence does not know what the illness was, but does not recall her mother ever seeing a doctor. She tells the case manager that she knows her mother and her aunt did not like her.

At 18, Florence ran away with Dave, who did mechanical work on cars. "He was my first and only boyfriend," she explains, weeping. Florence and Dave never married, and they had one child, Crystal. Last April, Dave died in a car accident on the interstate. Florence cries as she describes that night and the way the police came to her trailer and how kind they were to her. She describes how alone she has felt ever since.

Florence receives welfare. She completed eighth grade before her father "yanked me out of school to do housework. Said it was no place for a girl. A girl didn't need no schooling." Florence had enjoyed school, mostly for the companionship of other girls. "I'm shy of people, you know. But at school I had friends." Florence remembers school as hard, and she had trouble with subjects like math and science. "Mostly I sat there and worried about what would happen when I got home from school. It was always something: Mom was worse, I was in trouble, there was some big push to get in a harvest. I was glad when I quit."

Leaving with Dave had alienated Florence from her family. "Dave used to say, 'They're just mad 'cause they can't use you no more.'" For this reason, Florence has not seen her family since Dave's funeral, and they have made no attempt to get in touch with her even though they are only a few miles apart. The welfare agency reports that their workers have rarely seen Florence and have not as yet offered her any services for going to work, although she is on a list of single mothers they would like to make job-ready. Child welfare tells you that they cannot return Crystal until Florence has had intensive parent training and supervised visits with her child. They also tell you that they found her home worn, but immaculate.

Florence confides that she is terrified of going to work, that she feels useless, and that she probably has little to offer on a "real job." She also appears to be depressed, crying at intervals and hanging her head. Socially she is isolated both because of Dave's death and because her neighbors are fed up with her child-care practices. "The neighbors don't like me either," she says with resignation. The child-care agency is asking for parent training, but it is unclear who will offer that in this rural area.

What part of Florence's problem is a micro-level problem?

What part of Florence's problem is a mezzo-level problem?

What part of Florence's problem is a macro-level problem?

◆ Exercises: Designing Three Levels of Intervention

Instructions: Look at the four cases below and decide how you would intervene on three levels: the personal (micro), the contextual or social context immediately surrounding the client (mezzo), and the larger environment (macro).

1. Maria is paralyzed from the waist down following an accident three summers ago in a swimming pool. She is hoping to complete her degree in accounting, but she is complaining of depression and an inability to focus on school. When you see her, she looks anxious and tired. Her affect is flat, and she tells you nothing interests her. At the local college, she has had trouble finding appropriate parking and misses many days of class when the weather is bad because of the parking situation. One of the professors she must work with rather closely has made remarks about the difficulty of "other people getting around that wheelchair." She believes her boyfriend, who was with her the night the accident happened, has remained with her simply out of pity. When they fight about other things, she throws this up to him, although he vehemently denies it and tells Maria this is a hurtful accusation.

   Interventions on the micro level:

   Interventions on the mezzo level:

   Interventions on the macro level:

2. Mr. Groff is 93 and living alone in his home. He only stopped driving last year. He would like to get out more, perhaps go to the senior citizen's center. In addition, he would like to go to the Lions Club and to participate in a foreign policy club he belonged to for years. He tells you sadly that the members of the foreign policy club always seemed amazed at the reading he had done and the sound opinions he expressed, "as though I should be senile!" Since he stopped driving, he has lost contact with them. Right now he sees no reason to go to a nursing home and feels that if he had transportation he could continue to buy his groceries, prepare his meals, and care for himself generally. He tells you, however, that he would like to find a way to be less lonely.

   Interventions on the micro level:

   Interventions on the mezzo level:

   Interventions on the macro level:

3. Margie is in a sheltered workshop for people with developmental disabilities. She does well at work and has many friends. She lives alone with her mother, and her mother is not happy with the new level of independence Margie is developing. She often goes out with others from work and the supervisors for dinner on Friday night. She has joined a social group for individuals with disabilities much like hers, and they go bowling and to the movies. Margie has, since she went to the sheltered workshop, learned how to use the phone to make appointments with her doctor and dentist and how to ride the bus to and from both work and the social club, and she has been shopping to buy her own clothes twice with her case manager. When Margie's mother complains about all this, she tends to blame Margie for leaving her alone at night. "Since your father died, you're all I have," she tells Margie. Margie's response to this is to cry and stay in her room. Sometimes she has missed work, hoping to make her absences up to her mother.

   Interventions on the micro level:

Interventions on the mezzo level:

Interventions on the macro level:

4. Chris is a single father who is trying to work and raise three small children. His wife was killed 2 years ago in a traffic accident. After the initial shock and outpouring of support from friends and neighbors, Chris found himself alone with all the responsibilities and very unsure of himself. He would like to meet other men who have the same problems but cannot find any groups, even though he has been told about several men who are in the same situation. He tells you he is not sure what the best method is for disciplining his children, whom he describes as "good kids." Sometimes he feels he is too lenient with them, and at other times he is afraid he is unnecessarily strict with them. A local women's health center has groups for bereaved single parents, but Chris believes those would not be open to him. "It would be all women, wouldn't it?" he asks. In addition, he is having a hard time at work balancing the responsibilities there with parenting responsibilities at home. "Of course, I want to do a good job and get the promotions so I can support these kids through college, but I need to be home in the evening, or someone does, and I don't think that is always well received at work."

Interventions on the micro level:

Interventions on the mezzo level:

Interventions on the macro level:

Chapter 4

Cultural Competence

Introduction

Seeing each of our clients as unique individuals is the only way to accurately perceive them and to be constructive in the way we serve them. One key element of individuality is culture or subculture.

Most of our attitudes and perceptions are the result of our interactions with others throughout our lives. In time, these interactions come to seem natural. As professionals, we need to become aware of our personal ways of thinking about others and their situations. Is our thinking useful? Will it promote the well-being, self-esteem, and independence of our clients? Because we are a culturally diverse society, it is important for professionals in human services to respect differences and to seek to understand these differences whenever possible.

Culture and Communication

Each of us brings to any situation perceptions and attitudes that are influenced by our own culture. Our own ethnic group, family values, outstanding experiences, and cultural traditions all influence both the way we communicate to other people and what we believe other people mean when they communicate with us. Often we are unaware of the extent to which these factors color our interactions with other people.

In addition, we do not usually take the time to understand that others may come from a culture that differs from our own significantly. We may judge others' actions by the standards prevalent in our own culture. We may expect certain behavior we believe is appropriate and become annoyed when we do not see that behavior. We may misunderstand the communication of others, leading to lost rapport and opportunities. This is dangerous when we have accepted the professional responsibility for giving assistance to other people.

Your Ethical Responsibility

Ethically, you have a responsibility to take the time and make the effort to become familiar with cultures that differ from your own that you have extensive contact with as a social service professional. It is not ethical to simply assume you know all there is to know about a group because you see members of that group on a daily basis. Instead, you need to ask questions, take seminars, and gather information that will enhance your understanding of that group or culture.

When You Are Not Sure

It is not possible, on the other hand, to study and become familiar with all the different cultures you might encounter in the course of your professional lifetime. In your work, it is quite likely that you may encounter someone from another group whose culture is unfamiliar to you and whom you will see only briefly. What you need is a method you can use that will allow you to participate in those encounters and interactions competently.

Where Are the Differences?

Differences among people occur on a number of sociological levels. These differences can be overcome and understood, or they can become obstacles to good communication and understanding.

Cultures

Generally, cultures coincide with national or political boundaries. People living in one country have a culture that differs from the culture of those living just across the border. When we refer to culture, we are really talking about the culture assumed by an entire society.

This means that we in the United States have in common with one another a basic knowledge. We learned this knowledge through the socialization process—from our schools, parents, religions, and even television and magazines. Although each individual may see the culture just a bit differently and no one knows everything there is to know about it, people share enough in common to be able to relate to and cooperate with one another.

By the time we are young adults, the culture we carry with us in our heads is largely unconscious. Our culture influences how we communicate with other people, and it influences the way we determine what the other person means. In other words, what we say is affected by our culture, and, in turn, our interpretation of what another person is saying to us is colored by our culture. Because this process has become automatic for us, we are not aware of the significant influence our culture has on our interactions with others. Furthermore, if most of the time we are communicating with others from our own culture, we will assume that all people mean what we mean and see things as we see them. With this way of thinking firmly in place, there is a tendency to assume that our own culture is the better or correct way to be at any given time.

Subcultures

Within any given society, there are groups of individuals who, for the most part, follow the culture of their society but hold in common with each other somewhat different cultural ideas. This may be a religious group that holds ideas that are somewhat different from mainstream thinking about patriotism and serving in the military. It might be an ethnic group whose subculture is shaped by the discrimination experienced in each generation.

Subcultures usually are not completely out of step with the larger society's culture. There is, however, something about the subgroup culture that sets its members apart. It might be values, traditions, beliefs, lifestyle, or any combination of these.

Race and Ethnic Group

Important in understanding subcultures is understanding the terms *race* and *ethnic group*. According to Gudykunst and Kim (1997),* *race* refers to a "group of people who are biologically similar," and *ethnic group* refers to "a group of people who share a common cultural heritage usually based on a common national origin or language" (p. 20).

Racial groups often have distinguishing physical characteristics, whereas ethnic groups may be distinguished by their language, religion, or some other aspect of their culture. It is important to keep in mind that race alone is not a factor influencing communication; on the other hand, ethnicity with its culture can have considerable influence on communication. If the racial or ethnic group of your clients indicates a subculture that is unfamiliar to you, the potential for misunderstanding is increased.

---

*Material in this chapter and Figure 4.1 is adapted with permission from *Communicating with Strangers*, 3rd edition, by W. Gudykunst et al. Copyright © 1997 McGraw-Hill Companies.

How We Develop a We-Versus-Them Attitude

During the process of socialization, we learn that some groups are acceptable and others are unacceptable. The acceptable groups are seen by us as in-groups. We are more comfortable with in-groups than with groups we consider unacceptable. We see the members as being similar to us, and we expect the members to hold beliefs and values very much like our own, and to act and think as we would. When we talk about in-groups, we generally do so favorably, holding them in positive regard. We are better at predicting how members of in-groups will respond or behave.

Out-groups are those groups with whom we feel uncomfortable—groups with whom we have less inclination to interact on a regular basis. Generally we do not hold members of out-groups in a particularly favorable light. We may be suspicious of the motives of an out-group because we do not fully understand its culture. Using our own culture as the standard, we may find the out-group culture inferior. Members of the out-group may appear unpredictable, unreliable, or devious to us.

Strangers

When people do not act or think the way we believe they should, they seem strange to us. Many people you will encounter in the course of your work will seem like strangers to you. For example, Julio is a stranger to nearly everyone he sees on a daily basis. He, his little brother, and his mother live in a small city with others from Puerto Rico. When he is with his small group of friends and relatives, he is not perceived as strange. On the other hand, when he attempts to interact with the larger American culture, many see him as a stranger. His language, his behavior, and, in some cases, his attitudes appear strange to members of the larger culture. He is tolerated, and even given menial work, but he feels set apart. People he must meet and work with every day view him as a stranger because they know little about Julio's culture. They see him every day, yet he is in no way considered part of their group.

Julio went to the case management unit to seek services for his brother, who was diagnosed by the school psychologist as mentally retarded. There he encountered some problems. His accent and unfamiliarity with the language made it difficult for him to be understood. While the worker talked about residential placement and education, Julio resisted, indicating the family just needed help with the local school, where he felt his brother had been misunderstood because of a language problem. The local school had suggested Julio and his mother go to the case management unit because school officials did not believe they could provide adequate services. Julio felt their referral indicated insensitivity and an unwillingness to be concerned with keeping the family together and helping his brother function better in English. The vast array of services being offered at the case management unit was bewildering to Julio. He was inclined to simply withdraw from the situation and tell his mother to keep his brother at home.

To the worker at the case management unit, Julio seemed strange. She did not exactly use that word, but she wondered with some exasperation why he did not want to take advantage of the many services available to his brother. Why did he seem so reluctant to keep appointments with both the worker and the school? Why had he withdrawn his brother from school when this was clearly against the law for a child so young? To the case manager, Julio's behavior was inexplicable.

It is always the majority group that defines who is a stranger and who is not. The people who seem strange to us are not strangers to those with whom they hold common cultural traditions. If the situation was reversed and we found ourselves in a place where our cultural ways and values were different from the majority, then we would be the strangers.

Gudykunst and Kim (1997) use the concept of the stranger to define those whom we encounter who seem strange to us, whose ways of thinking and acting are unfamiliar, and who are not members of our in-groups. In other words, they are people who are close enough that we cannot ignore their presence, but they are unfamiliar to us and therefore seem like strangers. (Throughout this chapter, I will use the term *stranger* as it is defined here.) If people come from another culture, possibly from another country, it is entirely possible that they do not know enough about your culture to be able to relate easily to you. In addition, it is quite likely you do not have enough information about their culture to be able to make the new situation smoother for them.

As the human service professional, you are the person who can take the initiative in making the adjustment smoother for those who come to us as strangers. When people we might consider strangers have developed a good degree of competence in the majority culture and can communicate well, they will be healthier. Studies, however, indicate that it takes a long time for immigrants to adjust to the new culture and that if this maladjustment is severe or long-term, it can cause serious mental health problems as a consequence.

As the world community becomes more global, we can expect to encounter people from many different cultures who will seem like strangers, people who are different. Gudykunst and Kim (1997) make the point that we have internalized our own culture to such a degree that we believe it is innate in some way. They write, "anyone whose behavior is not predictable or is peculiar in any way is strange, improper, irresponsible, or inferior" (p. 357).

When people deviate from the familiar, we are likely to notice it instantly. We may feel anxious or surprised and uncertain. We may be forced to look more closely at our own cultural assumptions. Perhaps we are forced to conclude that aspects of our culture that we have taken for granted are not particularly useful. Our cultural identity may be challenged. Obviously it would be easier to avoid all this and stay away from strangers. Many people do just that, preferring not to experience these unsettling emotions. In human services, however, our work is all about encounters with people, and our purpose is to be helpful. Avoiding strangers would be irresponsible. For that reason, we need to know what to do when we encounter strangers.

Anxiety and Uncertainty

It is common for most people to feel uncertain or anxious when they are attempting to interact with people from other cultures. If we are consumed with our uncomfortable feelings, our communication with strangers will be impeded. We need to be able to manage our feelings during these encounters to provide for a constructive exchange.

Many times we attempt in some way to reduce anxiety or stress in these encounters. We project our notions about what the person means, giving us a certainty that might not be justified. We might try to develop theories about the other person that feature similarities. The more we believe a person is like us, the less likely we are to feel anxious. Thus, we might look for similar psychological reactions, similar group affiliations, and similar cultural aspects.

When Misaki came from Japan to study at a local college, she was the only person from Japan on campus. Other girls in her dorm invited her to join them for meals and to walk to classes with them, and Misaki did so. When the other girls laughed and talked about trivial matters, Misaki was silent. She rarely made small talk with the girls. They began to interpret her behavior as "too serious" and worked even harder to draw her into their discussions. Misaki was always pleasant but contributed little to these exchanges.

To the girls in her dorm, she seemed too serious; but to the resident assistant, Misaki appeared depressed. Ann, the resident assistant, based her opinion on the fact that Misaki never looked up when she spoke and never looked directly at Ann. Ann asked Misaki if she would like help with her sadness or depression. Misaki said "yes," so Ann made a referral to the campus clinic. There an intake worker decided that Misaki was indeed depressed and concluded it must be about leaving her homeland. To each question the intake worker asked, Misaki answered "yes." Yes, it was hard being here in America; yes, she missed her parents; yes, she had trouble understanding everything the professors said in class.

A counselor at the clinic recommended to Misaki that she join in more with the girls in her dorm and learn to "loosen up and have fun." In Japan, however, people who talk a lot are not viewed as particularly trustworthy. Those who use silence more frequently are considered discreet and trustworthy.

The girls in the dorm, the resident assistant, the intake worker, and the counselor in the clinic did not understand Japanese culture well enough to refrain from judging her by the standards of their own culture. Furthermore, in Japan people often assess what it is the speaker wishes to hear and answer "yes" as a means of keeping social harmony. They might not mean yes in precisely the way an American might interpret it. In addition, Japanese people often do not look directly into the eyes of someone with whom they are conversing. To look directly at another is a sign of defiance or aggression. Looking away is a sign of respect. The Americans took Misaki's behavior as an indication of shyness or depression because that is what the behavior would most likely mean in American culture. By fitting Misaki's behavior into American cultural meanings, the Americans did not have to feel anxious about how to interpret the behavior of a stranger.

American girls talk to each other frequently and often about trivial matters as a way of cementing their ties to one another. To the girls who befriended Misaki, this seemed normal. Her silence did not. In order not to feel anxious about her, they projected their own theories about her behavior onto her and concluded that she was sad about leaving her home in Japan. This was a normal reaction, understandable from their standpoint. The theory made Misaki seem more like them; thus, their theorizing reduced their anxiety.

We will unwittingly go to great lengths to resolve our anxious or uncertain feelings. Often what we do is inaccurate and not useful in promoting clearer communication.

Thoughtless Versus Thoughtful Communication

First, we need to find a way to control our anxious feelings to allow us to really be able to listen and communicate. If we are likely to feel anxiety when we talk to strangers and if this anxiety is going to interfere with a realistic understanding of these strangers, we are going to hear and communicate in a skewed or inaccurate manner. What is worse is that we may be only vaguely aware of this problem. The following sections discuss areas you can evaluate to make your communication more thoughtful and accurate.

Recognizing Our Tendency to Categorize

Think about what we do when we are communicating without thought. We categorize people; we assume there is only one correct or normal way to view things; and we are closed to information that does not fit with our cultural perspective. When we encounter someone who is different, we dump that person into one of our large categories or stereotypes. When someone's behavior does not fit or that person's thinking is strange to us, we are thrown off balance. To prevent that, we have categories all ready into which we can place such people. Because we do this habitually, we are not completely aware of our categorizing.

Actually, as you work with various sorts of people, you may find that you need to add many new categories to your conceptualizations of others. These categories, if more specific and definitive than those based on stereotypes, will be better predictors of behavior.

Looking for Exceptions

To become more thoughtful as you communicate, start to look carefully for the exceptions to your categories. If you think all Hispanics are loud, think about times when you have encountered Hispanic people who were not loud. If you believe all Muslims are militant, look for times when individual Muslims have expressed cooperation. If you believe all Jews horde money, seek out the times that Jewish people have been generous. In other words, recognize that the categories you have been using are likely to be much too broad to account for all the specific differences you may encounter in the people you serve.

Another way to look for exceptions to your categories is to seek differences in each specific individual. If you dismiss a stranger as coming from a group that is generally believed to be resistive to your efforts to help, you will have little success compared to recognizing the resistance and then looking for times the stranger was not resistive. If you have categorized someone as too talkative, look for times when that person was listening instead. If you are sure the people in a particular group are stupid, look for times individuals in that group made wise decisions or choices. Seeing others as individuals will make these exceptions important to you. As a competent worker, you will diligently seek these exceptions to gain a more accurate understanding of the people you are serving.

Checking Our Attributions

Most research shows that when we see a stranger's behavior as negative, we are inclined to blame that behavior on the stranger's character or disposition. When we see the stranger's behavior as positive, we are more likely to think this person is an exception and attribute the exceptional behavior to the environment or the circumstances. In other words, it appears that for many of us, giving up our stereotypes is very hard. We would rather see the exceptions to our stereotypes as something external to the stranger, and we are likely to blame behavior that seems to fit the stereotype on the personality of the stranger.

The opposite is often true as we go about attributing causes to our own behavior and the behavior of those we consider to be members of our in-group. If we see negative behavior in these people, we are likely to blame the environment or circumstances, while we often consider positive behavior a reflection of the person's character. The following list summarizes how we often see things:

Our positive behavior	Attributable to our good character
Their positive behavior	Attributable to the environment or the circumstances
Our negative behavior	Attributable to the environment or the circumstances
Their negative behavior	Attributable to their poor character

When we do this systematically, it reveals prejudice on our part. In addition, these systematic errors in attribution cannot have come about thoughtfully. They are thoughtless, automatic ways of looking at other people. As you become more thoughtful in your communication, become aware of how you explain the behavior of others.

Evaluating Scripts

We have all learned certain scripts for the activities we engage in frequently. For instance, if you meet someone you see often, but do not really know very well, you might say "Hi" as you pass that person. She might say, "Hi. How are you?" You would probably say something like, "Fine, and you?" She might then respond with "Just fine, thanks." By the time this exchange is completed, you may be several yards apart and walking in opposite directions. This constitutes a script for passing someone you see every day but do not know very well.

There are scripts for a variety of everyday activities. We carry them in our heads to be used when the appropriate situation presents itself. We have learned them first by observation and then from our own participation in these activities. The exchange demonstrated in the previous paragraph did not take much thought. Two people may pass each other every day and go through much the same exchange. They do not stop and consider what to do as each encounter presents itself.

We expect that people from our culture will respond to our "hello" with a "hello" of their own. If one individual does something different, we are thrown off balance. People from other cultures, however, have learned different scripts. For instance, a common area of misunderstanding relates to the fact that different cultures have different nonverbal ways of indicating that they do not want to be approached. Suppose you are indicating through your body language to someone from another culture that you do not want to be approached, and this person approaches you anyway. You may feel pushed and invaded when, in reality, the stranger could not recognize the signals. You could make a similar mistake. You might see a person you want to join you. You might wave to the person and point to your group, indicating that the person should come over and join you. To a person from an Asian country, this would be insulting. Waving people over, and especially using one finger to do so, is considered rude. We are looking at two different scripts.

Behavior or communication that seems strange to you may simply be a different script presenting itself. Stop and think about what the unexpected behavior means to the stranger. Is this offensive behavior, or does the stranger mean something quite different? Is there a possibility that you are misreading the signals or cannot recognize the signals from this stranger? Is it likely that the signals you are sending are not familiar to the stranger?

Checking Perceptions

Gudykunst and Kim (1997), who have written extensively on this subject, recommend that we simply check our perceptions with strangers to see if these perceptions are accurate. Instead of assuming that we know what a stranger means, we need to check. These authors recommend a three-step process:

1. Describe the other person's behavior, being careful to simply describe what was observed without evaluating or labeling the behavior.
2. Tell the stranger how you interpreted the behavior. In doing so, be matter of fact. Refrain from any hint of a negative evaluation of the behavior.
3. Ask the stranger if your perceptions are accurate.

Checking your perceptions is a good way to keep the communication between you and the stranger accurate and meaningful. It is important not to assume you know what the stranger means or what the stranger feels. Check with that person to see if what you perceive is correct.

Allowing Differences

It cannot be stressed enough that thoughtful communication is extremely important in reaching real understanding with strangers. Obviously, the better the understanding between you and a stranger, the more likely it is that you will be effective and competent in your assistance to that person.

Not all strangers will respond the same way to their new environment. Differences between the culture of the stranger and the culture of the host society may account for how a stranger responds. Large differences in verbal and nonverbal behavior, in norms or language, or in political and religious orientation can make adapting to the new surroundings more difficult. Where the differences are small, things may be easier for the newcomer. For example, someone from Canada would have less trouble adjusting to the United States than someone from Botswana. When you take this into account, you are able to look more thoughtfully at the stranger's attempts to adapt and be more helpful in that process.

In addition, recognize that there is a lot you do not know and be open to finding out more. When you are communicating with someone who is a stranger to you, put aside your goal for that conversation and begin to listen carefully for new information the person might be providing to you.

Finally, accept that there is more than one way to view something or to understand something. People have different perspectives, but that does not mean that some are superior to others or more correct than others. We may have been taught that this is so, but look at other ways to explain behavior besides your own perspective. Try to understand what perspective the stranger may have. This can be done only if you communicate thoughtfully.

Dimensions of Culture

Researchers in the field of communication have looked for ways to help us understand cultural differences even when we do not know the details of every culture. They have proposed that cultures have an underlying foundation of individualism or a foundation of collectivism. Cultures fall along a continuum, with no single culture being all one or the other; but many researchers believe that communication can be facilitated between people of different cultures if we know whether the stranger with whom we are communicating is from a culture that is primarily an individualistic culture or a collectivistic one. This tool is particularly helpful when we do not know all the particulars of a specific culture.

Individualistic and Collectivistic Cultures

Using information from Gudykunst and Kim (1997), we will look at some of the characteristics of cultures that are predominantly individualistic or collectivistic. Figure 4.1 summarizes some of the general differences between these two types of

FIGURE 4.1

Characteristics of Individualistic and Collectivistic Cultures

Individualistic Cultures

Individual More Important

- Individuals should look out for themselves and their families
- Promote self-fulfillment
- Emphasize individual initiative and achievement
- The in-group influence is very specific to times and place
- Individual goals are emphasized
- Tend to apply their value standards to everybody (universalistic)
- Emphasize needs and goals of the individual over the group
- Support unique individual beliefs

Have a More Vertical Culture

- People are expected to stand out from others
- Value is placed on freedom
- Maximizing of individual outcomes

Collectivistic Cultures

Group More Important

- Members of in-groups look out for each other in exchange for loyalty
- Require that people fit into the group
- Emphasize belonging to groups
- The in-group influence is very general over all situations
- Group goals are emphasized
- Tend to apply different value standards to members of their in-groups and to members of out-groups
- Emphasize the needs and goals of the group over the individual
- Shared in-group beliefs

Have a More Horizontal Culture

- People are not expected to stand out from others
- Value is placed on equality
- Cooperation with in-group members

cultures. Figure 4.2 lists some examples of countries that tend to be individualistic and some that tend to be collectivistic.

How Individualistic and Collectivistic Cultures Differ

First, individualistic cultures tend to place a higher value on the individual than on the group. Collectivistic cultures, on the other hand, tend to place more value on the group. Another difference lies in the way in which society is viewed. In individualistic cultures, there is ranking and hierarchy; collectivistic societies tend to be more egalitarian.

There is also a difference in the way the two cultural types use the surrounding context in communicating. In individualistic societies, the communication tends to be so direct that a person rarely needs to check the context to fully understand the meaning. In more collectivistic societies, context is extremely important. See Figure 4.3 for a summary of the communication differences between the two types of cultures.

FIGURE 4.2

Individualistic and Collectivistic Cultures

Countries That Tend to Be Individualistic Cultures	Countries That Tend to Be Collectivistic Cultures
(based on predominant tendencies in the culture)	*(based on predominant tendencies in the culture)*
Australia	Brazil
Belgium	China
Canada	Columbia
Denmark	Egypt
Finland	Greece
France	India
Germany	Japan
Great Britain	Kenya
Ireland	Korea
Italy	Mexico
Netherlands	Nigeria
New Zealand	Pakistan
Norway	Panama
South Africa	Peru
Sweden	Saudi Arabia
Switzerland	Thailand
United States	Venezuela
	Vietnam

Figure 4.4 highlights some of the specific elements that make communication different between individualistic and collectivistic cultures. As the comparisons in the figure indicate, there is plenty of room for misunderstanding. A person from a culture that values clear, explicit information might suspect someone from a high-context culture of being manipulative or confused. Someone from a horizontal culture might find someone from a vertical culture rude and boorish or incredibly selfish. If a client from a collectivistic culture waited to engage in services until he had group consensus, the worker from an individualistic culture might mistakenly think the client was resisting treatment or uninterested in help. If a worker from an individualistic culture encouraged a woman from a more collectivistic culture to look out for herself and leave an abusive marriage, the client might feel helpless and unsupported. Leaving the group might not be an option for her.

One common error is for people from individualistic cultures to assume the person with whom they are speaking from a collectivistic culture is speaking as directly and explicitly as they are. Individuals from collectivistic cultures can make the reverse mistake, assuming the person from an individualistic culture is only implying or speaking indirectly.

FIGURE 4.3
Communication Differences Between Individualistic and Collectivistic Cultures

Individualistic Cultures: Low-Context Communication

- Low-context communication is more precise
- Direct and explicit

Context Is Only Minimally Important

- Tend to use very direct communication
- Listener does not have to use context to obtain meaning
- Communication is less ambiguous
- More concerned with clarity as necessary for effective communication
- Communication is about the same for in-groups and out-groups
- Value saying what you think
- Value truthfulness
- Verbally direct, precise, and absolute
- "Yes" means agreement

Collectivistic Cultures: High-Context Communication

- High-context communication uses understatements, pauses, silences, or a shortage of information
- Indirect and implicit

Context Is Important in Determining Meaning

- Tend to use more indirect communication
- Listener must use context to obtain meaning
- Communication is more ambiguous
- More concerned with avoiding hurting others or imposing on others
- Communication is very different for in-groups and out-groups
- Value avoiding confrontations
- Value courtesy
- Verbally indirect, imprecise, and probabilistic
- "Yes" does not necessarily mean agreement

Privacy and Self-Disclosure

At different times, we feel open to interaction with other people or we feel closed and seek privacy. Different cultures regulate privacy needs in different ways. While individualistic cultures do so with physical boundaries, collectivistic cultures do so by psychological means. For instance, in collectivistic societies, people who might be encountered in general public situations are often seen and treated as nonpersons and simply ignored. In this way, the individual is protected from unwanted involvement. In individualistic societies, this would be seen as rude.

Time

Time is conceptualized differently in different cultures. How people conceive of time determines how they are likely to use it as well.

FIGURE 4.4

Specific Communication Differences

Individualistic Cultures

Privacy Regulation

- Use of physical barriers such as doors, walls, private rooms and offices, fences, hedges

Self-Disclosure

- More likely to self-disclose because privacy is protected through physical barriers

Monochronic Time

- Time is seen in discrete compartments
- Compartments are used to schedule events one after the other
- Actual time on the clock is more important
- Emphasize adherence to schedule
- Punctuality important

Face (Public Self-Image)

- Less emphasis on respect for elders and superiors
- Concern with saving one's own face

Persuasion

- Focus on the person they are trying to persuade
- Direct requests for what is desired
- Likely to threaten the person's security
- Likely to state negative consequences to a person if the person does not . . .
- May ingratiate themselves to the other (I really value you, therefore . . .)

Expression of Emotion

- Less concerned with using emotions to further group cohesion or harmony

Collectivistic Cultures

Privacy Regulation

- Use of psychological barriers such as speaking softly, treating one another with decorum, treating people in public as nonpersons, sending nonverbal cues that approach is not desired

Self-Disclosure

- Less likely to self-disclose to protect accessibility of others

Polychronic Time

- There are no compartments
- Can do more than one activity at a time
- Activities are more important than the time
- Emphasize completion of tasks
- Punctuality not so important

Face (Public Self-Image)

- Emphasis on respecting or giving face to one's elders or superiors
- Concern with saving the other's face

Persuasion

- Focus on the context in which the persuasion is taking place
- May use altruistic strategies (for the sake of the group, company, etc.)
- Likely to appeal to duty, concern for the whole group
- More likely to promise positive consequences if a person does . . .
- May imply a "good" person would do this

Expression of Emotion

- Display those emotions more likely to support group cooperation

(*continued*)

FIGURE 4.4 *(continued)*

- Display more of a variety of emotions
- More likely to express positive emotions with members of out-groups

- Not as tolerant of free expression of a variety of emotions
- Negative emotions toward others are expressed privately so as not to reflect badly on the in-group
- Negative reactions to members of the in-group are withheld so as not to disturb the harmony of the group
- Negative reactions to members of the out-group are more often expressed to increase the cohesion of the in-group

Information Seeking

- Try to get to know the person, such as characteristics, beliefs, past experiences, attitudes
- Look for personal similarities with members of an out-group
- Tend to self-disclose to strangers

Information Seeking

- Try to get to know the person's group affiliations, age, and status groups
- Look for group similarities with the out-group member
- Tend not to self-disclose to strangers

Conflict

- Prefer to deal with conflict directly
- Not too concerned that all parties save face
- May look for ways to integrate conflicting views or compromise

Conflict

- Prefer to deal with conflict indirectly
- Concerned that all parties save face
- May try to avoid the conflict or give in to the other

Face

It is common for people in individualistic cultures to talk about saving face. In sociological terms, *face* refers to a public self-image. In collectivistic societies, there is an emphasis on protecting the face of others, a concept that is less emphasized in individualistic cultures.

Persuasion

Different cultures use different methods for persuading people to undertake certain activities or to comply with specific requests.

Expression of Emotion

Different cultures express emotions differently and use the display of emotions to further the cultural values.

Information Seeking

In all cultures, people attempt to gather information that will clarify situations and reduce anxiety. Members of individualistic and collectivistic cultures go about this task differently. Interestingly, research indicates that in America, European Americans tend to self-disclose more than African Americans do. When close friendships are formed, the opposite is true. In close relationships, African Americans will self-disclose more than will European Americans.

Conflict

Look at the differences among cultures in dealing with conflict. Research suggests that "Chinese prefer bargaining and mediation more than North Americans, . . . Mexicans tend to avoid or deny that conflict exists, . . . Canadians prefer negotiation, . . . Nigerians prefer threats more than do Canadians" (Gudykunst & Kim, 1997, p. 282). In the United States, people are more likely to deal directly with conflict, looking openly for ways to resolve it. With all of these cultural differences in the preferences for handling conflict, it is important to approach conflict thoughtfully.

Obstacles to Understanding

We use a number of different mental mechanisms that can block clear communication. These mental mechanisms are used primarily to reduce anxiety when we encounter strangers. Often we are not aware of the extent to which we resort to these mechanisms. They are particularly present when we are engaging in thoughtless communication. The following sections discuss some of the obstacles that prevent real understanding.

Stereotypes

Some stereotypes are positive, and some stereotypes are held only loosely. Communication is most likely to be obstructed by rigidly held, negative stereotypes that can lead a person to make inaccurate assumptions and predictions about another person. Sometimes a person fits our stereotype of a particular group, but many other persons in the same group may not fit the stereotype at all. Becoming aware of our assumptions and questioning them is important.

Ethnocentrism

Ethnocentrism means that we use the standards common in our own culture to judge the behavior and culture of other people. It is important to understand that we are all ethnocentric to some extent. It is common to look at others through the lens of our own culture. The way our culture is arranged seems "normal" or "correct." Deviations from our culture, therefore, seem abnormal and incorrect. It is not that we consciously decide to employ ethnocentric tactics, but rather we are socialized into viewing the world in a particular way.

The antidote to ethnocentrism is cultural relativism. Using cultural relativism, we try to understand the meaning of others' behavior and communication within the context of their culture, not our own. When we use ethnocentrism to judge people from other cultures, we create barriers and distance. When we use cultural relativism to understand others, we diminish barriers and distance.

Prejudice

Gudykunst and Kim (1997) define prejudice as "judgment based on previous decisions and experiences" (p. 124). People hold prejudices against whole groups of people and against individual members of those groups when they are encountered.

Prejudice involves an attitude that generally stems from a negative stereotype. If you think all the people in a particular group are pushy and devious, you will probably decide that you do not like those people. Not liking those people is a prejudiced attitude that is based on the stereotype you hold in your head about members of that group. This easily leads to discrimination, in which you take pains to avoid being around these people whom you do not like. You might deny a member of this group a job for which the person is qualified or deny a family of this group housing in your neighborhood.

Conflict

When we are already suspicious or uncomfortable with a group of people, misunderstandings can turn into hostility and conflict very easily, particularly since we are likely to attribute the negative behavior of strangers to their personal characteristics, while attributing the negative behavior of in-group members to the situation. All the mental mechanisms described previously serve to make other groups seem less worthy of being understood and enhance the possibility that conflict will occur with individual members of a particular out-group.

Be aware of two points. First, misunderstandings may stem from mental mechanisms that are inaccurate or have obstructed real understanding on everyone's part. Second, once a conflict has occurred, the approach to resolution may be quite different from one culture to another.

Changing Attitudes

It appears from recent research that we can change our attitudes toward strangers or members of out-groups through a number of opportunities to interact with them positively. Stephan (1985) talks about ways to increase understanding and to create more favorable relationships among groups. For instance, an emphasis on cooperation, rather than on competition, is helpful. It is useful if those coming together have about the same status within their own groups and have some similarities in common with each other. Supporting the individuality of each member helps smooth things out. Voluntary contact and contact that is focused on substantive issues as opposed to superficial issues are more useful. Everyone involved should work toward a positive outcome.

The goal of intergroup cooperation and contact is to learn to see members of other groups as individuals rather than as representatives of our own biases and stereotypes. Gudykunst and Kim (1997) address this in their dichotomy between uncertainty-oriented people and certainty-oriented individuals. They write about an uncertainty orientation:

> Uncertainty oriented people integrate new and old ideas and change their belief system accordingly. They evaluate new ideas and thought on their own merit and do not necessarily compare them with others. Uncertainty oriented people want to understand themselves and their environment. (p. 185)

A certainty orientation is quite the opposite. The authors write:

> Certainty oriented people, in contrast, like to hold on to traditional beliefs and have a tendency to reject ideas that are different. Certainty oriented people maintain a sense of self by not examining themselves or their behavior. (p. 185)

When we are communicating thoughtfully, we can make a conscious choice to acquire more of an uncertainty orientation toward new situations and strangers. By remaining open, we can learn more.

We need to go one step further, however, by offering confirmation to others with whom we communicate. When you are working with people who are strangers to you, confirm for those people that they are valuable to you as individuals, that their experiences and concerns are important, and that you are willing to become involved in helping them to resolve their problems. When we deny that another person's concerns and experiences are valid and therefore imply that they are insignificant, we demean that person as an individual, and the opportunity for meaningful resolution and rapport is lost.

Competence

Workers who are adaptable to situations and flexible in choosing how to respond to situations do better in cross-cultural communication. These workers are intuitive and sensitive to what others might mean or need and are open to considering the interaction from a number of different points of view. Figure 4.5 highlights some of the points to remember about individualists and collectivists that might make this process easier.

FIGURE 4.5

Points to Remember in Cross-Cultural Interactions

Individualist Characteristics

- There is a degree of emotional attachment from their in-groups.
- Behavior cannot be accurately predicted based on group membership.
- Out-groups are not seen as extremely different from in-groups.
- Equal relationships where status is equal are preferred.
- People take pride in their own accomplishments.
- Arguments that emphasize harmony and cooperation are not very persuasive.
- Saying negative things about others is more likely.
- It is easier to separate criticism from the person being criticized.
- Long-term relationships happen less often.
- Relationships that contain more rewards than costs are more likely to be maintained.
- Initial friendliness is not considered a sign of an intimate relationship.
- Respect based on age, position, or sex is generally not as likely.

Collectivist Characteristics

- Emphasis is on group membership.
- Group membership can be used to predict the collectivists' behavior.
- When group membership changes, the collectivist behavior changes.
- Unique relationships, where one has more status than another, are comfortable.
- Competition is seen as threatening.
- Harmony and cooperation are emphasized.
- Keeping a positive public self-image (face) is a concern, and individualists can help them to maintain that.
- Criticism and the person being criticized are not seen as separate; thus, avoiding open confrontation is best.
- Deliberately cultivated long-term relationships work better.
- More formal initial interactions are preferred.
- Forced self-disclosure will cause a negative response.
- Respect for age and position is important.

Competence in cross-cultural interactions depends very much on the individual worker's commitment to give high-quality service to every person who comes for assistance. As you begin to practice, you will encounter more people from specific minority groups or cultural groups with which you are unfamiliar. Ethically you are responsible for developing an understanding of their cultures or subcultures, at least along the various dimensions outlined here.

Until such study has been completed, it is important to consciously and thoughtfully monitor your interactions with strangers. Make certain that you hear the significance of their concerns and experiences, that you respond in a way that lets them know they have been heard, and that you provide a respectful environment where problems can be resolved.

Summary

We know that it is not possible to know the particulars of every culture and respond appropriately to individuals from these cultures. While it is your ethical obligation to know more about the culture of people you see regularly in the course of your work, you will encounter people from different cultures from time to time whose culture you know nothing about.

To avoid problems, it is helpful to know whether a person comes from an individualistic culture or from a collectivistic culture. Once this is established, you are able to respond in keeping with the characteristics of those cultures. In addition, it is always a good idea to check your understanding when conversing with a person from another culture. What seems reasonable to you from the perspective of your own culture may not be reasonable at all to someone from another culture.

Students do better working among many cultures if they keep an open mind and are willing to discard stereotypes and listen for new information. This chapter is designed to give you a starting point for interactions with people from other cultures, but the hope is that you will learn more about other people and their values and norms as you take the opportunity to interact with people from cultures other than your own.

◆ Exercises: Testing Your Cultural Competence

Instructions: Look at the culture of each client described in the following scenarios, and decide what might be the underlying issue. What are you thinking about the client as you read each description? What are your first ideas about what constitutes the client's problem? Do you have a problem personally with the behavior of the client, and if so, in what way? The following brief explanations about cultural behaviors may help you answer the questions when you read the scenarios that follow:

- In many Asian cultures, members do not talk about family problems, feeling that these are private. They may also pretend that no problems exist.
- In most Asian cultures, crossing the legs and pointing the toe at another person is considered extremely rude. Because members of Asian cultures like to maintain harmony, they would not be likely to tell you directly that they were offended. In addition, in most Asian cultures, waving at another person or indicating that a person should join you by calling the person over with your hand or a finger is also considered extremely rude.
- Asians are not likely to make changes in the family or to engage in discussions about the family unless the male head of the household is present or is consulted. Furthermore, they are likely to tell you things are all right in order to maintain harmony. Things may not be all right. They may also tell you that you were helpful to them because they assume that is what you want to hear, not because it is true. Telling you what they believe you want to hear will maintain harmony.

- In most Asian cultures, group needs and considerations are more important than individual needs and considerations.
- In most Hispanic families, the man makes the major decisions and expects to be consulted about anything affecting the family. He would not be likely to take his wife's ideas or concerns into consideration. She would be expected to defer to the husband.
- Many Hispanic families allow mental health problems to persist for a very long time rather than admit that there is a psychiatric problem.
- In Hispanic culture, it is often believed that depression is due to a lack of religious faith.
- In Hispanic culture, mental health problems are often attributed to sin.

1. A man from Vietnam is in your office because his 11-year-old daughter has been having trouble in school. The school suggested the daughter be tested by your agency. You are doing the intake, but only the father has come into the office. He is very reluctant to tell you any specifics, but talks instead in extreme generalities. What might be the reason for his reluctance to talk to you in detail about his daughter's problems?

2. A Japanese family in the emergency room is seeing you because of a serious accident in which their teenage son was severely injured. During the course of the conversation, you cross your legs so as to be more comfortable. The family continues to talk to you in a polite but superficial manner, and gradually each member drifts away—to get a soda, to use the restroom, and so on. They are obviously resistant to sitting down with you again.

3. A Chinese woman is hospitalized for a serious infection, and her doctors think she seems depressed over possible home problems. You talk to her, and she appears to reassure you that everything at home is fine. When you come in the next time, she wants you to talk to her husband instead. He, too, is reassuring and pleasant. Later you ask the woman if your talking to her before was helpful, and she smiles and tells you it was. You are not sure.

4. You work in the school counseling office, and you have been asked to help a gifted young Vietnamese student fill out applications to several prestigious colleges. She is in line for a number of scholarships. She works on the applications, but with obvious reluctance, and indicates she cannot consider going away to school until the family has decided what she will do.

5. After the birth of her fourth child, a Puerto Rican woman is referred for depression by her family doctor. At the intake interview, her husband comes and answers all questions. He indicates that he will decide what she needs and what is to be done. The wife says very little and speaks only when she appears to feel her husband wants her to do so.

6. A Mexican American family brings an elderly aunt to the emergency room. The older woman is severely depressed and emaciated. She also appears to be nearly catatonic. She is admitted immediately to the hospital on an emergency commitment. You learn that this woman has been in severe depression for years and wonder why the family waited until things became so serious. Later, when you talk to the aunt, she is somewhat improved. She indicates that her pastor visited her and told her that her depression is due to her lack of religious faith. She tells you she agrees with this assessment. She tells you she believes that if her faith was stronger and she was less sinful, she would not feel like this.

7. A young Hispanic woman is admitted to the hospital, and the doctor believes she is showing obvious signs of schizophrenia. She is hallucinating and has not been eating. Her family tells you this problem is the direct result of her sinful behavior. According to them, she is too friendly with the boys in her class. The students often call each other to compare homework, and sometimes a group of boys and girls will go to a party or several boys and girls will walk home from school together. The family has tried to get her to cut off these friendships and to stay home and help her mother more. Because she did not listen, she is being punished.

Chapter 5

Attitudes and Boundaries

Introduction

The way we see other people and the way we relate to them as a result affects how things turn out in a relationship. The boundaries we erect or the boundaries we fail to observe can similarly have an effect on outcomes. In this chapter we look at attitudes that can be detrimental and boundaries that are useful, and those that are not. The purpose is to give you an opportunity to increase your awareness of attitudes and boundaries and to become more observant of your own ways of viewing other people, particularly other people you intend to help.

Understanding Attitudes

Attitudes are extremely important. The feelings you have about other people are bound to be communicated to those people one way or another. If your attitudes are positive and supportive, you will be more likely to establish rapport. If you feel superior or disdainful, no matter how well you try to hide those feelings, they will eventually be communicated to your client, and you will lose a working relationship.

Good human service workers have learned about themselves—their fears, sensitivities, and errors in judgment. In facing those things about themselves, these workers have come to understand themselves in a way that enables them to feel understanding and warmth toward themselves and others. If you are able to forgive yourself for the mistakes you make and the struggles you have had and see them as an important part of growing, you will recognize that you are basically all right. It is then much easier for you to understand others who are making mistakes and who are struggling with issues and problems. You know that the problems you have faced have provided valuable lessons. These personal struggles have helped you to grow into a more sensitive and insightful person. Problems and unfortunate decisions happen to everyone. With this personal understanding, you will be more inclined to see others' personal struggles as productive of growth, and not necessarily as a reflection of personal inadequacy.

Begin, therefore, with yourself. Be tolerant of your mistakes. Look at yourself objectively. Forgive yourself for errors in judgment, particularly errors that have taught you important lessons or helped you to grow. Recognize that part of being human is to struggle with issues and transitional problems, and that through this process we are often strengthened and given new insight.

Basic Helping Attitudes

You need to bring three basic helping attitudes to your work: warmth, genuineness, and empathy. Studies show that even in the absence of much formal training, workers who genuinely care for their clients and are committed to them will be able to help their clients make important changes and move toward better circumstances and increased emotional health.

Warmth

A worker needs to be friendly, nonjudgmental, and receptive. These three attitudes create a warm atmosphere, one that serves to put the client at ease.

In your presence, clients feel valued by you as a person. You communicate a belief to them that they are worthy of being understood. You do this through your actions, body language, and the way you listen to each person. In addition, you refrain from evaluating what clients say and the actions that they take. For instance, a warm person would say something like, "Tell me more about that." A judgmental person might be more likely to say, "Oh, well, you should never have done something so careless." In addition, you are receptive to what people have to say. You listen to what they tell you they have done and felt, what brought them to seek your assistance in the first place. When you say, "Tell me more about that," you are inviting the person to open up and talk safely with you. When you say, "Oh, well, you should never have done that," you have passed judgment and cut off further discussion. The atmosphere is no longer warm.

Part of being warm is not dominating clients. It means you respect your clients' right to make their own decisions. You may facilitate better decisions than the ones they might have made alone, but ultimately the decisions about their lives are their own, and you will respect that. Sometimes we are painfully aware that a decision is not the right one for the person to pursue. Later in this book we will talk about how you can give clients some of your thoughts in ways that people can hear and use your ideas more easily. Nevertheless, people may choose to ignore you and make their own decisions, and you will respect that. We have all made unfortunate decisions and concluded, as part of our growing process, that they were not very useful.

Some people think being a warm person means they must stand by passively, never confronting or giving the client another way of looking at things. A warm person is still able to facilitate change, and change is often painful. As you learn the skills in this course, you will pick up methods to use that help clients see things from more than one perspective and possibly see characteristics about themselves that are difficult to face.

Genuineness

You have heard the expression "be yourself" many times. This is a must for those who help others. Nobody relates well to a phony. People sense when you are not being authentic.

Perhaps you use slang that sounds forced, phrases you do not usually use. Maybe you are using them now to make clients think you are familiar with their lifestyle or culture. Maybe you put on a phony dialect or use profanity to seem more down to earth. You might pretend to be a physician, wearing a white coat and allowing your clients to call you "doctor." A client calls you "doctor," and you do not correct the impression. You might pretend to have degrees you do not have. You could use big words you know the client does not understand. None of this is authentic. You will be seen as a person who is rather foolish at best, and untrustworthy at worst.

Be open and truthful. Strive to be yourself, to present your authentic self to the other person. If you do not know something, say so. If you lost a client's forms, tell the client that and apologize. If a client asks about your credentials, tell the client matter of factly what they are.

Empathy

Empathy means putting yourself in the other person's shoes. To do this you must be able to comprehend what that person's needs and feelings are. In human services, we often say that we are able to listen with the third ear. We hear more than what the client is telling us. We hear the underlying emotions, desires, and worries. With practice we become proficient at this, and we develop a special sensitivity.

Part of empathy is being able to accurately communicate to the person an understanding of these underlying emotions. If you are able to put into words the feeling the person is experiencing right now, you are practicing empathy. To do it well, you will communicate in a way the other person can understand and accept, not in a way that is threatening or judgmental. An empathetic person would say, "You must have felt sick when you saw what the accident did to your car." Someone with little empathy would be more likely to say, "I'll bet you could have shot yourself when you saw what you did to the car. Do you have insurance? Bet you didn't have that either." Finally, empathy is not sympathy. It does not mean that you are so sad for people that you take their situations home and fret about them when you are away from work. It does not mean that you feel sorry for people and communicate the belief that they are poor souls or that their situations are without hope. Sympathy is what we often have for our friends and relations. Empathy is assessing where the client is at any given moment and being able to express that and support it. Sympathy is the common feeling we have for others in pain. Empathy is a basic clinical strategy for supporting people through difficult times.

On Being Judgmental

José, returning from a home visit in a neighborhood where many of the homes were run down and many of the residents were poor, was aghast. "I'm not going back *there*. That's a terrible place to live! Those people should think about how they live and what they are doing to their children." He continued in this way for several days. Eventually the supervisor had an opportunity to talk to him about his attitude and how judgmental it seemed. She explained to him that this is where his clients live and that service requires us to respect the home of another person and not judge it as inferior. Assuming the people who live in the neighborhood are responsible for the way the neighborhood looks and for the people who live there may not be altogether true. "You are not better than the clients you serve," she pointed out to him. "You may feel uncomfortable there, but you can't force a client to come to you here in the office just because you don't approve of the neighborhood in which your client lives or because you feel uncomfortable because the people who live there aren't like you."

There are human service workers who sit in judgment of clients, applying their own standards to people who are sick, who have been through trauma, or who have no ideas about alternative ways to approach their lives. There are people who say they are in human services to be helpful, but who are actually wary and distrustful of their clients. This is an attitude that has no place in the helping relationship.

For example, Rose, a new worker, was part of a planning team for a new shelter that was about to open for children who needed a place to stay before foster care could be found. These were children removed from their homes for physical or sexual abuse or extreme neglect. During the planning, it was decided that the children would earn points for good behavior and lose points when they violated policies of the residence. Children with 10 points or more would get special privileges, and those with no points would stay in their rooms temporarily and miss special activities. The director asked the group, "Where shall we start a child when she comes in new? Shall we start her with 10 points or none?" Rose was convinced that each new child should start with zero points and earn them. "How about starting each child with 10 points and letting her work to keep them?" the director suggested.

When the planning group ultimately adopted the director's suggestion, Rose was upset, thinking that the children would "just come in here and take advantage of us." She asserted that the children "need to know we mean business right from the beginning." The assumption that the children would automatically misbehave and take advantage of the staff was judgmental—adding that judgment to the problems the children were already experiencing would have been cruel. Rose's need to curtail and punish before any misbehavior had taken place would have put her negative attitudes into action in a destructive way.

Reality

Some human service workers say they have gone into this work to help other people, but the minute a client behaves in a difficult manner, they complain that they should not have to deal with this sort of person. Rita refused to sit down with the mother of a child who was in treatment and work with her on a solution to the child's behavior problems. Rita complained that the mother was a difficult person with whom to work. "She's always complaining about what we're doing. She thinks she has a better way. I just want to say to her, 'Look, if your way was so hot, you wouldn't have the problems you've got with Benny.' All she ever does is make stupid suggestions. I just wasn't going to get into that with her."

In human services, we are trained to deal with people who seem dissatisfied and upset. We expect to meet people who do not see things our way, who are challenging, or who question our decisions. Many of the people we work for will have an inaccurate perception of reality or difficulty expressing what concerns them, seem unduly sensitive, or be confused about following a plan. This is largely the reason our clients sought our help in the first place. If we only want to work with people whom we like and who agree with us, people who give us no trouble, we will be barely effective and more likely harmful.

How Clients Are Discouraged

There are many ways to discourage another person. You could set up a competition comparing the client to others or to yourself. You could push, force, or shame the client into moving toward some goal. You could spend an inordinate amount of time focusing on the client's mistakes or demand that the person do more or try harder. You could insist that clients do things your way, dominate clients by taking over or demanding perfection or unrealistic outcomes. You could treat clients like poor souls—as incompetent, bumbling people who need you to do everything for them. You could be insensitive by failing to notice positive changes or ignoring the good things clients accomplish. You could refrain from ever giving feedback except the most negative type. All of these responses discourage others from trying to do more.

Today, many individuals, some of whom hold degrees in fields unrelated to human services, are being asked to give direct care to clients who seem odd and unusual to them. For this reason, the clients may be frightening to these workers. In order to counteract feelings of uncertainty, such a worker may become extremely dominating and coercive. This gives a false sense of control. The domination and need to order clients' lives in inappropriate ways are discouraging to clients who are learning to take charge of their lives and make decisions.

An example of this occurred in a program for individuals recently released from an institution for those with mental retardation. A case manager working with the clients visited them every other day in their apartment, where she offered support to help them remain in the community. She enjoyed her work with the clients, and she had received good human service training. When the clients began to make jokes about the pounds they had gained over the years in the institution, she suggested they might want to exercise. Together they decided that walking around the apartment complex might be fun and a good way to meet their neighbors. For weeks the clients walked almost every day, but at different times of the day and not on days when the weather was too cold or snowy.

Later, the case manager's supervisor, a person with little human service experience, was upset that the case manager had not "scheduled the exercise." The supervisor felt that the clients should not be allowed to just say they would walk every day, "because they won't do it. We need to put that in their daily schedule, let's see, at 11:00 to 11:30 every morning. That way we can check on them and be sure they are doing it." The case manager asked, "But what if they skip one day, or feel like going at 3:00 in the afternoon?" The supervisor replied, "My point exactly. This way they have no choice, and they'll meet their goals. We'll look good for seeing that the clients' goals are implemented consistently. Set up a daily schedule for them, and see that exercise goes into it at 11:00." A person beginning to live a normal life in a community who has decided to take up an exercise program, and who has demonstrated a commitment to that program, does not need a professional to oversee the timing of it. This is an example of inappropriate control.

A very grave example of discouragement occurred in a partial hospitalization program. Kitty, a client in the program, suffered from severe schizophrenia and depression. Often she was immobilized with sieges of despair and delusions, with voices of many others talking to her in what she called a "confused conversation." Kitty described herself as afraid and appeared to the staff as dependent. The staff surmised that because Kitty had a master's degree, obtained before her first episode of depression, she was really capable of more independence. They developed a series of goals for her to follow, such as riding the bus, shopping at the mall, and handling arrangements for her insurance and transportation. The final step on the list of goals was for Kitty to prepare her tax returns because her degree had been in business.

From the start, Kitty had problems managing the goals. Feeling extremely depressed and occasionally hearing voices, Kitty found it alarming to be on her own in the city. In group sessions, Wayne, the group leader, held her up to ridicule. He encouraged the other clients to scold Kitty and accused her of refusing to help herself more. Kitty asked to reexamine her list of goals, but this was greeted with a refusal on the part of the staff and further insistence that she "get out there and try harder." Finally, Kitty decided to withdraw from the program. When she told the staff, they told her that unless she cooperated with the program set forth for her, she would not be allowed to come to the clinic for her prescriptions. These prescriptions, partially underwritten with public funds, were important in sustaining Kitty's connection to reality. Kitty finally called a friend of hers, a psychologist who worked in the state mental health system. When the behavior of the staff came to light, staff members were reprimanded and Kitty was able to obtain her prescriptions and counseling services elsewhere.

We need to examine what went on in Kitty's case. First, a client has the right to ask that goals be reexamined. It may indeed be that the goals are not truly in line with the capabilities of the client, and setting goals should always be a collaborative effort. Second, a client can always withdraw from service if the client determines the service is no longer useful or, as in Kitty's case, is actually harmful. The client has a clear right to determine what is good for and helpful to her, and what is not. Finally, the use of medication to coerce the client into doing what the staff has determined she will do is highly unethical.

All these factors combined in Kitty's case to create a discouraging atmosphere. On top of that was the denigration by the staff, particularly Wayne, who pointed out Kitty's deficiencies and ascribed manipulative motives to her failures without ever really working with her to plan goals at which she could succeed. It would have been hard for a person like Kitty to attempt any goals in such a negative situation.

Another example of discouragement happened in a transitional living arrangement for the mentally ill. This transitional living situation was one of many living arrangements with varying degrees of independence that helped clients move from hospitalization to independent living. Mario, who had persistent schizophrenia, had been placed in the last step toward independence, a small house with four other clients. At the time, Mario was on new medication, begun while he was in the hospital, which increased his ability to function considerably. While in the program, he adjusted well to the medication, obtained a job, and began to look for a new apartment.

This was all part of the plan. Finding a new apartment was difficult, however; while extremely ill many years before, he had presented problems for one landlord after another. Now, in spite of the obvious improvement, the client had a reputation for being a problem when he became ill, and no one was willing to risk his becoming a tenant. In the meantime, Mario collected furniture for a new apartment and continued to look at ads in the paper. Staff in the program assisted.

The time for Mario to remain in transitional housing expired. At that point, the case manager called the assistant director of the agency. The case manager was belligerent. He said the client was obviously "high functioning" and was therefore "stalling" in finding a place and moving on. He stated he knew nothing about the client's past history with landlords and was not interested. He reminded the program director that case management was responsible for the bills for the transitional housing, and they were going to stop paying for this service for this "manipulative" client.

"He obviously has no intention of moving and thinks we're all too dumb to see it," the case manager claimed. "Let him know he has 7 days to be out." Without asking for a meeting, without sitting down with the client or with the staff in the program, without looking at what might be going on and how the agencies could work together to facilitate a positive transfer to conventional housing, the assistant agency director wrote a peremptory and hostile eviction letter, making it clear that Mario had 7 days to find housing or he would be "evicted," and stating that Mario's case manager supported this decision and thus Mario should make no appeal to his case manager for help. Coming home from work, the client found the letter on his pillow and immediately deteriorated. Staff at his transitional living program had not been informed of the letter and discovered the client in a frenzy in his room, throwing things into garbage bags and crying. Sometime later he left the house.

When he did not return that evening, the staff became alarmed. They found and read the letter left in his room, but were unsure what to do. They notified the evening supervisor of another program, and together they were able to track Mario down in another state where he had gone to be with his sister. Much later, case managers and others began to put notes in the record that indicated work had been done to find housing with this client. The notes were made to appear as if they had been written long before he left the program. The notes were back-dated, a highly unethical practice. These notes contained indications that the client had been uncooperative during this time, something the transitional housing staff firmly denied.

In time, the staff in transitional housing were able to let the executive director of the agency know of the true nature of the incident. The executive director had been told this was a smooth leave-taking by the client. Reprimands followed, but these in no way made up for the damage done to the client's sense of self-esteem and confidence or the ground lost in this client's move toward independence.

Understanding Boundaries

There is always a danger that we will see ourselves in the clients we serve. Many of us will work in agencies that serve clients who have been through something we went through ourselves. We may meet a client whose situation is different but that person reminds us in some way of ourselves. Perhaps the person is our age or has the same interests we do. When clients remind you of yourself and you are unable to separate your circumstances from theirs, you will become a problem to the very person you are supposed to be helping. Sometimes we have not entirely resolved the issues in our own life. We may seek employment in an agency that deals with similar problems just to continue to heal. This is not useful. It means that the clients will be treated in the light of your own issues rather than with a completely objective focus on their own personal issues.

Seeing Yourself and the Client as Completely Separate Individuals

The Client Reminds You of You

A young woman volunteer who was in training to answer the hot line at a rape crisis center had been raped some years before. It was still an overwhelming event to her, the defining event in her life. She was not ready to begin to work with others who had been raped while her own emotions were so raw and intense. During the training, she would fret and stew over the information being given. She would constantly remind the trainer that this would not have worked for her in her situation because she was too upset or too badly injured. She pointed out her own circumstances and told the trainer to focus more on this type of situation. She gave details of her rape at every opportunity. She used her own situation to illustrate the trainer's points.

It was apparent that she was not ready to serve as a volunteer who would have direct contact with the clients. Why? She had not yet recovered from the trauma of her own rape, and it seemed likely that she would impose the circumstances and emotions of her own rape onto those of the caller. In that case, the caller's real problems might get lost as the worker went off on her own concerns and feelings. She was asked to take other work in the agency, and ultimately she left because she never was able to separate her rape from those of the clients the agency served.

Sometimes the client is trying to do something we accomplished ourselves long ago. The client reminds us of a time when we were vulnerable and uncertain. For example, in a welfare agency, a young woman, recently off welfare and now working as an income maintenance clerk, was helping a welfare client make plans to get off welfare. The worker was somewhat irritated by the client's concerns about day care and transportation. "Look," she finally blurted out, "If I can work every day, you certainly can!" In another situation, the similarities were too much for Yolanda, a human service worker, to tolerate. She went to great lengths to find differences between herself and the client. Working at a program for individuals recovering from alcohol abuse, she had trouble understanding how one of the clients could have "gotten into a mess like this." The client had regressed over the weekend and was drinking again. She came in seeking Yolanda's help, but Yolanda had been through recovery and this woman's "slip" reminded her of the hard fight she had made to stay sober and clean. What made it harder for Yolanda was that this woman was Yolanda's age, had two children the same ages as Yolanda's children, and lived two blocks from Yolanda. Instead of listening to where the client was at the moment, Yolanda became angry, asserting how hard she had fought to get where she was and telling the client to do the same. This woman's relapse threatened Yolanda's view of her own success. It became important, therefore, to demand that the client straighten up and never, ever think of doing this again. Her anger and refusal to start where the client was at the moment alienated the client. In subsequent meetings Yolanda pestered the client to tell whether she had relapsed since her last visit, and she admonished the client frequently about her "tendency to drink." Gradually the client drifted out of treatment.

The Client Reflects on You

There are other reasons that a human service worker might not separate from the client. As a case manager, you might become extremely involved in clients' problems and solutions because it makes you feel more important or competent if the clients solve their problems successfully. It may impress others if all your clients do well, and so you may cross the boundary and force clients to use your solutions. Sometimes, in spite of what we know about how good it is for clients to learn from their errors and struggles, and in spite of our belief that clients are responsible for their own lives, we also mistakenly believe that all our clients must be happy and successful if we are to look good. Again, we are focusing inappropriately on ourselves, and not on the clients' needs.

Erecting Detrimental Boundaries

Some boundaries are artificial and foolish. There is a very human tendency to make these two extremely unfortunate assumptions about people:

1. People who look like me will think and act like me.
2. People who do not look like me are not like me at all, but very different.

Neither of these assumptions is true, but we must watch for signs of them creeping into our thinking because these ideas erect negative boundaries that can make you ineffective.

Be very careful what you assume to be true of another person. A person may be of another race or culture and yet share many of your values and circumstances. A person who looks like you may be quite different in tastes, opinions, and way of life. If you assume a person of another race or religion has certain stereotypical characteristics, you will be dealing with a stereotype, and not with a real person.

When you view people in light of these assumptions, you no longer see individual differences. All Catholics, African Americans, Jews, Quakers, and Indians are not alike. If you view people based on your stereotypes of the groups from which they come, you will fail to discern individual differences. Failure to perceive individual differences is a failure to accurately perceive reality. Aside from this being a fundamental characteristic of mental illness, it is impossible to give excellent service to a client you see only as a stereotype.

Transference and Countertransference

Transference

Sometimes, when working with other people, you will find that you remind one of your clients of someone in their past. Sometimes clients are only dimly aware of that. They simply know that there is something about you that they really like or really dislike. This is transference, a collection of feelings and attitudes the client holds about you. Positive transference occurs when the client likes you, and negative transference occurs when the client does not. Understanding this is one more reason why it is important that you not take the feelings of clients personally.

In addition, clients can start out with positive transference toward you but then find those feelings changing. Perhaps a client hopes to make the relationship with you into a friendship. When you maintain professional boundaries, the client may reverse the positive feelings and the transference may become negative.

As a competent case manager, you will want to accept transference when it exists. It is not a good or a bad thing. It is something that commonly takes place in helping relationships. In other words, practice acceptance rather than becoming threatened and defensive. There will be times when clients' behaviors seem irrational, hostile, or even overly seductive. Acceptance of such behaviors while maintaining professional boundaries prevents barriers from developing and allows clients to continue to feel safe. In that environment, the clients may be able to reevaluate their feelings about you.

It is helpful, when clients respond in unexpected and seemingly somewhat inappropriate ways to the situation, to use reflective listening. This allows clients to know that you are not judging their behavior or attitudes and that you have heard them and want to understand. This, in turn, creates the safe environment you are seeking to maintain.

Countertransference

In countertransference, the case manager projects onto the client certain emotions and attitudes because the client reminds the case manager of someone from the case manager's past or because the client's issues and situation cause the case manager to identify with the client. This can arouse both positive and negative emotional responses from the case manager toward the client. A case manager may give special favors to someone who is reminiscent of an elderly aunt the worker once loved and who is now deceased. On the other hand, the worker may be inappropriately demanding when the client reminds him of a younger brother who was always bullying the worker when they were kids.

Acceptance of yourself and your feelings is extremely important here. We will meet people throughout our lives who remind us of other people. When it affects the way we work with our clients, then we need to be very aware of our feelings. Countertransference feelings are often a good warning signal that we have old issues we need to resolve. It is never acceptable to allow these feelings to interfere with service to your client.

Summary

Many, many good therapeutic approaches have been developed after years of study and trial and error. In addition, researchers have found that warmth, genuineness, and empathy have a profound effect on clients' ability to move forward and heal. Many students begin this course of study intending someday to become therapists and counselors. Learning how to convey these three essential elements of a therapeutic relationship is where a true therapeutic relationship starts.

Using the ideas in this chapter, you will recognize discouragement and know how to encourage and motivate your clients. Putting aside what you want for your clients and starting where your clients are gives them the footing they need to move to something better. The three basic elements of warmth, genuineness, and empathy form the underlying foundation for everything else you will do with clients. Even when you are uncertain about how to proceed, if you are using these elements, your actions will nearly always be viewed by clients as supportive.

In addition, it is important, for all the reasons stated in this chapter, to view each client as an individual person and to work very hard to understand what makes your client a unique human being. Using the individualistic and collectivistic models can help you to understand your client better, but then you need to recognize, through careful listening and observation, what it is that makes your client a unique person. Professionals work against relying on stereotypes, assumptions about groups of people, and personal feelings about certain problems and their solutions that will color the work they do with others. Take the time to see and hear the characteristics, circumstances, and interests of this person who is trusting you to assist in some way. Focus on what makes your clients separate individuals. Give your service based on what you know about your client as a unique person.

When workers begin to identify too strongly with their clients or find that they must assume some of their clients' responsibilities, they have blurred the boundary that makes both the worker and the client separate individuals. They cross that boundary in unproductive ways every time they assume that a client will be like them or will react as they would. These workers breach the boundary each time they handle a client's problem without collaborating with the client.

◆ Exercises: Demonstrating Warmth, Genuineness, and Empathy

Instructions: There are five grade levels of responses you might give to people who have come to you needing assistance in sorting out their problems and feelings.

Grade A: These responses are the most useful in establishing rapport and encouraging a continued dialogue.

- Centers on the client entirely
- Stays on the topic (responds to the client's feelings or the content of what the client has said)
- Addresses what is most important at that moment to the client
- Is respectful (indicates the client is an equal; indicates the client is a person worthy of being understood)
- Invites collaboration
- Shows confidence in the client

Grade B: These responses are helpful but could be better.

- Is somewhat confident of the client's abilities
- Minimal invitation to collaborate
- May briefly stray off the topic
- Is just a little superior

Grade C: These responses are usually made by someone who means well, but they are not especially helpful responses.

- Is pleasant, but superior
- Overly helpful without collaborating
- Introduces new topics that seem to the worker to be more relevant
- Misses the feelings
- Does not address the content

Grade D: These responses are not useful in establishing rapport and do not encourage a further exchange.

- Takes over with solutions
- Spends little time listening; is abrupt
- Moralizes and preaches
- Ignores the client's assets and strengths
- Shows minimal interest
- Does not indicate respect for the client

Grade F: These responses are mean-spirited and damage the relationship irreparably.

- ◆ Uses denigrating labels and descriptions of the client or the client's actions
- ◆ Shows no interest in the client
- ◆ Denigrates feelings of the client
- ◆ Denigrates the content of what the client has said
- ◆ Intimidates, humiliates, or threatens the client (berates and scolds the client)
- ◆ Leaves the topic for one entirely unrelated

Following are some vignettes that demonstrate the various grade levels of responses. Look at each response, and assign a grade to each one. Next, using the preceding material on grade levels, tell specifically why you think the response should receive the grade you assigned to it.

Vignette 1

A man has come to your agency for help after he was brutally beaten and robbed. The worker asks the man to tell her what happened. He describes the night the mugging took place, but as he approaches the actual incident, he finds it more and more difficult to talk.

The first worker's response: "This is really difficult for you. Would you like to wait a minute?"

Grade: _____   Reason: _____

The second worker's response: "Now, this is all over, Mr. Brown. It happened days ago. You need to be thinking about moving on and getting on with your life."

Grade: _____   Reason: _____

The third worker's response: "This must have been awful for you! Excuse me a minute." Turning to the secretary in another room, "I heard the phone ring, Sue. Was that the attorney calling? Tell him that we need that file before we can do anything for his client." Turning back to the client, "Now, where were we, Mr. Brown?"

Grade: _____   Reason: _____

The fourth worker's response: "I'm really wondering if you can handle this! I'm going to call mental health and set up an appointment for you. Why, you're a wreck!"

Grade: _____   Reason: _____

The fifth worker's response: "I can see it's difficult for you to talk about this. I'd like to work with you to see if we can find some ways to help you with some of these painful feelings. I have some thoughts that I think might help, and I'm sure you do too."

Grade: _____   Reason: _____

Vignette 2

A young woman enters a shelter after she and her boyfriend, with whom she is living, have had a fight. She has been badly beaten. She seems to want to talk and remains in the office even after the worker has completed the admitting forms. She is rather quiet, however, and does not volunteer much information.

The first worker's response: "Yeah, another case of the violent boyfriend. Here we go again. You'd think you women would stop seeing these guys before it gets to this."

Grade: _____   Reason: _____

The second worker's response: "Did he ever beat you before? I was just wondering because I'd think that if you'd been through this before, you would have left before now."

Grade: _____   Reason: _____

The third worker's response: "It sounds like you've had a rough evening. Do you own your own home? No, I was just wondering if you own your own home. It says here you live in a house, and not an apartment."

Grade: _____   Reason: _____

The fourth worker's response: "I was in your shoes once. Believe me, it was a long and difficult battle to get out of that mess. But I did. I just decided that it wasn't worth living like that—life's too short, and I got out!"

Grade: _____   Reason: _____

The fifth worker's response: "What you need is a good lawyer. You tell the staff that comes on in the morning that you want to talk to a lawyer. You can't just sit around and take this stuff!"

Grade: _____   Reason: _____

Vignette 3

A rape victim sees the volunteer in the emergency room. As the volunteer talks to her, she learns that the victim is afraid to go home. The man who raped her is an acquaintance in the neighborhood, and she is afraid that now that he knows she called the police, he will come after her.

The first volunteer's response: "It sounds like you could use a place to stay tonight. Would you like me to try to set something up for you?"

Grade: _____   Reason: _____

The second volunteer's response: "You're really afraid of this guy! Well, you're not going home tonight."

Grade: _____   Reason: _____

The third volunteer's response: "I can see that you can't handle this! I'll make all the arrangements. Don't worry about a thing. I'll get you a place to stay, and I'll set you up with an appointment at mental health."

Grade: _____ Reason: _____

The fourth volunteer's response: "How would you like to handle this tonight?"

Grade: _____ Reason: _____

The fifth volunteer's response: "Let's get off this gruesome topic. I mean, I know it's important to you right now, but it'll do you good to talk about something else. Tell me about your job."

Grade: _____ Reason: _____

The sixth volunteer's response: "You must be feeling so afraid of him."

Grade: _____ Reason: _____

Vignette 4

A man talks to the intake worker in a case management unit about his recent separation from his wife. He comments that he could have been a better husband, that he was stingy and went for days not speaking to his wife if he was annoyed. He thought he was making her see how he felt about things, but she left him, saying he was "uncommunicative." He seems depressed and bewildered by his wife's departure.

The first worker's response: "Sounds to me like you could use some communication workshops."

Grade: _____ Reason: _____

The second worker's response: "Did you have to go that long without speaking? I mean, what could she have done that made you that mad?"

Grade: _____ Reason: _____

The third worker's response: "You really thought you were getting through to her, so it must be hard to see her leave this way."

Grade: _____ Reason: _____

The fourth worker's response: "Only a fool would think what you were doing was 'communication'! Of course she didn't hear you, fellow!"

Grade: _____ Reason: _____

The fifth worker's response: "See, I think you should have tried marriage counseling before things got this bad. Not now, after she's already gone."

Grade:_____ Reason: _____

The sixth worker's response: "Well, if you had a better understanding of the way women think, you could have avoided this whole thing."

Grade: _____ Reason: _____

◆ Exercises: Recognizing the Difference—Encouragement or Discouragement

Instructions: Following are two vignettes. Decide what you would *do* or *say* to encourage the person, and then decide what you might *do* or *say* that would discourage the person. Actually picture yourself as an encouraging person, and then as a discouraging person. Remember your actions may be as important as your words. Write in your answers to share with the group.

1. A woman, the mother of two children, has been without a home for a number of months. She tells you she really wants a permanent place to stay. You know there are very few places she can go. You also know she has some talents and interests—strengths that might be to her benefit.

   You encourage her by

   You discourage her by

2. A man calls and says he was sexually abused as a child. It has come to haunt him recently, but he is not sure where he should turn for help.

   You encourage him by

   You discourage him by

◆ Exercises: Blurred Boundaries

Instructions: Following are some situations in which the boundary between the worker and the client has become blurred. Identify what went wrong and what needs to happen to correct the situation. Use the space provided to make notes.

1. Alice is very upset because she gave the client some names of people she thought might be helpful in solving the client's problem. Today she met one of those people at the local deli where she eats lunch and learned that the client has never been in touch with that person. She has been trying to call the client all afternoon to find out what happened.

2. Bill is feeling very proud of himself. He talked to a client who had very complicated problems this afternoon. He put everything down on paper, while the client sat by his desk and drank a soft drink. Then Bill decided on the best way to handle the situation. The client finished his drink, did just what Bill suggested, and reported that everything is fine now.

3. Mary Lou was once in a very abusive relationship. She was able, through much counseling and grit, to become assertive enough in her own behalf to get out of the situation. Today she is happily married and the mother of two lovely children. The client she is talking to is in just such an abusive situation and seems hesitant about leaving. Mary Lou wants her to leave and, using examples from her own life, assures the client she is certain the client will have just as happy a life as Mary Lou now has, if she will leave. Mary Lou remembers vividly how she felt when she was in the client's shoes and tries to make the client see how much better she will be if she leaves now.

4. Gloria was raped by her stepbrother when she was 16 and he was 23. It was a very difficult situation; law enforcement officials were called, and eventually the situation broke up her family. She is currently working at a rape crisis center and is talking to a client whose situation reminds her of her own. She says things like: "Oh, that wouldn't have done a thing for me!" or "I was too far gone to be able to handle it that way."

5. Carlos is working with a woman whose father is the president of a large bank in another city. She has become depressed and needs a referral to a therapist and perhaps a psychiatric assessment. Carlos is reluctant to talk to her about

needing "psychiatric help" because he assumes this would be offensive to someone as "upper class" as she is. Instead he suggests she "talk to someone for a little bit." Later, with the woman's permission, her father contacts Carlos and asks if there is anything he can do. Carlos is careful not to suggest short-term psychiatric hospitalization even though the father is offering to pay "for whatever she needs." Carlos is sure such a hospitalization would alienate the father.

6. Candy is working in a shelter for homeless men. She is new at her job and enjoys what she is doing. The fact that many of the men are in poor physical health and are unwashed is of great concern to her, and she works hard to meet the basic needs of the residents, such as food and clothing and a warm place to sleep. When she is working, she never asks the men to help with chores around the shelter even though that is a condition for their staying there. She thinks of her work as very loving and giving, and she sees the clients as hapless and uneducated. Therefore, when Paul comes to her and tells her he graduated from high school and finished a year of college before he got hooked on drugs, she is not certain she believes him. When he asks for help returning to college, she resists giving him information and support for attending the local community college.

7. Marissa is interviewing a client who has come in for help with her bills and job-readiness training. The client is the mother of a 2-year-old boy. Marissa is the mother of a 2-year-old boy as well. She considers herself an excellent mother. She prides herself on how she adapts her life around the needs of her child and how his needs come first. She is uncomfortable with the arrangements the client must make to accommodate her impoverished circumstances, and so Marissa lectures the client. "Children need stability, not instability and disorganization. They need to know you are there for them and not have continual disruptions. Does your son even know ahead of time when he will be staying with your mother and when he will be staying with you? You need to put this child first in your planning." Marissa is surprised when the client remarks quietly that seeking help so that she and her son can eat on a regular basis *is* putting her child first.

Chapter 6

Clarifying Who Owns the Problem

Introduction

Before you ever open your mouth, before you ever say a word to your client, you must be able to discern accurately who owns the problem. Who owns the problem?

*It is the person whose **needs** are not being met.*

It is not the person who is being rude and uncooperative. It is not the person who is ruining a party. Nor is it the person who is singing off-key and ruining a songfest. It is the person whose needs are not being met. You should know who owns the problem for three very good reasons:

1. *You will know who is responsible for solving the problem.* If you know who owns the problem, then you know who is ultimately responsible for solving it. If you know who is responsible for finding a solution, you will not assume the entire responsibility is yours. In other words, you will not accept responsibility for problems that are not yours. When you take over and try to solve other people's problems, or tell them how they should resolve their problems, you may be seen as meddling in their affairs or being pushy.
2. *Meddling is disrespectful.* This sort of meddling is disrespectful, even when you intend it to be helpful. It says clearly that you have doubts about the client's ability to figure the problem out and handle it on her own. You indicate that you are not sure other people have the sense and insight to know what is best for them.

3. *The client loses opportunities to grow.* Furthermore, when you take over with solutions, you interfere with what might be a very meaningful experience for the client. This person may grow from wrestling with this issue. It may be the opportunity needed to gain insight, learn a new skill, or try something that until now has been too frightening. If you attempt to take over with your own solutions and ideas, your client will miss this valuable opportunity. Clients can never say, "I did this myself!" Instead, they will have to say, "My case manager did this for me."

Kentaro, working in a sheltered workshop, was learning a new job on the assembly line. He seemed to quickly pick up his responsibilities, but he was having trouble keeping up. Over and over the worker monitored his progress and gave him tips for improving his speed. The worker stood behind him and grabbed the pieces Kentaro missed. Finally, the worker was called away to the phone. When he came back, he discovered that Kentaro was sitting so that he faced the assembly line from a different position. Now, with better visibility, the client was catching each piece that came toward him and making the necessary adjustments. The worker later said he felt foolish for standing over Kentaro all morning when it turned out the client knew all along how to solve the problem.

Agnes wanted to have a better relationship with her mother. She confided this to her worker one day, and the worker set about helping her solve the problem. While the worker spoke to her about poor communication, mother and daughter relationships, and family therapy, Agnes decided to buy a pretty card and send it to her mother. In the card she told her mother how much their relationship meant to her and how much she wanted them to be friends. She enclosed a little lace handkerchief, and sent the package off to her mother. Soon her mother called Agnes, and they began to talk. Agnes, who knew herself and who had lived a good portion of her life with her mother, understood how best to solve her problem. Listening and helping Agnes talk about the relationship with her mother might have been a better course of action for the worker.

Keep your clients in a position of authority over their lives to the greatest extent possible. Remind clients of how much of the resolution of the problem is their own doing. Point it out to them. You might say, "Let's look at all the things you've done to make this happen." Make sure your clients have the opportunity to feel pride in their part in solving the problem. Let clients see they can help themselves more (even if it is only a little bit more) the next time, rather than turning to their case manager to solve the problem for them.

If the Client Owns the Problem

Let us suppose your client comes in and tells you she cannot stand living with her mother anymore. Her mother is verbally abusive and rejecting. Your client is unhappy. Obviously this client's need for a pleasant home environment and her need to be appreciated by her mother are not being met. The client owns the problem. Does the mother own the problem? She does not appear to. This method of communicating with her daughter seems to work for her. She shows no discomfort or guilt about any pain she might be causing her daughter. It seems to meet some need of hers to communicate in this way. The mother does not have a problem in this situation, as her needs appear to be met.

There are several important ways you can respond to your client's situation. First, listen. Then, rather than providing a solution, be a resource to your client. Give her options. Tell her about services with which you are familiar that might be helpful to her. Ask her for her ideas. What is she looking for? What does she want to happen? Leave the final decisions up to her. In this way, you make sure that the client retains a position of power in her own life, and you act collaboratively. You are the expert on available services, but she is the expert on her own life.

Now let us change the story a little. Your client brings in the same problem, but she has a moderate developmental disability. The problem still belongs to her, but now you make a conscious decision to get a bit more involved and a conscious decision about the extent to which you will get involved. Just because someone tells you about a problem does not mean you must solve it. As a case manager or worker, there will be times when it is important to give more help than others. A wise worker will know how much to help and when to stand back. These are strategic decisions.

Deciding how much to become involved is important when the client has a problem with you. For example, a client may come into your office and tell you that he cannot stand the way you sit in front of a cluttered desk and talk to him. He claims he feels disorganized by your clutter and wants you to have your desk cleaned off when he comes in. In this case, you may make a conscious decision to let him own this problem because there is no way to clean the desk off in the middle of a busy day when you know he is coming in. You would thank him for his comments, give a word or two about why that might not be feasible, and tell him you will continue to keep your office as it is for now.

On the other hand, the client may be upset with you because you are always late. His need for punctuality is obvious; your being on time means to him that you are expecting him and that you value his time. His need is not being met. In this situation, you might decide to help own the problem. You recognize that you have been somewhat disrespectful. You can justify it with your busy schedule, but you also can do better. So you acknowledge the problem, thank him for his comments, and offer to be more punctual. You have made a conscious decision to become involved in the solution to his problem.

It Is Not Uncaring

Sometimes we feel guilty about not doing more. Sometimes others tell us that we should be doing more. After all, we are the person's case manager. Why are we not extending ourselves further? Sometimes the clients themselves are the ones to accuse us of not caring or of being indifferent. Knowing who owns the problem and allowing that person to resolve it is not an uncaring action. In fact, you would never refuse to help a client simply because you determined the problem belonged to the client.

When you allow clients to work on their own issues and problems, you respect their right to privacy and self-determination. In addition, you give them an important opportunity to grow and work on their own behalf. Solving one's problems effectively is part of emotional health and maturity. To the extent to which clients are able, we want to encourage them to do as much for themselves as they can.

It Is a Strategic Decision

The extent to which you become involved in helping clients solve problems that belong to them is a strategic decision. This is another difference between the professional approach to relationships and a friendship you might have away from work. In the professional relationship with your client, you want to decide strategically how much help to give and the extent to which you will step in. The decision is based on your knowledge about the client and about how this opportunity can be used to help your client grow.

A woman who is blind might need more help negotiating the transportation system than one who is depressed. A person who is illiterate and from a rural village might need more help working with the Social Security office in the city than would an urban lawyer. A child might require more support than an adult to carry out a personal decision.

The strategy lies in knowing your client's strengths and limitations and tailoring your involvement to those factors specifically. In this way, you avoid taking over simply because that is the easiest thing to do or because you see all clients as helpless. Your involvement is just to the point the client needs help or ideas and no further.

In certain cases, even though the client owns the problem, you may find yourself taking over and resolving it almost entirely alone. Suppose you are working with a single, 17-year-old girl, disowned by her family because of her pregnancy. She has just delivered her first child for whom she has made adoption arrangements. The child, however, is severely disabled and retarded. The doctors feel the care required by the child can never be undertaken by a 17-year-old girl living alone, and the prospective parents have now withdrawn their bid to adopt the infant. In this case, you work out arrangements for the care of the infant, solving the infant's need for a safe, medically appropriate environment and solving the mother's problem of what to do with a handicapped child she believed would be going to the home of another couple. In this case, you would consult with the mother throughout the process, possibly even taking her to see the facility where her baby will receive care, but you would handle most of the actual arrangements. If you did not understand the concept of who owns the problem, you might be tempted to ignore the mother in the process of solving this problem. If the mother were older, married, having her second child with this handicap, and supported by her family (or in any number of different circumstances), your response and the extent of your involvement would change as well.

When the client owns the problem, *carefully* decide the extent to which you will be involved. Test your hypothesis about how much the client can handle alone. Be ready to take on more responsibility or give more responsibility to the client as you move toward a solution. Watch your involvement to be sure you are not obstructing the client's opportunities to grow or to exercise self-determination and independence.

Be a Resource and a Collaborator

You will have at your fingertips information that can help the client solve a problem. You may have the names of agencies, phone numbers, contact people, and addresses for services. You will also be familiar with policies in various agencies and within large social service systems, such as child welfare and mental health. You will often be more familiar with the law as it pertains to the client's situation. This makes you a valuable resource to a person attempting to arrive at a solution.

Bring the information and facts to the client, and then collaborate with the client on the solution. It is the client who is most aware of which solution will work and which ones are impractical. Together, with your knowledge of the system and your clients' knowledge of their personal lives and circumstances, you will be able to construct a useful approach to clients' problems.

If You Own the Problem

If you are having a problem, that is, your needs are not being met, you will understand that the resolution of the problem is ultimately your responsibility. This applies to personal problems, and it also applies to problems you might have in the course of your relationship with your clients. What if it is the client who is always late? Whenever the client is late, you find you are behind for the rest of the day. This is not the client's problem. The client may find it perfectly acceptable to get to your office at approximately the time he is scheduled to see you. He may have scheduling problems or punctuality problems; but in this case, he does not own this problem. You do. Your need to stay on schedule and see everyone you are scheduled to see before 5:00 p.m. is not being met. Therefore, you are the one who is responsible for bringing it up. Do not expect that others will guess there is a problem.

In bringing up a problem we are having with another person, we are asking for that person's assistance in resolving it. Just as you make decisions regarding how much you will become involved in resolving someone else's issue, your clients have the right to determine the extent to which they want to help you. It is conceivable that the client will see your point and make some changes. It is also possible that the client will decide that it will have to be your problem because it is preferable to be late for whatever reason or because being punctual is an inconvenience. There are ways to solve problems like this one; but for now, as the first step, you need to be clear about who owns this problem.

If You Both Own the Problem

Sometimes you both have a problem. Suppose a client needs evening appointments, and you work only during the day. Or perhaps a client wants to shout and yell about her situation, and you find that too unnerving to do a good interview. These are opportunities to negotiate. You, as the worker, have to be able to sort out in your own mind who owns what problem, and you must be able to initiate some negotiation around these issues.

When you both own the problem, you should not view it as a win–lose situation. If the client sees it that way, you need to point out other ways of looking at the situation. Perhaps he can see another worker who does work at night, or perhaps he can come in during the day sometimes and you can stay late sometimes. Maybe she can yell with less intensity, and you can overlook the rest of it. It might work to transfer the client to another worker, one whose schedule is better suited or one who can better tolerate the yelling. There are many ways to negotiate a solution. When you work on a solution collaboratively with the client, you provide the client with an important experience in problem solving. As the worker, you invite the client to join you in this effort.

Margaret had been ill with schizophrenia for a very long time. Rejected by most of the community and most of her strictly religious family, she found solace and support among the workers in the mental health system. In the course of her illness, she had been hospitalized and knew the staff at the hospital well. She had encountered the various members of the crisis team and knew them too. She had a case manager whom she found supportive. Margaret found countless reasons to call workers within the system. Night and day she called with tiny questions, not so much because she could not resolve the problems herself, but because she found contact with these supportive people comforting. Sometimes she would call to ask what time she should go to bed. She might call to ask if she should eat one frozen dinner rather than another. Should she go out for a walk tonight or not? Should she buy a new pair of shoes or not?

Margaret's incessant calling began to create a problem for already busy workers. They grew exasperated. Margaret had a need to feel their support, and the workers had a need to get things done with other clients. Finally, a solution was worked out with Margaret and all the workers in the system who regularly received calls from her. It was decided that a man on the crisis team who shared her religion and genuinely liked her would be the person she would call. When he was off duty, a backup person was designated. Margaret was then allowed only one call a day. She was to save all her questions for that one call. Everyone agreed to this plan.

Although Margaret tested the plan many times initially, everyone stuck to the agreement. Eventually Margaret began to make the calls more meaningful, asking for help with real problems. Undoubtedly, this one call a day helped to sustain her and helped her to live more comfortably in the community rather than in an institution. It also allowed the workers to focus on other clients.

In this situation, both the workers and the client had a problem, and their needs conflicted. By collaborating on a solution, rapport was not lost, and both the workers and the client gained valuable experience.

Summary

Knowing who owns the problem is an important first step in working with clients. This allows us to understand who is ultimately responsible for resolving the problem. Once we recognize that many of the difficulties our clients bring to us are theirs, we need to determine the extent to which we will assist in problem resolution. Both the determination of who owns the problem and the decision to get involved are the first strategic decisions you make in your work with clients. Your involvement must be tailored to the clients' strengths and capacities so that you do not take over where a client is competent or take from clients the opportunity to grow and learn from their experiences.

For many, deciding that the clients own the problem can be seen as uncaring. In reality, you are not abandoning clients with their problems. You are, instead, making decisions about how much clients can do for themselves and where you will be most helpful. In the long run, we want our clients to be able to take some pride in the fact that they participated in solving their own problems and learn from that experience.

◆ Exercises: Who Owns the Problem?

Instructions: In the following situations, identify who owns the problem. As you study each case, decide whether it is you, as the worker, who owns the problem; whether the client and perhaps the client's family owns the problem; or whether both you and the client own the problem at the same time.

1. A woman you have placed in temporary housing is angered by the loud music of her neighbors. She appeals to you to do something about it. Who owns the problem?

2. You work at a victim/witness resource center where you assist the victims of crime to handle the emotional and technical ramifications of the crime before they go to court. The husband of a victim, a woman who was carjacked by a teenager one night, takes you aside and asks you to persuade his wife to drop the charges. He tells you confidentially that it would be better for his wife if "she didn't have to go through this." Who owns the problem?

3. The mother of a rape victim, with whom you have been working, calls and says that ever since the rape, her daughter has been crying and unable to eat or sleep. She tells you it is urgent that she know exactly what happened to her daughter, but that her daughter refuses to talk about it. She asks if you can tell her what happened. Who owns the problem?

4. You are talking to the victim of a violent crime in the emergency room. Her boyfriend barges in and demands to know "what's going on." Who owns the problem?

5. You have placed a woman in temporary housing after she left her home following severe abuse by her husband. The husband calls demanding to know where she is and tells you he will get his lawyer and sue you if you do not tell him. Who owns the problem?

6. You are working with a support group. One of the participants tells you on the side that another participant is monopolizing the group's time with frivolous details and asks if you will do something. Who owns the problem?

7. You accompany a victim to court. The defendant's family meets you in the hall and tells you that you and your agency are responsible for their son being on trial. They claim the whole thing is trumped up, and they think you should persuade the client to drop the charges. Who owns the problem?

8. You are arranging for housing for a woman who is in a homeless shelter. Her parents come to see you and ask you to see that she also goes to therapy. They tell you she has never "seemed right," and they ask you to give them your opinion of her mental status. Who owns the problem?

9. You have developed a goal plan for a child. The parents agree with the plan, which involves summer camp and other recreational activities over the summer, all with a therapeutic program. The teacher calls to tell you that this

child can hardly benefit from school and that sending him to camp is a waste of the taxpayer's money. What he needs, she tells you, is therapy. Who owns the problem?

◆ Exercises: Making the Strategic Decision

Instructions: Following is a basic situation, with a list of scenarios in which the circumstances surrounding the situation are different. Decide what you would do in each case.

Situation: Hannah recently went blind due to an accident with chemicals at the company where she worked. She is asking for a service plan that will help her regain some independence.

1. Hannah is a PhD chemist with the corporation where the accident occurred. She has received a huge settlement from the corporation's insurance company. The corporation has said she can come back to work if she can be retrained in some way, possibly with computers. Hannah has a supportive husband and many close friends. How do you help?

2. Hannah was a custodian at the small chemical engineering company where the accident occurred. The company had little insurance, and it has no interest in hiring her back for any reason. The company did give her $5,000 at the time of the accident, and the hospitalization plan and workers' compensation helped pay the initial medical bills. Hannah lives alone and has few friends. How do you help?

3. Hannah is mildly mentally retarded and worked as a custodian at the company where the accident occurred. The company gave her $5,000 at the time of the accident, and the hospitalization plan and workers' compensation helped pay the initial medical bills. Hannah lives with her parents, who are very supportive, and she has two older siblings who also give support. The family has been working with Hannah to help her decide what to do next, and they have found a place where she can answer the phone and give standard information. This company is delighted to have a real person to do this,

as the answering machine option seemed too impersonal. Hannah will need some training. How do you help?

4. Hannah is a student working on a chemical engineering degree. She worked part time to pay her school expenses at a large chemical corporation. She wants to remain in school. Her family is supportive of this, but they live in another state. Hannah's roommates seem hesitant about her returning to live with them in their downtown apartment now that she is blind. How do you help?

5. Hannah is a student working in a small chemical lab while completing a chemical engineering degree. She wants to remain in school. Her family is supportive of this, but they live in another state. Hannah wants a seeing-eye dog, has a landlady who is afraid of dogs but who might accept one, and needs to learn how to negotiate the town and the campus as a person who is blind. She has numerous supportive friends. How do you help?

6. Hannah is a student working on a chemical engineering degree and doing a chemical engineering internship at a chemical plant near the college. She wants to remain in school. Her family is supportive of this, but they live in another state. Hannah was using this job to pay for her education. Now Vocational Rehabilitation will help, but Hannah must fill out countless forms. Hannah is depressed and frightened by her blindness and spends days at home alone. How do you help?

7. Hannah had a fairly ordinary chemical technician's job at the company when the accident occurred. She and four other people were blinded by the accident. Hannah has told you she wanted a lawyer while she was still in the hospital, and she also feels the group should meet regularly to talk about the accident and their anger. The others have agreed. Hannah tells you of

the state office of services to the blind and wants help connecting to that office. How do you help?

8. Hannah had a fairly ordinary chemical technician's job at the company when the accident occurred. The company offered to pay all her medical benefits and a small stipend to support her while she trained for another kind of work, not to exceed 5 years. Hannah lives alone and has few friends. She makes it clear to you that she is not interested in receiving any help from you. She rejects services that you know could help her to begin training and asks you to leave her alone. How do you help?

Chapter 7

Identifying Good Responses and Poor Responses

Introduction

This chapter provides some concrete examples of good and poor responses. Those called "poor" are poor in the sense that they tend to block communication and prevent the worker from hearing what is really important. The examples of poor responses are followed by examples of good or constructive responses that encourage another person to talk and feel comfortable doing so. Like learning to drive a car, we learn step-by-step the ways to structure responses that will facilitate good communication.

It is not enough, however, for you to look at these responses and do the exercises. You will build a skill in identifying which responses are inadequate and which actually enhance the communication, but this will not teach you to automatically use good responses rather than poor ones. This chapter is a start, but there is no substitute for practice. In later chapters, you will learn to use constructive responses with more understanding of how they promote rapport and clarity. Even this understanding, however, will not help you to make an automatic response that is therapeutic if you have not practiced.

This chapter clarifies which responses are most likely to promote rapport and which are most likely to promote withdrawal and defensiveness.

Twelve Roadblocks to Communication*

Dr. Thomas Gordon's (1970) *Parent Effectiveness Training* outlined twelve specific ways we often block good communication, setting up barriers to real understanding and dialogue. I have adapted these roadblocks to fit the kind of poor communication that sometimes happens in the human service setting. These responses are not helpful in talking with other people. They serve to obstruct rapport and block any constructive resolution of the problem, and they often serve to make our clients feel inferior or demeaned.

In the examples of poor responses provided in this chapter, notice the implied superiority of the worker. Individuals who come seeking assistance already feel unsure of themselves and uncertain about what to do. Workers who come across as all-knowing or judgmental are not helpful. An attitude of superiority—giving clients the sense that the worker is "talking down" to them—is harmful to the relationship and makes real communication and rapport difficult.

In addition, notice how hard it would be for a client to trust and be open after hearing the poor responses. What does one say to a person who appears to be convinced that she is superior? Most clients stop talking or resort to pleasantries after that, and real communication is blocked. Why continue being open if the responses are not empathic? Let's look at some examples of such negative responses.

Ordering, Directing, Commanding

The first roadblock involves giving the person an order or command. The assumption made by workers who do this is that they have all the correct answers or all the best solutions and ideas. There is no dialogue or collaboration. In the following examples, the workers take charge without including their clients.

- "I don't care what anyone tells you! You have to go see that lawyer!"
- "Go right back over to the courthouse and get those forms!"
- "Leave your house and find another one."
- "Look, just go over and apply for the job."

Warning, Admonishing, Threatening

Warning of consequences if the person does something is the second roadblock. Workers who do this do not want their clients to follow certain lines of action. Rather than discuss their clients' inclination to act in a particular way, they warn the client instead.

---

*Adapted with permission from *Parent Effectiveness Training*, by Thomas Gordon. Copyright © 1970 Random House, Inc.

In this next series of responses, the workers are again operating from a superior position without consulting their clients.

- "If you take that suggestion, you'll be sorry!"
- "You'd better not do that if you know what's good for you!"
- "I can tell you that something like that won't work!"
- "You won't get your medications if you don't attend group regularly."

Exhorting, Moralizing, Preaching

The third roadblock is telling clients what they should or ought to do. Again, such workers display the belief that they are superior to their clients and have all the answers. In several of the responses that follow, you can hear the workers imposing their own moral values on their clients. Listen to the "shoulds" and "oughts." Workers using these two words speak as though what they are saying is a universal given rather than a personal choice or value.

- "You should know that doing that is wrong!"
- "You shouldn't think like that."
- "You ought to see a counselor."
- "You ought to be more concerned."

Advising and Giving Solutions or Suggestions

Telling clients how to solve their problem is a fourth roadblock. When workers believe their clients have nothing useful to contribute to the resolution of a problem, they will make unilateral decisions without their clients' input. Some of the following responses indicate the worker's exasperation with the client. Workers who tell clients how to solve their problems believe that their way of seeing the clients' problems is the only way to see them. The clients are treated as though they are hapless or inadequate for not seeing their problems that way as well. Here are some worker responses that illustrate the point.

- "Why don't you just call your husband?"
- "I suggest you stop seeing this person today."
- "It would seem to me that you should just stay home."
- "Why don't you simply tell him to stay away?"

Lecturing, Teaching, Giving Logical Arguments

The fifth roadblock involves trying to influence with facts, arguments, and logic. In this next series of responses, the workers sound as if they believe their clients are incompetent. Only the workers know the whole picture. These responses by workers do not encourage real discussion of clients' feelings and problems.

- "I am going to give you the facts about domestic violence. If this doesn't change your mind, I don't know what will."
- "Look at it this way, the longer you put up with this, the more she gets away with it. People always try to get something for nothing. It is human nature. Your task is to stop it now."
- "Now what you need to do is call the police. That will circumvent any action on their part and free you to move to another location."
- "Now look, you have two choices. You can either stay or leave. That's what you have to decide."

Judging, Criticizing, Disagreeing, Blaming

Making a negative judgment or evaluation of clients is the sixth roadblock. In the responses that follow, the workers see themselves as judges of their clients' behavior. Instead of being supportive, these workers are grading their clients' behavior. Their responses can only serve to demean a person who is grappling with problems and feels unsure. Here are some examples of such demeaning worker responses.

- "You aren't thinking clearly."
- "You're very wrong about that."
- "I couldn't disagree with you more."
- "Your plan is faulty because you never did your research."

Praising, Agreeing

The seventh roadblock is offering a positive judgment or evaluation, or agreeing. Sometimes workers really cannot tolerate the pain clients express about certain situations. In the sample responses that follow, the workers are certainly well-meaning, but their responses cut off any meaningful discussion or further exploration and relieve the workers from having to deal with the real pain their clients might want to talk about.

- "Well, I happen to think you did just fine."
- "You'll figure this out. Don't worry."
- "It will all work out for the best. You'll see."
- "You're smart enough to know what you need to do."
- "You're bright. You know what to do here."

Name-Calling, Ridiculing, Shaming

Making clients feel foolish is the eighth roadblock. Perhaps workers who give responses like those that follow are just fed up. They may tell themselves they have a right to express such degrading sentiments because they put up with so much from their clients. Only very untrained and unprofessional workers would ever resort to name-calling, but when it happens, the workers generally try to excuse what they have said by claiming they have endured long-term disgust or exasperation. Here are samples of responses from exasperated workers.

- "You're an idiot to do that."
- "Okay, smarty, do it your way. You'll see."
- "What you're doing is totally ridiculous!"
- "You act like you never finished first grade!"

Interpreting, Analyzing, Diagnosing

The ninth roadblock consists of telling clients what their motives are, or analyzing their actions. Sometimes, in order to feel vastly superior to their clients, workers will engage in surprise revelations. They often do this to show their clients that they know more about their clients' inner conflicts than the clients do. In the responses that follow, the workers are informing the clients of their motives and underlying intentions, as though their clients lack self-awareness.

- "You're just upset because you haven't heard from the lawyer."
- "I think you really wanted to press charges but you just can't admit that."
- "You don't really believe that about her. I know that you are just saying it because you wish it were true."
- "What you really mean is that you don't want to see him anymore."

Reassuring, Sympathizing, Consoling, Supporting

Trying to make people feel better or trying to talk them out of their feelings is the 10th roadblock. The following responses are offered as a way of comforting clients, but they serve to cut off real discussion of painful feelings. Telling clients you know how they feel or you understand what they are feeling is not convincing, even if you have had similar experiences. Listening to the feelings is better than cutting them off. Following are responses by workers that tend to cut off clients' expression of their feelings.

- "You'll feel better in the morning."
- "All new mothers go through this at one time or another."
- "Don't worry. Things will work out."
- "I know exactly how you feel!"
- "I understand how you feel."

Probing, Questioning, Interrogating

The 11th roadblock concerns trying to find motives, reasons, and causes. Clients do not always tell their concerns in logical sequence, and there are good ways for workers to go back and fill in the gaps without sounding as though they are in a superior position. In the following examples, however, the workers are actually prying into their clients' motivations and intentions—areas the clients may not be fully aware of or ready to discuss.

- "Just when did you start to feel this way?"
- "Why do you suppose you went there that night?"
- "Do men ever tell you that they feel violent toward you?"
- "What were you really trying to do when you saw her?"

Withdrawing, Distracting, Humoring, Diverting

Trying to get clients to focus on something other than the problem is the 12th roadblock. Sometimes workers are overwhelmed by what their clients have told them. They may feel helpless to make a real difference or offer substantive help. Perhaps they realize that all they can do is listen, but listening is painful and difficult. To save themselves from these uncomfortable feelings of inadequacy and helplessness, workers may resort to responses like the ones that follow.

- "Just forget about it!"
- "C'mon! How are things at church?"
- "Let's see, you could always run over him in your car." (chuckle)
- "Let's turn to other things in your life."

Using the Phrase "I Understand"

It is tempting to want to comfort clients who are upset with the phrase "I understand." Sometimes workers say to clients, "I understand how you feel." Often, however, this sounds trite. Most of us can never fully understand exactly how a client feels. Another phrase some workers use is "I understand, but. . . . This phrase is even worse. In addition to the fact that we cannot fully understand a client, the *but* in the phrase tends to negate the client's very real feelings and push the worker's perspective instead. Make it a point to refrain from soothing clients with phrases such as "I understand" or "I understand how you feel," and certainly refrain from saying, "I understand, but. . . ."

Useful Responses

In this third section of the book, you will be looking at and practicing responses that enhance communication. Following are several categories of responses that you may find useful as you construct answers to the exercises in this section of the book. Learning to structure good responses is a little like learning to drive a stick-shift car, rather than an automatic one. For years your communication responses to other people have been automatic. They probably worked because you were in relationships other than professional ones. In our friendships and family relations, people communicate in shorthand. These relationships are generally positive and familiar, so others do not need to guess what it is we are saying.

Now, as a professional, you are responsible for creating an environment that makes clients feel comfortable and safe enough to be open. Clients will not know you very well, if at all, when they come to see you. Therefore, you are in charge of communicating in a way that builds rapport and collaboration in regard to the clients' problems. This means that at first you will have to think carefully about how you are going to respond before you do so.

The good response examples that follow contain openers that you can lift right off the page to get you started on the exercises you will find in later chapters on communication. Use these initial phrases to structure constructive responses. Gradually, as you practice, you will begin to sound more like yourself, and your responses will not seem as rehearsed. At first, however, you need to practice effective ways to answer what another person has said. Using the responses provided here will help you to get started in this process.

Ways to Start Responding to Feelings

When clients are talking to you about something that involves an emotion or feeling, it helps them to feel comfortable and understood if you can identify their feeling and say that back to them. When you do so, it is best to structure a single sentence and say nothing more. Anything that you might add to this could take the conversation away from where they are and over to something you have introduced. Be very careful about this. Here are some useful openers to use when you respond to feelings.

- "That must have made you feel . . ."
- "You must feel . . ."
- "You must have felt . . ."
- "That must have been . . ."
- "It sounds like you're really feeling . . ."
- "How [sad, upsetting, wonderful] . . ."
- "Sounds like you really feel . . ."
- "You must be . . ."
- "You must feel so . . ."
- "It sounds like you felt . . ."

Ways to Start Responding to Content

There are times when you might indicate you heard accurately by responding to the content of what your client has said. In this way, you confirm that you are hearing what the client has told you and confirm for the client how important the details are to you.

- "So, it's important to you that . . ."
- "You're really concerned about . . ."
- "So you were [he/she was] . . ."

- "Right now you want . . ."
- "So, in other words, . . ."
- "So what happened was . . ."
- "So you decided to . . ."
- "You really need . . ."
- "You're hoping that . . ."
- "It sounds like they [he/she] . . ."
- "So they [he/she] just . . ."
- "So you just . . ."

Ways to Start a Closed Question

There are times when you need facts or specific information. Questions that require only a single answer are often referred to as closed questions. Here are some ways to start a closed question.

- "What is your . . .?"
- "Where did you . . .?"
- "Who is . . .?"
- "When were you . . .?"
- "Where do you . . .?"

Ways to Start an Open Question

When we are listening to clients give background about their concerns and problems, our questions need to be more open to solicit the information clients believe is significant. Here are some ways to start an open question.

- "Can you describe . . .?"
- "Can you tell me a little bit about . . .?"
- "Could you talk about . . .?"
- "Could you describe more about . . .?"
- "Can you tell me a bit more about . . .?"
- "Can you fill me in on . . .?"
- "Could you clarify that a little bit more for me?"
- "Can you tell me something about . . .?"
- "Could you say something about . . .?"

Ways to Start an "I-Message"

There will be times when you are concerned about something the client has done or said. You may be worried about something the client intends to do or something the client has not done. In the roadblocks to good communication earlier in this chapter, many of the ways workers brought up their concerns were confrontive and superior. A better way to bring up our own concerns is to indicate that these concerns belong to us. We do this by using the word "I" first. These responses can consist of several sentences and should sound tentative rather than judgmental or decisive.

- "I feel..."
- "I'm just concerned that..."
- "I'm wondering if..."
- "It appears to me that..."
- "I need to understand..."
- "I'm not clear about..."
- "I need to kick something around with you."
- "I'm having a problem with..."
- "I'm uncomfortable that [with]..."
- "I guess what worries me is..."
- "I think what I'm most concerned about is..."

Useful Ways to Begin a Firmer "I-Message"

There are times when you need to act in behalf of clients. Another person may be unintentionally interfering in some way. This may call for an invitation to help, and that invitation must be worded in a way that is more authoritative, but not offensive. Here are ways to be clear about what you want or need.

- "I need you to..."
- "It would be very helpful if..."
- "I wonder if you could help us by..."
- "Could you..."
- "Would you please..."
- "We need your help to..."

Ways to Show Appreciation for What Has Been Said

When clients bring something to your attention that is of concern to them, it is a good idea to let them know you appreciate what they have to say. Here are some ways to start appreciative responses.

- "Thank you for bringing this up."
- "It was good of you to tell me about this."
- "I appreciate your thoughts about this."
- "Thanks for telling me."
- "It's helpful to me to know this."
- "What might I [we] do to clear this up?"
- "Can you tell me more about what happened?"

Specific Questions Useful in Beginning to Disarm Anger

When clients express anger with us or our organization, it is not constructive to argue with them. Showing a genuine interest in what they are telling us is better for maintaining a good relationship. Here are some questions to ask that indicate a genuine interest on your part. By using these responses, you indicate that you really want to understand the problem the client is experiencing with you or your organization. Do not ask the person all of these questions; one or two of them will indicate a real willingness on your part to grasp the issues. Too many questions can make the client feel he or she is being interrogated.

- "How did I [we] offend you?"
- "What did I [we] do?"
- "When did I [we] do this?"
- "How often did I [we] do this?"
- "What else about me [us] upsets you?"

Examples of Ways to Agree When Practicing Disarming

When we are not acting in a professional capacity, it is common to feel very defensive when someone criticizes us. Usually, however, there is a kernel of truth in what the other person is expressing even though it might seem exaggerated or trifling to you. Here are some responses you can use to let clients know that you can see and accept the truth in what they have told you.

- "I'm sure I could do better at times."
- "We probably could do things a bit differently."
- "There are people who have had more experience than I have."
- "It may be that we could do things differently."
- "Probably we're not always aware of these problems."
- "It is very possible that we overlooked this."
- "I certainly can be forgetful at times."

Sample Response When You Cannot Change

After a heated exchange, an angry client may be expecting that you will change the way you do things. Sometimes you are not able to change things. Maybe you are blocked by the law or because of how a change would affect other clients or staff. When that happens, you need a pleasant way to let the client know you cannot make the requested changes. Here is an example of what you might say.

- "I understand your point. We're going to have to continue this way for now, but it was helpful to hear your concerns."

Sample Response When You Find You Can Compromise

At other times, clients make useful suggestions, and the requested changes can be made. Here is an example of how you might respond in such a situation.

- "I think there are some ways we can solve this problem."

Ways to Start Collaboration

Nothing really useful can happen for clients if there is no collaboration. Even when clients will be doing most of the work, the word "we" can soften this fact and create a team approach to the problem. In this way, you let clients know they can trust your intention to be supportive without taking over and forcing a solution. Collaboration has another useful purpose. When done well, it prevents your giving the impression that you feel superior and that you see clients as being helpless and inadequate. Here are some ways to begin collaboration.

- "Perhaps we can . . ."
- "Maybe we can [could] . . ."
- "Let's [look at this together, look at your options, see what we can find out about this]."
- "We can [could] . . ."
- "Why don't we . . ."
- "We might . . ."
- "You and I together can [could] . . ."

Ways to Involve the Client in Collaboration

Sometimes clients do not participate. You make suggestions, and the clients simply go along with them. If this happens often, the clients are not collaborating or participating in solutions to problems they own. There are ways to help clients become more involved. Here are some examples.

Start with an I-Message

- "I'm wondering if . . ."
- "It occurs to me . . ."

Finish with a Question or Comment That Invites Collaboration

- "What do you think?"
- "I'm wondering what you think."
- "What thoughts do you have?"

- "Maybe you see it differently."
- "You probably have some ideas too."
- "But it's important to me to know how you see it."
- "But I think what would really be helpful is to hear your ideas about it."
- "How do you see it?"
- "What are your suggestions?"

False Praise versus Positive Feedback

Earlier in the chapter in the discussion of roadblocks to communication, some examples of ways workers might praise clients were presented. These statements do not contain real information clients can use. It is all right to give people positive feedback, but not to say something trivial that contains no information clients can use in the future when they encounter difficulties.

For instance, suppose a client worked on and solved a tax problem. Rather than just praising the fact that she solved the problem, it might be better to point out information about the client she can use in the future. Here is an example of how to do that.

- "I thought you handled the people at the tax office very well. You asked the right questions and didn't get flustered, and I think that really helped to resolve the problem."

Now the client has been given feedback that identifies traits that might be helpful to her in the future: She seemed capable of talking to others and asking the right questions, and she was able to communicate without becoming flustered. This kind of response is much better than one like, "See how smart you are?"

Following is another example of praise that contains useful information for the client.

- "I think it has taken real determination for you to stay sober this long. I'm just impressed with how you have managed an entire week like this."

Again, this is a statement that gives the client useful information: The worker believes the client has "determination." This is something he can rely on in the future when times are tough. Thus, such a response is better than something like, "Good for you! You're still sober!"

Minor Problems

The following examples demonstrate some of the minor problems you might encounter during your communication with your clients.

Minor Problem One. You assess your client's feelings incorrectly. For instance, you might misinterpret a client's underlying feelings and thoughts. You might say, "You must have felt sick when you saw what the accident did to your car." The client might respond by telling you she really did not feel sick. Instead, she was angry—furious, in fact—at the other driver who stood there and screamed at her. It is always possible that clients may correct you in this way. This is positive. It allows clients to make you aware of what they are really feeling and thinking, bringing you much greater clarity.

Minor Problem Two. Your mind wanders. At times you may not be listening attentively. Something has happened at home; you just finished handling a personal problem; or you hoped to go home before 4:00 and now it is 5:00 and this may take some time. Your mind leaves the immediate situation and wanders to your personal concerns. Of course you do not want this to happen often, but it will happen. If you are practicing good body language, sitting in a way that communicates interest and attention to the client, these momentary shifts in your focus will not be damaging to your relationship.

Major Problems

The following are examples of major problems that can occur during your communication with your clients that are not at all useful.

Major Problem One. You cannot wait to pass judgment. Sometimes workers listen to clients, but their minds are full of judgments they want to make about what the clients have said. Rather than truly listening, these workers are judging the clients in regard to how well the clients handled their situations, whether the clients were smart or stupid, and whether the clients were on top of things or lax in taking care of the situations.

Such workers cannot wait for clients to be quiet so they can give an authoritative judgment. Rather than listening, these workers are preoccupied with what they plan to say in response. This is unprofessional listening. We might do this with our friends and relations, but it has no place in a professional relationship.

Major Problem Two. You ignore the client's feelings. Another way to miss the important issues is to focus entirely on content and never hear the meaning this situation has for the client. Instead of commenting, "How difficult it must have been," the worker goes on about the actual details. "You mean you went to the corner of Fourth and Market, and this man came from—what—the east, I guess, and asked you for directions to the capitol? And then you stepped off the curb toward the car?" There is a place for this kind of listening, but when you do this exclusively and never talk about feelings, important opportunities are missed for healing and building rapport.

Major Problem Three. You cannot wait to offer the solution, to give advice. Important opportunities are lost for rapport and understanding if the worker does not acknowledge the feelings a client is expressing. Some workers rush right past the feelings to the solutions. Rather than saying, "You must have found that painful," such a worker would say something like, "Well, you'll need to see a lawyer about this. There is a good one around the corner that we use a lot, and I can probably get you in to see her in the next day or so." Anyone can tell a client he needs a good lawyer. Only a very good listener is able to respond with empathy to the underlying feelings present in the client's story.

Summary

This chapter has provided you with a sense of how good and bad responses sound. Good responses are constructive responses that promote rapport and build trust; poor responses block rapport, understanding, and further exploration. Knowing how these two different kinds of responses sound, however, and actually using them are two different things. To become proficient, you must practice.

In each chapter in this third section of the book, different types of responses are discussed along with what they are intended to accomplish in a therapeutic sense. Each chapter contains a series of exercises. To do these exercises, at least initially, turn back to this chapter and refer to the examples of useful responses provided in it. Use these sample openers as a springboard to developing constructive replies of your own.

◆ Exercises: Identifying Roadblocks

Instructions: Following are various scenarios illustrating workers' responses in a variety of situations. Examine the responses in each case and decide whether the worker is blocking communication or enhancing it. Do the worker's responses cut off further communication from the consumer or seem to encourage the person to continue. Mark your answer after each vignette.

1. Carlos is afraid his mother is dying. He is talking to the worker in the hospital emergency room about an "attack" his mother seemed to have when she could not breathe and turned blue. She was brought to the hospital in an ambulance, and Carlos is waiting to see whether she will be all right. He is distraught. The worker says, "You certainly did the right thing to call the ambulance. Don't worry she'll be all right. We have very good doctors here." Can Carlos continue to express his anxiety freely?

    Enhanced   Blocked

2. Anita and her family moved, and her parents feel Anita is not adjusting well to the move. Anita wants to return to her old school to be with her friends. Her parents ask the worker to talk to Anita about her desire to return to her former school. Anita talks about how strange the new school is and how much she misses her old friends. The worker replies, "Tell me something about your friends where you used to live." Can Anita continue to tell the worker what she misses about her old school?

    Enhanced   Blocked

3. Elvita has decided to leave an abusive relationship, but she feels guilty leaving her abuser's children behind. She talks about how she knows that once she leaves, she cannot have any more contact with the children; and she is worried about how that will affect these children whom she has come to love and wants to protect. The worker asks, "Just when did you start to think of these children as if they were your own?" Can Elvita continue to discuss her concerns about her abuser's children?

    Enhanced   Blocked

4. Ed suffers from chronic mental illness and needs medications to maintain his mental health. Recently he went to several workshops on the use of supplements and vitamins to maintain mental health. He wants to discuss these ideas with his worker. He makes it clear that he is not really thinking of going off his prescriptions, but he would like to consider trying these supplements in addition to his medication. The worker says, "It sounds like you really got a lot out of that workshop." Can Ed continue to explore the things he learned at the workshop with the worker?

    Enhanced   Blocked

5. Shawna wants to go to college. She attended a poor rural school where most of the students do not go on to college. Her scores for the entrance exams were very poor in math, and she feels unsure that the developmental course being offered to her at the college will really help her catch up. She seems anxious and uncertain. The worker says, "You don't seem to quite understand what developmental courses are. Look at the number of people who take them. Look at how many of those people finish school. You need to think about this a little less emotionally." Will Shawna feel comfortable in the future talking about her concerns about going to college with this worker?

    Enhanced   Blocked

6. Ada is very upset over the divorce settlement. She got the house and the children, but very meager support and only a small amount to go to school to upgrade her skills. As she speaks with the worker, she is crying and expresses the belief that she cannot make it. The worker replies, "Look, get another lawyer. You're going to have to just face the fact that you had a lawyer who wasn't serving you. Go back to court! Reopen the case! Make a stink!" Will Ada be able to talk about her divorce with this worker?

    Enhanced   Blocked

7. Lindsey is an alcoholic and tells her worker she wants to stop but doesn't know how. She tells the worker that for a while she stopped drinking while she was going to AA meetings, but she stopped going and began to drink again when she reunited with old friends. The worker says, "Look, you

either do what you need to do or you don't. Don't come in here crying about how you stopped AA. That's your responsibility to go there—so go!" Can Lindsey continue to talk about options for not drinking with this worker?

Enhanced   Blocked

8. Reynaldo just lost his job and is frantic about how he will pay the rent. He talks to the worker about how he will pay his rent and whether he will be eligible for unemployment. In the course of the conversation, he mentions his fear of going home to face his wife. He does not believe she will understand. The worker says, "Well, you're just upset because you're afraid of your wife and what she's going to say about this." Will Reynaldo want to continue to express his worries with this worker?

Enhanced   Blocked

9. Tonda is discussing her need for help with a depression that she says started several months ago. She talks about the amount of time she has missed at work and how it has reached a point where she sleeps most of the day. The worker says, "Tell me a little bit about what was going on when this all started." Can Tonda continue to discuss her depression with this worker?

Enhanced   Blocked

10. Persis has been clean for 9 months and comes into see her case manager about the fact that she is so tempted to use again. Persis asks if there is something more she can do. The worker says, "Oh, come on. Nine months it's been. Get down to business and focus on the good things in your life. Its all up to you whether you use or not." Can Persis continue to explore her temptation to go back on drugs with this worker?

Enhanced   Blocked

Chapter 8

Listening and Responding

Introduction

Listening to others is a healing activity. For that reason, it is very important in effectively helping others. Although case managers do not practice therapy as we think of it in a counseling setting, they do have many opportunities to listen to others. At intake and during the course of the relationship as problems and issues arise, the case manager can offer listening as a first and important step in the resolution of clients' problems.

Writing in the *American Journal of Psychiatry*, Dr. Stanley W. Jackson (1992) talked about the importance of listening:

> The effective healer in the realm of psychological healing tends to be someone who is interested in talking with and listening to the other person. And these inclinations are grounded in an interest in other people and a curiosity about them. Further such healers have a capacity for caring about and being concerned about others, particularly about those who are ill, troubled, or distressed.

Describing those who seek our help, Jackson wrote, "He seeks to be listened to, to be taken seriously, and to be understood, as crucial aspects of this process." Finally, he talked about the process itself:

> The attentive listening of a concerned and interested healer can, and often does have a compelling effect on the sufferer. The sufferer often enough responds by telling more about himself, by revealing more.... The

relationship is deepened—more is said, more is heard, more is understood, more of a sense of being understood is experienced.

Listening to another person in a way that indicates our concern for that person is important in the healing process. Reflective listening is a method that allows you to demonstrate such concern and interest in other people.

Defining Reflective Listening

Reflective listening is a term used to describe therapeutic listening and responding—a way of listening that is most helpful to clients. This method for listening to others has three purposes.

1. Reflective listening lets clients know you have heard their concerns and feelings accurately.
2. Reflective listening creates an opportunity for you to correct any misperceptions.
3. Reflective listening illustrates your acceptance of where the client is at that moment.

When a client talks to you, there are two aspects to which you can listen and respond:

1. The *content* of what the client has said
2. The *feelings* that underlie what the client has said

Responding to feelings is empathic and is, therefore, the most useful kind of response.

When you accurately respond to the feelings the client is experiencing, the person feels heard. Someone is really listening. When clients feel that you truly hear them and that you hear the feelings they are expressing, even when they do not explicitly describe those feelings, they begin to develop trust and rapport with you, making it easier for them to fully talk with you about their problems and issues. As you saw in the discussion of roadblocks to good communication in Chapter 7, there are many responses that are barriers to trust and rapport. You want to provide a safe, accepting environment where clients feel free to express themselves. For this reason, it is important to learn how to provide empathic responses that will further a constructive relationship with your clients.

Responding to Feelings

When you let another person know that you have heard the feelings that person is expressing at that moment, you are being empathic. *Empathy* is the ability to hear accurately the underlying feelings and emotions that clients are expressing when they speak. Clients may tell you how they feel in actual words, but much of our understanding of other people's emotions comes from their facial expressions, body language, tone of voice, mood, and choice of words. In listening to feelings, we are listening to all of that as well as the words clients speak. In this way, we gain an understanding of the underlying emotions and concerns.

It is important to really listen. Instead, many of us are tempted to think while other people are talking. We think about how wrong they are. We think about what they could do instead. We think about what advice we should give them and how to solve their problem. What we really should be doing is listening for the feeling and determining the degree of that feeling. For instance, a person may be angry or furious or just annoyed. Another person may be a little wistful, sad, or openly depressed. Can you tell the difference when you listen? Of course you can, when you are really listening for the feelings.

Responding to feelings involves the following two steps:

1. Identifying the feeling
2. Constructing a single statement that includes that feeling

This single sentence that includes the other person's feeling is called an empathic response. This is a specific way to practice empathy for clients, to acknowledge clients' feelings and concerns. We use a single sentence because to add more often distracts the client or moves the conversation away from the central concern. A single sentence allows clients to know that they have been heard and that they are welcome to continue on the same track; they are reassured.

Reflective listening does not include advice or solutions. A reflective listener does not tell the other person to feel another way or to look at the problem from another perspective. A reflective listener does not judge the message or the feelings. See Figure 8.1 for some examples of correct and incorrect responses in different situations.

In the following dialogue, based on the situation in which a client has wrecked a new car, notice the way the worker stays with the client throughout the exchange:

FIGURE 8.1

Correct and Incorrect Responses in Various Situations

To a person whose new car was damaged in an accident:

Correct: "You must have felt pretty terrible about the accident."
Incorrect: "You should call your insurance dealer first before you get all upset."

To a person who just won money in a lottery:

Correct: "That must have been thrilling!"
Incorrect: "You may be thrilled now, but I don't think you really know what to do next. Better get a good accountant!"

To a person complaining that he did not get the correct change from the cashier:

Correct: "It sounds like you had some trouble with the cashier."
Incorrect: "Next time you go to pay your bill, try getting the manager to take your check and stay away from the cashier."

CLIENT [*sighing as he sits down*]: I wrecked my car yesterday on my way to work.

WORKER: It sounds like you feel pretty bad about it.

CLIENT [*sighing again*]: I do. I guess I should be happy no one was hurt, but I just got the car.

WORKER: It was brand-new and perfect.

CLIENT: I know. I picked it out and ordered it special. It had everything I wanted. I don't know, in a way it was my fault. She ran the stop sign, but I wasn't really paying attention.

WORKER: You're sort of blaming yourself for this.

CLIENT: Oh, I did. I still do. The police said she was clearly in the wrong. But now I'm going through all this unnecessary stuff with insurance and using a loaner car and trying to get a new car.

WORKER: You must feel so disrupted.

CLIENT: Yeah, I do.

Listen now as the same client speaks to a worker who is not trained in reflective listening. Notice how the worker pursues her own agenda and how the client begins to sound defensive and ultimately stops participating:

CLIENT [*sighing as he sits down*]: I wrecked my car yesterday on my way to work.

WORKER: You wrecked your car? How did you do that?

CLIENT [*sighing again*]: I guess I should be happy no one was hurt, but I just got the car.

WORKER: Well, what happened?

CLIENT: The other driver ran the stop sign, but I wasn't really paying attention. In a way, it was my fault.

WORKER: Well, you can't drive and think about 10 other things. When you are driving a car, you have to pay attention to what is going on around you. If you're daydreaming, it doesn't work. You can't do that when you're driving.

CLIENT [*sounding defensive*]: Well, I wasn't really daydreaming or anything. I just didn't notice her. You can't always see everything the other drivers intend to do before they do it.

WORKER: I guess you can't, but sometimes I think there are just too many drivers out there anymore.

CLIENT [*nods*]: But now I'm going through all this unnecessary stuff with insurance and using a loaner car and trying to get a new car.

WORKER: Well, that's all part of it. You wreck your car, and you're tied up for months with all the bureaucratic paperwork. And they never give you what you need to buy another one just like it.

CLIENT: Uh-huh.

Let us look at another example of good listening. Notice how the worker in this next example identifies the strongest feeling present in what the client is saying and how the client almost always responds positively to that recognition:

CLIENT [*tears welling up in her eyes*]: I never went through this before.

WORKER: It sounds like you are devastated.

CLIENT [*nodding and crying more openly*]: My dad died, last week. He . . . he . . . well, he had been in dialysis, but he seemed so good Sunday night. Then Monday the nurse called me at work—oh, I guess around 10:00—and suggested I come in, but she didn't say it was an emergency or anything.

WORKER: You must have felt you didn't have to rush, that you had a little bit of time.

CLIENT: Well, no, I went in as soon as I finished up what I was doing, and here he was already in intensive care. His breathing was so labored, so hard for him . . . [*cries*].

WORKER: That must have been a shock!

CLIENT: It was! I couldn't believe it. That was my dad lying there. He just fixed my electrical outlet 2 weeks ago. We went out to eat for his birthday. I just couldn't believe he would go now.

WORKER: It was all so sudden.

CLIENT: Oh yes, and then they are talking to my mom and I about how to make him comfortable. He knew me and all, but he couldn't talk. And you know how they say people need permission to die? Well, I told him it was okay to go [*cries*]. I told him he gave his life a good shot and he could go [*whispering*]. And he did [*cries*].

WORKER: That must have been so difficult for you.

Now observe what happens in this situation when the worker's listening skills are inadequate. Notice in this example how the worker brings the conversation around to a more cheerful topic. In this case, the worker may very well be protecting himself from feeling the enormous pain of the client:

CLIENT [*tears welling up in her eyes*]: I never went through this before.

WORKER: Like what?

CLIENT [*crying more openly*]: My dad died last week. He . . . he . . . well, he had been on dialysis, but he seemed so good Sunday night. Then Monday the nurse called me at work—oh, I guess around 10:00—and suggested I come in, but she didn't say it was an emergency or anything.

WORKER: I hope you went right in!

CLIENT: Well, no, I went in as soon as I finished up what I was doing. I didn't think she meant I had to hurry, and here he was already in intensive care. His breathing was so labored, so hard for him . . . [*cries*].

Chapter 8   Listening and Responding   **155**

WORKER: Did he have a living will? That would have helped you to know how to handle this.

CLIENT: I don't think he did. I don't know. Mom and I made the decisions. We knew he couldn't go on much longer, and we didn't want him to suffer. I couldn't believe it. That was my dad lying there. He just fixed my electrical outlet 2 weeks ago. We went out to eat for his birthday. I just couldn't believe he would go now.

WORKER: We never really know when death will strike, do we? We just have to look on the bright side, at all the good times we had with people while they were here. We know our parents won't live forever.

CLIENT: It isn't that I thought he would live forever. It was just so sudden or something. We didn't have much warning really. I guess in that respect I can say he didn't suffer, you know, like in a long illness for years and years.

WORKER: See. There's something to be thankful for. There is a silver lining in everything.

CLIENT: Sure.

Did you notice that the client stopped crying. She took the cue from the worker that crying and continuing with the painful story about her father's death was being discouraged. It must have been clear to you as well that a significant part of the story was left out. The first worker received more information about what really happened by saying less. The second worker said more, but cut off part of the story and, therefore, did not receive as much information.

Good listeners stay with clients until their emotions are drained off. If a client cries, we know we are helping that person to face and come to terms with intense emotion. Clients who are supported through this process by skilled listeners heal better than clients who have been forced to shut down their feelings in front of the worker and deal with them alone.

Responding to Content

When you respond to the content of what clients say, you are usually doing it to check the accuracy of the information you believe you heard. Listening to content gives you clarity and helps you understand the facts. Generally, we listen to content less often than we listen to feelings. Figure 8.2 provides some examples of correct and incorrect responses in terms of listening to content.

Responding to content is a good way to help people who have just been through a traumatic event. By repeating facts of the event back to the clients, the clients can begin to integrate their particular experiences into the whole of their experiences, and their healing is facilitated. In fact, the sooner people begin this process after a traumatic event, the more readily they may be able to heal in the future. Here

FIGURE 8.2

Correct and Incorrect Responses in Listening to Content

To a person upset over having to wait for a ride:

Correct: "So you went to the park about 4:30, and they didn't come until 7:00."
Incorrect: "Those people sound like they need a watch!"

or

Correct: "In other words, the people who were to pick you up have done this to you before."
Incorrect: "You better find someone else to ride with. I can line you up with a party."

is an example of a worker who listens to the content of a client's discussion of a traumatic event:

CLIENT: [*looks pale and shaken, and is silent*]

WORKER [*responding first to feeling*]: It seems like you've been through something pretty terrifying.

CLIENT [*nods*]: I . . . Can I tell you? It was . . . in the parking garage at the hotel. Not late or anything. I heard this person get off the elevator as I . . .[*is silent*].

WORKER: You had gone to the parking garage to get your car.

CLIENT: Yes, and as I was walking toward the car, and it was at some distance, I thought I heard the elevator, and then someone started walking along behind me.

WORKER: The person was walking behind you, but at that point you thought the person was just going to a car.

CLIENT: Right. And just as I was ready to get in my car, . . . I mean, I almost made it, and he grabbed my coat and just pulled, just pulled as hard . . . just pulled me backward.

WORKER: So, in other words, you were grabbed and pulled down from behind.

Notice that the worker rephrases the facts the client gives so that the client hears them again. It is not uncommon to find that through this listening process, unpleasant memories that the client has blocked begin to surface in the supportive atmosphere created by the worker. At this point, some people might say the client is lying or making up things because the story has changed somewhat. More often, however, the client is beginning to remember more of what actually happened because the worker is encouraging and has created a safe environment.

Positive Reasons for Reflective Listening

There are some specific therapeutic reasons for employing reflective listening.

Self-Acceptance

Arnold Beisset (1970), writing about Fritz Perls ideas, talks about Perls' paradoxical theory of change. The theory asserts that people change only when they are able to accept themselves exactly where they are right now.

Judgments about where clients should be only engages them in defending how they came to the place they are now. This wastes clients' energy and the valuable time you have to work on healing. The most healing, and therefore the most therapeutic, practice is reflective listening. By saying "You must be angry," you accept the fact that the client is angry. If you say "You should try to stay away from those awful people," the client then has to explain why she has not done so or cannot do so. In this situation, some clients say nothing and decide you do not really understand.

Drain Off Feeling

In the human service profession, you will meet people in all sorts of life crises and difficulties. Some of the circumstances are very traumatic, and considerable reflective listening will be required on your part if the clients are to begin the healing process. A woman who has been raped will start coming to terms with it sooner and heal more readily if she encounters a good reflective listener soon afterward. An older person can prepare for the end of life and feel comfortable about his past life if he can talk about it with a good reflective listener.

Human service workers have been criticized for not listening long enough. Some take only a few stabs at it, and then move into problem solving: Where will this person stay tonight? Who should I call? What facts do I need to open this case? The importance of your role in trauma, in healing, and in helping clients to grow cannot be overestimated. You play that role in large part by practicing good reflective listening.

Points to Remember

Listen Reflectively Long Enough

Do not cut short this important piece of the client's healing process because you feel pressed for time. Be sure you go over the situation thoroughly once and, if you can, review it several times. In cases of violence, reviewing the content several times, along with listening to feelings, helps the victim begin to hear the story and come to terms with it. Reflective listening, in this case as in others, promotes healing.

Solutions Come Later

Do not rush to the solution phase of the interview. Even if you have ideas, wait until the emotion has been drained off. If the client would obviously feel comforted to know there are solutions or resources, tell him about them, but then demonstrate reflective listening at another point in the interview.

You cannot confront the issues you feel are important if you have not done your reflective listening first. If you do, the client may go along with you, but not as well or with as much involvement as she would if she felt heard and understood. For instance, if you immediately explore your concerns about where the client will stay tonight instead of acknowledging the loss of her home in a fire just hours ago, she will not be as ready to work with you on solutions. Her mind is on her many losses, and her emotions may be ranging from guilt to anger. Listen first. Likewise, if you try to help a young couple with the details of their baby's funeral without listening to their story about the baby and the baby's death, you will be taking care of the details that matter most to you, but the clients are likely to experience you as unfeeling and impersonal. By starting where they are, you can help them to move toward the matters that must be addressed. Most important, you help them to integrate this experience into the whole of their life experiences, making it easier for them to ultimately accept the reality.

Reflective Listening Does Not Mean You Agree

Just because you say to a client, "You must feel very angry," that does not mean you think the client should feel angry or should not feel angry. You are simply acknowledging where the client is right now.

You Could Be Wrong

Suppose you say to a client, "It must have made you sad to see your parents go through that." The client responds, "Well, not really. I think I felt more anger than sadness." This is a good exchange. Here you get important, corrected information that allows you to follow the client's concerns more accurately.

Mind Your Body Language

To facilitate the interview, lean toward the client, look the client in the eye, nod, and look interested and enthused. While the client is talking, do not fiddle with things on your desk, lower your head to write, stare out the window, or glance at your watch. Give body language signals that indicate you are being attentive to what the client is saying. Do not stand over clients talking down at them. If the client is in a wheelchair or is a small child, get down to a level where you can make eye contact. Pull up a chair so that you can look at the person directly.

Summary

Good listening is one of the most supportive and healing techniques you will practice in your work with other people. The opportunities to provide solace through good listening skills are numerous and occur in many diverse settings where people come for help. What you give to people in uncertain circumstances and difficult times is the gift of truly being heard and understood. You bring with you the warmth and interest in people that makes them feel valued. Their story is an important story to you. Their anxiety or sad feelings are noted and responded to. Whether or not you are able to effect a positive resolution to people's problems, your listening skills will always provide the support people need to take up the tasks of their lives and go on.

◆ Exercise: How Many Feelings Can You Name?

Instructions: In a group of no more than four people, see how many feelings you can name in 10 minutes. Remember that there are many different degrees of the same feeling.

◆ Exercises: Finding the Right Feeling

Instructions: When responding to feelings, it is important to know the intensity of the feeling. It is very important to reflect to clients an accurate reading of what they must be feeling. All feelings have varying degrees of intensity. For each word listed here, list other words that mean the same thing but indicate varying degrees of the feeling identified by the original word. The first one is done for you as an example.

HAPPY: *overjoyed, exhilarated, glad, delighted, cheerful, ecstatic, merry, radiant, content, elated, euphoric, ebullient, chipper, bouncy, bright, joyful, pleased*

SAD: _____

CONFUSED: _____

TENSE: _____

LONELY: _____

STUPID: _____

ANGRY: _____

◆ **Exercises: Reflective Listening**

Reflective Listening I

Instructions: People communicate words and ideas, and sometimes it seems appropriate to respond to the content of what someone has just said. Behind the words, however, lie the feelings. Often it is most helpful to respond to the feelings.

Following are statements made by people with problems. For each statement, first identify the feeling; write down the words you think best describe how the person might be feeling. Next, write a brief empathic response—a short sentence that includes the feeling. Refer to the sample openers provided in Chapter 7 under the heading "Useful Responses."

1. "When I was in court, the defense attorney really pounded me. You know, like he thought I was lying or didn't believe me or thought I was exaggerating."

    FEELING:

    EMPATHIC RESPONSE:

2. "Those dirty, lousy creeps! Everything was fine in my life, and they really, really ruined everything! I don't care if I go on or not."

    FEELING:

    EMPATHIC RESPONSE:

3. "I know you said this is temporary housing and all, but I never had a place like this place. I can't stand to think I have to move again sometime, and God knows where I'll go."

    FEELING:

    EMPATHIC RESPONSE:

4. "This whole setup is the pits. He gets to stay in the house after beating me half to death, and I have to go to this cramped little room. Does that make sense?"

    FEELING:

    EMPATHIC RESPONSE:

Reflective Listening II

Instructions: People communicate words and ideas, and sometimes it seems appropriate to respond to the content of what someone has just said. Behind the words, however, lie the feelings. Often it is most helpful to respond to the feelings.

Following are statements made by people with problems. For each statement, first identify the feeling; write down the words you think best describe how the person might be feeling. Next, write a brief empathic response—a short sentence that includes the feeling. Refer to the sample openers provided in Chapter 7 under the heading "Useful Responses."

1. "When I was a little kid, my mom and dad got along okay, but now they fight all the time, and my mother says my dad is on drugs and has a girlfriend. Home is like hell."

    FEELING:

    EMPATHIC RESPONSE:

2. "I just can't go out in the car. All I hear is the screech of tires and the awful thud and scrape of metal. I thought I was dying. I can see it all before me as if it was yesterday."

    FEELING:

    EMPATHIC RESPONSE:

3. "We have a neighborhood problem here! Yes we do! A real big idiot lives in that house. A real nut! He trimmed my own yard with a string trimmer and threw stones all over my car. Ruined the paint!"

    FEELING:

    EMPATHIC RESPONSE:

4. "I never meant to get pregnant. I know everyone says that, but I didn't! I can't think straight. What about my job and school and all my plans? I feel sick. I feel all the time like I'm going to faint."

    FEELING:

    EMPATHIC RESPONSE:

Reflective Listening III

Instructions: People communicate words and ideas, and sometimes it seems appropriate to respond to the content of what someone has just said. Behind the words, however, lie the feelings. Often it is most helpful to respond to the feelings.

Following are statements made by people with problems. For each statement, first identify the feeling; write down the words you think best describe how the person might be feeling. Next, write a brief empathic response—a short sentence that includes the feeling. Refer to the sample openers provided in Chapter 7 under the heading "Useful Responses."

1. "I can tell you now, I just can't go back there. I just feel as if my husband will kill me one of these times."

    FEELING:

    EMPATHIC RESPONSE:

2. "I can't stand those people! They made fun of that retarded kid night and day. I hope they get theirs!"

    FEELING:

    EMPATHIC RESPONSE:

3. "I've been clean for 8 months! If you had told me this would happen a year ago, I'd have laughed in your face."

    FEELING:

    EMPATHIC RESPONSE:

4. "Sometimes it kind of makes me sick to think of all the stuff I did when I was drinking. I'd like to go and take it all back, but how do you ever do that?"

    FEELING:

    EMPATHIC RESPONSE:

Reflective Listening IV

Instructions: People communicate words and ideas, and sometimes it seems appropriate to respond to the content of what someone has just said. Behind the words, however, lie the feelings. Often it is most helpful to respond to the feelings.

Following are statements made by people with problems. For each statement, first identify the feeling; write down the words you think best describe how the person might be feeling. Next, write a brief empathic response—a short sentence that includes the feeling. Refer to the sample openers provided in Chapter 7 under the heading "Useful Responses."

1. "When I took that test, it was really hard. And I guess I was nervous. I mean, I couldn't think of any of the answers."

   FEELING:

   EMPATHIC RESPONSE:

2. "Those lousy creeps! They're always snickering and making fun of other people, especially people who have a handicap. They make me sick!"

   FEELING:

   EMPATHIC RESPONSE:

3. "I know Jim said we could be buddies at swim practice, but I'm probably not as good a swimmer as he is. I feel sort of silly trying to swim with him. Maybe he would like to have a better buddy."

   FEELING:

   EMPATHIC RESPONSE:

4. "This whole setup is the pits. This other guy gets the tutor, and the teacher tells me to go home and see if my mother can tutor me. She never had this math. Math isn't even her thing. Does that make sense?"

   FEELING:

   EMPATHIC RESPONSE:

Reflective Listening V

Instructions: People communicate words and ideas, and sometimes it seems appropriate to respond to the content of what someone has just said. Behind the words, however, lie the feelings. Often it is most helpful to respond to the feelings.

Following are statements made by people with problems. For each statement, first identify the feeling; write down the words you think best describe how the person might be feeling. Next, write a brief empathic response—a short sentence that includes the feeling. Refer to the sample openers provided in Chapter 7 under the heading "Useful Responses."

1. "Well, every time I go off my meds, I get kind of crazy. My minister is really putting the pressure on me to quit and let God take over my illness."

   FEELING:

   EMPATHIC RESPONSE:

2. "The people at the halfway house are so nice to me, compared to the way things were with my family."

   FEELING:

   EMPATHIC RESPONSE:

3. "You have some nerve, having the therapist see my son every week for 6 months, and then you refuse to tell me more than 'he's doing better.' How do I know he's doing better?"

   FEELING:

   EMPATHIC RESPONSE:

4. "I've been on the streets since 1972, and I never slept inside a night until now. I don't know, I just can't seem to stay out like I used to without getting this cough."

   FEELING:

   EMPATHIC RESPONSE:

Reflective Listening VI

Instructions: People communicate words and ideas, and sometimes it seems appropriate to respond to the content of what someone has just said. Behind the words, however, lie the feelings. Often it is most helpful to respond to the feelings.

Following are statements made by people with problems. For each statement, first identify the feeling; write down the words you think best describe how the person might be feeling. Next, write a brief empathic response—a short sentence that includes the feeling. Refer to the sample openers provided in Chapter 7 under the heading "Useful Responses."

1. "I just can't go to court. I just can't face those guys. I will freeze up, and it will all come back—what they did to me. I just can't go through with this!"

   FEELING:

   EMPATHIC RESPONSE:

2. "You don't expect us to take Alfred into our home, do you? He is very mentally ill—tore up the house several times. I really—well, I know he's my son, but I just can't deal with the way he's been in the past."

   FEELING:

   EMPATHIC RESPONSE:

3. "I can tell you what scares me most. It's being by myself at the house one night and having him come back. I don't know if I can go on living there."

   FEELING:

   EMPATHIC RESPONSE:

4. "I just can't go to class. Not after making a fool of myself the last time. I got every answer wrong when the teacher called on me, and people were making fun. . . . It was terrible!"

   FEELING:

   EMPATHIC RESPONSE:

Chapter 9

Asking Questions

Introduction

When listening to another person's difficulties, we might find ourselves asking a lot of questions. We usually mean well. In part, we do this to find out more so a solution can be quickly devised. We also do this as a way of filling in the gaps when our reflective listening skills are not strong. It may be easier for the listener to say "Did you have any money?" or "Where did the man say he lived?" than to simply say, "That must have been so hard on you."

Sometimes when we listen, we feel nervous about what the other person expects from us. After all, if we are the worker, should we not have all the answers? If we do not have an answer just yet, we can stall for time by asking a lot of questions until we do.

Often, however, the client hears these questions as prying. You may ask questions at a rate the client is not ready to answer. For instance, you may be asking questions further ahead in the story, throwing the client off. Clients may feel pushed to reveal more than they intended or be distracted from the line of reasoning they were following. They may become defensive and their communication guarded if the questions seem to pry or to imply there is only one way to have handled things.

When Questions Are Important

Obviously, at times questions need to be asked. The three times it is important to ask questions are as follows:

1. When you are opening a case or chart on a person and need identifying information (closed questions)
2. When you are compiling information for assessment and referral purposes and need facts to do that properly (closed questions)
3. When you are encouraging the client to talk about his or her situation freely to better understand which aspects of it are important to the client (open questions)

Closed Questions

A *closed question* is one that requires a single answer. For example:

WORKER: Where do you live?

CLIENT: 346 Pine Street.

WORKER: How long have you lived there?

CLIENT: Oh, about 6 years.

WORKER: Have you ever been seen here before?

CLIENT: Yes, in 2001.

WORKER: And who did you see then?

CLIENT: Dr. Langley in outpatient.

WORKER: Did she prescribe any medication?

CLIENT: Yes, she gave me a prescription for Prozac.

WORKER: Do you still take that?

CLIENT: No, I stopped a few months ago.

Closed questions are most often used when opening a case or when compiling information for an assessment. In both of these instances, however, clients will need to talk about what has brought them into the service, and you will not rely exclusively on closed questions. Nevertheless, some closed questions are appropriate here to gather the basic information. The client can respond with a simple answer because the questions to do not ask for expressions of feelings, descriptions of circumstances, or explanations of problems.

Open Questions

Open questions serve the purpose of giving clients more opportunity to talk about what is important to them. By asking open questions, you receive more information about a client's situation. In answering open questions, the client can talk about feelings, underlying causes, supporting circumstances, and personal plans.

Open questions have been shown to put clients at ease. Workers using these questions are not perceived as prying but as expressing real interest in other people or a genuine desire to understand their situation. You can use open questions to obtain examples or elaboration of the problem and to clarify certain aspects of the other person's story.

Often an open question begins with "can" or "could," but there are other ways to start such questions. For example, you might say, "Tell me a little bit more about your divorce." Typically open questions look something like this:

WORKER: Can you tell me about the night your father left?

CLIENT: Well, my mother had been arguing with him for some time. I could tell he was getting angry. I don't think I really blame her for his leaving. He had done many things to her that she had every right to be angry about. But I guess for him it was the last straw. Anyway, we were having dinner and she began on the same topic of the house. He just put down his fork and got up from the table and walked out of the house.

WORKER: Can you describe your relationship with him after that?

CLIENT: Well, he did come back to the house for his things from time to time. He got an apartment nearby, and I used to stop there on my way home from school. We never stopped seeing each other, and we never talked about my mother. I can't ever remember him asking me how she was or, for that matter, saying anything mean about her.

Would the worker have gained as much information by conducting the same conversation using closed questions? This example demonstrates that the client would have been much less forthcoming:

WORKER: When did your father leave?

CLIENT: Oh, August of 1995.

WORKER: Did your parents argue much before he left?

CLIENT: Sure, yeah, a lot of the time.

WORKER: Why did he go?

CLIENT: Well, they disagreed over money.

WORKER: After he left, where did he go?

CLIENT: He got an apartment near us.

WORKER: Did you ever see him after that?

CLIENT: Yes, pretty much.

Would the client have felt investigated with these short closed questions fired at him, one after the other? Did the worker really understand how the client felt about the divorce and the contact with his father?

In the second example, in which the worker used closed questions, there was room for the worker to assume things that might not be true. For instance, the worker might have assumed that the client blamed his father for leaving. In the first example, in which the worker used open questions, the client's elaboration on the situation demonstrated that this clearly was not the case.

Questions That Make the Client Feel Uncomfortable

Avoid the Use of "Why" Questions

If you ask someone why they did something or did not do something, you imply that you believe the person should have handled things differently.

- "Why didn't you call the police?"
- "Why did you go there?"
- "Why were your children out that late?"

Do Not Ask Multiple Questions

If you fire off a string of questions, the person can feel interrogated. You may sound impatient, and you can confuse the client.

- "Did you see the other person? Did you turn right around then and call the police about it? Did you get a license plate number? Were you standing close to the window?

Do Not Change the Subject

If the client is talking about how she learned of her mother's death, do not start asking questions about her mother's prearranged funeral. Let the client continue to talk about her mother's death until it seems that she wants to turn to the prearranged funeral. Never ask about something out of curiosity. Do not ask, for example, about the prearranged funeral because you are thinking of getting one for your mother and want to know more about it. Ask questions that stay on the topic the client has selected. If you do ask questions on another topic, make sure the topic is relevant and the questions will actually clarify the client's situation for you.

Here are some examples of questions that change the subject:

- "I heard about the kids before, but where do you work?"
- "So, she died on Saturday, and now you are seeing a lawyer about the will?"
- "That's real neat about how your car looked before the accident. Do you have adequate car insurance?"
- "So, your mother died on Saturday, and you're living in a house by yourself?"

Sometimes questions such as these can disrupt the entire discussion.

Do Not Imply There Is Only One Answer to Your Question

You can ask questions in a way that implies there is only one thing the client should have done or thought or said.

- "Didn't you go to the police?"
- "Did you *tell* the other person what you heard?"
- "Did you see to it that he knew what you were thinking?"

Do Not Inflict Your Values on the Client

You can also ask questions based on your own value system. The client, however, may have other values. For example, you may value truthfulness at all costs, whereas your client may come from a group that values group harmony and not hurting another person's feelings. Questions that imply that your value system is better are not useful.

- "Did you tell her how you felt before you just walked out?"
- "Did you tell her the complete truth?"
- "Don't you value truth above everything else in this situation?"

Do Not Ask Questions That Make Assumptions

You can word questions in such a way that they make it clear you are assuming you already know the answers.

- "You called the police, right?"
- "You wanted to go to the store, didn't you?"
- "He was being a fool, wasn't he?"

A Formula for Asking Open Questions

Figure 9.1 contains a formula for asking open questions. In the figure, the open question is broken into parts. You can interchange the parts, by choosing one part from each column, to construct good open questions that encourage the other person to feel safe in talking and expressing feelings and opinions. Use this formula in the exercises at the end of this chapter to construct effective open questions that invite others to be open and talk freely with you.

Some Tips for Asking Open Questions

Learning to ask open questions takes practice. It is easy to ask a closed question, such as "Where do you live?" or "How old are you?" When intending to ask an open

FIGURE 9.1

Formula for Asking Open Questions

Openers	Directives	Add-ons/Softeners	Object of the Question
Can you*	share	a little bit more about	your husband
	describe	a little bit about	your childhood
	explain	a little more about	your medication
	summarize	something about	what the move was like
	outline	the problems with	the move
	spell out	the larger picture	regarding the move
Could you*	talk	a little more about	what your dad said
	give me	a bit more about	your illness
	tell me	something more about	your job
	help me understand	something about	your relationship with your kids
	clarify	a bit	the situation

*It is fine to leave the "can you" or could you" out of the questions. In this case you would make a request such as "Share a little bit more about the fire."

question, we often start out well and then unwittingly close the question. Some examples of what can happen are presented next.

A Question That Is Not Really Open. "Tell me a little bit about how you got here?" "How you got here" is a closed question and the client can answer, "I came over in the car."

To Open That Question Try This. "Tell me about getting here." The client is more inclined to say more, such as "Well, I came over in the car, but it was scary. I kept looking in my rearview mirror to see if he was following me."

Words That Snap Questions Closed Are How, Why, What, When, Where. You may not be able to avoid using these words in some of your open questions, and using these words in questions is perfectly all right. To leave them out might mean your question doesn't make sense. However, when our purpose is to draw clients out and make them feel comfortable about talking to us in depth, we want our questions to be as open as possible. When you are about to use one of these words—how, why, what, when, or where—see if you can leave it out for a more open question.

INSTEAD OF: "Tell me a bit about how you found out about your husband's cheating?"

ASK: "Tell me about finding out about your husband."

INSTEAD OF: "Can you describe why you left him?"

ASK: "Can you describe leaving him?"

INSTEAD OF: "Could you tell me a little bit about what the doctor said?"

ASK: "Could you tell me a little bit about visiting the doctor?"

INSTEAD OF: "Can you summarize for me when you left?"

ASK: "Can you tell me about leaving?"

INSTEAD OF: "Tell me a bit more about where you were that night."

ASK: "Tell me a bit more about that night."

If we look at one of those pairs of questions carefully, we can see that the two questions are asking for somewhat different information. For example, in responding to the question "Tell me a bit more about where you were that night," the client might tell you where she was and in addition give you more valuable information beyond that: "I was down by the railroad tracks. I think I thought I could jump a freight or something like that. I just wanted to get away." When you say "Tell me about that night," you are asking him for much more, and he may be inclined to tell you many more details: "I was feeling terrified. I didn't know who these people were or why they had singled me out. I didn't know what to do or where to go so I went down by the railroad tracks. I think I thought I could jump a freight or something like that. I just wanted to get away. I saw it starting to get light. No one came, and finally I got up and snuck home." In this last example we know a lot more about the night in question, and we have some idea about the client's perceptions and feelings as well.

Summary

Asking questions helps us to understand our clients and the issues that are bothering them. Asking too many questions, however, can give the impression that we are desperately seeking some sort of solution. Keep in mind what you learned about who owns the problem. The problems clients bring to us are theirs. They need someone to listen to their concerns and sort out the best way to approach a solution. We help clients do that by listening and asking open questions that encourage them to tell us more about what has brought them to us for help.

Combine open questions with active listening to feelings and to content to create a safe environment for clients to talk to you and begin to work on problem solving. Ask closed questions sparingly; confine them to times such as when you are opening a case or you need information to make a proper referral.

◆ Exercises: What Is Wrong with These Questions?

Instructions: Read the questions that follow and decide what makes them bad questions. In writing your criticism, look for questions that assume there is only one answer, inflict values on the client, make the client defensive, make assumptions, cut off discussion, or change the subject.

1. A woman is telling a worker why she has come to the shelter tonight. Right in the middle of her gripping tale about what was going on at home only a few hours before, the worker says, "How long has this been going on?"

2. A worker has listened to a young mother talk about how she dropped out of school and got pregnant and has no skills. Finally the worker interrupts to ask, "Did you have to get pregnant? Didn't you know about birth control?"

3. A man calls and says he is depressed. He has felt depressed for some time and is now thinking of suicide. The worker asks, "Where is your wife? Are you divorced?"

4. A man is telling you about the night he witnessed a murder. The victim was his brother-in-law, and although he was never very close to him, he feels that maybe he could have stopped his death in some way. The worker asks, "Why don't you just go and ask the police?"

5. A woman has come into temporary shelter with a lot of debts. She has been out looking for work today and is discouraged about not finding anything yet. She sits down tiredly in the worker's office and talks about what her day was like. The worker asks, "Did you have to get so many debts?"

6. A man wants to know if his wife is all right after she has been raped. He is sitting with a worker in the waiting room while his wife is being seen in the emergency room. The worker answers his question with one of her own: "How much does your wife mean to you?"

7. A patient in a partial hospitalization program for the chronically mentally ill tells the worker that when the group went to the mall, one of the patients took a pair of socks without paying for them. The worker asks, "You told someone right away, didn't you?"

8. A woman is telling about the time her coworkers waste when the supervisors are out at meetings all day. The worker responds, "Why don't you say something?"

9. A woman tells a worker about a long and difficult marriage she has endured. She mentions abuse, both verbal and physical, and talks about her own failing health in recent months. The worker asks, "Why can't you just bring yourself to divorce him?"

10. A man is trying to sort out whether or not to leave his employer. He feels that the small company is poorly run and that he could do a better job if he went out on his own. On the other hand, he likes his employer, and he feels sorry for him and the mess he's made of his business. He knows that if he leaves, things will really fall apart. The worker asks, "Don't you value loyalty?"

◆ Exercises: Which Question Is Better?

Instructions: Read the following questions and decide which of them are better than others. Place a check mark next to those you think are good questions, and then explain why you think they are better than the ones you did not check.

☐ 1. The worker to a woman in the hospital waiting room whose baby just died of pneumonia: "How old was your baby?"

☐ 2. The worker to a woman who is grieving after her husband died in a hunting accident: "Could you tell me about your husband?"

☐ 3. The worker to a teenage boy who is afraid of failing a math course and losing an opportunity to get a scholarship: "Can you tell me a little bit about this math course?"

☐ 4. The worker to a young woman who has just discovered her best friend and her boyfriend have been seeing each other behind her back: "Can you tell me something about your best friend?"

☐ 5. The worker to an elderly woman whose dog of 15 years has died: "Couldn't you get another one?"

☐ 6. The worker to a man who is requesting food for his family after running out of unemployment compensation and being unable to find a job: "Can you describe the sort of work you would be looking for?"

☐ 7. The worker to a woman in a shelter who has been out searching unsuccessfully for a house or apartment for herself and her two children: "Where all did you look?"

☐ 8. The worker to a single mother who has been referred for parenting skills training: "Could you tell me something about the problems you have been having with Johnnie?"

☐ 9. The worker to a man with developmental disabilities whose mother, with whom he has always lived, died unexpectedly: "What did your mother die of?"

☐ 10. The worker to a woman who was accosted and assaulted in her neighborhood and is afraid of calling the police: "Can you tell me a little bit about what happened tonight?"

◆ Exercises: Opening Closed Questions

Opening Closed Questions I

Instructions: Following are some vignettes in which the worker asks closed questions. Write an open question you think might work better in each situation, and be prepared to tell why you think the closed question is not useful.

1. A human service worker in the emergency room is talking to a man who was hit on the head before he was robbed. He seems to be having trouble getting the story out, but he wants to tell the worker everything that happened. The

worker has been with the man a long time. She thinks that it is late and that the man ought to get to bed and rest now. The worker cuts off the discussion with, "Aren't you tired, Mr. Jones?" What open question would you have asked Mr. Jones to help him wrap up his story?

2. The human service worker is trying to learn what happened that resulted in Mrs. Peters being without housing. Mrs. Peters says she has been "on the street a while now." The worker asks, "Have you been on the street for 2 years, 3 years?" What open question would you have asked to learn more about what happened to Mrs. Peters to make her homeless?

3. The human service worker is on the phone with a woman, the victim of child abuse. The woman tells how she has felt recently, how she needed to call, and then sighs and says, "Oh, I don't know how to begin." The worker asks, "Did your father do this to you?" What open question would you have asked that would have helped the woman start telling the story in her own way?

4. A child is talking to a youth worker while he waits for his mother to get a place to stay. "We've lived in 16 places," he announces, "and I'm only 7." The worker says, "What school did you go to last?" What open question would you have asked to help the child talk about what all this moving has been like for him?

5. A man calls a hot line and tells the mental health worker he wants to die. The volunteer asks, "Does this have to do with being abused as a child?" The man is startled and says, "Why, uh, no. Not really." The worker asks, "Well, what's the problem?" What open question would you have asked to help the man talk about what was troubling him?

Opening Closed Questions II

Instructions: Put yourself in the place of the worker in the following vignettes, and decide what question you would ask in each situation. Write an open question that you think might work better than the one asked by the worker, and be prepared to tell why you think the closed question is not useful.

1. A worker is interviewing a man in the food bank. He tells the worker that he and his children have not eaten for 24 hours and that he has spent most of that time getting referred around town until he finally got a voucher to come to you for food. The worker asks, "Why don't you have any food?" What would you ask?

2. A woman is referred to the social service department in a large hospital after having a stroke. She is somewhat incapacitated and has had a lot of therapy while hospitalized. Now she is going home and needs therapy at home. The worker asks, "What kind of therapy do you want?" What would you ask?

3. A man and woman have been referred by the county Children and Youth Services for parenting skills training. They are poor and have had their four children removed from the home. They have been told the children will be returned when they complete the course and demonstrate they can use the skills they learned in supervised visitations. The worker asks, "Are your children good kids?" What would you ask?

4. An elderly woman has been having trouble caring for herself in her own home. Twice now, in the middle of the night, she has called an ambulance and has been taken to the hospital for chest pains. When her heart is checked, she is found to be in good health, if a little frail. The worker who is looking into what could be going on asks, "Are you afraid to stay at home alone?" What would you ask?

5. A young woman and her baby have been given a voucher for temporary shelter after she lost the apartment in which she was living. She was evicted for back rent, and her rent fell into arrears only when she was laid off several months ago. She has worked, but she cannot earn quite what she was making before. The worker doing the intake interview asks, "What kind of work have you been doing?" What would you ask?

◆ Exercises: Try Asking Questions

Instructions: Look at the case histories that follow and, for each one, write four closed questions and four open questions that you might ask the client.

1. Annette came to your office needing her prescription filled. She was in Marywood Hospital, a private mental hospital, and was discharged on Tuesday. She was given prescriptions, but has no money to fill them. She has no job and probably is eligible for prescriptions paid for by the county. You open a case on her.

    YOUR CLOSED QUESTIONS TO OPEN HER CASE ARE:

    1.

    2.

    3.

    4.

    YOUR OPEN QUESTIONS TO LEARN MORE ABOUT HER ARE:

    1.

    2.

    3.

    4.

2. Marie was a client of a partial hospitalization program. She was loud and demanding, but she often felt hurt upon learning that others were afraid of her or reacted to her as if she were angry. As a result of an encounter in the partial program, she is sent to you, her new case manager, to see if there are ways to help her that might work better. You need to understand more clearly what has happened from her perspective and what sort of program she might fit into.

   YOUR CLOSED QUESTIONS TO BECOME ACQUAINTED WITH HER CASE ARE:

   1.

   2.

   3.

   4.

   YOUR OPEN QUESTIONS TO LEARN MORE ABOUT HER PROBLEMS AND DESIRES FOR TREATMENT ARE:

   1.

   2.

   3.

   4.

Chapter 10

Bringing Up Difficult Issues

Introduction

There will be times when you have a concern about something the client has said or done. You may be concerned for your client's well-being, and you do not want your client to do something harmful or continue to behave or think in ways that are destructive. Occasionally you will have a problem because the client has in some way interfered with your ability to do your job well. As noted earlier, when your needs are not met, you are responsible for resolving the matter or, at the very least, for bringing your concerns out in the open where they can be discussed and examined by the client.

Bringing something out into the open is called *confrontation*. To most people this means an angry, accusing action. In social services, however, it means matter of factly bringing something out to gain a better understanding and perhaps to make meaningful changes or take important new steps. When you bring up your point of view, you are holding reality as you see it before the client for the client to consider. The client is in no way obligated to see things your way, but now both points of view are known and considered. Many opportunities to grow and make constructive changes will be discovered when you use confrontation.

The decision to use confrontation is another strategic decision. This chapter examines when confrontation might be a useful tool to help you and your client explore differences and resolve possible conflicts.

When to Use Confrontation

Discrepancies

There are times when a client will communicate two different messages. Confrontation can help the client see the discrepancies and can offer an opportunity to look at the situation and at the person in another way. Some examples of discrepancies follow.

The Client Says One Thing but Does Another. Dalia tells you that she really wants to go to the job-training program and that getting a job is a top priority for her, but she does not register for the classes. On the other hand, she has numerous excuses for not registering, some of which do not seem entirely believable.

The Client Has One Perception of Events or Circumstances, and You Have Another. Harold thinks you are uncaring and self-involved. He got this idea because you did not come to work the Friday after Thanksgiving even though the office was open. He was off work that day, and he wanted to make an appointment with you so that he would not have to miss work at another time. Your perception is different. To you it was reasonable to be off work the Friday after Thanksgiving because there was only a skeleton staff working that day. You also needed to take a day off before the end of the year or you would have lost some of your accumulated time. Clients rarely come in on this date, and there was a crisis team to cover any crisis that might have come up. To Harold you seem uncaring, while to you your actions seem reasonable.

The Client Tells You One Thing, but the Client's Body Language Sends a Very Different Message. Andrea tells you that she is "fine," that she feels "okay," and that "everything is all right." She looks, however, as if the opposite is true. She speaks in a monotone, looks at the floor as she speaks, and appears depressed and disheveled. These are clues that the spoken message and the unspoken message do not match.

The Client Purports to Hold Certain Values, but the Client's Behavior Violates Those Values. Paul tells you he "likes everyone" and "accepts" everyone. He tells you ethnic differences are unimportant to him and he finds them enriching. In one of his meetings with you, he tells a decidedly racist joke that obviously denigrates an ethnic group.

All of the examples discussed here are situations that contain discrepancies that deserve to be addressed. Doing so will help to clarify the issues and help you and your client come to understand one another's point of view. Ignoring discrepancies interferes with understanding between you and your client because of conflicting perceptions.

Other Reasons to Use Confrontation

There are other reasons besides discrepancies for using confrontation. It can also be used to bring out in the open behavior or communications that seem to interfere with clients meeting their goals. Following are some examples of such situations.

The Client Has Unrealistic Expectations for You. Marcy expects that you will drop everything to see her or to take her phone calls. She does not want to see anyone else in the agency and does not think she should have to see anyone else at night. You are her case manager, and she wants you to be there when she needs you.

The Client Has Unrealistic Expectations for Him- or Herself. Miguel has been in a partial hospitalization program for a number of months and has been sick for about 4 years. Stress seems to trigger his schizophrenic symptoms, and regulating his medication is difficult. He is very good at cleaning and janitorial tasks around the center, and there is a good supervised janitorial program for clients in which they hold a regular job and clean actual establishments. Miguel is set on going to work at the highway department and getting a job driving a steamroller. He applies for the job repeatedly but gets no response.

The Client Asks for Assistance, but Actions Indicate the Client Is Not Interested. Serena asks you to help her find suitable housing so she will not have to stay at the shelter any longer. You have some leads she could pursue, but she breaks appointments, calling in to say she was detained and will reschedule. She does not follow up on the leads you give her, and the two apartments she went to see that were suitable she turned down for minor problems, refusing to live there.

The Client's Behavior Is Contradictory. Art comes in to group and tells the group he will stop drinking. He never misses AA meetings, gets a good job, and begins to help others stop drinking. Later you learn that he is actually drinking in spite of what he says in group and at AA meetings and that he goes to AA on Tuesday and Thursday and to his favorite bar on Friday and Saturday nights. Art's behavior is contradictory in another way. While he talks to newcomers in the group about how helpful it is to stay in group and how wonderful the agency is, he has been denigrating a certain member of the staff outside the building where he goes to smoke during the break.

The I-Message in Confrontation

Because the problem is yours and the observations are your own, confrontations should begin with or include a reference to you. The term used for these statements by Dr. Thomas Gordon is "I-messages" because they contain the words "I" and "me." Confrontation is not helpful, as we have seen, if statements contain the accusatory "you." Figure 10.1 shows some examples of correct and incorrect I-messages to demonstrate the difference between them. The first example consists of messages to a client who was late on Tuesday; note the use of "I" in the correct version and the use of "you" in the incorrect version.

A complete I-message usually contains four parts:

1. Your concerns/feelings/observations about the situation
2. A nonblaming description of what you have seen or heard—of the behavior
3. The tangible outcome for you as a result or the possible consequences for the client
4. An invitation to collaborate on a solution

FIGURE 10.1

Examples of I-Messages

To a client who was late on Tuesday:

Correct: "I'm concerned that you were late on Tuesday morning. It got my day behind more than I wanted, and I spent a lot of time trying to catch up."

Incorrect: "You were late on Tuesday, and you held me up. My whole day was behind, and I spent a lot of time trying to catch up because of you."

I-messages broken into the four parts:

Correct: "(1) I think what concerns me is (2) your being late for the last four appointments has (3) caused a lot of scrambling on my part to catch up the rest of the day. (4) Can we look at what is happening here?"

Incorrect: "(1) You were (2) late for the last four appointments and (3) you caused a lot of scrambling on my part to catch up the rest of the day."

Correct: "(1) It just seems to me that you could get in trouble (2) if you follow through on your plan to yell at the District Justice. (3) It might cause him to be even tougher on you. (4) Let's look at this."

Incorrect: "(1) If you (2) go out there and yell at the District Justice, (3) all you are going to do is get yourself in a lot of trouble. (4) My advice is to cool down."

The second part of Figure 10.1 provides more examples of messages given to clients, with each message broken into the four parts. Compare the correct and incorrect messages. Note the following about the incorrect ones: They begin immediately with the accusatory "you" rather than "I," and they contain no invitation to the client to collaborate on a solution (in the second example, the worker gives advice instead).

The Rules for Confrontation

There are ways to talk with a client about the issues that concern you. An important goal is to do so in a way that allows the client to hear you and make use of what you have said. We all benefit from the feedback of others, but the manner in which it is given often interferes with our ability to accept and use that feedback.

The following text discusses rules for making I-messages less threatening and more acceptable to the listener. Figure 10.2 contains examples of correct and incorrect messages for each rule. As you read about each rule, examine the sample messages in Figure 10.2 under the heading for that rule. Note that in the correct messages the speaker emphasizes "I" and "me," taking responsibility for the observations and concerns, whereas in the incorrect messages, the emphasis is on "you."

FIGURE 10.2

Examples of I-Messages Based on Rules for Confrontation

Be Matter of Fact

To a person whose goals are unrealistic for the present:

Correct: "I need to talk with you about something that bothers me. It seems to me that some of your goals are a bit further down the road. I'm wondering if we could look at some preliminary steps for you to take first to help you get ready."

Incorrect: "You better reconsider! You're not at all ready to undertake a job like that. Let's get cracking on some training first, something to prepare you. You don't just walk in and get the best job right away."

Be Tentative

To a person who may not be seeing all of the issues with his mother:

Correct: "I'm wondering about this problem you're having with your mother. I could be wrong, but when you describe the way she talks to you, it sounds as if she is angry for some reason. What do you think?"

Incorrect: "Your mother is obviously angry at you!"

Focus on Tangible Behavior or Communication

To a client who is frequently late for appointments:

Correct: "I have a problem with the number of times you have come for your appointment late. Maybe we should take a look at it together and see if you can make some arrangements that will fit your schedule better. For example, you were 20 minutes late on July 10th, 1 hour late on July 17th, and 45 minutes late on July 24th. I need to talk about what is happening here and see if we can come up with something."

Incorrect: "You're always late. Every time we have an appointment, you come in when you feel like it."

or

"I'm really upset with you. You're never on time."

Take Full Responsibility for Your Observations

To a person who needs housing but is doing little to obtain it:

Correct: "It appears to me as if the sessions we have together to get you better housing aren't as important to you as I first thought. What I mean is that to me it seems you have other more important priorities. I'm basing this on the fact that you never went to see the three apartments that were available to you. Can we talk about where you are right now with this and where we should go from here?"

(continued)

FIGURE 10.2 *(continued)*

Incorrect: "I can see you don't care about housing."

or

"The way it appears, housing certainly isn't a high priority for you! You never follow through."

Always Collaborate

Correct: "How can we look at this differently?"

or

"What can we do to change this?"

or

"Is there something we should be doing differently?"

or

"How can we resolve this?"

or

"Let's look at this together."

Incorrect: "You better do things differently."

or

"You need to change things."

or

"I hope you can figure out how to handle this thing."

or

"You need to find a solution here."

or

"You better take a good look at this yourself."

Do Not Accuse the Other Person

To a person who is frequently late:

Correct: "I find it a bit difficult when you aren't in the day we are open. Someone has to run back on another day to open the food bank for just one person. Maybe we could work out something together that would make getting here the day we are open easier."

Incorrect: "You're never here when the food bank is open. Then you think we should drop everything and run out here just to open up for you."

Do Not Confront Because You Are Angry

To a person who is having trouble maintaining sobriety:

Correct: "I'm concerned that you are drinking when you are away from the program and not talking about these relapses in the group. I think to me it seems untrustworthy not to be honest in group. What are your thoughts on this?"

(continued)

FIGURE 10.2 *(continued)*

Incorrect: "You can't come to group and lie to people about your drinking. You've been drinking outside group and you're lying about it when you don't bring it up. Plain and simple, it looks to me like you aren't being honest with us."

Do Not Be Judgmental

To a person who needs permanent housing but is not pursuing it:

Correct: "Can we take another look at your priorities and see where housing for you and your children fits in? I was under the impression that this was pretty high on your list, but you haven't kept the four appointments we had to discuss it."

Incorrect: "If I were you, I'd make housing a top priority. You have two children, you're living in a shelter, and you aren't doing a thing to change the situation. That's what I call irresponsible."

Do Not Give the Client a Solution

To a person having trouble remembering appointments:

Correct: "Let's see if there is a way to resolve this."
or
"There probably are some different ways we could approach this. I have some thoughts, and you probably do too."

Incorrect: "Go get an appointment book. Write all of our appointments in the book, and that way you won't forget."
or
"You should get an alarm clock that works and have your landlady call you up every morning. That way you can't miss."

Be Matter of Fact. Do not become excited or judgmental or petulant.

Be Tentative. You could be wrong in your observations. For that reason, it is not helpful to present yourself as though you know everything.

Focus on Tangible Behavior or Communication. *Tangible* refers to what you can observe. Sometimes when we bring something up for discussion, we tend to be vague about what the actual problem is. We might generalize or just describe our feelings about it. This is not enough information for the client to use to make a meaningful change.

Take Full Responsibility for Your Observations. If you recognize that what you observed is what *you* observed and that it is perfectly all right for your observations to be incorrect or different from another's observation, it will be easier for you to take responsibility for your observations. If you are wrong, the perception can be corrected, particularly if you have been tentative and nonjudgmental.

Always Collaborate. Share responsibility for finding a solution or an understanding.

Do Not Accuse the Other Person. It may be tempting to blame or accuse the client for the situation. Refrain from doing that because it prevents the client from hearing you.

Do Not Confront Because You Are Angry. Sometimes it is tempting to use confrontation to punish a client who has made you angry. In these situations, you might use public humiliation or denigrate the person as a person. Again, the client will not hear the important message.

Do Not Be Judgmental. Do not sit in judgment of the client, as the worker does in the incorrect example in Figure 10.2.

Do Not Give the Client a Solution. Because of your position with regard to the client, who is already having problems, any solution you give will be seen as imperative. We want clients to develop their own solutions. Even the words should and ought sound like imperatives to the client and are best avoided.

Asking Permission to Share Ideas

There will be times when you will want to offer information or suggestions. For example, suppose you are working with a man who wants to stop drinking. You have some ideas about how he might go about that. Rather than giving the solution, ask permission to share some ideas. You might say, "I have a couple of ideas that might be helpful to you, but I want to be sure it is all right with you to share these now." Or you could say, "There are some things my clients have done in the past that worked well for them. Would you mind if I shared a few of these with you?" In this way, solutions and advice are given only with the client's permission, leaving the client in charge of his situation and free to reject the offer of ideas.

The opposite approach would be to simply give the advice. You could even start your message with "I." You might say, "I think it would be better if you stayed away from the bar and went to AA meetings instead." You may feel this is an I-message, but you have given a solution without permission. There is the very real possibility that you could make the client defensive, arguing against the very thing you see as a good solution. It is better to ask permission to share the idea first before plunging in. When giving your ideas, do so tentatively and ask for feedback from the client.

For example, Naoko was working with Paul on housing. Paul, who suffered from schizophrenia and had a problem with alcohol, was not happy with the place he lived. Most of the people there had drinking problems as well, and Paul felt they tempted him to drink more and skip his medications. On the other hand, Paul told Naoko that these people were accepting of his illness, friendly, and often very helpful. Naoko had some ideas about where Paul could move where he might feel secure and have friends, but not be with the people with alcoholism. Before Naoko gave these ideas she said, "You know I was thinking of a couple of places that might work for you if they have an opening. Would you mind if I told you about them?" In this way, Naoko made it clear that the ultimate decision was Paul's and she was only offering suggestions.

It is always best to have more than one idea to share with clients so that they feel there is a choice. Emphasize that the choice is theirs to make and that they would know best which of these ideas, if any, would work for them.

Confronting Collaterals

There may be times when someone is interfering with the client's treatment or your ability to interact effectively with the client. For instance, some years ago a night-shift nurse supervisor in the emergency room took it upon herself to keep the interview room open. Even though the room was there for workers to interview victims of domestic violence, violent crime, or rape, the nurse would barge in, in the middle of the interview, and try to clear the room. Such situations generally include something someone is doing that

1. Adversely affects the client
2. Adversely affects your work with the client

In situations like this, you need a firmer message. The message would

1. Not sound tentative
2. Be pleasant, but firm (smile, but mean what you say)
3. Contain an implied or explicit request for help

Examples of correct and incorrect messages to the nurse in the emergency room who is trying to clear the interview room are shown in Figure 10.3.

In confronting other people, it is tempting to throw out the rules and simply show our annoyance or exasperation. The problem with that approach lies in the fact that we need to work with other people and the agencies they represent. In this field, we must be able to communicate well with one another if we expect to help the people we serve learn better ways of communicating. Your anger directed toward the nurse in the emergency room can affect relations between your agency and the entire emergency room staff. If this is an important part of your work, such strained relations will affect patient care. Remaining firm, but diplomatic, often prevents such problems.

On Not Becoming Overbearing

It is a little tricky to stay where the client is and still express your own concern. Sometimes a technically correct I-message is really about your agenda and is not sensitive to the client and where the client is with the problem at the moment. Such an I-message comes across as intrusive.

FIGURE 10.3

Sample Messages for Confronting Collaterals

To the nurse in the emergency room who is trying to clear the interview room:

Correct: "I need you to help me complete this interview. I expect to need this room for about 45 minutes, and then I will have all the necessary information."

or

"Could you give us another 45 minutes to complete the interview? This must be done before the patient leaves."

Incorrect: "Oh dear, we'll only be a minute, and I need this information too. May we stay awhile longer?"

or

"I thought we could use this room any time. What seems to be your problem?"

For instance, a woman is suddenly widowed. Her husband died in an accident on Tuesday night. You went to the home as part of the crisis team the night it happened because police said she was extremely upset. Tonight you are doing a follow-up visit. When you talked to her the first time, you learned that she is the second oldest of five children. Her brothers and sisters do not live nearby, and she made no move to call them in spite of your suggestion that she do so and your offer to do it for her. You feel that family can be very supportive at a time like this. You have reached this conclusion because you and your family are close and supportive. In this situation, you might send I-messages like those that follow. The parts that are italicized actually express a view or opinion belonging to the worker and do not leave any room for the client's perception.

- "I will honor your request; however, *I feel you may be avoiding a source of real help.*"
- "*I'm uncomfortable that* you don't want your family to be aware of your husband's death. *Family support can be very comforting, and I'm sure that they will not be inconvenienced.*"
- "*I'm not clear* about why you want to keep this from your family. *I feel that they would want to know.*"
- "*It seems to me* that going through this alone *will be very rough for you.*"
- "*I feel that talking to your relatives will be very helpful.*"
- "*I have a problem with you wanting to do this alone.*"

Suppose it turns out that some years ago this woman was in trouble. She was a rebellious teenager and left school and ran away from home. Her parents seemed not to care, and when she attempted to return home at age 19, they told her she had caused them enough grief and she was not welcome there. She moved here, went to college, got a master's degree, and married a local dentist. She feels better off without her family who has never offered her support in the past. She does not tell you all this because she just met you and she does not know you well enough to go into all the reasons why she left home and is estranged from her family.

Think about such possibilities very carefully when you frame an I-message. Be sure that while you speak your concern you leave plenty of room for the fact that you do not know everything and that you could be very wrong. Sounding tentative helps.

Summary

Providing our own point of view must be done carefully and with considerable tact. Our goal is to introduce another perspective, and we want the client to be able to hear and use what we have to say. It is often helpful to ask permission to introduce our ideas. Once we begin to express our view of things, it is best to sound tentative and to invite clients to respond to the ideas we have raised. We do not want to convey a know-it-all attitude that imposes on the client the solution and viewpoints we think are best.

◆ Exercises: What Is Wrong Here?

Instructions: Look at the following confrontations, and identify what is wrong with the way each one is expressed.

1. To a person who is drinking and taking tranquilizers: "That's a dumb thing to do!"

2. To a person who is driving without a driver's license: "You're just doing this to tempt fate."

3. To a person who is always forgetting to take his insulin: "I'm sick of these so-called lapses of memory. You must want to feel sick most of the time!"

4. To a person who bounced three checks in 3 months because she cannot seem to balance her checkbook: "Go take an accounting course, for heaven's sake!"

5. To the person who has lamented not spending enough time with his son: "Children are important. They grow up fast. You only have so long to spend with them when they are kids. You need to keep that in mind."

6. To the person who had trouble completing a high school equivalency exam and is now talking of becoming a doctor: "You need to be more realistic about what you can and can't do. Think of some other career."

7. To the woman who has completed 10 weeks in a rape victim support group and is still unable to work or leave the house much, but who says she is fine and getting over it: "It doesn't seem to me like you're getting over it. If you wanted to get better, you would force yourself to go out more."

8. To the man who complains about his neighbors but spends time on his porch yelling at the children, which starts neighborhood feuds and tensions: "You're always yelling at them. Of course they fight with you!"

9. To the woman who has been in a wheelchair for several months following an accident in spite of her doctor's feelings that she could now be up walking with crutches: "You need to get out of that chair and practice walking. Obviously you get something out of sitting in that wheelchair."

10. To a child who says the other kids do not like him, but who is always hitting the other children and calling them provocative names: "You're half the problem, you know. Stop yelling and hitting everyone, and they'll like you better."

◆ **Exercises: Expressing Your Concern**

Expressing Your Concern I

Instructions: In each of the vignettes that follow, you have a problem—a concern about something affecting the client. For each of these situations, construct an I-message from you to the client. Be sure to follow the rules for confrontation. Make certain you sound tentative and ask for collaboration. Rather than a single sentence, try using several sentences to soften and put forth your ideas.

1. A woman, who has been the victim of grave physical abuse, is currently staying in a shelter where you see her. One night she comes in drunk and tells you, "Hey, it doesn't hurt as much this way." The next day you approach her with an I-message expressing your concern.

2. A woman calls and says her husband is really a dear. He has done many wonderful things for her, and she is feeling guilty about calling you, but he does keep her confined to the house and slaps her a lot. You use an I-message to express your concern.

3. A man with two children needs temporary shelter. His oldest, a daughter, is old enough to drop out of school; and in the course of placing him, you learn that he has encouraged her to do just that. He tells you he needs someone at home to look after the place, now that they have one, and to see that the younger child is taken care of. You use an I-message to express your concern.

4. A woman, the victim of a violent crime, is using a prescription medication her doctor gave her to help her with the anxiety of facing the perpetrator in court. Lately you feel she has been abusing her medication. Her speech seems slurred, and you often see her slip one of the pills into her mouth. You use an I-message to express your concern.

5. A woman has not come out of her house since she suffered a major injury at work. Although her doctors say she will be able to return to work if she goes to rehabilitation, she refuses to go and cites her concern for her fragile recovery. You have talked to her many times by phone and invited her to attend support groups at the rehabilitation center where you work and to see a counselor, but she never comes, and you are becoming aware that she is terribly fearful. You use an I-message to express your concern.

Now return to the first set of exercises called "What Is Wrong Here?" and construct better I-messages for each situation described there.

Expressing Your Concern II

Instructions: In each of the vignettes that follow, you have a problem—a concern about something affecting the client. For each of these situations, construct an I-message from you to the client. Be sure to follow the rules for confrontation. Make certain you sound tentative and ask for collaboration. Rather than a single sentence, try using several sentences to soften and put forth your ideas.

1. A man who has been sitting by his wife's side since she slipped into a coma is weary and has neither eaten nor slept for over 24 hours. You approach him with an I-message expressing your concern.

2. A woman who is refusing to take medication that would prevent her from having a psychotic episode comes to you and says she is not sure what to do. She does not feel well, but she would like to be able to handle things without medication. You use an I-message to express your concern.

3. A man whose wife just left has told you he wants to give up his job and simply leave the area, having no further contact with either his ex-wife or his children. You are concerned that he has not had time to think this through. You use an I-message to express your concern.

4. A woman staying in the shelter where you work has left her baby in the care of others repeatedly and gone out. She says she is going to the store or to look for an apartment or a job, but others let the baby lie in the crib and cry. You have had to feed and change the baby on several occasions. You use an I-message to express your concern.

5. A man is waiting for his Social Security disability check to start. He has a serious heart condition and has been told he should not be out in extremely cold or hot weather. You stop by on a home visit and discover he is out on a cold day shoving piles of snow off the driveway. He tells you it is not that cold and this is not "shoveling." You use an I-message to express your concern.

◆ Exercises: Expressing a Stronger Message

Instructions: In each vignette that follows, you have a problem with the behavior or actions of someone; this person's behavior is affecting the goals of your work with the client or is adversely affecting the client. For each vignette, construct a firmer message that explicitly or implicitly requests this person's help.

1. You are interviewing a man who appears to be quite delusional in the hospital emergency room. The new security officer at the hospital does not seem to understand that the behavior is part of an illness, and he keeps entering the room and asking, as if the patient cannot hear, "Is he giving you any trouble? Do you want me to take care of him?" Your message expresses your need to continue the interview and your need for privacy.

2. You have been working with a man who was beaten and robbed. Because of the injuries, he has been unable to work. His employer calls you several times, saying he thinks the man is simply "freaked out" and needs to get over it. The boss tells you that he has told the man this on several occasions, and says that the man just yells at him. You need the boss to understand the severity of the situation, and you feel it would be helpful if he did not keep calling the victim with his negative opinions. Your message expresses your need for the boss to work with you and the client more constructively.

3. You have been working with a child in temporary housing. You have discovered the child is very artistic, and you have found an artist who is willing to volunteer time to teach the child on Saturday mornings. The mother of the child is upset and tells you that it is impossible "the kid has any talent" and that "anyway, he's got chores on Saturday morning." Your message expresses your need to see the child's potential fully realized.

4. You are interviewing a rape victim when her boyfriend barges into the room and demands, "What's going on in here?" Your message expresses your need to continue the interview.
    (Note: Do not allow another person in the interview room with the client until you and the client have decided *privately* whether that person should be there. In other words, do not discuss, in front of the boyfriend, whether the boyfriend or anyone else can stay. In such situations, never ask the woman, *in front of the man*, if it is all right for the man to stay during the interview. Lead the man outside when you give him your message. Later, when you and the woman are alone, you can ask her whether she would like to have him present, but *always make it appear that the decision to have him wait outside is yours*. It is possible that she is afraid of him and will feel compelled to agree to his staying if she is asked about it while he is in the room. If she is fearful or embarrassed, the quality of the interview will be compromised.)

5. An elderly woman is trying to decide what to do about her need for help. The decision is between staying in her own home with assistance, or selling her home and entering a nursing home. She is very torn. You have arranged for help, which seems to be working well, and you visit her each week. During your visits, the woman discusses with you her options. The decision is a difficult one for her. When you visit her, a woman who lives next door invariably appears and offers her advice and expresses her doubts that the woman should be alone. Your message to the neighbor expresses your feeling that her behavior is not helpful.

Chapter 11

Addressing and Disarming Anger

Introduction

People do become angry. They express anger and hostility in ways we might find quite unpleasant. We can expect that there will be times when the people with whom we are working will forcefully express their anger. As professionals, it is helpful to view the anger as a clue to other underlying issues or as a clue to problems that need to be resolved. Using the anger to help us better understand the other person is better than reacting to it defensively or personally. When people are angry, it is not about you. It is about frustrations and concerns in their own lives. If you are an effective, reflective listener, you will hear these underlying causes and feelings, and you will respond in a manner that disarms rather than provokes the anger.

Common Reasons for Anger

When clients are angry, it is often because of one of the common reasons listed here.

The Client Is Angry About Something the Agency Has Done. The agency in which you work will have policies and regulations that you must follow. Sometimes the agency is bound by state and federal laws as well. These laws work better for some clients than for others. Clients who feel that the agency's policies have caused them to be treated unfairly or with insensitivity to their particular circumstances may react angrily.

The Client Is Angry about Something You Have Said or Done. As noted earlier, there will be times when the client or the client's friends and relations will have a problem with something you have said or done. Without your intending that it should happen, a client may completely misunderstand what you have said or may misread your intentions. On the other hand, you may not always be completely tuned in to where the client is at any particular moment and may unwittingly say or do something the client finds upsetting.

The Client Is Fearful. Many clients are frightened by the turn their lives have taken. The changes that have occurred that brought them to your agency may make them feel as though their lives are out of control. They may attempt to reassert control through the use of anger, and they may lash out at you because you are the safest target or the closest person at the moment.

The Client Is Exhausted. Some clients you see will be exhausted. These people may have been grappling alone with an issue or problem for a long time, or the circumstances they are facing now may be taking all their energy. They sense that they may not be able to carry on, which may cause them to direct anger at you.

The Client Feels Overwhelmed. Other clients feel overwhelmed by problems. They may feel that they cannot handle all that is facing them. Sometimes they feel the extent of the burden is unfair, and so they lash out at you.

The Client Is Confused. Some people are confused by policies, circumstances, others' reactions to them, or the steps they must take to right a difficulty. Rather than admit to feeling confused, some clients become angry and blame the system or you or your agency.

The Client Feels a Need for Attention. Some people feel insignificant and demeaned. It may have nothing to do with you, and it may very much relate to a lifetime of living in the margins or having one's problems or contributions trivialized. These people need to feel valued and worthwhile. The problem for you is that your best efforts may not always be good enough. Sometimes such people are extremely tuned in to slights and suspected rejection. They may become angry with you for reasons that you feel are unfair or unwarranted. As always, you are the professional person and need to speak to the condition of the client in a professional manner.

People become angry for many reasons. Knowing how to disarm anger is important. It will enable you to move toward a more meaningful dialogue and a better resolution.

Why Disarming Anger Is Important

You cannot be as effective in your work if you are dealing with a client who is angry. The client cannot be expected to move the relationship to another level; but you, as the professional, can be expected to practice the techniques that will allow the relationship to move beyond the anger. The major reasons for disarming anger are as follows.

Eliminates an Obstacle to True Understanding. Disarming anger diffuses the anger, making it less of an obstacle to true understanding. People who are angry cannot really hear each other. If you are genuinely interested in why the client is reacting in this manner, you need to reduce the anger so that you can better understand what is fueling these strong emotions.

Shows Clients You Respect Their Message. Disarming anger shows the other person that you respect the message even if the way it is expressed is not helpful. By moving to another level beyond the anger, you can indicate to angry clients that their concerns are important to you even when you are having trouble with the way they are addressing these concerns.

Enables You to Understand the Problem. Disarming anger allows you to become aware of the actual problem. Only when you have disarmed the anger can you and the client actually address the underlying concern. As clients feel heard and understood, they are more likely to begin to collaborate with you in looking at their problems and the solutions.

Allows You to Practice Empathy. Disarming anger allows you to practice empathy, seeing the situation as the other person is seeing it. Disarming anger is an important part of establishing rapport. If you become angry yourself, you are caught up in your own feelings and needs at the moment. On the other hand, if you think about the reason the person is angry and you speak to that situation or to those feelings, you are responding empathically. This lets the client understand that you are not going to engage in an angry exchange, but you are going to respect the client's concerns and feelings.

Focuses Work on Solving the Problem. Disarming anger focuses on solving the issues and problems, and not on who is to blame. Disarming anger techniques do not allow for exchanges of blame. Angry clients may hope for such an exchange with you wherein they blame you and you defend yourself, often by blaming them in return. The purpose of disarming anger is to fix those things that legitimately need to be fixed.

Many people sound angrier than they mean to. They are often anticipating the angry response of the other person. As human service workers, we read anger as a signal that the client's needs have not been met, and we focus on resolution of the problem that has caused the angry emotions, regardless of whether we think the client's anger is legitimate.

Avoiding the Number-One Mistake

Countless times human service workers encounter people who are openly angry. Many of those workers choose to take that anger personally. Taking anger personally is the number-one mistake when dealing with an angry person. It is a foolish mistake to make.

As noted earlier, people become angry for a number of reasons. Some of these reasons have nothing to do with the worker specifically. Other times the anger may be caused by something the worker or the agency has done, and the anger may be rude and denigrating. Nevertheless, beyond disarming the anger, it is important that when you encounter an angry client, you refrain from taking the anger personally. A worker who chose to take the anger of a client personally might end up in a conversation something like this.

CLIENT: Where the hell were *you* on Tuesday?

WORKER: What do you mean?

CLIENT: Where the hell were you? I came in to get a voucher for food, and you weren't here.

WORKER: Why are you shouting at me? I wasn't here, but you don't have to shout.

CLIENT: I do have to shout! You say to come in here for a voucher, and I did that, and you were not even here. Where the hell were you?

WORKER: Look, Mr. Peters, I don't have to tell you where I was. If you came in and I wasn't here, why didn't you tell someone else what you needed? I'm not the only person who can help you.

CLIENT: I get so damn tired of the way you guys act like prima donnas. Who the hell gave you the right to tell all of us when to come and when to go? You say come in, I come in, like a fool, and *you* decide you'll just go someplace else.

WORKER: Well, if that's the way you feel, you certainly don't need *my* help. I've spent quite a lot of time with you, may I remind you? You have gotten a lot from this agency. I'm not sure I'm going to put up with this shouting at me.

CLIENT: Well, what are you going to do about it? I can tell you that you are a piss-poor caseworker if I want to. I can't do much else around here, but I *can* do that!

WORKER: You're an idiot. Go out and get the voucher from Mrs. Charles, bring it back here, and I'll sign it [*begins reading papers on her desk*].

In this example, the relationship is damaged, and there is an unsatisfactory resolution. Bitter feelings remain for both the worker and the client.

There is a better way to handle situations like this one. This chapter will explain how to use a four-step process to deal with anger. The central question you want to ask yourself is this: Can I feel empathic toward this angry person and hear the pain behind all this anger—or am I likely to get into a power struggle with this angry person to show I won't be pushed around? Empathy is the professional response. Power is the unprofessional response.

Erroneous Expectations for Perfect Communication

Some human service workers have the erroneous expectation that their clients will give them no trouble. In their view, clients not only will never get angry, but they will follow suggestions, be appreciative, and never raise doubts, criticisms, or resistance. This sort of thinking is a trap, and workers who fall into it often become exasperated or punitive with clients who become angry.

We all have had bad times in our lives, and we look back on those times later and think, "I wasn't myself then." These times may have been isolated incidences, or they may have been prolonged periods when we were under a lot of stress. The people who seek our help are under a lot of stress. In addition, many of them have problems precisely because they have trouble communicating easily with others. Anger and other forms of negative communication may be all they learned.

Expect anger, disarm it, and treat it matter of factly. In this way you will not allow a client's anger to bar your work with the client, nor will you carry completely unrealistic notions in your head that clients won't or shouldn't get angry. They will get angry, but you will know what to do.

For example, Jane was a worker in a home for three individuals with mental illness. Kip had a bipolar diagnosis and was doing well. In fact, maintained on his medication, he was pleasant and cooperative. He was working at a local supermarket and seemed about ready to move to an apartment of his own. Then it was discovered that the medication he was taking, Lithium, was adversely affecting his liver. Liver function tests came back showing this deterioration. Doctors immediately removed Kip from the Lithium and placed him on an alternative medication.

Almost at once Kip's personality turned irritable and angry. He accused Jane of spying on him, and he became erratic about going to work. When the residents in the home went shopping for their groceries, he either sat in the van with his arms folded, refusing to get out, or he created scenes in the supermarket about things he wanted to buy that would have shattered the careful budget he and the others had constructed.

His outbursts in public were embarrassing to Jane, and in the home she often endured a lot of his anger. Jane's approach was twofold. She actively advocated for a reexamination of Kip's medications, and she was firm with Kip but never angry. Many times she told him she understood that he was not feeling like himself. She refused to take anything he said personally. On more than one occasion, his accusations actually made her laugh, and Kip laughed with her, recognizing momentarily how silly his accusations were.

Jane's superiors, and particularly the treating psychiatrist, all believed that Kip could have become dangerous had Jane not steadfastly refused to escalate the situation or take it personally.

The Four-Step Process

In his book *Feeling Good*, David Burns (1980) suggests a four-step process for disarming anger. The material in this section is adapted from his book. First, we will look at the individual steps, and then we will look at how these steps work in actual practice.

1. *Be appreciative.* It is frightening enough to tell people you are angry about something they have said or done. You will put clients at ease if you can say something like "I appreciate your coming to me with this" or "It is helpful to know how you are feeling about this" or "Thank you for bringing this up."
2. *Ask for more information.* A client who is upset may be skimming the surface of an issue. To understand the issue better, ask for particulars. Do not grill

the person or sound defensive. You might say, "Can you tell me when this happened?" or "I guess I'm not sure when this happened. Can you help me out?" or "How often did this happen?"

3. *Find something with which you agree.* Never make up something just to sound agreeable, but see if there is not some little piece of what the client has said with which you can agree. You might say, "I think we have probably done this in the past." or "I can see where you would feel that way." or "There probably was a lapse the day you are referring to."
4. *Begin to focus on a solution.* Focusing on a solution should involve *collaboration* whenever possible. Remember, however, that the client owns the problem; the extent of your assistance is a conscious and strategic decision that you must make.

Begin with your objective point of view. Listen to the client's point of view. Then decide if you will make changes or leave things as they are. You might, after explaining your point of view, say, "I can see where you thought that. I think from now on I'd like to write you ahead of time." or "I can see where you thought that. Right now we are really short-staffed, so writing to you ahead of time isn't really an option. I'm glad you brought this up. In the future, we will take another look at it." Own your perceptions and own your decision regarding the problem. Use "I," not "you." Let us return to the situation we looked at earlier and see a more effective approach for handling the problem.

CLIENT: Where the hell were *you* on Tuesday?

WORKER: I'm not sure I know what you mean.

CLIENT: Where the hell were you? I came in to get a voucher for food, and you weren't here.

WORKER: What time were you here on Tuesday?

CLIENT: Oh, about 2:00. You say to come in here for a voucher, and I did that, and you were not even here. Where the hell were you?

WORKER [USING ACTIVE LISTENING FIRST]: Well, this must have been really inconvenient for you. I appreciate your telling me about this. Did you ask anyone else to help you?

CLIENT: No, I didn't. I didn't know I could.

WORKER: Sure you can. I can see where you would think I didn't care about your getting food when you expected me to be here.

CLIENT: I know. We didn't have any dinner Tuesday night. Just potato chips and cheese—oh, and there was a little milk left.

WORKER: I'm really sorry that happened. Let me see that you get the food you need today, and let me explain better than I did the other day how this works. If I or any of the other workers tell you to come in for a voucher, then you can come right to the office, and whoever is doing the intakes can take your information and see that you get the food you need. This shouldn't have happened this way, and we don't want it to happen again.

CLIENT: Thanks.

As is rarely the case, all the elements of the four-step process are present in this exchange. In this example, the worker asks for more information with genuine interest ("What time were you here on Tuesday? Did you ask anyone else to help you?"). She goes on to express appreciation ("I appreciate your telling me about this."). She indicates that she agrees with the way the client viewed the situation ("I can see where you would think I didn't care about your getting food when you expected me to be here."). Finally, she moves on to focus on a solution ("Let me see that you get the food you need today, and let me explain better than I did the other day how this works.").

The worker in this example does some other things that make it clear she is not going to take the client's anger personally. She uses reflective listening ("Well, this must have been really inconvenient for you."), letting the client know that he is being heard and respected. She also takes some responsibility for the mix-up ("and let me explain better than I did the other day how this works.").

We might change this vignette just a bit. Perhaps the worker actually did explain to the client on the phone before he came in how the agency works. There are many reasons he might not have heard her: anxiety over trying to make sure his kids would eat that night, anger over having to go to the agency in the first place, uncomfortable feelings of helplessness or inadequacy over his inability to fix his situation on his own, and the stress of not eating and having hungry children at home.

Although the worker may not know specifically what has generated the angry outburst, she is fully aware that there are forces at play in this man's life beyond his need for her to be present when he arrives at the agency. For that reason, she remains respectful throughout the entire exchange, and she moves with genuine interest and concern through the steps of disarming anger. In other words, she does not take his anger personally and feel a need to confront it with anger of her own.

What You Do Not Want to Do

There are a number of things you need to avoid doing. Figure 11.1 contains examples of these things. The incorrect example for each point illustrates what you want to avoid, and the correct example shows you a better way to handle the situation. As you read, refer to the figure and compare the correct and incorrect examples that illustrate each point.

Do Not Become Defensive. Do not fall into the trap of defending yourself. It is okay to have made a mistake or to be wrong. If you begin to defend yourself, it makes the other person angrier, and you lose an opportunity to really resolve the problem.

Do Not Become Sarcastic or Facetious. When you thank people for their comments or agree with something they told you, it is possible that you will sound sarcastic or facetious. This is especially true if you are feeling defensive.

Do Not Act Superior. It is all right for you to be wrong in your perceptions or behavior, and it is all right for the client to be wrong too. If you feel especially

FIGURE 11.1

Examples of What Not to Do

Do Not Become Defensive

To a person who feels the worker did not spend enough time with her:

Correct: "I might have cut the interview short."

Incorrect: "I'm doing the best I can. I certainly gave you the time you needed!"

Do Not Become Sarcastic or Facetious

To a man who works and is frustrated because he needs a later appointment but keeps getting an early morning appointment:

Correct: "I'm glad you brought this up again. We really do need to get this straight."

Incorrect: "Here we go again! Thanks for telling us, again, how inefficient we are."

Do Not Act Superior

To a woman who thinks her daughter should have different services:

Correct: "We ought to look at this more closely. I'm glad you told me about this. You may be right."

Incorrect: "The services have been chosen for your daughter by professionals in the field of child development, and they know what it is she needs."

Do Not Grill the Client

To a man who believes his aunt is being neglected by the agency:

Correct: "Tell me more about what you see happening with us and your aunt. We may need to look at this situation more closely."

Incorrect: "When exactly did we fail to come out to your aunt's house? How often did this take place, and did she ever tell us about this before? We need to know specifics before we can determine if this is a real problem. What other problems did you encounter with us?"

threatened or angry at your clients, it may be tempting to denigrate them in some way, pointing out how little they actually know about the situation or how little experience they have and how much more knowledgeable you are.

Do Not Grill the Client. In order to better understand the problem from the client's point of view, you will need to ask questions. Avoid grilling the client by asking numerous questions, one after the other, in a doubtful tone of voice. If clients are nervous, you will only make their nervousness worse. Most people grill another person in a triumphant attempt to prove the other person wrong. That is not your goal here. Your goal is to genuinely try to understand.

Look for Useful Information

You can benefit from the feedback you are receiving if you really hear it. Sometimes the client is bringing you valuable information that will help you to make constructive changes in yourself or in your agency.

In one agency, there were a lot of angry clients calling for help. They all had been discharged from a certain program without follow-up services or with follow-up services that had not been confirmed. The agency was grateful for the clients' feedback and developed a questionnaire for the receptionist to use when such calls came in. Gradually, a picture emerged of precisely what was wrong and how to fix it. In this example, an entire agency benefited from the clients' feedback. A more efficient operation will keep clients from returning with recurring problems and will save money and time for other clients.

Managing an Angry Outburst

On rare occasions, people become so angry they seem to be about to lose control. Their demeanor moves from rational expressions of anger to increased belligerence, threats to the safety of others, or actual aggression toward people and objects in the vicinity. Research shows that staff people play an important role in defusing these explosive situations. An even tone of voice, continued reflective listening, and relaxed movement work best.

Lisa, a nurse in a community program for the mentally ill, discovered Phil eating lunch one day with a gun lying by his plate. He had been angry about his medications earlier in the day, but that problem seemed to have been resolved. Instead of quietly approaching Phil and suggesting the gun be left with the nurse until the end of the day, Lisa became hysterical. Rushing about the room, she loudly began to clear out the startled patients, thrusting them through the door. "Call the police, call the police," she kept shouting to other workers. Phil, alarmed by her actions, grabbed his gun and pointed it at her. He began to yell at Lisa, "Just shut up, shut up, before I shoot you. Be quiet." Lisa dashed from the room and cleared the entire building. Police came from every direction. The area was cordoned off, and a standoff ensued into the afternoon.

Lisa's loud, hysterical tone of voice, her panic, and her hurried actions all combined to make Phil agitated. Before long, the situation had escalated. What Lisa should have tried first was asking Phil to come with her to another part of the building. If Phil left the gun at his place, another worker could have secured it. If he brought the gun with him, Lisa might have said matter of factly that perhaps it would be better to leave the gun with the staff for the time being. If Phil gave her the gun, she could have taken steps to secure it.

Even if Phil were resistant and wanted to keep his gun, the staff could have asked the clients to bring their lunches into the group rooms for after-lunch groups. If they made this request in a tone of voice that indicated that it was nothing out of the ordinary, clients would have complied. In the meantime, police could have been called to come quietly and help to disarm Phil.

In another situation, Jim, a young mental health case manager, was working with Alex. Alex wanted to go into the hospital, fearing that he was getting sick again and would hurt someone. On that particular day, there were no beds, and Jim's supervisor suggested he help Alex find an alternative to hospitalization until a bed was available. Jim was afraid of Alex, who spent most of that day sitting in the waiting room. Each time Jim explained that no beds were available yet and that an alternative needed to be found, Alex grew more belligerent.

The last time Jim returned to report that there were still no available beds, he did so in what he thought was a very firm manner. Reasoning that Alex seemed about to become uncontrollable, Jim assumed that if he approached him with a firm, superior tone of voice, he could keep Alex from getting any angrier. In fact, Jim's superior tone was harsh and was heard by Alex as denigrating. He began to shout and pound the wall to demonstrate to Jim "just who is in charge here." Remaining matter of fact, practicing empathic reflective listening, and remaining calm are important in maintaining a controlled situation. If you or your clients are in danger, certainly the first thing to do is to secure the safety of everyone. However, situations that escalate because workers fuel them—inflaming the client's anger by becoming loud, agitated, or angry themselves—can rapidly spiral out of control. Remaining calm and moving deliberately to prevent a dangerous situation from worsening is the responsibility of the professional.

Summary

Disarming anger is an important skill used to preserve your relationships with your clients and to prevent anger from escalating. The goal is to reach an understanding about the problems or concerns that are fueling the anger and to resolve those where possible. Becoming angry yourself can only escalate the situation, making real problem solving and collaboration with the client impossible. In previous chapters you have learned many techniques by which to convey to clients their importance and your interest in what they have to say. Use these to advantage when dealing with a client who is angry. Remain matter of fact, refuse to take the anger as a personal insult, and reflect back the underlying concerns and feelings of the client.

◆ Exercises: Initial Responses to Anger

Instructions: In the examples that follow, formulate an initial response to the anger and criticism you hear. On a separate piece of paper, look at the steps for disarming anger, and use those that seem appropriate. The four steps are: (1) thank the person for the comments, (2) ask for more information, (3) find some point on which you can agree, and (4) begin to look for a negotiated solution.

1. A man is coming to your agency for assistance after a violent crime. He wants you to do more for him than you think is wise. You have been very helpful in ways you could, but you have also insisted he do some things for himself because you do not want him to become dependent. He is frustrated, and one day when you suggest to him that he try to call his lawyer himself, he blows up and yells, "This crazy place, sucking up the taxpayers' money—and for what? I get so sick and tired of your trying to make me do everything when that's what you're paid for. A bunch of idiots is what you are! Incompetents! Sure, I can do it myself! If I wanted to do it myself, I wouldn't have come to you, would I?" What is your initial response?

2. A woman who is in your shelter feels neglected. Twice you are interrupted when you are talking to her because of severe emergencies. You apologize both times and continue your discussion with her, but you are short-staffed and things at the agency are unpredictable. The second time this happens, when you are able to get back to her, she cannot remember what she had been saying. That upsets her. She says, "You all sure can find plenty of reasons to avoid talking to me. Every time I sit down to talk about my case, you get up and run off. Now I can't remember where we were. I don't see you running off when you talk to Alice or Cindy. Just seems like every time I need help, well, you have something more important to do." What is your initial response?

◆ **Exercises: Practicing Disarming**

Instructions: Following are some opening sentences said by angry clients. It is up to you to develop the exchange, including more information regarding what the client is angry about and the responses of the worker. You do not have to use the disarming steps in any particular order. See if you can add some active listening and open questions as you go along. See if you can put yourself in the clients' shoes and empathize with their feelings.

1. CLIENT [*talking loudly, and banging his fist on the desk*]: I have a beef to pick with you! Little jerks run this agency, a bunch of little jerks! You tell me I'm a mental case and then give me medicine that makes me feel like a nut case.
   WORKER:

2. CLIENT [*barging past the receptionist to the worker's office, obviously angry*]: My kids and I are hungry! Know what that means—to be hungry? We're hungry and you . . .
   WORKER:

Chapter 12

The Effective Combination of Skills

Introduction

It is always tempting to go back to old ways of communicating. A client doesn't take her medications, another begins to drink again after extensive rehabilitation, a third fails to keep his appointments, and yet another seems unable to make a decision to remove herself from a dangerous situation. In such situations, we may become exasperated and lecture, admonish, and argue the points we think are important. We know all about good communication, but we tell ourselves this is an exception—that all those good communication skills we learned may work for clients who are compliant and appreciative, but this client is not and therefore a tougher stance is required.

When we become exasperated and begin to argue with people, it is extremely doubtful that those people can hear what we have to say. If being effective means helping people to move in directions that promote their health and well-being, then we have thwarted that goal with our irritation. Everyone (clients included) resists listening to an irritated, argumentative person. We justify our harsher tone by telling ourselves that this particular person needs a "wake-up call" or a "reality check." But in reality we are venting our own frustration at the expense of the client.

No matter how justifiable our anger may appear to be, there are far better ways to approach clients. You already know most of them. In this chapter, we will look at how to combine the skills you have already learned with some special techniques to effectively talk to clients like those just described. These techniques are ways you can use what you have learned to minimize an adversarial relationship with clients and develop a truly collaborative and productive one instead.

Much of what is described in this chapter comes from motivational interviewing, a special technique used to facilitate behavior change. When you use these techniques, you will be following the spirit of motivational interviewing and the spirit of the approaches outlined in the previous chapters of this book. That spirit is respectful of each person and values each person as unique and capable. To actually do motivational interviewing with all the various tools and nuances takes training and practice, something you may choose to pursue in your career.

Combining Skills and Attitudes

Let's begin by looking at the skills and attitudes you learned in the previous chapters. In Chapter 1 on ethics and professional responsibilities, you learned the importance of respect for the person and your responsibility for caring for people who are emotionally vulnerable. The following skills and attitudes were stressed.

- *Acceptance* of clients where they are at the moment they reach for help is one of the most important and facilitating attitudes.
- *Informed consent* engages clients in the process of making decisions about their services and treatment.
- *Self-determination* requires an attitude of respect for the person's choices and the ability to honor the person's choices.
- *Not insisting on your solutions* is yet another way that the client's choices and views are honored.

Chapter 2 on case management covered additional ways to respect clients. For example:

- *Individualized planning* requires that we see each client as a separate and unique individual.
- *CASSP, recovery, resiliency,* and *self-determination models* that come from federal and state governments mandate that we consider the client's strengths, ideas, and choices and approach clients with hope and vision. (See Section 2 for methods for demonstrating respect.)
- *Cultural competence* requires case managers to understand and relate appropriately to cultures other than their own.
- *Nonjudgmental attitude* allows us to listen and accept what the client brings and where the client is without a need to pass judgment as to whether the client is good, stupid, smart, or a bad person.
- *Motivating and encouraging* are important in instilling hope for something better, faith in oneself, and the possibility of meaningful change. This requires a good look at the person's strengths.
- *Collaboration* is yet another way to show respect for people, involving them in the process of planning and making important changes. Here we actively work with clients to support their vision and ideas.
- *Separate people* is another attitude that commits the case manager to keeping the boundaries between who is the client and who is the case manager clear and free of our own emotional intrusions.

The skills and attitudes listed here exhibit hope, demonstrate respect, and foster self- determination. We want to, and indeed we must, use these skills and convey these attitudes if people are going to trust us and begin to make the changes in their lives that are most useful.

Next we learned communication skills—the very skills that demonstrate our attitudes toward other people. Let's review what we know.

- *Reflective listening* demonstrates considerable acceptance for where clients are at the moment and shows our interest in what they are thinking. Our respect in turn fosters self-acceptance and enables clients to move forward.
- *Open questions* are another way to show we want to go where the client thinks is most important and hear what the client feels is most relevant.
- *I-messages* are as nonintrusive as possible, are owned by us, invite the client to explore with us, and always consider the possibility that we might be wrong.
- *Disarming anger.* Even here, when the client is angry, we invite criticism, refuse to be defensive, and appreciate the information—all ways to accept and respect the concerns of the person without needing to respond in kind.

These communication skills are tools that give us an effective way to demonstrate respect, encouragement, and concern for our clients.

All of us feel better in the presence of someone who respects us, is not judging us, and is hopeful about our situation. We begin to relax, to talk, to explore ideas, to be ourselves. In this type of situation, it becomes safe to hope about the future. This is exactly why you learned these attitudes and skills: so that the people who seek your help will trust you and your intentions and, therefore, be able to work on changing their situations.

So why, you might ask yourself, would we as case managers ever resort to arguments, demands, irritation, and anger? It isn't necessary if we practice the attitudes and skills we have learned, and learn how and when to apply them. What we need to do now is learn to strategically apply these tools to help clients when they are in our presence. In other words, we will move beyond just giving appropriate responses to giving strategically chosen responses.

Communication Skills That Facilitate Change

Make It Safe to Explore

Using reflective listening from the start is important in setting a climate in which exploration of the problem is safe. You might start an interview the first time you meet the client with questions that show your interest in the person's point of view.

- "I would like to know more about how you see this situation."
- "Tell me what you feel is most important here."
- "What do you feel we should address first?"

These are simply considerate ways to address clients in any interview, but the questions indicate that you value clients and their agenda for themselves. It respectfully allows them to set the priorities.

Steer Around Initial Worries

Sometimes clients come in believing we will prescribe the best course of action. Betts was sure the case manager was going to recommend a dietitian who would put her on a stringent diet. Kipp came in convinced that the case manager would tell him he had to stop drinking before he could be helped. A good case manager might say something like this:

- "Wow, you're really moving ahead of things. Today I just want to know how you see the problem and what you think about it."
- "You're way ahead of me here. I just want to know what you think about your situation."

Articulate Self-Determination

When it comes to changing a situation or behavior, state the obvious.

- "In the end, what happens here is entirely up to you."
- "You are free to choose either alternative."
- "You will be the one to decide what happens here."

For many people, this sense of personal autonomy is relieving and takes away one reason for taking an adversarial stance with the case manager.

Help People Talk About Change

Arguing with you about why they should not change convinces people that they should not change. The opposite is also true. When clients tell you why they should change, they are very likely convincing themselves that change is possible and can be done. What you want to do, therefore, is engage people in what Miller and Rollnick (2002) refer to as "change talk." Using your skills, ask open questions about change. Rather than asking why a person doesn't change, ask instead about how that person sees change occurring.

- "Tell me a little bit about how you would like things to be."
- "Can you give me some ideas about how you might bring this about?"
- "What do you think might be a good place to start?"
- "Tell me something about what you have considered doing to change the situation."

When clients respond to questions like these, be sure to reflect the responses back to them. This way clients hear the responses twice.

- "So, in other words, you thought you could cut down gradually by smoking one cigarette less each day for a month?"
- "What you really want is to be free of your symptoms and go back to school."

With comments like these, you place clients in a position in which they are the ones arguing for and articulating change.

Discuss Discrepancies

People become ambivalent because discrepancies exist between the way things are and the way they would like things to be. The more a person deals with these discrepancies, the more likely it is that the person will move toward change. The idea here is to allow the person to discuss why it would be an advantage to change.

For example, Trudy did not want to take her medication because she felt it labeled her as mentally ill. On the other hand, she recognized that she not only felt better on her medication, but she was also more productive. Consequently, she went on and off her medication with predictable swings in mood. Here is what a good case manager might ask:

- "Tell me a little bit about what is negative in the way you are taking your medication now."

Here the case manager elicits from the client herself what might be impractical or negative about her use of her medication. This is more effective than the case manager lecturing the client. A good case manager also might say:

- "Tell me about how things would be if you took the medication consistently."

Again, the case manager is allowing the client to talk about the advantages, rather than listing them for her. A case manager with poor insight and skills might be tempted to ask instead:

- "Well, why don't you just take the medication the way it was prescribed?"
- "Do you really think this is not a problem for your health?"

Open questions about what Trudy values or would like to see in her life 4 or 5 years from now also illustrate the difference between the way things are and the way the client would like things to be. For example:

- "Let's put aside how hard it might be to change and tell me how you would like things to be in 5 years."
- "Tell me something about what values you have that make you consider staying on the medication."

Again, reflect the responses to such questions back to the person, so they are heard twice.

It may be easier for people to change when they can see a clear difference between the way things are and the way they want them to be. Ask questions that will help your clients see that discrepancy. Look for ways to allow people to discuss the disadvantages of their present situation and the advantages that could be had if things were different.

- "What worries you most about your situation?"
- "Tell me about the concerns you have right now."

In these questions, the case manager is asking the client to discuss disadvantages.

The case manager might also ask:

- "How would things be different if you decided to do this?"
- "What are the main reasons for making a change like this?"
- "If you stayed off your medication, how do you think things would be different?"

In these questions, the case manager is setting the stage for the client to recognize why it would be advantageous to make changes. It is not the case manager telling the client why changing would be a good thing. It is the client telling the case manager.

As always, reflect back what clients tell you so they hear it twice.

Allow People to Express Ambivalence

If clients feel safe with you, they will talk more openly. For that reason, you will be more likely to hear people talk about their ambivalent feelings if you use good communication techniques than if you use techniques that do not value or appreciate the client. When clients tell you about their ambivalence, you know you are doing something right. Focus, using reflective listening, on what the client is concerned about.

For example, Jose knows he should diet, but he tells you that doing so would mean a damper on family get-togethers, denying himself the food he loves, and eating food that seems boring to him. On the other hand, he wants to live a long life, see his children grow up, and knows that his present weight has caused his diabetes and high blood pressure. Through reflective listening, the case manager accepts these concerns as making sense within the context of Jose's life. A good case manager might say:

- "So it would be hard to eat food without much taste, particularly at family gatherings where there is lots of good food."

Here the case manager accepts the client's concerns. A poorly skilled case manager might be tempted to say:

- "You don't have too many options if you want to reduce your blood pressure."

In this response, the case manager argues for the going-on-a-diet side while the client is forced into taking the no-diet side of the discussion.

Bring Out Confidence

Consider a lack of confidence part of normal ambivalence. Some people will be more confident that they can pull off a change than others will be. Ask for expressions of optimism and confidence:

- "Tell me about your personal strengths that will help you succeed here."
- "If you decide to change, what do you think will work for you?"
- "Tell me about the confidence you have that you can do this."

These questions allow the client to express explicitly what the client has that will contribute to success.

Generally clients have made some changes in their past. Talk about that:

- "You said you wanted to drop out of school, but in the end you didn't. You graduated. Tell me how you did it."

Ask for details so that your clients have to talk about their successes and will hear how they overcame obstacles.

Pima did not want to finish high school. She was having some trouble with English, she liked being home with her mother doing housework, and she did not have hopes of going on to college. But Pima stayed in school and graduated. The case manager explored this situation to highlight Pima's strengths:

- "What made you decide to stay in school after all?"
- "How did you manage to keep going?"
- "Why do you think you were so successful in completing high school?"
- "What strengths did you use to see it through?"

Of course, you would not ask such questions in rapid-fire order. Everything the client says you would reflect back and explore. These kinds of questions help clients to talk in some detail about previous successes and to tell the case manager about those successes, rather than the other way around. Talking about their own success tells clients why they can probably succeed in making an important change in their lives now.

You might also ask clients to list for you the positive strengths and characteristics they see in themselves that will help them get through a change in their lives. Again, by using reflective listening between questions, you can encourage clients to tell you what strengths they have, rather than your telling them.

Facilitate Commitment

Another important approach is to elicit intentions to change from the client. A case manager might ask:

- "Can you describe what you would be willing to try at this point?"
- "Tell me about what you intend to do from here."

Generally, at some point, people will agree to a plan they believe will work for them. If you ask permission to share that plan with others, it often strengthens a person's resolve to follow through. For example, are there family members the client wouldn't mind inviting to hear about the decisions that have been made? Are there other workers who might be invited to hear about the change? Always ask permission to do this, make sure it is the client who does the telling, and accept any hesitance to share the plan with others.

Reflect the Opposite Side

Sometimes a person is reluctant to make a change. In this situation, it can be helpful if you carefully take the opposite side. That is, you reflect the reluctance back without sarcasm. For example, Trudy did not want to take medication, even though she had been too depressed to work. The case manager said:

- ◆ "You really feel that taking medication is a sign of weakness and will label you a 'mental patient,' and it seems better to you to be depressed and unable to work at this time rather than take the medicine."

It is important to hear the matter-of-fact tone the worker is using, rather than a sarcastic, facetious tone. The case manager has reflected back the reluctance and even added the other side of the situation, what it will be like without the medication. In this case, the client responded by saying:

- ◆ "I suppose I should take the medication if it would really get me back to work."

Here the case manager's empathic reflection of her client's reluctance, along with highlighting the obvious consequences, caused the client to rethink her reluctance in a new light. Now it is the client who argues for positive change.

Trapping the Client

The client expresses ambivalence. She is not sure she wants to change her behavior. The case manager tells her why she should want to change. The client tells the case manager all the reasons why she shouldn't want to change. She talks about how it is too late to change. She admits this behavior has some negative consequences, but she focuses on all the positive rewards she gains from it. In the process she convinces herself that she does not want to change and that she probably couldn't if she tried. The case manager concludes the situation is hopeless, the client has already made up her mind and doesn't want to change, and so the case manager stops really trying.

Another client is an alcoholic, and the case manager uses the aggressive form of confrontation with him. The case manager readily tears the person down in an effort to get him to "take a really good look" at himself. The case manager tells him he could change if he wanted to, and that the problem is he is too lazy, too self-centered, and too much of a "cry-baby." Most of us would lose trust in a situation that produced that kind of confrontation. When the client drifts away, the case manager decides that the client is unmotivated and hopeless and labels the client "resistant."

The problem in the two scenarios just described is that arguing with clients about changing and confronting clients with what bad people they are generally won't help them make constructive changes. Research backs this up. People stay and work on their situations and problems more often when they feel the environment is safe, they are in control of their own situation, and someone will listen to their vacillation on the way to changing.

In the two instances described earlier, well-intentioned case managers used techniques of dubious value and unwittingly further trapped their clients in their negative situations. People change when case managers use the attitudes and skills you learned in the previous chapters. Therefore, we will look next at how to enhance these skills and use them strategically.

From Adversarial to Collaborative

Brainstorming

Spend some time with the person who is having trouble considering how to bring about desired changes. Ask the person to list as many ideas as she can think of for making the changes. You add some ideas too. As the ideas are proposed, list them without judgment.

Jenny and her case manager were brainstorming about what to do about Jenny's abusive marital situation. Jenny offered several ideas during brainstorming that her case manager felt were impractical and even dangerous. For instance, Jenny suggested that she and her husband continue to live together and seek counseling. The case manager knew from experience that in most such cases, the mere mention of abuse before a counselor, provided the abuser went for counseling, could result in more abuse after the counseling session was over. Nevertheless, the case manager said nothing until all the options were on the list and no one could think of any others. Then, while going over the various options, the case manager asked permission to share her experiences with this particular course of action.

In brainstorming, if all the options are laid out, usually a solution appears. Sometimes several solutions appear, or a good one is developed by combining elements of several different ideas.

Offering Information and Advice

In one case management unit, the clients were told what they needed to do. Phillip resented being told by his case manager that he needed to go to the welfare office; he had hoped that a change in his medication might mean he could get a job. While he felt he might need welfare at the moment until he "got on his feet," he resented never being able to talk about what he hoped would come next.

As a case manager, you should offer your own ideas only

1. After you have fully listened to and explored those of the client
2. After first asking for permission to do so
3. When you believe it can help the client or you need to warn the client about a threat to the client's safety

It is arrogant to approach people as if we have all the answers for their lives. It is respectful and collaborative to offer ideas after we have heard theirs. Our purpose is to have people work together with us, not be put off by us.

Summarizing

Miller and Rollnick (2002), in their book *Motivational Interviewing*, discuss the importance of a good summary. If you are skilled at reflective listening, you will be able to do summarizing well. Miller and Rollnick suggest three types of summaries that reflect back to clients important points that they need to hear again. If your summary hits most of the important points, clients will move again to discussions of how the changes can take place.

Collecting Summaries

In collecting summaries, you simply pull together the important points you have heard thus far. These should be short so they do not interfere with the person's train of thought. You can end these with the question "What else?" to keep the person going on the same topic. Here is an example by a case manager:

- "What you have said so far is that you are interested in quitting drugs, particularly marijuana, and you think if you stay away from school you would be less likely to have access to it. You feel pretty sure your friends won't understand and may even make fun of you if you tell them that you want to quit. What else?"

Linking Summaries

In a linking summary, you bring together and link important points, some of which were made earlier in the discussion.

- "You have decided that you want to stay away from school to avoid your friends and access to drugs. You feel this will help you to stop using drugs. On the other hand, you also think it would be a good idea to get your high school diploma, and you are hoping to use it to go to the community college for a degree in math."

Notice that the case manager is using reflective listening and is matter-of-factly acknowledging the fact that there is ambivalence about what to do in this situation.

The case manager in the previous example also uses the words "on the other hand" rather than "but," and there is a reason for this. When you use the word *but*, you tend to negate all that was said before it. You want to acknowledge both sides of the situation. The case manager also could have said: "And you also think it would be good...," or "At the same time, you think it would be good...."

Transition Summaries

In transition summaries, you are preparing the client to move forward, whether toward another interview with you or one with the provider where the client will be referred. Your transition summary might go something like this:

- "Let me see if I can summarize where we are before we stop today. You are thinking about dropping out of school in order to avoid drugs and the friends you have that push them. You feel that these friends would not understand your plan to stop using drugs and would not support your plans to stay in school and attend the community college. You feel you should get your high school diploma, and you are willing to explore how to do that with the counselor you will be seeing next week."

Summaries help people clarify, organize, and start again. These summaries are one of the ways the case manager shows acceptance and prepares the way to move forward.

Case Manager Traps

Coming Off as a Know-It-All

It may be that you have seen dozens of clients similar to the person sitting in front of you now. You believe you know what works and what doesn't work, so you offer a prescription. Do this, this, and this, and everything will be fine. But when we behave and talk as if we have all the answers, we inadvertently place people in a passive position wherein they allow us to take over without volunteering much in the way of useful suggestions.

You do not have to fix the situation for your clients. They will do that for themselves if it is to be done. All they need from you is the space and collaboration to find their way to their personal vision of how things can be better, and then their capabilities will take them there.

Another Look at Resistance

As noted earlier, people are, to varying degrees, ambivalent about changing their situations. When a person does not readily accept ideas for change and proceed to implement them, we often label that person "resistant." Actually, we will do better to see this as a part of ambivalence, a normal phase through which one often passes on the way to change.

In some situations, this resistance becomes pronounced. If the client continues to resist, becomes more resistant, or actually drops out, it is time for the case manager to take a look at her- or himself. Generally, these situations have to do with how the case manager has responded rather than a personal defect in the client.

A case manager who is able to use reflective listening when talking to a client will find the client less likely to remain "resistant." For example, Maddie told her first case manager that she didn't want to stop dating Phillipe because he had a lot of money and bought her "nice things." This case manager responded with, "Oh for heaven's sake. He's abusive! He has hit you three times. That's what you came in here about. You want to *stay* in this relationship?" Maddie left the case manager irritated and concluding that the case manager "didn't have a clue." Later Maddie voiced this same ambivalence to another case manager who responded like this: "So in spite of the fact that he has hit you several times, you like the gifts he can buy for you." Maddie agreed. The case manager went on to ask: "Tell me what things would be like without this man in your life." Then Maddie began to talk about going back to school. The case manager practiced reflective listening. In Maddie's mind, as she left this second case manager, she felt some hope that she could get along without her boyfriend and that this case manager might be able to give her the support she needed to make the difficult break with him.

What we tend to call resistance can actually be seen one of two ways: as the person's unwillingness to change, or as a normal part of contemplating a move toward a change that may include unknowns and disruption. Depending on which way the case manager views resistance, the response can be angry, exasperated, and irritated, or it can reflect the client's very real concerns with acceptance. You want to be the case manager who uses reflection rather than exasperation.

Arguing

Some case managers, either because it is easier or because they were trained that way, use an argumentative style with clients on the assumption that arguing for a good change will force the client to change. Some people do hear such arguments and change, but for the most part arguing for change forces people to become defensive. What are they defending? The way they are, the reasons they haven't changed until now, the way the situation is.

Think about how you would react if someone said to you: "Look, school is hard. We all know that. You have homework, deadlines, tests, a tough schedule. We know all about that. But if you don't start to take this whole thing seriously and get your act together, you are going to fail. No excuses. We can come up with plenty of excuses. You don't need any more excuses. You better begin right now to get organized. Stop daydreaming about getting the degree and knuckle down now and do the work. Otherwise your life is on the fast track to nowhere!"

So, you think to yourself, "Is this person going to be quiet so I can talk? Anyway, I'm doing okay. How soon can I get out of this office? This guy hasn't a clue about what my life is like and isn't interested either." This isn't a very constructive, collaborative, or respectful relationship. This kind of case manager–client relationship is going nowhere.

Seeing the Client as Hopeless

Just because people argue against change does not mean they are dead set against it. Some case managers are tempted to give up at this point. They hear the client giving reasons the change can't happen or won't work, and they decide the client is right.

Maybe the client is right, but before you jump to that conclusion, it is important to shift the discussion to a point where the client is talking about what change would be like, how it might happen, and what things would look like if there were no obstacles and the client got there finally. People often come to us with no hope and little vision. They have lost faith in themselves and lost their hope for the future. The transfusion, if there is to be one, comes from the case manager who uses reflective listening and asks the right questions to help the client begin to envision change.

This is another way of steering around obstacles. Here is an example of how such an exchange might sound:

CLIENT: I can't see any way out of this mess.

WORKER: Right now it looks pretty hopeless to you.

CLIENT: Well, yes.

WORKER: Tell me a little bit about what brought you here.

CLIENT: My wife left, I don't know where she is, and I feel like I'll never get my marriage back together again.

WORKER: You'd like to get your marriage on track again?

CLIENT: Yeah.

WORKER: Tell me about your marriage.

CLIENT [*talks about a troubled relationship and his wife's complaints that he is rarely home and is not interested in the children*].

WORKER: When you talk about getting the marriage back on track, what would your marriage look like then?

CLIENT [*describes a better relationship, including his being more attentive*].

WORKER: I know things look bleak now, but let's take a minute and try to think of all the ways you might be able to bring this about. What ideas do you have for starters?

Some case managers might listen during an exchange like this—using good reflective listening and even asking good open questions—and conclude that the client is right and the marriage situation is hopeless. In this example, however, the case manager goes directly to the better vision (You'd like to get your marriage on track again.). Later she asks for information about what his on-track marriage might look like. This brings the client to a point where he can begin to envision change. Finally, the case manager suggests they look at options for change anyway.

These are just a few of the ways case managers begin to gently steer clients toward a positive vision of the future. When the case manager remains hopeful and encouraging, the client receives a transfusion of these positive attitudes from the case manager and begins to look in a new direction. When the case manager assumes that all is hopeless because that is what the client says, it is the case manager who has taken the transfusion, and it is not a very constructive or helpful transfer. Nor is it the reason the client sought the case manager's help—so that they could both feel equally bad about change. Case managers are responsible for maintaining a positive attitude and helping clients explore solutions to their situations in a hopeful way.

Summary

This chapter has looked at ways you can enhance the communication skills you have learned and make them more effective. We have emphasized respect, client autonomy, and collaboration with clients. We have moved away from adversarial relationships with people wherein we argue, cajole, and grow exasperated. All of this is in line with recent thinking about how people change and how some situations, formerly thought to be permanent, can be changed in a positive direction.

When a client fails to envision a better tomorrow, resists changing, drifts away, or gives up, it may be because the case manager or other person working with that client has not made it safe enough for the client to explore reluctance and ideas for making things better. Based on the information in the previous chapters and this one, you now have the skills to create a safe environment in which clients can overcome their reluctance and ambivalence, and envision and make changes in their lives.

Chapter 13

Putting It All Together

Introduction

You are now at the point where you can practice holding entire conversations with clients using all the skills you have learned. At first, this will seem awkward and mechanical to you. You will hesitate as you try to decide whether to use an active listening response or an I-message. You will feel that you are engaging in a dialogue that is halting and unsatisfactory. With practice, the skills become second nature. Your responses will be smooth and sound unrehearsed and genuine. The following exercises are designed to help you begin to put all the skills together in the same conversation.

◆ **Exercises: Putting It All Together**

Exercise I

Instructions: Follow the instructions for each question based on the communication skills you have learned in class.

1. You have been called to an elderly woman's home. The family is upset that she is refusing to leave the home for an evaluation at the hospital even though she can no longer walk, is incontinent, and cannot get to the kitchen to fix meals for herself. She lives alone. When you arrive, you find her daughter and son-in-law exasperated from their attempts to convince her to go to the hospital for a medical workup, as her doctor has recommended. You enter the room, and after introducing yourself and finding a place to sit down near her, you ask her an open question. Write your open question.

2. The woman tells you why she is not going to the hospital. "I don't want to," she says, "Why should I? I'm an old lady. I've lived a full life. I want to die right here. Harry [her husband] died down at the hospital. He thought he was coming home, and he never did. He didn't want to go down there, and we all made him go. We thought he would get well, come back home. He never did. I'm certainly not going through that." Write a word that describes the feeling you think the woman is expressing, and then write your empathic response.

FEELING:

EMPATHIC RESPONSE:

3. You are quite concerned about this woman being at home alone. As you sit there, you can see how extremely frail and weak she is. After a while, you express a very gentle I-message or concern that *you* feel regarding her being home alone. Write your comment here.

4. In response, the woman answers, "You know, I never said I wouldn't go anywhere! I just said I wouldn't go to that godforsaken hospital where Harry died." Write an opening sentence that shows you are beginning to collaborate on a solution that might work for her and still accomplish what is needed.

Exercise II

Instructions: Follow the instructions for each question based on the communication skills you have learned in class.

1. You are seeing a 40-year-old man for the first time. He has a diagnosis of schizophrenia. This is a chronic condition that started when he was 19 and went away to college. Today he has come in to see if you can help him with a better place

to live. He tells you he just wants to "live somewhere else, that's all." You sense that he is upset. You ask him an open question. Write your open question here.

2. In response, the man looks away, and then slowly begins to talk about the kids in the neighborhood. He says they make fun of him and try to stop him when he walks home at night. "I get sort of sick when I see them. The other night I stayed out in the alley most of the night. It just seems like they are out to get me. They throw bottles at me and call me 'psycho.' I don't know. I just stayed out so they wouldn't get me." He looks sad and embarrassed. Write a word that describes the feeling you think the man is expressing, and then write your empathic response.

   FEELING:

   EMPATHIC RESPONSE:

3. You are quite concerned about the stress of this situation for him, knowing stress can trigger a relapse. You are not clear what else he does during the day or what friends and family he might have for support. You ask him an open question about his activities. Write that question here.

4. The man tells you that he is enrolled in Goodwill during the day and that he has been taking the bus on his own to the center where he works in the retail shop. "When I have to take the bus, I stand on the corner, and they always see me. Or when I get home and get off the bus, they seem like they are waiting for me." Write a word that describes the feeling you think the man is expressing, and then write your empathic response.

   FEELING:

   EMPATHIC RESPONSE:

5. You still want to determine if this man has any supports other than Goodwill. Write the open question you will ask him.

6. In response, the man answers, "My family got funny on me years ago. I have a sister. She lives in Lemoyne, and she always has me come over at Christmas. She is the only one that bothers with me. The family always acts nice at first, but I can tell I get on their nerves. I don't stay real long." Write a word that describes the feeling you think the man is expressing, and then write your empathic response.

   FEELING:

   EMPATHIC RESPONSE:

7. The man continues, "But I have this friend from Goodwill—Paul. He told me I could come to his house if things get bad. He didn't want me to stay in the alley like I did." Write a response to the content of this statement.

8. The man goes on to say, "Yeah, Paul is a real good friend. The other day when I ran out of Mellaril, he lent me some of his until I got my prescription filled down at the county." You are concerned about his use of another patient's prescription. Write your I-message to express your concern here.

9. The man says, "Well Cindy, down at Paul's apartment building, she works for the county, and she got upset too, like you. She said Paul ran out of his stuff too soon to get a refill, and they had to see the doctor especially to get him more pills." Respond here to the content of his comment.

10. Now that you know what supports are in place, you need to know what he thinks about finding another place to live. Ask the man an open question to learn what ideas he has about finding another place, and to begin collaborating on a solution. Write the open question here.

11. The man answers by saying, "Well, I was thinking I could get into the program Paul is in. It's part of Goodwill. They told me I was doing good and didn't need to be in that apartment building, but I know a lot of the people there, and I could, well, feel better if I lived there—or down near there somewhere." He is referring to a personal care boarding home that is sponsored by Goodwill. Write a statement that indicates you want to collaborate with him on the issue of a new place to live.

Exercise III

Instructions: Follow the instructions for each question based on the communication skills you have learned in class.

1. Mrs. Sylvestri is worried about her son, Manuel. She tells you that he seems to have trouble concentrating in school and that the teachers have told her he is "a daydreamer." He is falling further and further behind, and she is wondering if her son is reacting to the recent death of his father in a construction accident. She says, "I don't know if you saw it on TV or not. He was working on that sewer project down in Carsonville, and the walls of the trench fell in on him. All his buddies were there, trying to dig him out. It was on the news." You respond with active listening. Write a word that describes the feeling you think the woman is expressing, and then write your empathic response.

    FEELING:

    EMPATHIC RESPONSE:

2. Mrs. Sylvestri seems grateful for your understanding and goes on to say that Manuel saw the newscast of the accident at a friend's house. "He was over there playing about the time the news came on," she said, "I hadn't gone to get him because I had so much to take care of, the hospital and then the funeral home and calling his brother to decide what we were going to do. And Manny saw it on the news. The neighbors didn't know, not yet." Ask an open question about her husband.

3. She tells you he was a good father and a good provider, that Manuel is their only son, and that they were unable to have other children. They came together from Puerto Rico 9 years ago and worked hard to buy a small house in Carsonville and serve the community. "Now he is gone, just when Manny is about a teenager, and..." Give an active listening response. Write a word that describes the feeling you think the woman is expressing, and then write your empathic response.

   FEELING:

   EMPATHIC RESPONSE:

4. Mrs. Sylvestri asks you if you can help with Manny. She tells you what a "good kid" he is and how much he helps around the house. "He has cousins, all his uncles and aunts, they live in Carsonville or around, so he has family, and me, but he won't pay attention in school. He hurts." Ask her an open question that will help you to know what she might have in mind for Manuel.

5. Mrs. Sylvestri responds with the fact that the school wants him tested for attention deficit disorder, but she does not think he is "mental or anything." Instead, she believes he is grieving and says, "I don't know what you do for a kid who just lost his father like Manny did. I don't know." Using an I-message, suggest the children's Arbor House that specializes in children and grief.

6. She looks interested. "Are there other kids, that many other kids who have problems like Manny? So sad to think. What do they do there?" You describe the group sessions and the activities they have for the children and the age range of children Arbor House accepts. Then you move toward collaborating with her on a way to engage in these services. Write your comments here.

Exercise IV

Instructions: Try this exercise as often as you need to in order to become more proficient in the communication skills. Find a partner with whom to practice the skills. Use a tape recorder and tape your conversations.

1. First, you be the worker and let your partner play the part of a person who is seeking help for a personal problem or condition. Play the tape back. Critique your efforts with your partner, looking at ways you might improve your responses.

2. Ask your partner at the end of the dialogue how your responses felt to him. Did he feel reassured, understood, supported? Did your partner feel genuine interest and concern on your part?

3. Next, reverse roles, letting your partner be the worker while you take the role of the client. Again, tape the conversation and go over the tape together, looking for ways to improve your partner's skills.

4. Give your partner feedback about how his responses felt to you.

5. Once you have made a good tape of you as the worker responding to the client, hand it in to your instructor or play it for the class. Be prepared to receive additional pointers for improvement. At this stage in your training, every word can be examined. Soon, however, you will begin to know exactly what to say.

Chapter 14

Documenting Initial Inquiries

Introduction

In many agencies, phone inquiries are logged on the computer and kept on file there. The New Referral or Inquiry form used in this text contains the kind of information the client would be asked for during an initial call to the agency, particularly if the person were asking for an appointment. Learning to gather this information properly is important to ensure that the person's situation is handled well from the beginning.

This first form is used to take information from people calling *on the phone* to obtain services. You are to ascertain what the problem is, in brief, and set up an intake appointment in which the caller will be seen in person for a more in-depth history and evaluation. Remember to use all the communication skills you have learned in previous chapters to make the client feel at ease while describing the problem. Asking for help is difficult, but it is less so if the phone worker is empathic and accepting.

PLEASE NOTE

You cannot accept a case and fill out this entire form on the word of another person. The other person can refer the client to your agency, but the client must call in order for the intake to be valid. Exceptions to this rule exist when (1) the client is incapable of calling due to a mental health emergency (other forms are used for this situation); (2) the client is a child (a parent or guardian can call for the child); (3) the client is a very infirm or frail older person (a family member or friend can call for that person); or (4) a person needs an interpreter to communicate.

Guidelines for Filling Out Forms

The following guidelines apply to filling out all forms:

1. Use black ink. Never use a pencil to fill out a form.
2. Do not use correction liquid on forms; it is not permissible.
3. Be sure to sign and date any form you complete or note you write.

Steps for Filling Out the New Referral or Inquiry Form

A typical form for phone inquiries is found in the Appendix. It is titled "New Referral or Inquiry." Use the following step-by-step process when filling out this form. Make a photocopy of the blank form in the Appendix at the back of this book, and fill it out by following these steps:

1. Place the client's name, sex, date of birth, and address at the top of the form.
2. Place a home phone number on the form, and the work number of the client if the client is working.
3. The person will either:
    a. be a minor and have a parent or guardian, in which case you circle or underline "parent" on the form and write in the name of the parent, or
    b. be an adult with a spouse, in which case you underline or circle "spouse" on the form and write in the name of the spouse, or
    c. be neither of these, in which case you write N/A in big letters on that line.
4. If the person is employed, place the name of the employer on that line. If the person is not employed, place N/A on that line.
5. If the person is in school, place the name of the school (complete with what kind of school—college, elementary school, high school) on that line. If the person is not in school, place N/A on that line.
6. The client will either be:
    a. a self-referral, meaning the person found out about your agency through the phone book or a friend and called in on his or her own. If that is the case, write "self" on that line. Most calls are self-referrals; or
    b. referred by a doctor or other professional. In that case, place that person's name on the line. You are asking the client, "Who referred you to our services?" Answers might be Dr. Graham Smith or Attorney William Burns.
7. Under the section marked "Chief Complaint," always tell why the person called *today*. Do not say the person called today because her husband is abusing her. The husband may be abusing her, but what made her go to the phone today?

Here are some reasons people might give for calling today:

◆ Today the person decided she cannot go on.
◆ This morning, his employer insisted he get help.

- She saw a medical doctor within the last 48 hours who told her she needs counseling.
- He just had a fight with his spouse and is afraid of what he might do.
- He just hit his child.
- She thinks she will hit her child and has called for help to stop herself.

In filling out the "Chief Complaint" section, capture why the person called on this date and not on some other day. Begin this section with "Client (or the person's name) called today because . . ."

Capturing the Highlights of the Chief Complaint

You have a small space and can use very few sentences to describe why the client called today and not some other day. In thinking about what the client has told you about why he or she called, choose the most important points. Here are some examples:

- John Haulik called today because his employer requested he seek help for drug problem (crack). In last 2 weeks, he has missed or been late to work every day. Sleeping on the job and cited for safety violations. Client sounded distressed and anxious to begin treatment.
- Jane Wilson called today after a serious fight with her husband involving physical abuse. Jane states husband has been verbally abusive in past, but not physically. Client is hospitalized and looking for alternative safe living arrangements upon discharge. Client sounds depressed, but cooperative.

Following are some guidelines to keep in mind for capturing the highlights.

Keep the reasons from being too complicated. Do not make these first cases psychiatric emergency situations that need either immediate attention or a commitment. In other words, in this first exercise, do not create clients who are hearing voices, are contemplating suicide, have made a suicide attempt, or are a danger to others.

Be very specific. Do not use general descriptions such as "her husband beats her" or "she lives with an alcoholic" or "he has been having a hard time at work." Tell when the last beating was, what the most recent problem with the alcoholic husband was, and what the most recent problem was for the client at work.

Keep the reason for the call brief. Do not include a lot of background information, as that will be acquired when you do the social history at the time of the evaluation. Give just enough background information to let the next worker know the context of the client's problem. For example:

- Client called today because she was severely beaten by her husband on Tuesday during an argument over dinner. Client was hospitalized and is seeking alternative shelter. There is a history of domestic violence, which the client feels has worsened in the last 9 months.
- Client called today because his employer warned client that without evidence of treatment for problems with alcohol, employment may be terminated or suspended. Client admits to drinking while on the job today. There is a pattern of binge drinking followed by missed work and problems with coworkers.

Evaluating the Client's Motivation and Mood

Complete your note with a single sentence that indicates how the client seemed to you. For example, you can mention how the client sounded. Did the client seem depressed, glad to have reached you, relieved to be getting help, guilty over what has happened? Did the person seem eager to engage in services, skeptical that you can help, cynical about complying with forced treatment, or cooperative?

Here are some examples of sentences that might summarize how the client seemed to the phone worker:

- Client expressed a desire to begin treatment immediately and seemed angry.
- Client seemed depressed by the circumstances but motivated to follow through with services.
- Client expressed skepticism that anyone could help him but seemed motivated to seek help.
- Client was tearful and seemed depressed during the interview.
- Client seemed agitated by these recent developments and somewhat unwilling to follow agency procedure.

Steps for Completing the New Referral or Inquiry Form

The following steps complete the process described in the previous section, which ended with Step 7.

8. Under "Previous Treatment," keep the notes brief—just note when, where (and with whom if you know that), and for what. Keep from being too wordy in this section. For example:
   Correct: Seen in June of 1989 for 6 months by Dr. Piper, Waldenham Clinic, for postpartum depression.
   Incorrect: Susan saw Dr. Piper at the Waldenham Clinic, 432 Muench Street. She started to see him in June of 1999 after her first son was born and continued to see him for 6 months. He was treating her for postpartum depression.
9. The intake is "taken by" you. *This is the first place your name is to appear on this form!* Put the date of the intake next to your name.
10. Under "Disposition," note the name of the person to whom you refer the new client for intake and the date of the intake appointment. In many settings, the person who handles the phone inquiries is not the same person who sees the clients when they come in for their first appointments. For training purposes, we will assume that you will be doing both the phone inquiry and the client intake, in which case you would write your own name, along with the date of the intake appointment, on that line.
11. Under "Verification Sent," write "Yes" and the date. The date you use here is the date you send out the verification form, usually the same day on which you take the phone inquiry.

Figure 14.1 shows a New Referral or Inquiry form that has been filled out correctly. Look at the form to see how the worker filled in each element.

FIGURE 14.1
Sample New Referral or Inquiry Form

Wildwood Case Management Unit
New Referral or Inquiry

Client _Karen Elaine Markley_   Sex _F_   DOB _4/9/72_

Address _1234 Pleasant St._

_____ _Anytown, PA_ _____   ZIP _01234_

Home telephone _555-555-5555_   Wk telephone _555-555-5555_

Parent or Spouse _John H. Markley_

Employer _Evansville Township_

School _NA_

Referred by _Dr. Walter E. Carmichael_

Chief complaint and/or description of problem

Client called today because she suffered an incapacitating anxiety attack at work. A coworker took her to Dr. Carmichael who referred client. She states that she suffered first attack 4 years ago following birth of son. These attacks are increasing in frequency, particularly at work. Client sounded distressed and was tearful at times. She seems eager to begin treatment.

Previous evaluation, services, or treatment _Was seen by Dr. Allen Peters, Winston Clinic, from 6/96 to 7/97 for general anxiety and agoraphobia_

Taken by _Marcia Andrews_   Date _9/13/09_

Disposition _Referred to Marcia Andrews for intake 9/21/09_

Verification sent _Yes (9/13/09)_

After a person has inquired about services from your agency, it is important to bring the person in for a more thorough history and evaluation of the problem if the person is seeking services. You will set up an appointment for the caller on the phone at the time of the call or soon after you hang up. The next step is to send a letter verifying or confirming this appointment.

Steps for Preparing the Verification of Appointment Form

The purpose of the verification letter is to confirm for clients the appointments that were made with them for an initial intake in the office. In this way, the agency hopes to cut down on the number of missed appointments and the number of hours reserved for clients that are not used by the client. (Blank copies of the forms referred to in this section can be found in the Appendix.)

Today many agencies have more clients than they can see easily. Long waiting lists are the result. An agency cannot afford to waste an hour on a client who does not come in for a scheduled appointment. Although it may give the individual worker a much-needed break and time to catch up on paperwork, it is an hour for which the agency will not be reimbursed because no services are given. For that reason, most agencies send out a verification letter to remind clients of the appointments that are reserved for them.

Following is a step-by-step procedure for filling out the Verification form. A blank Verification form can be found in the Appendix at the back of this book. Make a photocopy of that form and follow these steps to fill it out:

1. On the Verification form, be sure that the date you send it out is the same date you said you sent it out on your New Referral or Inquiry form.
2. Be sure to address the client by name.
3. Fill in the date, time, staff, and location of the interview. The date is the date you listed under "disposition" on the Inquiry form. You can decide on a time. The staff person will be you. The interview will take place at the Wildwood Center.
4. Sign your name. Your signature should line up precisely under "Sincerely" and over "Case Manager." Do not sign out to the right.

Figure 14.2 contains a sample Verification of Appointment form with all the information added. Look at the form to see how the worker addressed each element.

The next step in the process is when the person actually comes to the agency for a more thorough evaluation of his or her situation. This is sometimes called an intake appointment. In this chapter, we have practiced phone intakes; in Chapter 15, we will turn to the first appointment and examine how to prepare to meet the client for the first time.

FIGURE 14.2

Sample Verification of Appointment Form

Wildwood Case Management Unit

Verification of Appointment

Date *9/13/08*

Dear *Mrs. Markley:*

This letter is to inform or remind you that you have an appointment scheduled:

Date: _____*9/21/08*_____

Time: _____*2:30 p.m.*_____

Staff: _____*Marcia Andrews*_____

Location: _____*Wildwood Center*_____

Please contact me if you have any questions or if you need to reschedule.

Sincerely,

Marcia Andrews

Case manager

Summary

Taking an intake from a client on the phone requires two important skills. The first is skillful communication, something you have been working on previously. Using the skills you have acquired, you will be able to draw the client out and learn the reasons for the call. In addition, you will need good observation skills. Your task, during this first phone call, is to assess the needs of the person calling and assess the degree of distress the person is experiencing.

On your New Referral or Inquiry form, you will need to be able to document not only what the client shared with you on the phone but also the way the client sounded, how motivated the client seemed, whether the person's conversation with you seemed reasonable, and how distressed the client seemed to be. As you practice your communication skills, begin also to practice listening to the tone of voice and the underlying emotions the client may not express directly.

◆ **Exercise: Intake of a Middle-Aged Adult**

Instruction: Using the blank form in the Appendix titled New Referral or Inquiry, develop a client intake. You may use any problem that would ordinarily come to the attention of a social service agency. Your client should be an adult, at this point, calling on his or her own to seek services.

In developing your client and your client's problem, read the American Psychiatric Association's *Diagnostic and Statistical Manual of Mental Disorders* (APA, 1994) and look at books and articles on specific problems (such as domestic violence, alcoholism, divorce, depression). Look at the chapters in the companion textbook, *Fundamentals for Practice with High Risk Populations* (Summers, 2002), for information on how your client might be feeling and what issues or problems the client might be facing when he or she makes the first call to your agency.

If time permits, do several adult intakes with each client having a different reason for calling.

◆ **Exercise: Intake of a Child**

Instructions: Using the blank form in the Appendix titled New Referral or Inquiry, develop a client intake for a child, a person under 16 years of age. In this case, a parent or guardian would be calling on behalf of the child. A doctor, a school counselor, or a teacher may have referred the parents to you, or the parents may have felt they needed help and sought your services without a referral. Typical issues confronting children are problems with school, behavioral problems, and adjustment problems to events such as divorce or the death of a parent.

In developing your client and your client's problem, read the *DSM-IV* and look at books and articles on specific problems common to children. Look at chapters (particularly those on children's mental health and on mental retardation) in the companion textbook, *Fundamentals for Practice with High Risk Populations* (Summers, 2002), for information on how your client and your client's parents might be feeling and what issues or problems the client's parents might be facing when they make the first call to your agency.

◆ **Exercise: Intake of an Infirm, Older Person**

Instructions: Using the blank form in the Appendix titled New Referral or Inquiry, develop a client intake for an older person, a person over 80 years of age. In this case, a child or close friend or neighbor would be calling on behalf of the client. A doctor may have referred the caller to you, or the caller may have felt the client needed help and sought your services without a referral. Typical issues confronting frail, older adults are problems with self-care, independent living problems, untreated medical conditions, malnutrition, and depression and anxiety.

In developing your client and your client's problem, read the *DSM-IV* and look at books and articles on specific problems common to older people. Look at the chapter in the companion textbook, *Fundamentals for Practice with High Risk Populations* (Summers, 2002), for information on how your client and the concerned caller might be feeling and what issues or problems the caller might be facing when making the first call to your agency.

Chapter 15

The First Interview*

Introduction

You have spoken to the person by phone, and you have arranged for the person to come into the office for an interview. This is the first interview for the client. Even if this person was at one time a client of the agency, we will assume the case has been closed for some time.

The purpose of this interview is to establish the following basic information about the person:

- Strengths, including external support systems, talents, successes, capabilities, and positive attitudes and events the client defines as a success
- Weaknesses, including gaps in the external support system, lack of experience or information, negative attitudes, and events the client defines as failures
- Current problems that caused the client to seek help *now*
- Potential problems
- A sense of who the client is

Your Role

You have three tasks to accomplish in this first interview. First, listen and convey an accurate understanding of clients' perceptions about themselves and their problems. When you convey this understanding, it does not mean that you necessarily agree with them, but it does mean that you have heard them accurately. To do this well, you need

---

* This chapter is based on *Where to Start and What to Ask*, by Susan Lukas. Adapted with permission of W. W. Norton & Company, Inc. Copyright © 1993 by Susan Lukas.

to allow clients to proceed in their own words. As they talk to you about what led to their seeking help, you can reflect back their feelings and perceptions about their situation, responding to feelings and to content. In this way, you sort out with the client what is important.

Second, you formulate a professional understanding of what it is the client is experiencing and what this person will need while being served by your agency.

Finally, strive to establish rapport with clients so that they feel comfortable with you and with your agency. Some people, no matter how hard you try, will never warm to the interviewer, but most people respond positively to a worker who is warm, genuine, and empathetic.

The Client's Understanding

In most cases, clients have recognized the need for help; but in a few cases, clients may feel they do not need to be in your agency. The courts mandate that some clients seek help or face jail or the permanent removal of their children. In situations in which clients feel forced to come to your agency, you may encounter hostility. In either case, you must indicate that you have heard all of their concerns about being there. You can convey this through your ability to reflect back how clients are feeling about being in the agency.

Even when clients believe they need help, they may not be clear about what their problems are or how the agency can help them. They may be clear that the current situation is painful, but unclear about how to describe it. They may know things seem out of control, but be unable to describe the impact their situation is having on them emotionally. They may hope that there is help available without understanding what kinds of resources there are or how these resources could help them specifically.

Preparing for the First Interview

If you did not perform the telephone intake, you will want to look at the intake material that is available before the client arrives. As you do this, ask yourself what more you should know about the client's difficulties. What details need to be clarified? Where are there particular gaps in the information that need to be filled in?

If the client was in your agency before, read past records to fill out the picture of this person. Look at past medical difficulties, medications the client might be on, or medications that were prescribed previously while the person was in treatment.

As you begin to form a picture in your mind of this person, remember that the information you have was collected by others who saw this person under other circumstances. This may not be the whole picture, and it may not be an entirely accurate picture. Rely heavily, therefore, on your own insight and your own competence to form an accurate picture of the client.

Let's look at the specific case of a woman seen by various case managers, physicians, therapists, and psychologists, who conducted some tests. The woman had a problem with anger and had been asked to leave the home of several family members where she had been staying. At last she was residing in a group home. A psychologist was asked to do an evaluation for possible organicity (problems in the brain that would cause anger and loss of control). In reading the chart with the many records in it, the psychologist came across an early note by the case manager: "Client created a scene at the local Giant food store last week over the fact that another customer took the last head of lettuce as she was reaching for it. Crisis intervention was called. Client was taken to her home." About a year later, in another note, a therapist noted, "Client made several scenes in the past at the Giant where she shops. Apparently she gets upset over the fact that there is not more produce in the store. Management has called Crisis Intervention." Still later a new case manager wrote, "Client apparently creates violent scenes at the food stores when she feels there is not enough produce. Crisis was called on several occasions. Will advise client to stay away from food stores." Finally, several years later, a doctor prescribing medication noted, "Client was barred from shopping at any local food stores several years ago because of violent outbursts of rage over a lack of store items she meant to purchase. These outbursts resulted in contacts with Crisis Intervention and indicate a difficulty with anger control and poor communication skills."

Between the individual notes in the chart, there was no other reference to outbursts at the food store. It appeared, from looking at the chart carefully, that each person who mentioned the incident was summarizing the previous note and magnifying it in the process. Think how differently you would approach this client if the first note you read was the doctor's note as opposed to the original case manager's note.

In this example, you do not know if the client changed her story each time she met someone new or if the workers read the charts and records and misinterpreted the information. There are other reasons the notes you read may not be accurate. The person who wrote a note might have been hurried in her assessment. She might have felt hostility or prejudice toward the client for some reason. The note may have been made by someone who was inexperienced in interviewing. For all these reasons, you will have to rely on your own insight and competence in doing your assessment.

If you see inconsistencies in the previous history, make a note of them for further exploration.

Your Office

Most case managers have an office or place where they see clients. Sometimes case managers share an interview room. Look at your office or interview room. Be sure it is a place in which you would feel comfortable while confiding in another person. Is it warm and comfortable or utilitarian? Are there comfortable chairs? Is it free of harsh lighting? Are the walls attractive?

It is probably best not to have personal pictures sitting about because you cannot be sure how your clients will view these or what meaning they may find in them. A picture of a happy, smiling 3-year-old may be upsetting to a person whose children were just removed from the home or to someone who is struggling to find shelter for her own 3-year-old. It can create a barrier, and you are seeking to diminish barriers.

In your office, there needs to be a comfortable place for the client to sit facing you. You want her to be able to talk to you in a normal tone of voice, but you do not want her to feel crowded by your presence.

Meeting the Client

From the very beginning, you want clients to know that you respect them, that you wish to be helpful, and that you will be relating to them as a professional, and not as a social acquaintance. The interview begins with your first introduction.

1. Begin by going to the waiting room to meet your clients. Do not make them find their way through the halls to your office.
2. Introduce yourself as Ms., Mrs., or Mr. _____. Or say, "Hello, my name is Jim Pellam." Do not say, "Hi. I'm Jim" or "Hello, my name is Jim." You did not spend all those years in school to earn this degree in order to be simply "Jim."
3. Make a mental note of your first impressions. How do the clients respond to your greeting? What do they say first? How do they look?
4. How do the clients react to your office? Do they seem comfortable? Do they appear to feel awkward? Do they readily sit down or wait to be invited to do so?
5. If clients start talking, show interest in what they are saying. Often the first things the client tells you will hold the most significance.
6. If clients ask about your credentials, tell them about these matter of factly. It is part of informed consent for clients to know who is seeing them. There is no need for you to sound defensive. Do not go into personal details about yourself, however. If a client insists on knowing if you have ever had children or if you are old enough to know how to help her, point out respectfully that the purpose of her visit is to understand the issues and problems she is experiencing.
7. Describe the agency and explain its purpose to clients who are unclear about it. Some individuals come to a case management unit and expect to see a doctor or a psychologist. Give information about the types of professionals that staff your agency and what they do.
8. Make certain that you or someone else has described payment arrangements to the client.
9. Make sure that you or someone else has explained confidentiality and the limitations of confidentiality to the client. Be sure the client is given information on the Health Insurance Portability and Accountability Act (HIPAA). Clients need to know that their diagnosis may go to their insurance company. It is not necessary to go into every exception regarding confidentiality verbally, but let them know that under circumstances where they might be in an emergency, information may be shared.

Taking Notes

It is all right to take notes during your interview. For one thing, you are collecting very basic information, and you want to ensure that it is accurate. Let the client know that you are taking notes to make certain that you have accurate information.

During other contacts with the client, jot down significant phrases or information. You can reconstruct your contact in short notes after the client has gone.

Collecting the Information

Allow your clients to tell their story in their own way, using their own words and expressions. Help them to begin talking about why they are here by asking an open question such as "Tell me a little bit about why you are here today" or "Can you tell me something about what brought you here?" While the client is talking, remain emotionally neutral. Do not recoil in horror or gasp or squeal with delight. Do not tell the client how you would have felt under the circumstances. This is not about you. While the person answers your question, reflect back the content and feelings you hear.

If clients come from a different race, religion, or culture or have different values from yours, be aware of that without judging them. As we have seen, some case managers are tempted to judge clients using themselves as the standard. In other words, these case managers see themselves as the standard against which everything should be compared. By doing so, they miss the unique circumstances and characteristics that make the client a separate person. This diminishes the case manager's ability to be truly helpful.

Asking for More Clarification

During the interview, ask for clarification. Use open questions primarily ("Can you tell me a little bit more about your father?" or "Could you describe your relationship with her before you were divorced?"). It is all right to ask closed questions if you need further clarification ("Bill is your boss?" or "You lived there how many years?"). Avoid too many closed questions so that your interview does not take on the tone of a grilling.

Avoid "why" questions as much as possible. Even when you have taken special care to ask them respectfully, a person may experience them as prying. Sometimes a "why" question actually asks clients to give an understanding of what motivated their actions or the actions of others. You may be asking for a level of insight clients have not yet developed. In that case, they can only feel incompetent and uncomfortable.

Sometimes clients know why they behaved in a certain way or why something happened, but the reason is upsetting to them or they are having trouble recognizing and talking about it. A "why" question can make them think that you will probe for answers and push them to talk about things they are not ready to discuss.

Finally, clients may tell you a great deal more than they had intended to tell the first time. They may go home upset with themselves and embarrassed by the amount of self-revelation in which they engaged. It may be so uncomfortable to them that they do not return to continue with your services. In that case, it is possible that you have intruded into the client's personal information too quickly. As the person conducting the interview and, therefore, the person with the most power, you have an obligation to protect the client from this kind of intrusion. A good way to protect clients is not to go too far beyond what they appear comfortable talking about.

Intrusions and discomfort of this sort can be avoided if you recognize from the very beginning that *the facts and circumstances of the client's life and problem belong exclusively to the client*. Clients are under no obligation to tell you more than they feel comfortable revealing. This means that you focus on the information clients can give you freely without probing and without discussing feelings and motivations.

What Information to Collect

The most important piece of information is to understand why the client is here now as opposed to last week or last month. Some of this information may be on the phone Inquiry form, but your task in this first interview is to develop that information more completely. The reason the client has come to the agency now is often referred to as the "presenting problem."

In addition to the presenting problem, you want to understand the extent to which this problem has interfered with the client's ability to function socially, occupationally, and personally. Is this person able to work? Are the client's most important relationships feeling any strain? Is the person taking care of personal hygiene and other needs? You might ask questions like the following:

- ◆ "Can you tell me something about how things are going at work?"
- ◆ "Could you describe how things are at home?"
- ◆ "Can you give me some idea of how this has affected your daily routine?"

Individuals who are alone, or who perceive they are isolated, are at greater risk for stress and suicide than those who have a good support system in place. Does the client have a support system or seem to be all alone? To find out, you might ask such questions as these:

- ◆ "Tell me a little bit about your family."
- ◆ "Tell me something about your friends."
- ◆ "Can you describe what you do in your spare time?"

Client Expectations

No service or treatment plan is entirely useful unless the client has participated in developing the plan. During this first interview, ask clients what it is they would like from your agency. You might ask them questions such as these:

- "Can you describe how you think we might be able to help you?"
- "Tell me a little bit about the services you had in mind."
- "Can you share with me some of your ideas about services you would like from us?"

Often clients do not know what services are available or what services they need. Together explore what your agency has to offer, and describe various alternatives for clients to consider. By the end of this first interview, you and the client need to have developed a tentative plan for services.

Social Histories and Forms

In Chapter 16 we will look in more detail at how information is collected. Most agencies have a standard format that gives you the foundation for creating a social history. Many agencies have a form that covers the essential information you need to develop a treatment or service plan and to give ongoing support and service to a client.

Wrapping Up

Here are some tasks to complete toward the end of the interview.

1. Ask clients if they have any questions, and answer these questions thoughtfully. This is part of giving clients information they need to give informed consent.
2. Work with clients to define their problem in language they can understand. This is very important because it gives you and your clients a mutually clear definition of the presenting problem.
3. Talk to clients about what they expect as a result of coming to the agency. Ascertain what their goals are for themselves, the sort of service they are looking for, and the expected outcome. You might say, "Tell me something about where you would like to be a month (or 4 months, or whatever) from now."
4. Give clients some information about what will happen next. If the case is to be presented to a panel or treatment team, tell clients that, and tell them how long it will be before they will have information about a formulated plan for them. If they must go on a waiting list, tell them that, and give them information about where they can get services more quickly. Let them know what will happen after this first interview with you. Never let clients leave wondering what will happen next.
5. If clients are to return to you in a set amount of time to discuss the implementation of the plan that has been developed with them (or for some other reason), be sure to give them a card stating the time and the date of the next appointment. If someone must bring them to their next appointment (such as a parent, guardian, group home worker), be sure that person is aware of the time and date as well.

The Client Leaves

Rise at the end of the interview to indicate that the session is complete. It is always a good idea to walk the client back out to the waiting room.

Be aware of something social service workers refer to as the "door-knob syndrome" wherein a client begins to tell you something of great significance just as he is leaving. He may have saved this information for last deliberately because it is painful and he did not want to discuss it in depth. In any case, let clients who bring up significant issues at the very end know the session will not continue and that they should bring the subject up with the therapist or with you the next time they see you. Do this in a warm and interested manner. Do not appear to scold.

Do not allow clients to leave your office if you believe they are a danger to themselves or to others. If what they choose to bring up at the end indicates to you that this is a possibility, you will need to explore that further or see that someone else is available to do so.

After the client has left, do not go to the receptionist to place the client's name in the appointment book and discuss the client with the receptionist; and do not use the client's name where other clients in the waiting room can hear. Do not discuss your session in the hall or in another case manager's office where other clients can overhear your comments.

Summary

You now have a considerable amount of information about the person you have just interviewed. Your initial phone contact is documented on the New Referral or Inquiry form. The initial assessment will be documented according to a format used by your agency.

In Chapter 16, we turn to how these social histories and forms are handled by agencies. We look at two general ways agencies arrange initial information about their clients. One is the social history and the other is the assessment form. Our next step is to arrange the information we have assembled in at least one of these formats

Chapter 16

Social Histories and Assessment Forms

Introduction

Every agency has a different way of taking and recording relevant client information during an initial intake process. Some use assessment forms, which typically are specific to a particular high-risk population. Forms such as these can be found at the end of each chapter on a high-risk population in *Fundamentals for Practice with High Risk Populations* (Summers, 2002). In that textbook, you will find all the information you need to begin to develop a client from a population of interest to you. After using those forms, you will be able to move easily to other similar forms for specific populations. In this book, I provide a generic form to help you become accustomed to assessment forms.

    In some situations you will be asked to take a social history, either as a supplement to assessment forms used by your agency or in place of these forms. Just as the assessment forms in different agencies may differ, the format for a social history will vary from agency to agency. Nevertheless, having written social histories in the classroom, you will be able to more easily adapt to whatever format is used in your agency.

What Is a Social History?

A social history provides the following information:

1. A description and history of the presenting problem (the problem that brought the client into the agency)
2. Background information on the person's life
3. The worker's impressions and recommendations

Taken together, these three sections of the social history give a picture in summary form of where clients were when they came to the agency seeking assistance. In this way, the social history functions as the baseline or foundation for decisions about services and for measuring clients' progress. It also gives some direction to the problems that will need to be addressed. We will look at each of these sections individually, giving you examples of each one, so that you can see how the social history is developed.

Layout of the Social History

Social histories always use subheadings set out to the left of the text. This is done to help people find relevant information quickly without reading an entire text to find buried pieces of information. In most agencies the outline of subheadings is the same for all clients so that workers are familiar with the outline and know exactly where to look for information. Figure 16.1 is a typical outline for a social history.

It must be stressed that the outline shown in Figure 16.1 is one of any number of formats. For instance, if you worked in an agency that dealt with criminal offenders, the

FIGURE 16.1

Typical Outline For a Social History

Description and History of the Problem

Presenting Problem (includes the reason for referral, what the client is requesting, and how the client sees the problem)

Background Information About the Person's Life

Family of Origin
Birth and Childhood
Marriages and Significant Relationships
Current Living Arrangements
Education
Military Service
Employment History

Medical History
Legal History
Social and Recreational Interests
Religious Activities
Client Successes, Strengths, and Resources

Impressions and Recommendations

section on Legal History might be called Criminal Justice Background, and that section might be closer to the top of the outline. If you worked in an agency that served the needs of victims of domestic violence, the agency might place the section on Marriages and Significant Relationships right after the presenting problem to augment the information on the presenting problem. If you were working with children, you might include a section on School Adjustment and drop the section on Education. In an organization devoted to helping people with their addictions, you would probably have several sections related to the course of the addiction and attempts to overcome the addiction in the past. Both Criminal Justice History and Medical History would become more prominent in that outline.

In the chart or record, a social history may appear on different-colored paper so it is easily identifiable in the folder. The history will have identifying information on each page so it is not separated from the record in which it belongs.

In the text that follows, we look at each section of the typical social history more closely. Examples are provided to demonstrate how to write these summaries.

How to Ask What You Need to Know

If you follow the outline in Figure 16.1, you will have assembled a considerable amount of personal information. Clients who are giving a social history probably aren't very familiar with you or the agency, and talking openly about each of these aspects of their life may be difficult. For that reason, use plenty of open questions.

Certainly you will not use all open questions. Asking, for example, how many brothers and sisters a person has is a closed, but useful question. You might, however, follow that with an open question, "Tell me a little bit about them." In another example, you might ask the closed question, "Were you ever in the military?" followed by, "What were the dates of your military service?" Then you could follow up with an open question such as, "Can you describe your military service?"

Open questions soften the interview, making it less prying so that clients can choose the significant details to reveal without feeling grilled. Asked with respect and a genuine interest in the clients, the questions at these initial interviews can be helpful to people in sorting out for the first time the factors in their lives that are relevant and significant.

In each section that follows, open questions are given that you might use to solicit information in that section. These are only examples; you should become proficient in asking open questions on your own.

1. Description and History of the Presenting Problem

The first section is the Description and History of the Presenting Problem. In a brief summary, the background to the presenting problem is documented. This is done in no more than two or three paragraphs. Usually only one paragraph of summary is needed.

Agencies may differ in what they call this section: Background Information, Presenting Problem, or History of Presenting Problem. Some break this section into two parts: Presenting Problem and Background to Presenting Problem. For our purposes, we will call the first section Presenting Problem and will include both the problem and the background to that problem in this section.

Following are two examples of a Presenting Problem section in a social history. The first is written about Kate, a 47-year-old woman who contacted the agency requesting help for a long-standing depression. The second example is written about Carlos, a 38-year-old Mexican man who recently entered the country and is having problems adjusting to the new culture.

Presenting Problem

Kate Kate is a 47-year-old married woman with no children who called requesting help for a depression she states has lasted almost 2 years. Kate describes the depression as beginning after a serious episode with the flu and the death of her mother approximately 2 years ago. At the time her mother was ill, Kate did not follow doctor's recommendations that she take off work and stay home. She was very involved in caring for her mother, who subsequently died. Kate states she was not aware of being depressed until after the funeral, but grew depressed during the 7-month period in which she and her husband cleaned out her mother's house and settled her mother's affairs. She describes this work as "heart wrenching" and involving several legal difficulties. Currently Kate describes her depression as characterized by hypersomnia, an inability to go to work several days a month, and a loss of interest in social activities and friends. She states she is here in part because her husband insisted she get help.

Carlos Carlos, a 38-year-old male Mexican citizen, contacted the agency at the suggestion of his boss, Ronaldo Rodriquez. Carlos states he came to the United States from Mexico because his only family is living here. His brother and parents came to this country in 1982. His brother received a good education, went on to medical school, and currently practices medicine in Maryland. Carlos was left behind with an aunt when the family emigrated "because I was hard to handle." Last year the aunt died and Carlos came to the United States to join his family, "who are all I have." Carlos has been here for 8 months and is not sure if he wants to stay or return to Mexico. He describes feeling "out of place" in American culture, particularly compared to his brother and his brother's lifestyle. He states he has no commitment to Mexico but believes he would be more comfortable in familiar surroundings. In addition, he states his parents are "putting pressure on me" to remain in this country and get a better job. He describes them as critical of the few friends he has made and his lax attendance at church.

In each of these examples, we see the information the worker assembled as being most relevant to the immediate difficulty. We have a picture now of why each of these people called the agency and what might have precipitated the request for help.

Questions you might use include:

- "Can you tell me a little bit about what happened?"
- "Can you describe this problem a little for me?"

- "Could you give me some idea of what's been going on lately?"
- "Can you tell me a little bit about what brought you here today?"

Client's Appraisal

Always ask the clients what it is they are seeking. A client new to the system may not know exactly what services are available or have only a partial understanding of what a service actually is or can accomplish. When you ask for the client's expectations, you may have to describe and explain what is available and how the service works, not only at your agency but also in other places in the community if these are relevant.

Ask clients for their assessment of the problem. Valuable information may be found in listening to how clients view what is going on in their lives.

Questions you might use include:

- "Tell me a little bit about what you see as the main problem."
- "Could you tell me something about what you think is important here?"
- "Could you give me some thoughts on how you see the problem?"
- "Do you have any thoughts about the service you would like to have from us?"
- "Give me some ideas you have for how you feel we could best help."

2. Background Information About the Person's Life

As noted earlier, this part of the social history has a number of sections on various aspects of the client's personal history. We will look at each of these.

Family of Origin

Here you document the relevant information about the family of origin, the family into which the person was born. Information on the parents, their occupation, siblings, outstanding characteristics, or information on the family would be placed here.

Questions you might use include:

- "Can you tell me something about your brother?"
- "Could you describe your parents for me?"
- "Tell me a little about what your family was like."
- "Can you describe what your home was like?"

Birth and Childhood

In this section, you want to note if the pregnancy and birth of the client were in any way complicated. Ask about important features of the person's childhood and what the client remembers. You want to elicit comments from the client that give a flavor of the client's perceptions during this period of life. Was it happy or fraught with conflict? As a child, did the client feel appreciated or ignored? Was the client asked to shoulder very adult burdens or allowed to remain a child?

Questions you might use include:

- "Can you tell me something about your childhood?"
- "Tell me a little bit about what growing up was like."

Marriages and Significant Relationships

In this section, you will document the marriages of the client. Be sure to include here all significant relationships, whether the couple actually went through a marriage ceremony or not. If the client lived for several months or years with someone, note that here. Some clients will have more than one marriage or relationship. A sentence or two on each is important, such as when it took place, how long it lasted, and why the marriage or relationship ended. Information about the current relationship of the client to an ex-spouse is also relevant. In addition, always mention children, their ages, whether they reside with their parents, and where they are now. If the children are no longer in the home, document the degree of contact the parents and children have.

Questions you might use include:

- "Tell me a little bit more about her [him]."
- "Can you describe something about what that marriage [relationship] was like for you?"

Current Living Arrangements

In this section, give a brief description of the home, how the client feels about the home, and who lives there.

Questions you might use include:

- "Tell me a little bit about your home."
- "Can you describe your life when you are home?"

Education

Document here the person's highest level of education. Note, too, any difficulties or successes the client experienced while in school.

Questions you might use include:

- "Can you tell me more about school?"
- "Can you explain a little bit about your problems in school?"
- "Tell me a little bit about college."

Military Service

If the client served in the military, give the details of that service here in a summary. Always mention the type of discharge from the military and the status as a veteran. If the client was never in the military, simply state "No military service."

Questions you might use include:

- "Can you tell me about your military service?"
- "Could you describe a few of the things you did in the service?"

Employment History

Here you will document the type of employment the client has held. Note breaks in employment and give the reasons for the period of unemployment. Also indicate how the client views the work she has done. If the person never held a job, write "No employment history."

Questions you might use include:

- "Tell me a little bit about working there."
- "Can you give me some examples of the work you did?"

Medical History

Medical history will be extremely important to medical personnel who may be called to assess and give service to your client. A psychiatrist or a nurse may spot a possible underlying medical problem based on the information you assemble in this section. Ask about childhood illnesses and any other illnesses, allergies, or surgeries.

Questions you might use include:

- "Tell me a little bit about your health."
- "Could you describe this surgery a bit more for me?"
- "Can you tell me a little bit about the polio?"
- "Can you describe those allergies?"

Legal History

In many cases clients will have no legal history. Write "No legal history" if this is the case. However, involvement in a lawsuit or criminal case, as either the defendant or plaintiff, is usually an important source of stress. Petty criminal activity that is current gives insight into how clients view authority and their place in society. Previous criminal activity may show how much some clients have been able to turn their lives around or may indicate an unfortunate pattern.

Questions you might use include:

- "Can you explain a little about the lawsuit?"
- "Can you tell me about those early encounters with the law?"
- "Could you tell me a little bit about what brought you into contact with law enforcement?"

Social and Recreational Interests

Because we are always interested in the strengths of our clients, we want to note what it is that interests them and the social and recreational activities in which they participate.

If a client has no activities to report, be sure to note this as well. It gives important clues to the client's social involvement or withdrawal. Ask if this lack of social involvement has always been present or whether it is more recent in the client's life. Recent lack of interest in activities that used to be important can be a sign of depression. Note what interests the client most and what activities the client pursues.

Questions you might use include:

- "Tell me a little bit about what you do in your spare time."
- "Fill me in on what you do for fun."
- "Can you tell me a little bit about what you like to do most?"

Religious Activities

Some clients are very involved in their church, synagogue, or mosque. Others are not so involved but hold firm spiritual beliefs that they find very sustaining. Still others have neither religious involvement nor any interest in spiritual matters. Ask clients about their religious affiliation and activity or involvement. For clients who do not have anything to report, explore with them any spiritual beliefs they might have that give them strength and comfort. This sort of strength and comfort is often enormously helpful to people as they recover or cope with illness and difficult problems. This is a sensitive area, however, so move on if you feel your clients are reluctant to discuss their beliefs. For some clients, this line of questioning may be construed as your attempt to push a specific religion. Be sure to note, matter of factly, a client's discomfort with this topic.

Questions you might use include:

- "Could you tell me about your synagogue?"
- "Could you describe some of the beliefs you feel are most helpful to you?"

Client Successes, Strengths, and Resources

This is a section you may not find on most social history outlines. As much as we want to see clients as whole people, several factors—agencies, their policies, the pressure of time—often prevent us from exploring anything other than problems with clients. This focus on the negative aspects of people's lives often causes workers to create a skewed picture of the people they want to help and to register barely disguised surprise over the successes clients have had that come out during their social histories.

Asking clients what they are most proud of, or what things they consider accomplishments, makes it clear that you expect a client to be a whole person, not a collection of problems. It is good practice for you too, as you will get into the habit of asking about and documenting the positive aspects along with the difficulties.

Questions you might use include:

- "Tell me a little bit about the things that make you proud."
- "Can you tell a little about the things you consider successes for you?"

In addition, note here the strengths and resources your client brings to the situation. Personal skills, financial assets, and social supports are all important to note in this section.

3. Impressions and Recommendations

This last section in the social history contains your own impressions and recommendations. Much of the information included here about your client is referred to as a mental status exam.

First give a brief one- or two-sentence summary of what you have already written. Include the way the client appeared during the interview, and any problems you see with memory or reality, anxiety or depression.

Then, give your recommendations for services that might be considered when creating the treatment or service plan for the client noting the client's input into these recommendations. Further details on writing impressions and recommendations are found on p. 264.

Capturing the Details

Sometimes when people are taking social histories for the first time, they are inclined to write the barest number of details. They might write something like this: "Alice worked at Kmart for 4 years." In addition, it would be useful to know when she worked at Kmart, what she did there, and why she is no longer there. Figure 16.2 provides some other examples.

Your history should be a concise summary of the main points of a person's life, but too much brevity can leave a number of unanswered questions that, if answered, would shed considerable light on the client's life and problems now. Figure 16.3 shows a completed

FIGURE 16.2

Capturing the Details

Fair	Much Better
Madelaine's health is good. She states she had one surgery in 1998, but since then she has been fine.	Madelaine's health is currently good. She had an appendectomy in 1998, but since that time she has been fine.
Marie is the mother of two children.	Marie is the mother of two teenage children. Oliver, age 12, lives at home, and Michael, age 17, is currently in a boot camp in Mount Allen. She states she and Oliver get along well and that he is doing well in school. She sees Michael every other weekend and is hopeful that the boot camp experience will help him in the long run.

(continued)

FIGURE 16.2 *(continued)*

Bill is currently active socially.	Bill states he has a number of friends and sings in his church choir. Last summer he joined a local baseball team and intends to this summer as well. He likes sports and goes to games with friends.
Carl describes his childhood home as happy, but today does not know where two of his siblings are.	Carl describes his childhood as happy. He talks about a close relationship with his parents before their death and a number of activities, such as scouting and wrestling, that he participated in with his family's support. Carl has two sisters whose whereabouts are unknown. He states that at the time of his parents' death they were already married and living in other states. He went to live with the family of a friend to finish high school and then went into the Army. During that time they lost touch with each other.

social history on Kate, the 47-year-old woman described earlier who contacted the agency for help with a long-standing depression. Examine the figure carefully so that you can see how a completed history is constructed.

Who Took the Social History

Generally agencies have you sign your social histories after a phrase such as "taken by," "submitted by," "prepared by," or "filed by." This goes at the end, and if you have credentials such as BSW or MSW, these follow your signature. However, in the example shown in Figure 16.3, the name of the worker who took the history is typed in at the top of the history so that anyone in the agency can quickly see who did this history. It is not appropriate for you to place your name anywhere but in the designated places.

Social Histories in Other Settings

Limited Time for Intake

As a case manager having ongoing contact with your client, it may be possible to assemble an entire social history like the one discussed in this chapter. Certainly developing this complete picture of the client at the time of intake is best practice.

FIGURE 16.3

Example of a Completed Social History

NAME Kathryn (Kate) Carter   Agency # 04587
SOCIAL HISTORY   Date: *7/10/2009*

Prepared by: Winston Cramer

Presenting Problem

Kate is a 47-year-old woman who called requesting help for a depression she states has lasted almost 2 years. Kate describes the depression as beginning after a serious episode with the flu and the death of her mother approximately 2 years ago.

At the time her mother was ill, Kate did not follow doctor's recommendations that she take off work and stay home. She was very involved in caring for her mother, who subsequently died. Kate states she was not aware of being depressed until after the funeral, but grew depressed during the 7-month period she and her husband cleaned out her mother's house and settled her mother's affairs. She describes this work as "heart wrenching" and involving several legal difficulties.

Currently Kate describes her depression as characterized by hypersomnia, an inability to go to work several days a month, and a loss of interest in social activities and friends. She states she is here in part because her husband insisted she get help.

Client believes she needs medication "to jolt me out of this." She blames herself for letting it go so long but says she felt it would lift on its own. She also states she didn't want to disturb her husband with the problem. She is asking for a session with a "doctor" and a prescription. She seems uncertain that she needs therapy, stating "I don't think there is anything wrong in my life, really."

Family of Origin

The client's father died when she was 6 years old, and Kate describes feeling responsible for her mother most of her life. She describes her childhood as a happy one. A number of aunts and uncles took an interest in her, and she grew up with a number of cousins close by. She described happy family gatherings for holidays.

She depicts her mother as living off the Social Security that came after her father died and unable to sustain a consistent work history. She states her mother sought her advice often, and the client feels she made many of the important decisions for the family. At present only one aunt remains and is in a nursing home, and client's cousins have moved out of the state. Client has some contact with them at Christmas.

Birth and Childhood

Pregnancy and birth were uneventful. In addition to what is noted above, the client and her mother never had enough money. "That's why I think my aunts and uncles took an interest in me." She spent weeks away from home in the summer at the homes of her cousins and often went to camp with them. Her mother would come for family picnics and was always warmly received.

(continued)

FIGURE 16.3 *(continued)*

Marriages and Significant Relationships

Kate has been married to her husband for 25 years. They have one daughter who is 20 years old and currently a student at the University of Minnesota. She is studying engineering. Kate remembers the pregnancy as easy, but she suffered severe and incapacitating depression immediately following. She was unable to return to work at the end of her maternity leave, thus losing her job.

She describes her husband as "steady" and reports that he is an accountant with a local accounting firm. Kate wanted more children, but he discouraged her, fearing she would again suffer postpartum depression. As a couple they are fond of going to symphony concerts and plays. Her husband is a model railroader, and Kate helps with the activities of the club from time to time.

Her daughter is "quiet like her father." She did very well in school and got a scholarship to the university. Kate worries about her in that she has had few friends and no boyfriends. She is concerned that she "may be prone to depression the way I am."

Current Living Arrangements

Kate and her husband live in a three-bedroom home on a half-acre in Meadowview. The couple has been married 25 years. Except when their daughter is home from college, the couple lives alone. Kate has a cat that she is very fond of. She describes her home as "in need of work" and says that she would like to do more to fix it up but is not able to find the energy. The couple has lived in this house since they were married.

Education

Kate has an associate's degree in early childhood education. She recalls that she did well in school and it was suggested she go on in college and become a teacher, but her mother discouraged her due to the financial situation of the family. She has rarely used this education. Recently Kate started taking courses at the local college to improve her computer skills but is not taking any this current semester.

Military Service

There was no military service.

Employment History

Right after Kate got her degree, she worked for 3 years in a day-care center, but she was attracted to a job as an office manager in a small insurance firm. She has done office management for the last 27 years except for a time when she was off for a prolonged postpartum depression. This occurred at the time of the birth of her only child, a daughter. Following this episode she obtained an excellent position in a large law firm and has, until now, moved up steadily with promotions and pay raises.

Medical History

Aside from the postpartum depression and the bad flu she suffered 2 years ago, Kate reports her health is good. She had few childhood illnesses and has a medical check-up about every 3 years. She denies using drugs, and states that she never smoked and that she will have a glass of wine once or twice a year when she and

(continued)

FIGURE 16.3 *(continued)*

her husband go out to dinner. Recently, along with the depression, she has noticed that she has more headaches. She has not seen a doctor about these.

Legal History

There is no legal history to report.

Social and Recreational Interests

Kate is very interested in sewing and has made all the curtains and draperies for her home. "I would make my own clothes, but I haven't the time with working." She is also an avid reader of mystery novels and does some "modest gardening" on the weekends. She talked at length about her cat and the pleasure she gets from being with her pet. Since her depression, she notices a gradual withdrawal from activities she used to enjoy.

Religious Activities

Kate states she is a Methodist and she and her husband regularly attend the church just 6 blocks from their home. She used to sing in the choir but dropped out after her mother died and has not been able to "find the strength to add that to my list of things to do." She and her husband used to be active in Sunday school, but she doesn't want to go anymore, and he has dropped out too.

Client Successes, Strengths, and Resources

Client was unclear what she could list as successes. She denies that raising her daughter was an accomplishment or that helping her mother to the extent she did was important. "I was just doing what anybody would have done." She smiled and shook her head, unable to think of anything she would list as a success.

Client feels she can be open with her best friend, Sue. She reports no financial problems or marital problems.

Impressions and Recommendations

This is a 47-year-old married woman, mother of one adult daughter, who presented with depression that began 2 years ago following the death of her mother. She is a competent, but modest, person who is coherent and oriented × 3. Her appearance was very neat, and she sat with her hands folded in her lap and on the edge of the chair. Her affect was flat, but she seemed concerned that she give accurate and useful information to the worker.

She reports a loss of interest in activities that formerly gave her pleasure. This and hypersomnia have increased recently, causing her to seek help. Husband supports this. During the interview client had difficulty discussing herself and her accomplishments. She tends to minimize her successes and focus on things she could have done better.

She is requesting medication and, after a discussion with CM, agreed to three sessions of counseling and an appointment for a psychiatric evaluation. Recommend medication and psychiatric evaluation with Dr. Crumlich and three initial sessions with Bay View Counseling Services.

Today, however, many agencies do not have the opportunity to spend the time it takes to assemble such a history. Often the client is in and out of service, sometimes in a matter of days, at the direction of the funding source. Many managed care organizations and insurance companies have severely limited the amount of service a client may receive. This is particularly true for adult services in areas such as mental health or drug and alcohol agencies.

Brief Intakes

In some agencies, the emphasis during intake is on the presenting problem, the background of that problem, and your impressions and recommendations. In all cases, you still would be expected to discuss the services you provide with the client and to seek the client's input; and you would be expected to document this discussion. Unfortunately, you may not have the time to do this thoroughly or to note many of the other aspects of the client's life in the history. This happens when clients are given only a few days of service by their insurance company or other funding source.

When the client will not be with you very long, it is important to focus on the most immediate problem. Therefore, carefully document that problem, and talk about the most important points in the background to that problem. For example, when Harry came for services, he was recovering from a stroke in which he lost the use of his left hand and foot. The intake focused on the level at which Harry functioned before the stroke, the stroke itself, and the goals Harry wanted to pursue in recovering from the stroke. His acrimonious relationship with his brother in another state was not covered in detail, although the worker noted it in the intake material and, in her assessment, indicated that this relationship may have contributed to the recent stroke due to the client's anger and agitation over things that had been said in the week before the stroke. Left out of the history were extensive details about previous health problems unrelated to the present stroke, social interests, client accomplishments, military and legal histories, and details about his childhood.

In the current environment, brief intakes may be required more than we would like because of the limited time we have with a client. When the intake must be brief, the goal is to put sufficient focus on the immediate problem and the background to the problem to provide treatment for the client without delay.

Writing Brief Social Histories

A brief social history has three parts:

1. Presenting problem
2. Background
3. Impressions and recommendations

Presenting Problem

In the presenting problem section, describe why the person came into your agency. What precipitated his admission? Why is he here? Here is an example explaining Fred's presenting problem.

> Fred is a 26-year-old unmarried male who returned Sunday evening from a 2-week trip to the Philippines and Japan. On admission he was accompanied by his mother and was complaining of hearing voices, some confusion, and a lack of coordination. He states he had these same feeling briefly in September, but they cleared within several days. During that episode, he describes rigidly maintaining his routines as a means of dealing with these symptoms. Client further reports feeling as if he is standing outside himself watching his condition. He recognizes that he "is not right."

Background

In the background section, describe the client's background briefly along with any additional information regarding the presenting problem. Here is some background information on Fred.

> Fred was attending the wedding of a high school friend in Manila when he became ill. He was traveling with friends of his and the groom. He states that he left New York at 5:00 p.m. on a Sunday afternoon and arrived in Manila 19 hours later at 3:00 p.m. the same day. He reported that the celebration went on for several days, during which time he drank a considerable amount of alcohol and slept very little. Toward the end of the journey he began to experience confusion and could hear his friends voices, but not what the voices were saying. He came here immediately upon return home.
>
> Fred is employed as a computer analyst for ProWeber, where he has worked for the past 4 years. He currently shares his apartment with another male whom he describes as a childhood friend. According to client, they rarely see each other and travel in different social circles.
>
> Fred is the oldest of two boys. His parents separated while he was still in high school and were subsequently divorced. The divorce is described as amicable. Father lives in Alabama but returns for holidays and graduations. When asked about his father's side of the family, client replied, "that whole side of the family is crazy." He did not elaborate further. When discussing his mother's side of the family, he reports that his aunts and uncles are supportive and have always shown considerable interest in him and his other cousins.
>
> Fred graduated from high school and completed one year of college, but dropped out after he experienced intense stress. He claims his grades in both high school and college were "good."

Currently Fred is not dating anyone and socializes with a group of people with whom he went to high school. They have returned to the area after completing college. He expresses an interest in music and cars. He denies drug use, but says that he and his friends drink on the weekends.

Impressions and Recommendations

Impressions and recommendations come at the end of all social histories, regardless of the length or method in which the history was taken. After taking the social history use this section to express your impressions of the client. In addition, include your recommendations for what needs to happen to support the client in the present situation. Later, in Chaper 18 we will discuss how to write better impressions.

First Sentence

Begin with the same sentence you used to open your social history:

> Lisa is a 42-year-old married woman, the mother of two girls ages 10 and 12, who is complaining of depression and lack of energy.

You can use this comprehensive sentence to open the social history and again to open your impressions and recommendations.

Next Two or Three Sentences

The next sentences can further describe the client's situation:

> She states that her depression began 4 months ago and has persisted during a time of marital strain. She reports that she has trouble waking up, is unable to work at home or at her job effectively, and has neglected parenting responsibilities. She further states husband is threatening divorce and appears to be seeing another woman.

Next State Your Impressions

Give your impressions of the client in the following areas:

- Functioning
- Affect
- Vegetative functions
- Insight
- Motivation (for change or help)

Here are the case manager's impressions of Lisa:

> Client appears to have impaired occupational and social functioning accompanied by insomnia. Her affect is blunted, and at times she was tearful. She

has good insight about her current marital situation and the role it may play in her depression. In addition, she expresses a desire to obtain help and "change some things in my life."

You will have a much better idea about how to address the areas listed above after you have read Chapter 18.

End with Recommendations

End with a recommendation for what you believe should happen next. Do not use the word "I." Recommendations for Lisa are as follows:

> Client is requesting a therapist, with possible marital therapy in the future. Recommend psychiatric and medication evaluation of her depression and referral for six sessions of individual counseling, initially to address depression and marital issues.

When writing your recommendations, state the number of sessions, days of hospitalization or group therapy sessions, and the reason for this recommendation. For example, "six therapy sessions with Carlos Baldini to address anger management."

The points in the Impressions and Recommendations will have been elaborated upon in the social history itself, and the history will include details on each of the points not included in the Impressions and Recommendations. This section allows others to get a brief summary of the client's situation and what your impressions were at the time you took the intake. For a physician in a hurry, or for another case manager dealing with a crisis in this client's life, reading your impressions and recommendations can be an invaluable place to start.

Common Errors When Writing a Social History

- People don't "admit" things unless we are sticking them with a hot poker. They tell us things. "Adele admitted her address is 2346 Lincoln Way" sounds adversarial. Instead try, "Adele gave her address as 2346 Lincoln Way"
- Don't state things as a fact if they are things you don't know personally or have not observed personally. Use "according to the client" or "the client stated."
- Don't recommend something without saying what it is for. For example, "recommend psychiatric evaluation for depression" not "recommend psychiatric evaluation." Not "recommend 12 counseling sessions at Susquehanna Counseling," but "recommend 12 counseling sessions at Susquehanna Counseling to address loss of job and depression."
- Leaving gaps in the history. "She lives with 4 other people," but we haven't a clue who they are; or "they were married 10 years and divorced 3 and have a 20-year-old son." What is the explanation for that?

Using an Assessment Form

Because of the limited time in some agencies and the need to be sure that specific questions are covered in the initial interview, many agencies provide an intake or assessment form. The form contains certain information the funding source requires, and use of the form makes that information easily accessible. This assessment form may be very similar to but a bit longer than the phone Inquiry form you used when learning to do phone inquiries. These forms usually have names like Initial Assessment Form or Intake Evaluation Form. Other intake or assessment forms may be lengthy and contain numerous questions to determine the client's needs and capabilities.

Remember, when you are using a form, that it is important to stop and ask open questions as you go through the form. This increases rapport and reduces the sense on the client's part of being grilled by you. Long forms that spell out what questions need to be answered create the potential for you to begin to sound like an interrogator. You may be asking, "Name? Address? Phone number?" and then move on to more involved questions such as "When were you married? How many children? Names and ages of your children?" Where is the warmth and empathy in such questioning?

The assessment form does contain many of the questions you need to ask to create a more complete picture of the person. If clients seem unwilling to answer any of the questions, move on to others in a matter-of-fact way. Do not try to persuade clients that they should answer something they feel uncomfortable discussing. Chances are this information will readily come out as you establish rapport.

In addition, most forms have a place for interviewer comments. Be sure to take advantage of these spaces to elaborate on what the client has told you. This is where your notes give a more individualized picture of the client.

The assessment form is simply an outline of what is important. If your intention is to fill in all the blanks on the form and close the interview, you have not really conducted an adequate interview. Put these spaces to good use by filling them with relevant comments or summaries.

In one agency, a worker took the information required on the form. He also carefully inquired and documented additional information in the interviewer comment spaces. After one interview with a client, his supervisor came into his office and said, "We aren't here to make friends. That form should only take 15 or 20 minutes to complete." This supervisor is an example of a person who is poorly trained in establishing rapport and does not understand the importance of the first contact for the future success of the client.

It is expected that you will talk with the client, that you and the client will discuss the situation, and that the client will volunteer additional information. Most forms soliciting information from clients are focused on the clients' problems and deficits. In order to round out a complete picture of the client, you need to look for strengths. Take the time to do so—and remember, people only share such information when they feel comfortable with you. If you sound like a machine or rush through a series of questions, the client will not connect with you at all.

A blank Intake Assessment Form is provided in the Appendix at the end of this book. In addition, the companion book, *Fundamentals for Practice with High Risk Populations*

(Summers, 2002), provides assessment forms for eight high-risk populations. These forms are tailored to each specific population and contain detailed inquiries into common issues for each population. You may use those forms as you create and follow a client.

Taking Social Histories on a Computer

In some agencies case managers are asked to take the information from the clients and place it in electronic forms on a computer. This is seen as more efficient than taking a social history and then having it typed up. However, case managers have raised two valid concerns about this form of history-taking: First, can the case manager look at and engage the client if the case manager is typing on a computer? Second, does the electronic form have enough space to allow for the real details of the client's life and current problem? These are legitimate concerns, and I hope you will work for an agency that has addressed these possible obstacles. In some agencies a flat screen computer allows the case manager to engage the client, who sits facing the case manager at the side of the desk. In this way a large bulky computer is not obstructing eye contact and engaging the client.

The need to know the particulars of a client's situation is important because the goal is always individualized planning. If the electronic form you use does not allow for individualized descriptions of the client's problem, the plan is jeopardized. Even when using electronic forms, there should be plenty of room to give particular information about your client and to spell out in detail what the client sees as the major problem and wants to accomplish by coming to your agency.

The Next Step

Having completed the initial intake with the client, it is time to begin to put together a chart for the client. Charts or files are kept in a particular order. The order of the contents is precise, making it easier to find information (see Arrangement of the Client's Chart in the Appendix). Sometimes information is color-coded. For example, financial information may be on yellow paper and assessments on blue.

As for the social history in the chart, check these points before filing it:

1. Keep heading with the content. Many put the heading for something on the bottom of one page and the content on the following page. They should stay together.
2. Bold all your subheadings so they are easily found.
3. All social histories should be stapled together.
4. All social histories must be typed so they can be read easily and quickly.

It is important to maintain your charts in the order specified by your agency and to return them promptly to the records section of your agency or file them properly.

In addition, it is important to make sure that the charts are locked up safely when you leave for the night and that no one has access to them but those who should.

Finally, never remove a chart from the agency. The possibility that the information could be lost, stolen, or read by others is too grave.

Summary

When clients come in for their first interviews, we are there to collect important information that will illuminate the problems the clients are experiencing. Our task is to assess and document the details of clients' problems as well as the background to the problems. When clients must be served quickly, we are asked to focus more closely on the reasons the clients are seeking help and the histories of their immediate problems. In all cases, however, your information will serve at some point as the foundation for the development of services and treatment. Accurately understanding clients and assessing their moods and motivation gives others valuable information with which to work.

If you are asked to use a form to collect information, be sure to ask questions and discuss the clients' situations with them. Note the information you obtain on the form so that the form will better illustrate each particular client's needs and concerns.

Finally, it is important to keep in mind that you may be the first person from your agency whom the clients will meet. Their contact with you needs to be positive for them to move on and begin to heal and resolve old issues. As a representative of the agency, you are responsible for setting a tone that is warm, accepting, and safe so that clients can talk freely about what has brought them to seek help.

◆ Exercises: Practice with Social Histories

1. On a single sheet of paper, write a note on how Kate appears to you from the social history (see Figure 16.3 in this chapter). What are your impressions of her? What do you think she would be likely to do or not do? How likely is she to commit suicide following this visit? How readily can she stand up for herself? What strengths and supports does she have? What contradictions do you see in looking at her life?
2. Write up a social history of Carlos using the presenting problem paragraph provided in this chapter to begin the history. Invent other information as needed. This will give you practice in organizing information.
3. Take a social history from a friend or classmate. Be sure to explain that the person does not have to answer any question that is uncomfortable and that the person can make up information to fill in the gaps. The important thing is for you to practice taking a social history and then organizing the information in a useful format such as the one discussed in this chapter.

◆ Exercises: Assessment of a Middle-Aged Adult

Instructions: Using one of the blank assessment or evaluation forms found in the back of each chapter in the companion textbook, *Fundamentals for Practice with High Risk Populations* (Summers, 2002), develop further one of the clients for whom you did a phone intake. Choose the assessment form that fits your client's problems. Develop details about the client's life and gather information relevant to the reason the client called the agency based on information that you found in *Fundamentals for Practice with High Risk Populations*.

In developing your client further, piece together the circumstances you believe might be reasonable for a person who has this particular problem. Assign the client a socioeconomic situation, amount of schooling, and other particulars. Develop as well your client's problem by again consulting the current *DSM*, if relevant, and books and articles on this specific problem. Look at the chapter in the companion textbook, *Fundamentals for Practice with High Risk Populations*, related to the assessment form you chose to use for your client. Think about how your clients might be feeling as they come in for the first time and what issues or problems clients might be facing for which they are looking for help.

Or

Develop a believable social history on the client you have chosen, consulting the same material so that you are familiar with the issues and common problems faced by clients in this population.

Or

Use the generic assessment form in the Appendix at the back of this book, again consulting relevant material and the current *DSM*, to create a believable client.

◆ Exercises: Assessment of a Child

Instructions: Using the assessment form for children found in the back of Chapter 3 on children in the companion textbook, *Fundamentals for Practice with High Risk Populations* (Summers, 2002), develop further the child for whom you did a phone intake. Develop details about the child's life and gather information relevant to the reason the parent or guardian called the agency.

In developing your client further, piece together the circumstances you believe might be reasonable for a child who has this particular problem. Assign the child's family a socioeconomic situation, amount of schooling, and the other particulars. Develop as well the child's problem by again consulting the current *DSM*, if relevant, and books and articles on this specific problem. Look at the chapter on children in the companion textbook, *Fundamentals for Practice with High Risk Populations*, and think about how you, the parent (or guardian), and the child might be feeling as the child comes in for the first time and what issues or problems the family might be facing for which they are looking for help.

To complete this assignment, you may use the chapter on children's mental health (Chapter 3) or the chapter on mental retardation (Chapter 7) found in the companion textbook, *Fundamentals for Practice with High Risk Populations.*

Or

Develop a believable social history on a child, consulting the same material so that you are familiar with the issues and common problems faced by children and their families.

Or

Use the generic assessment form in the back of this book, again consulting relevant material and the current *DSM*, to create a believable client.

◆ Exercises: Assessment of an Infirm, Older Person

Instructions: Using the assessment form in the back of Chapter 8 on older people found in the companion textbook, *Fundamentals for Practice with High Risk Populations* (Summers, 2002), further develop your client who is an older person, a person over 80 years of age. In this case, a child or close friend or neighbor may be present when you do the assessment and, depending on the condition of the older person, may give you most of the information. In addition, you may need to go to the person's home to meet with the person because the client is too infirm to come to the office.

In developing your client further, piece together the circumstances you believe might be reasonable for an older person who has this particular problem. Assign a socioeconomic situation, amount of schooling, and the other particulars, such as marriages, number of children, former occupations, and interests. In developing your client's problem, read the current *DSM*, if relevant, and look at books and articles on the specific problem your older person appears to have. Look at the chapter in the companion textbook, *Fundamentals for Practice with High Risk Populations,* for information on how your client and the concerned caller might be feeling and what issues or problems the caller might be facing when meeting with you for the first time.

Or

Develop a believable social history on the client you have chosen, consulting the same material so that you are familiar with the issues and common problems faced by clients in this population.

Or

Use the generic assessment form in the Appendix at the back of this book, again consulting relevant material and the current *DSM*, to create a believable client.

◆ Exercise: Creating a File

Instructions: At this point, you need to create a file on the people you are seeing as clients. Create a separate file folder for each client you intend to follow throughout the remainder of the course. Place the client's name on the tab of the file folder—last name and then first name, so that the cases can be filed alphabetically by their last names. Place the New Referral or Inquiry form on top, followed by the verification letter you sent. Under that, place the long assessment form you used, clipping the pages of that form together.

Chapter 17

Using the DSM

Introduction

Many students wonder why they need to learn about the *Diagnostic and Statistical Manual of Mental Disorders* (*DSM*; APA, 2000) when it appears to be a tool used exclusively by mental health practitioners. Actually the *DSM* is a valuable tool you will use in many different settings. Although the majority of clients in the broad human service system do not have mental disorders, the *DSM* sometimes helps to define what the client is experiencing and what that person needs. For instance, clients who come to agencies as victims of abuse or assault often suffer from posttraumatic stress disorder. Workers in agencies dealing with the problems of growing older will encounter people who have dementia or symptoms that resulted from a stroke or other long-term, debilitating illness. Those who work with children in a variety of settings will encounter children who have learning difficulties. Familiarity with the language and process of the *DSM* enables you to participate in planning for the client more competently.

Is *DSM* Only a Mental Health Tool?

Today, with deinstitutionalization of the mentally ill, those with mental disorders come for services at many social service agencies, and more often than in the past, we see people who have more than one problem. You might be working at a shelter for victims of domestic violence and do an intake for a woman who also suffers from bipolar disorder. Clients no longer fit into neat boxes with no overlapping problems. For that reason, it is important to be familiar with this system.

The *DSM* is the language of insurance companies and other funding sources with regard to behavioral treatments such as drug and alcohol treatment or treatment for those with mental health problems or mental retardation. In addition, the *DSM* contains information about situations and problems that may not constitute a mental disorder but may be the focus of attention in a clinical setting. Many of these situations come to the attention of social service agencies not equipped to treat them. You will need good information to make sound referrals.

Your ability to understand the *DSM* and your acquaintance with the various classifications of mental disorders will enable you to be more conversant with others in the field and to recognize a mental disorder when you encounter one.

Cautions

Having spelled out why the *DSM* is important in human service practice, it is equally important to understand that most people who come for services in social service agencies are not suffering from a mental disorder. The *DSM* cannot be used to help you understand every client. If you try to give a psychiatric label to everyone you see, you will unnecessarily burden individuals who are well but are grappling with life events and disruptions.

In addition, the *DSM* comes from the medical model. That is, the model suggests that individuals are labeled with an illness and are then treated as sick. This is a view of the client that can cause you to lose sight of the fact that the client has strengths and successes. Although a diagnosis is useful to clinicians in providing treatment, to case managers it can have the subtle effect of diminishing the client as a whole person.

The agency where you work will have policies and guidelines about using the *DSM*. Many agencies do not rely on the manual at all. Agencies that do rely on the manual generally are required to give diagnoses in order to be reimbursed for services. When you must rely on the *DSM*, be very careful not to categorize people or to allow their diagnoses to color your complete understanding of them as individuals.

Who Makes the Diagnosis?

You are not studying the *DSM* to make final diagnoses. The actual diagnosis is made by a physician or a senior staff person with a PhD. Nevertheless, the *DSM* contains a language that is universally understood. Your experience with this language and with the mental disorders in the manual will facilitate your communication and reports to those responsible for giving the diagnoses. It could happen, on a rare occasion, that a harried emergency room physician with a waiting room filled with medical emergencies would turn to the emergency worker from a social service agency and ask that the worker give a provisional diagnosis to facilitate admission to the hospital (where the diagnosis will be reevaluated in less pressing circumstances). Further, it is becoming common practice for insurance companies and other payers to require a diagnosis at the completion of intake. Case managers responsible for intakes may need to give a diagnosis at the time of the intake so the agency can be reimbursed. Such diagnoses may be changed later by senior professionals, but case managers need to be familiar with the common diagnoses seen in their agencies.

It is important for you to keep in mind that additional clinical information is *always* needed to help round out the picture and make the best diagnosis and treatment plan. Much of that additional information in many settings will come from your histories and notes.

This chapter is based almost entirely on the work of Anthony L. LaBruzza (1994), whose book *Using DSM-IV: A Clinician's Guide to Psychiatric Diagnosis*, gives excellent background on how we arrived at the current *DSM* and how to use it effectively.*

Background Information

Until the 1600s, physicians used a patient's horoscope to diagnose mental disorders. Medieval physicians looked at the four humors to account for differences in human personality and temperament. The humor that predominated accounted for the patient's disposition—with blood accounting for a happy temperament; choler contributing to a fiery, competitive temperament; phlegm resulting in a cold, delicate disposition; and bile causing melancholy.

Psychiatry Attempts to Classify Mental Disorders

In colonial times, most individuals with mental illness were managed at home by their families. Many were abused and exploited or were confined to workhouses and almshouses in which varying theories about the reasons for their illnesses caused harsh treatment in most cases. Between 1800 and 1860, a number of people became concerned with placing those with mental illness in "asylums" in which a more humane approach and more respect for the patient would be the rule. Such treatment was referred to as "moral treatment" (LaBruzza, 1994). Dorothea Dix was active in this movement; and when her attempts to start a federal asylum program failed, she became instrumental in founding state hospitals in Pennsylvania and New Jersey, which bear her mark to this day.

Mental illness was little understood; and in the census of 1840, people were classified as either sane or "idiocy/insanity." The shift from the asylum to treatment, research, and education occurred in the late 1800s and early 1900s. At that time, research was beginning to provide a clearer picture of the anatomy of the brain, and the diagnostic system became more refined. By 1880 there were seven categories of mental disorder.

---

*Adapted with permission from *Using DSM-IV: A Clinician's Guide to Psychiatric Diagnosis* by Anthony L. LaBruzza in collaboration with José Méndez-Villarubia. Copyright © 1997, 1994 Jason Aronson, Inc., an imprint of Rowman & Littlefield Publishers, Inc.

Diagnosis continued to be the focus of research. Wilhelm Greisinger (1817–1868) in Germany looked at the mental disorders as diseases of the brain, an organic view. Another German, Emil Kraepelin (1855–1926), looked at syndromes or collections of symptoms and made statistical records of the symptoms patients exhibited, the course of their diseases, and the outcomes. His goal was to be able to accurately predict the outcome of a disorder for a patient based on certain combinations of symptoms. He used a behavioral and descriptive approach that made it easier for others to use his concepts.

Others also contributed their views of the brain and nervous system in creating a diagnostic classification system. Most influential in the United States was a Swiss-born psychiatrist, Adolph Meyer (1866–1950). Mental disorder, in his view, was a response to psychosocial stressors. This view was widely accepted because individuals drafted into the military during both world wars appeared to break down under the stress of combat. Had his view continued to be influential, mental illness would have been seen today as an adaptive response. Instead, mental disorders gradually came to be seen as discrete psychiatric diseases.

In the 1920s, the American Psychiatric Association (APA) decided to find a way to standardize the medical terminology psychiatrists used. A national conference in 1928 looked at how diseases were named. The classification system that emerged focused only on the most severe forms of mental disorders, those that would most likely cause the patient to be institutionalized. The classification became broader when World War II veterans returned with less severe disorders. In the 1940s, there were 10 types of psychoses, 9 neuroses, and 7 disorders related to behavior, intelligence, and character. In 1952, the APA published the first *Diagnostic and Statistical Manual*.

In an attempt to keep up with international changes in the way mental disorders were classified, in 1965 the APA revised the original manual and brought out the second edition, *DSM-II*. This manual seemed to return to the Kraepelian descriptive model for diagnosis. Those who did the revisions eliminated terms that implied a particular theory of etiology (or cause) for the disorder. This successfully did away with Meyer's idea of seeing mental disorders as a response to stress. Nevertheless, psychoanalytic terminology remained because psychoanalysis was still quite popular and influential among psychiatrists.

The 1950s, 1960s, and 1970s

At this point, the manual was still quite unreliable. Psychiatrists would give different diagnoses to the same symptoms, making replication of research impossible. Anthony LaBruzza (1994) stated, "[T]he possibility that two psychiatrists would agree on the same diagnosis in the 1950s and 1960s was nearly random." In the 1960s, psychiatry was out of favor with the public as famous court cases pitted psychiatrists against each other in what appeared to be a nebulous theoretical system, and movies like *One Flew Over the Cuckoo's Nest* introduced moviegoers to the possibility that institutions were punitive and that the staff in such places were not much healthier than the patients. This was a time when all authority was challenged, and a number of books challenged the authority of psychiatry, particularly Thomas Szasz's book, *The Myth of Mental Illness*. Many saw psychiatry and psychiatric diagnoses as stigmatizing and as wielding undue social control.

In addition, insurance companies began to cut back on the amount of psychiatric care for which they were willing to pay, in part because the diagnosis of mental illness was unreliable and there seemed to be no consensus on the best treatments. No studies had been conducted to determine which illness responded to which treatment.

Psychiatry Becomes More Medical

The third edition of the manual, *DSM-III*, came out in 1980. Every edition of the manual since *DSM-III* has been an expansion or refinement of that document. This manual relied on a more medical research–oriented model of disease, and it also relied more heavily on the Kraepelian use of descriptions. In addition, it was no longer slanted toward psychoanalytic descriptions or causes; in fact, causes were, for the most part, left to research to determine. Responding to the concerns voiced about psychiatry, the third edition of the manual contained 14 discrete and specific mental disorders with very explicit descriptions. These descriptions had operational criteria that allowed them to be measured statistically. All references to unconscious motives were removed, and the clinician based the diagnosis strictly on what could be seen.

The changes in the third edition of the manual could be summarized as follows:

1. There was every attempt to use clear English, and not mental health scientific jargon.
2. Disorders were labeled, and not people.
3. *Patient* was dropped in favor of words like *person* or *individual*.
4. The manual was tested for reliability for the first time by clinicians using it in the field.
5. A multiaxial system was adopted to give a fuller diagnostic picture of the person.
6. Decision trees were included to help the physician rule out similar disorders and narrow the diagnostic choice to one.
7. The words *disease* and *illness* were dropped in favor of the word *disorder*.
8. All the pet theories about causes of disorders were eliminated.
9. Each disorder had a working definition that contained operational criteria (criteria that could be observed and measured).

After publication of *DSM-III*, psychiatrists were far more likely to make the same diagnosis for the same set of symptoms. This enabled research to be done more effectively, particularly field trials of medications that treated specific psychiatric symptoms. In other words, it became more likely that practitioners would all agree on the diagnosis for certain clusters of symptoms, regardless of where they were practicing. If everyone was seeing the same thing when they looked at a cluster of symptoms, then it was possible to treat that cluster of symptoms in various ways to determine the best approach to alleviating the symptoms. Now clinicians could communicate reliably in a common language about diagnoses. This common language facilitated good research. Pharmaceutical companies supported this research for products they developed for these specific disorders.

How We Got to *DSM-IV* and *DSM-IV-TR*

With all the field testing that took place as a result of *DSM-III*, revisions were inevitable. Thus, in 1987, *DSM-III-R* (or revised) came out; this edition included 27 new categories and revisions to some older diagnoses. The number of categories went from 265 to 292. An appendix contained further categories requiring additional research.

The *DSM-III-R* made another important shift that will affect your work with the document. It moved from the *monothetic diagnosis* to the *polythetic diagnosis*. The old *DSMs* used the monothetic diagnosis. They gave a series of symptoms that constituted a disorder, and unless all of them were present you could not use the diagnosis. This meant that a diagnosis was only as useful as the least useful item in the series of symptoms. In a polythetic approach, the series of symptoms is given, and the patient must have several, but not all, of them. This improved the reliability of diagnoses.

Another important shift was the move to give a patient more than one diagnosis if the patient met the criteria for more than one. Previously the clinician had to choose the diagnosis that was most obvious or urgent. Other diagnoses that coexisted with the first diagnosis or were, perhaps, part of a larger clinical problem were not mentioned. This narrowed the clinical picture of the patient. Now a fuller clinical picture was possible. The *DSM-III-R* also lined up with the new version of *International Classification of Diseases (ICD-10)*, which made it easier for American clinicians to talk to clinicians internationally.

The *DSM-IV* contained as few changes as possible, and those changes were based on good research with empirical results. To establish the empirical basis for changes, the work committees (those committees working on various classifications) systematically reviewed the literature for different diagnostic categories, reanalyzed previous data, and conducted field trials to make certain the diagnoses were reliable in many different settings and in many different types of clinical work. The *DSM-IV* also did away with all sexist language.

The *DSM-IV-TR* (or text revision) refined the diagnostic categories still further. Other refinements and new *DSMs* can be expected as research and experience combine to increase our understanding of mental disorders.

Using the DSM

What You Will Find in the *DSM-IV-TR*

The following are some of the features you will find in the recent edition of the manual.

1. Every disorder has a name, numerical code, the criteria needed to give the diagnosis, the subtypes of the disorder, the specifiers, recording procedures, and examples that illustrate the disorder.

2. Associated features and associated disorders may include such items as clinical features that may be present but are not always seen in the disorder; disorders that precede, often co-occur, or generally follow the disorder in question; typical laboratory findings; physical signs and symptoms; and typical medical conditions.
3. The typical age at onset and any cultural and gender-related information.
4. The prevalence of the disorder, the incidence, and the risk.
5. A description of the typical clinical course of the disorder.
6. Any complications that might be applicable to the disorder.
7. Typical predisposing factors discovered through research.
8. Family patterns if there are genetic or suspected genetic components to the disease.
9. Differential diagnoses or disorders that share similar symptoms and information on how to distinguish among similar disorders. (LaBruzza, 1994, pp. 57–58)

Making the Diagnosis

The patient receives a diagnosis along five separate dimensions, referred to as axes. Each axis gives different information about the patient, providing a more accurate clinical picture than would be possible with a single axis. This is called a multiaxial diagnosis. The diagnoses entered on each axis have both names and numbers, the numbers being useful for insurance and billing purposes. Each axis serves a different purpose. Figure 17.1 contains an outline showing what information is coded on each axis.

A Closer Look at Multiaxial Assessment

Axis I

All clinical syndromes listed in the *DSM* are coded on this axis *except* personality disorders and mental retardation. The primary diagnosis, or reason a person is seeking treatment, generally is the diagnosis appearing on Axis I. However, if a person is seeking help for mental retardation or a personality disorder, there may not be an Axis I diagnosis.

If there is more than one Axis I disorder, the primary diagnosis is listed first and often is qualified with the phrase "Reason for visit" or "Principal diagnosis" (unless the principal diagnosis is on Axis II; LaBruzza, 1994). If the clinician does not use one of these phrases, the Axis I diagnosis is always considered to be the primary diagnosis.

The following are the disorders coded on Axis I:

1. Disorders usually first diagnosed in infancy, childhood, or adolescence (except mental retardation, which is coded on Axis II)
2. Delirium, dementia, amnesia, and other cognitive disorders
3. Mental disorders due to a general medical condition not elsewhere classified
4. Substance-related disorders
5. Schizophrenia and other psychotic disorders

> **FIGURE 17.1**
>
> **Dimensions Used in Multiaxial Diagnosis**
>
> **Axis I**: All clinical syndromes listed in the *DSM-IV* are coded on this axis *except* personality disorders and mental retardation. Axis I includes developmental disorders and other conditions that might be a focus of clinical attention.
>
> - V71.09   No diagnosis on Axis I
> - 799.9   Diagnosis deferred on Axis I (meaning too little time or information to establish a diagnosis)
>
> **Axis II**: Coded on this axis are personality disorders, mental retardation, significant maladaptive personality traits, and habitual defense mechanisms.
>
> - V71.09   No diagnosis on Axis II
> - 799.9   Diagnosis deferred on Axis II
>
> **Axis III**: This axis is used for all general medical conditions that are relevant to planning and understanding the patient's diagnosis. *International Classification of Diseases (ICD-10)* codes can be used here.
>
> - None (meaning no medical conditions)
> - Deferred
>
> **Axis IV**: Psychosocial and environmental problems that affect the prognosis, management, or treatment of the case are coded here.
>
> **Axis V**: This axis is for the rating on the Global Assessment of Functioning (GAF) scale, which is usually a single number between 1 and 100 indicating the current level of functioning the patient possesses.

6. Mood disorders
7. Anxiety disorders
8. Somatoform disorders
9. Factious disorders
10. Dissociative disorders
11. Sexual and gender identity disorders
12. Eating disorders
13. Sleep disorders
14. Impulse control disorders not elsewhere classified
15. Adjustment disorders
16. Other conditions that may be a focus of clinical attention

When there is no diagnosis on Axis I, the clinician writes V71.09 on the axis.

Axis II

Axis II is used to code personality disorders and mental retardation. This was done to be sure relevant personality factors would be part of the entire diagnosis. It also makes mental retardation a separate factor on a separate axis in the patient's general diagnosis. *Of all the disorders listed in the* DSM, *only mental retardation and the learning disorders require diagnostic testing before the diagnosis can be given.* If a patient meets the criteria for more than one personality disorder, all of them should be coded on Axis II. In addition, the clinician can write in any significant maladaptive personality traits or habitual defense mechanisms on this axis. These items have no code number.

The absence of an Axis II disorder is coded V71.09. If the practitioner suspects there may be an Axis II disorder but is not sure, the deferred code, 799.9, is used. You will find that insurance companies are not pleased with Axis II diagnoses due to the amount of costly treatment required. This treatment can be intense and time consuming.

There are 11 categories of personality disorder.

1. Paranoid
2. Schizoid
3. Schizotypal
4. Antisocial
5. Borderline
6. Histrionic
7. Narcissistic
8. Avoidant
9. Dependent
10. Obsessive-compulsive
11. Personality disorder not otherwise specified

In addition, borderline intellectual functioning is also coded on Axis II (V62.89). When there is no diagnosis on Axis II, the clinician writes V71.09 on the axis.

Axis III

Often, individuals with severe mental disorders also have general medical conditions that affect the prognosis, treatment, and even the understanding of patients' situations. Any general medical condition that is relevant should be coded on Axis III, along with any medical history that may be relevant to the current problem.

Axis III is not meant to indicate the mind and body are entirely separate entities. Axis III is separate in order to be sure the full picture of mental and medical disorders is recorded. People with medical conditions often feel less well psychologically. Axis III also alerts the physician to the possibility that the patient is on medications that might interfere or interact negatively with psychotropic medications that might be prescribed for the mental disorder.

In some cases, it is the medical condition that has caused the mental disorder. If this is the case, the medical condition is recorded on Axis III, and the mental condition is recorded on Axis I with the phrase "due to . . ." (for example, Axis I might read "major depressive disorder, single episode, due to hypothyroidism," while Axis III would read "hypothyroidism").

If no medical condition exists, write "Axis III: None." If it is suspected that there may be a medical condition but there is not enough information, it is coded "Axis III: Deferred." The clinician can note in writing any significant symptoms or physical signs that were observed that need further evaluation.

Axis IV

Axis IV should list any psychosocial stressors or environmental problems that appear to have an impact on the conditions noted on Axes I, II, and III. The clinician looks at what has happened to the client, particularly in the last year. Some stressors happened a number of years ago. For instance, a diagnosis of posttraumatic stress disorder (309.81) on Axis I may have Vietnam War on Axis IV as a stressor that is affecting the current condition of a Vietnam war veteran.

The *DSM* lists "other conditions" that may be the focus of clinical attention. These codes begin with the letter V and are listed on Axis I. They refer to problems people encounter in life that might cause them to seek professional help. It might be bereavement (V62.82), school problems (V62.3), or any number of situational and relationship problems that have come to clinical attention. After further treatment, a discrete mental disorder sometimes emerges and the diagnosis is changed at that point. At other times the client just needs help adjusting to the circumstances.

The V codes were developed to outline broad general categories of psychosocial stress a person might experience.

1. Problems with primary support group

    ◆ Childhood (V61.9)
    ◆ Adult (V61.9)
    ◆ Parent–child (V61.20)

2. Problems related to the social environment (V62.4)
3. Educational problems (V62.3)
4. Occupational problems (V62.2)
5. Housing problems
6. Economic problems
7. Problems with access to health care services
8. Problems related to interaction with the legal system/crime
9. Other psychosocial and environmental problems

If stress from a specific stressor is the main reason a person is seeking help, the V code for the stressor should go on Axis I, and a description of the exact stressor should go on axis IV. For example, if a person is having trouble on his job, you would put V62.2 occupational problem on Axis I, and on Axis IV you would write, "difficulty adjusting to additional responsibilities" or "problems with supervisor."

Note: These V codes should not be confused with V71.09, which is the code used on both Axis I and Axis II to indicate that no clinical condition is present on that axis.

Much psychosocial stress has to do with problems in the person's support system. This can include births, deaths, separation, divorce, remarriage, abuse, neglect, and significant illness. When looking at the person's social environment, you might find social isolation, lost friendships, retirement, relocations, and cultural differences as contributors to the current difficulty.

The "other" category can be used to record natural disasters and catastrophes such as floods or earthquakes or problems related to professional caregivers, for example, a nursing assistant who is rough and seemingly threatening. The term *other* is used for any stressor that does not fit into the other categories. After the category is listed, the clinician should write out the specific stressors within each category (unemployed, mugged, best friend was killed, and so forth).

There are positive stressors such as weddings or the birth of a child. These positive stressful events are not coded on Axis IV unless they create a clinical problem for the patient.

Axis V

This axis is reserved for the patient's number on the Global Assessment of Functioning (GAF) scale. How well a person functions or does not function will affect any treatment plan developed and may affect insurance payment, research options, and the overall assessment of the person. A single rating of how the person is functioning at the time of the evaluation is given on Axis V. You will find the GAF in your *DSM*. The number assigned the patient should reflect the person's "current level of psychological, social, and occupational functioning at the time of the evaluation," according to Anthony LaBruzza (1994, p. 79). He further pointed out that "impairment due to physical, and environmental limitations is excluded from Axis V"(p. 79). For example, if a person were impaired because of a stroke and therefore unable to get around, this reduced functioning would not be part of the assessment. Nor would circumstances such as poverty or a poor education be included in the assessment. The assessment looks at how well people are functioning beyond their environmental and physical limitations.

The number given on Axis V is a number from 1 to 100. Zero indicates that there has not been enough time to adequately assess the functioning. The scale is divided into 10-point segments, with 1 to 10 being the lowest functioning and 90 to 100 being the highest. Most individuals requiring inpatient hospitalization have a GAF score of 50 or less. The scale has been criticized for making it possible to a greater degree to abuse reimbursement, forensic, and disability situations.

Use of Codes V71.09 and 799.9

These two designations are used only on Axis I and Axis II. You need to know what these numbers mean when you see them. On both Axis I and Axis II, the codes indicate the following:

- ◆ V71.09 means there is no diagnosis on that particular axis.
- ◆ 799.9 means the diagnosis was deferred, presumably because there was too little time or information to make a diagnosis.

Making the Code

All the disorders in the *DSM* have a numerical code. The code has three whole numbers followed by a decimal point and one or two additional numbers. The form of the codes looks like this: XXX.XX. The last two numbers in the code give the diagnosis more specificity.

Let us take an example. A person comes in with an obvious depression. In *DSM-IV* terms, this is called a "major depressive episode" (296._ _). The number 296.21 indicates the person's condition is mild, 296.22 means moderate, 296.23 means severe but without psychotic features, and 296.24 is severe with psychotic features. A person in partial remission would get 296.25, and a person in full remission would get 296.26. We know that the Axis I diagnosis will be 296._ _. By choosing the proper digits to follow the decimal point, we create a more accurate clinical picture of this person.

The fifth digit is generally used to identify four things:

1. Subtypes
2. Modifiers
3. Course of the disorder and severity
4. Additional information such as reason for visit; provisional diagnosis; and the diagnoses of not otherwise specified, unspecified, or deferred.

Subtypes

When the clinician codes a diagnosis, the manual may require that the clinician "specify type." This refers to subtypes within a specific diagnosis. For instance, the diagnosis may be a delusional disorder (297.1), but there are seven distinct types of delusional disorders, including jealous, persecutory, grandiose, and so forth. The fifth digit is used to assign the subtype the clinician is diagnosing.

Modifiers

The manual may require that the practitioner "specify if" when coding a diagnosis. These are modifiers that allow the clinician to indicate if certain factors are present in this particular diagnosis. For instance, if the diagnosis is pedophilia (302.2), the practitioner will be asked to specify if the person is sexually attracted to males, females, or both (LaBruzza, 1994).

Modifiers for Past and Present

It is always understood that the diagnosis is a present condition. Sometimes, however, it is useful to note a past history of a particular diagnosis. A diagnosis from the past is modified with the phrase "prior history." In this case, you might write: "Posttraumatic stress disorder (309.81), prior history."

Modifiers for Course of the Disorder and Severity

The fifth digit is also used to specify the status of the remission or the degree of severity. Severity is usually either mild, moderate, severe, or psychotic. Each of these degrees of severity, specified by the fifth digit, indicate the intensity of the signs and symptoms and the degree to which the person's functioning is impaired. Mild means the person's symptoms just minimally meet the criteria for the disorder. Severe means the person meets the full criteria with intensity and is severely impaired in functioning.

Remission is usually either "partial remission" or "full remission." Partial remission means the person meets some of the criteria for the disorder but is no longer showing the full criteria that were present when the original diagnosis was made. You might also use this specifier to indicate that a person who had been in full remission is now showing some of the criteria again. Full remission means all the signs and symptoms of the disorder have disappeared but the diagnosis is clinically significant at present.

Additional Information

Reason-for-Visit Modifiers

Beginning with the *DSM-IV*, there was a shift toward multiple diagnoses. If the person fits the criteria for more than one disorder, then all of the disorders are listed. This means that the practitioner needs to identify the disorder that brought the client in for treatment or the disorder that will most likely be the focus of treatment. This is done by placing the phrase "principal diagnosis" or "reason for visit" beside the primary diagnosis.

List the primary diagnosis first with the modifier ("reason for visit" or "principal diagnosis"), and then list the other diagnoses under it in order of importance. Generally, the primary diagnosis is on Axis I. On occasion, it will be on Axis II, in which case you need to make sure to use the modifier on the Axis II diagnosis.

Provisional Diagnoses

When it is not clear what the diagnosis should be, the clinician needs to indicate that uncertainty. Some clients are uncooperative or impaired to the point that they cannot give much information. If the clinician has a strong idea of what the diagnosis probably is, a diagnosis is written with the term *provisional* after it.

There are some disorders that *must* initially be modified with "provisional." These would be disorders where a time lapse is needed between episodes in order to confirm the diagnosis. For example, panic disorder (300.01) requires at least one panic attack, followed by at least a month of persistent worry about having more attacks. A clinician who sees someone who appears to have panic disorder but had the panic episode only 2 days previously cannot give the client that diagnosis with a degree of certainty. Thus the word *provisional* is used until enough time has passed to confirm or revise the diagnosis.

Not Otherwise Specified

Sometimes a client comes in with most of the symptoms of a particular disorder and the practitioner thinks she knows what the diagnosis should be, but the signs and symptoms do not quite fit the criteria as they are outlined in the manual. All the major classes of mental disorders have a "not otherwise specified," or NOS, category. The practitioner would write NOS after the diagnosis in this sort of case.

For example, a person might have symptoms that do not meet the full criteria for any one disorder but meet some criteria for several different disorders, giving a mixed version of the disorder. Or you might encounter a person who has an obvious mental disorder, but it is not found in the *DSM*. Perhaps it is a characteristic of the person's culture, or it is something being researched that has not been given a code yet. In another situation, the clinician may not know the cause of the disorder. The mental disorder he is seeing might be due to the medication the person is on, the general medical condition the person has, or the stress of the individual's life. This may need to be sorted out before giving a certain diagnosis. Finally, clinicians who lack enough information to be sure of the diagnosis can use the NOS category. After getting good information, the diagnosis can be changed.

Unspecified and Deferred Diagnoses

There is an "unspecified mental disorder" category that cannot be used when psychotic symptoms are present. The number is 300.9. This is used when there is some certainty that a mental disorder exists, but there is inadequate information to make a clear diagnosis. Later it can be changed to a specific disorder, unless it is found that the symptoms do not meet the criteria for any specific disorder.

If there is inadequate information to make any diagnosis, the number on both Axis I and Axis II is 799.9, "diagnosis deferred." Today most private and public insurance agencies insist that a diagnosis, even if provisional, be given at the very first person-to-person contact. This means that in some locations it is case managers who are giving those provisional diagnoses.

Summary

The *DSM* is a complex manual. It takes practice and good clinical skills to use the manual effectively. Nevertheless, entry-level individuals are being asked to understand the categories of disorders and discuss diagnoses with clinicians. In this course, we begin to look at how you would use the manual in your work as a case manager.

As you practice, you will begin to understand more clearly how disorders are defined and treatments are assigned. As you work with the *DSM* over a period of time, these axes and the diagnoses that go on them will become more familiar to you and easier to use. You will also be able to note such diagnoses more quickly with practice.

◆ Exercises: Using the *DSM*

Instructions: See how many of the following exercises you can complete. These are designed to familiarize you with where different material is located in the *DSM* and how conditions are coded on the five axes. When it comes to actual diagnoses, there will always be debate about what diagnosis to use. In other words, don't expect that there is only one right answer. Try to seek the best answer instead. After discussion, in which you will no doubt cover many of the issues raised in a real work situation, assign the diagnosis you feel is most appropriate.

1. It seems to you that Jim is having trouble in school. The teacher reports that Jim can read and speak well but has trouble writing out his thoughts in a coherent and organized manner. You suspect the diagnosis is _____, and you know that _____ must be done to confirm it.

2. The doctor asks you to estimate a GAF for a woman who is being seen by you in the ER. Her family says she has been confused recently, and today she left some pots on the stove and forgot to attend to them. The kitchen caught fire. In talking to her, she seems somewhat unconcerned or unaware of the gravity of the situation. She also seems unable to find the ladies' room when you direct her there, and you end up going with her and leading her back to the interview room. The abbreviation GAF stands for _____. You assign her a GAF of _____. You place the GAF on Axis _____.

3. A man comes in and indicates he is suffering from severe depression. He appears to have a flat affect and some tearfulness. In the course of the interview, you learn that he is an intermittent cocaine user. How do you code these two disorders? Think carefully!

4. A woman has breast cancer and has been depressed since the diagnosis was first given. Her family reports that she seems to be getting worse. How do you code these two disorders? Think carefully!

5. A patient is being admitted to the psychiatric unit, and the doctor is unclear whether she is seeing a personality disorder or a clinical syndrome. She needs to get the patient admitted quickly and knows the doctor on the floor will have the time to sort this out. What does the doctor most likely write on Axis I? What does she most likely write on Axis II?

6. The psychologist laments to you that she knows the client has a dissociative disorder but goes on to say that although it looks similar to dissociative identity disorder, she cannot quite see two or more distinct personality states. You think of what diagnosis?

7. For each of the following, indicate on which axis it should appear:
   Migraine headaches _____
   Housing problems _____
   Cancer _____
   Schizophrenia, paranoid type _____
   Borderline personality disorder _____
   A broken leg _____
   A divorce _____
   A lost job _____
   Severely impaired social and occupational functioning _____
   Dementia of the Alzheimer's type _____
   Domestic violence _____
   Mental retardation _____
   Inhalant intoxication _____
   Histrionic personality disorder _____

8. If you know that the diagnosis for schizophreniform disorder is an episode of the disorder lasting at least 1 month but less than 6 months, and you must make the diagnosis without waiting for the recovery, you would mark the diagnosis_____.

9. Describe two clients:
   Client 1 has 296.21, major depressive disorder, with melancholic features. Describe the symptoms, and tell the axis on which this diagnosis will go.

   Client 2 has 296.33, major depressive disorder, with catatonic features. Describe the symptoms, and tell the axis on which this diagnosis will go.

10. All personality disorders have as the first three digits _____.
11. All anxiety disorders have as the first three digits _____.
12. Depressive disorders have as the first three digits _____.

13. Schizophrenia has several subtypes. Describe a person whose diagnosis is 295.10.

14. How does this person differ from a person with a diagnosis of 295.30?

15. Assign a GAF to this person: A man is seeking counseling for depression following the death of his wife. He has been preoccupied and forgetful at work and finds himself crying alone at night. The GAF is _____.
16. Assign a GAF to this person: A man tells you he has been anxious lately. He makes vague references to neighbors and a plan the neighbors have that worries him but does not elaborate. He also mentions the need to use only stores that stay open 24 hours a day in order not to be involved in the neighborhood plan. He believes his neighbors have had an influence in Washington beyond what their numbers would indicate but attributes it to their "plan." He is working and reports he recently received a raise. He has few friends and enjoys his job as his main source of socializing. The GAF is _____.
17. Assign a GAF to this person: A woman was brought from her apartment by ambulance to the hospital emergency room after neighbors who were concerned about her called for help. She is unwashed, smells bad, and is mute. Attempts to communicate with her are in vain. She looks past the worker and does not appear to hear anything addressed to her. She is very thin and has bad breath. The GAF is _____.
18. Assign a GAF to this person: A man is about to take his state psychology boards. He has made nearly straight As in graduate school. He is happily married and the father of two daughters. He plays tennis on the weekends and is an expert cook. He and his wife hold season tickets to the symphony, and he is a deacon in his church. He is complaining of rapid heart beat and sweaty palms. The GAF is _____.

Chapter 18

The Mental Status Examination

Introduction

The mental status examination (MSE) is based on your *observations* of the client. It is not related to the facts of the client's situation, but to the way the person acts, how the person talks, and how the person looks while in your presence. A mental status examination can be an abbreviated assessment done because someone appears to be in obvious need of hospitalization, or it can be an elongated process that takes place over several interviews. The MSE always has the same content, and you write your observations in roughly the same order each time.

Although a formal MSE would be done by a physician or psychologist, you will do an informal MSE in which you systematically look at the client's thinking process, feeling state, and behavior. You will want to understand the way the client functions emotionally and cognitively.

Much of the examination is done by observing how clients present themselves at the interview and the manner in which they spontaneously give information about themselves and their situations. The examination is not done separately but is an integral part of the assessment interview. Questions that relate to mental status are framed as part of the overall assessment and not as a separate pursuit. There will be times when you or a clinician might ask for psychological testing to confirm your evaluation of the client, but during your own MSE of the client, this is not done.

Some of the terms you will learn in this chapter are not necessarily words you will use in describing your clients and their appearance or behavior. This chapter is meant to familiarize you with the way some professional practitioners describe their clients. If you know these terms, you will be able to follow the notes and discussions better.

What to Observe

Your mental status examination of the client involves observations of the following:

- General appearance
- Behavior
- Thought process and content
- Affect
- Impulse control
- Insight
- Cognitive functioning
- Intelligence
- Reality testing
- Suicidal or homicidal ideation
- Judgment

A good case manager is a good observer. You pick up many details about the client, all of which are relevant to understanding the client's mental status. In a sense, you watch for the most obvious and the most subtle visual and verbal clues as to who your client is. Use what you see and hear to give you direction in regard to what questions to ask.

How to Observe

Throughout the interview note how the client communicates verbally and nonverbally and how the client behaves. In addition, you look at the content of the communication. You are looking at both *what* the client tells you and *how* the client tells it.

As clients talk about why they came to your agency for services and about the main problems they are confronting, you will make some judgments about how they functioned in the past and how well they are functioning currently. You will note how clients tell their stories. Is the person cooperative and friendly? Does he appear to be relieved and eager to talk to you, or is he mute, guarded, and uncooperative? Is she weepy and hesitant as she speaks, or is she forthright and stern? Does the person twist a tissue in her hands or rock back and forth in her chair, or does she use appropriate gestures? Does he relax during the interview or remain guarded and uncooperative?

At times you may need to assess clients' mental status through the observations of others who are close to them. Your clients may not always be able to tell you much about past events or functioning, and you will need to turn to others for that information. If there is no reliable source, you may not be able to perform a complete MSE that has a clear degree of certainty.

Documenting Your Observations

To back up your observations, use both descriptions of the client's behavior during the interview and direct quotes made by the client in the interview. In this way, you carefully document your observations and your resulting conclusions.

When you describe the person, be sure that your values and prejudices do not appear in your notes. Use adjectives that describe the client, but are objective. All editorial comments and value judgments should be omitted. Figure 18.1 defines some general terms that are commonly used when documenting observations of clients.

FIGURE 18.1

General Terms Used in Documentation

Primary language: When you see this on a form, give the person's native language, and if it is not English, tell how well the person functions with English.

Presenting problem: In one or two sentences, tell why the client is coming to see you *now*. Use the person's own language.

Past psychiatric history: Use incomplete sentences. Give dates, approximately how long, and summarize if there is much detail.

Functional ability: Note particularly if the person is able to display and carry out age- and stage-appropriate skills and tasks. Also note any recent change.

Moods/emotions: What does the person or the person's family say?

Physiologic: What does the person or the family say about the person's appetite, sleep, and sexual activity?

Thinking: What is the person saying about how she is thinking? Are you able to follow her thinking?

Perception: Are there any hallucinations?

Orientation/cognition/memory: Does the person think he can find his way? Does he know where he is? Does he remember well?

Mental status examination: This is a word picture that tells what the person looks like *now*, not all the time.

Mental Status Examination Outline

Anthony LaBruzza (1994), in his book *Using DSM-IV*, provides a good outline for the mental status report that you will complete after the interview. He stated that his outline is not meant to be followed precisely, but it does give the major points and a framework to determine what is important. The outline shown in Figure 18.2 provides the major categories you must cover in a mental status report.

FIGURE 18.2

Outline For The Mental Status Examination

The Mental Status Examination

    I. General Description
        A. Appearance
            1. Dress and grooming
            2. Physical characteristics
            3. Posture and gait
        B. Attitude and interpersonal style

(continued)

FIGURE 18.2 *(continued)*

    C. Behavior and psychomotor activity
    D. Speech and language
        1. Rate
        2. Clarity, pitch, volume, tone, quality, and resonance
        3. Abnormalities
II. Emotions
    A. Mood
    B. Affect
    C. Neurovegetative signs of depression
III. Cognitive Functioning
    A. Orientation and level of consciousness
    B. Attention and concentration
    C. Memory
        1. Immediate registration, retention, and recall (a minute or less)
        2. Recent memory (a minute to days or weeks)
        3. Remote memory (weeks to years)
           a. Memory for recent past
           b. Memory for distant past
        4. Client's subjective report of memory difficulties
    D. Ability to abstract and generalize
    E. Information and intelligence
        1. Fund of knowledge
        2. Estimate of intelligence
IV. Thought and Perception
    A. Disordered perceptions
        1. Illusion
        2. Hallucinations
        3. Depersonalization and derealization
    B. Thought content
        1. Distortions
        2. Delusions
        3. Ideas of reference
        4. Magical thinking
    C. Thought processes
        1. Flow of ideas
        2. Quality of associations
    D. Preoccupations
        1. Somatic
        2. Obsessions and compulsions
        3. Phobias
V. Suicidality, Homicidality, and Impulse Control
VI. Insight and Judgment
VII. Reliability
VIII. The Environment

Source: Adapted with permission from *Using DSM-IV: A Clinician's Guide to Psychiatric Diagnosis* by Anthony L. LaBruzza in collaboration with José Méndez-Villarubia. Copyright © 1997, 1994 Jason Aronson, Inc., an imprint of Rowman & Littlefield Publishers, Inc.

This section discusses the outline for the mental status examination and report in detail, defining terms to use and identifying items on which to focus for each category you will cover in mental status examinations and reports. Pay particular attention to the terms that have **Always** in boldface in the descriptor, as these are important items to which you must *always* give attention.

I. General Description

A. Appearance

1. Dress and Grooming. You may find the person's appearance to be average, meticulous, slightly unkempt, or disheveled. The person may have body odor, no makeup, makeup that is skillfully applied, or garish makeup.

- *Meticulous:* The appearance is too perfect, unusually so.
- *Skillfully applied:* The person is made up to look like a model.
- *Garish:* The person looks outlandish.
- *Self-neglect:* **Always** indicate when you think this is present. It involves such things as having body odor or looking disheveled and unkempt. Dress would be dirty, stained, or rumpled. This can be a sign of a mental illness such as depression or schizophrenia.
- *Dress:* You may find it casual, business, fashionable, unconventional, immaculate, neat, stained, dirty, rumpled.
- *Immaculate:* This means the person is too neat.
- *Unconventional:* Use this term to refer to clothes that are inappropriate to the setting.
- *Fashionable:* This is fine unless the person looks like something out of *Vogue* in an office in a small town or average city.

2. Physical Characteristics. Note those features that are outstanding. Look at body build, important physical features, and handicaps. Note voice quality. Is it strong, weak, hoarse, halting?

3. Posture and Gait. Note gait and any need for devices such as a cane or crutches. Look at coordination and gestures. For instance, does a right-handed person make most of her gestures with her left hand? Something like this could be a clue to neurological difficulties. Does the person limp or appear to slump? Does the person seem unsteady or shuffle?

B. Attitude and Interpersonal Style

Look at the attitude the person has with you. You may find it cooperative, attentive, frank, playful, ingratiating, evasive, guarded, hostile, belligerent, contemptuous, seductive, demanding, sullen, passive, manipulative, complaining, suspicious, guarded, withdrawn, or obsequious.

- *Hostility:* **Always** note when the person is hostile.
- *Uncooperative:* **Always** note when the person does not or cannot cooperate.

- *Inappropriate boundaries:* **Always** note if the client is too friendly, touches you, or attempts to draw you out personally.
- *Seductive:* too close a relationship too soon; might call you by your first name or touch you
- *Playful:* jokes, uses puns, self-deprecating humor
- *Ingratiating:* goes along with whatever you think; wants to please
- *Evasive:* talks, but gives nothing
- *Guarded:* is more reserved than evasive; contributes the bare minimum, often with suspicion
- *Sullen:* angry and somewhat uncommunicative
- *Passive:* barely cooperates, needs to be led; generally without overt hostility
- *Manipulative:* asks for special favors, uses guilt, solicits pity, threatens
- *Contemptuous:* superior, sneering, cynical
- *Demanding:* sense of entitlement
- *Withdrawn:* volunteers little, appears sad

Watch your own emotional reactions to the client. They will give you important clues. Also pay attention to the person's *facial expression*. You may find it pleasant, happy, sad, perplexed, angry, tense, mobile, bland, or flat.

- *Bland:* intense material, but looks casual
- *Flat:* no facial expression
- *Mobile:* rapid changes in facial expression and mood

C. Behavior and Psychomotor Activity

Look at the quality and quantity of the client's motor activity. You may find the patient is seated quietly, hyperactive, agitated, combative, clumsy, limp, rigid, or has retarded motor function. You may find the client has mannerisms, tics, twitches, or stereotypes.

- *Seated quietly:* uses normal gestures, but does not move around much
- *Hyperactive:* is busy with hands and possibly feet
- *Agitated:* cannot sit still (could be secondary to antipsychotic medication)
- *Combative:* looks ready to hit, threatening
- *Awkward:* unable to manage activity like sitting in the chair or writing; drops things (may be part of the illness or reaction to medication)
- *Rigid:* sits like a tin soldier
- *Mannerisms:* these are unconscious repetitive actions
- *Posturing:* the person assumes certain postures and holds them inappropriately
- *Tics and twitches:* less voluntary body movements
- *Stereotypes:* four mannerisms strung together
- *Motor hyperactivity:* **Always** report this when you see a lot of hyperactivity, restlessness, and agitation. It may indicate a manic state, reaction to medication, or anxiety.
- *Motor retardation:* **Always** report this when you see the patient moves slowly, in a constricted manner and with minimal motor responses. Speech and

thought are slowed, often depressed. Depression can give the appearance of cognitive impairment.

- ◆ *Mannerisms and posturing:* **Always** indicate mannerisms you see and any posturing.
- ◆ *Tension:* **Always** note tension, particularly if the person seems tense and the interview does nothing to relax the person.
- ◆ *Severe akathisia:* **Always** note severe restlessness. Sometimes it may be part of an illness, and sometimes it may be due to medication. If the physician believes it is due to an illness and increases the medication, the person may grow much worse. Therefore, try to establish when it started, how long it has gone on, and whether it has grown worse recently.

Always note the following when present: pacing, fidgeting, nail biting, trembling or tremulousness (a common side effect of lithium carbonate and tricyclic antidepressants), and abnormal movements such as rocking, bouncing, or grimacing (particularly strange facial movements).

- ◆ *Tardive dyskinesia:* **Always** note this condition if you see it or suspect this is what you are seeing. It occurs among psychiatric patients who have been on antipsychotic medications over a long period of time. The term literally means "late appearing abnormal movements" and seems to involve the muscles of the face, mouth, and tongue. Sometimes the trunk and limbs are also affected.

These movements can be slow and irregular (athetosis) or quick and jerky (choreic). All the movements are brief, involuntary, and purposeless. A person may twist the tongue and lips, make odd faces, bounce or tap the feet, or actually writhe and squirm in the seat.

- ◆ *Catatonic behavior:* **Always** note this behavior. It is generally a sign of severe depression or schizophrenia, catatonic type. It generally appears as a rigidity of posture wherein attempts to reposition the person are rigidly resisted. The person may voluntarily pose in bizarre and inappropriate ways. In waxy flexibility, the limbs of the person will remain in the position in which they are placed.

There is also a catatonic excitement wherein the patient engages in almost continual, purposeless activity that is nearly impossible to interrupt. Sometimes the patient engages in echolalia (repetition of everything that is heard) or mimics and imitates others during this episode.

D. Speech and Language

Speech is important because it is the primary means of communicating. Important to note are such things as rate, clarity, pitch, volume, quality, quantity, impediments, use of words, the ability to get to the point, and articulation.

You may find speech to be a normal rate, slow, hesitant, rapid, pressured, monotonous, emotional, loud, whispered, mumbled, precise, slurred, accented, stuttering, stilted, rambling.

- *Pressured:* often rapid but constantly talking; cannot be interrupted (often a sign of a manic episode). Person appears to have racing thoughts.
- *Monotonous:* no variation in tone
- *Emotional:* very expressive
- *Accented:* note a native accent and also if the patient seems to accent certain words or syllables
- *Impoverished:* may say very little either because of depression or because he is being interviewed in a language other than his native one; may also indicate a lack of facility with language
- *Neologisms:* **Always** note when the person makes up entirely new words with idiosyncratic meanings. (This can occur due to aphasia or brain injury due to accident or stroke.)

You should be able to identify any *neurological language disturbances*. Strokes, head trauma, and brain tumors can cause patients to lose their facility with language. Try to determine if the client has always had a language difficulty. Patients with schizophrenia may use loose associations as they talk. Those in a manic state may be prone to flight of ideas.

- *Aphasia:* loss of ability to understand and produce language; damage usually to left hemisphere of the brain (left-handed people often have this in the right hemisphere)

The type and extent of aphasia depends on location and extent of brain injury.

- *Global aphasia:* can neither speak nor understand, read, write, repeat words, or name objects
- *Broca's aphasia:* can understand written and spoken language, but has trouble expressing own thoughts verbally
- *Wernicke's aphasia:* inability to understand language and uses fluent, bizarre, nonsensical speech (The person may also act strangely and appear euphoric, paranoid, or agitated. It is easy to think this is a psychotic thought disorder, but in schizophrenia the person is generally able to write and speak in her language, repeat words, and name objects.)
- *Dysarthria:* difficulty articulating due to problems with the mechanisms that produce speech. This sometimes produces distorted or unintelligible speech. The person usually can read and write normally. Ask the patient to repeat "No ifs, ands, or buts" to hear dysarthria better.
- *Perseveration:* defined as the persistence "in repeating a verbal or motor response to a prior stimulus even when confronted with a new stimulus" (LaBruzza, 1994, p. 113). The client may give the same answer to different questions, stay on the same subject, or repeatedly return to the same subject.
- *Stereotypy:* "constant repetition of speech or actions" (LaBruzza, 1994, p. 113). The patient may pull a shoe on and off, twist and untwist the hair, or repeat the same phrase or word over and over. These behaviors appear to be ritualistic and are common in childhood autism.

Give verbatim examples of what the client has said to support your assessment of speech.

II. Emotions

A. Mood

This is the way a person is feeling at any given time. You may find it euthymic, depressed, sad, hopeless, empty, guilty, irritable, angry, enraged, terrified, expansive, euphoric, elated, sullen, dejected, or anxious. Ask yourself, what seems to be the dominant mood of the person?

- *Euthymic:* normal mood
- *Expansive:* feels very good and is getting better
- *Euphoric:* out-of-sight happy
- *Anxious:* worried and distressed

B. Affect

Affect refers to the underlying flow of moods. This would be the outward expression of the emotional state. You can see it in the way patients use and position their bodies and in their tone and manner of speaking. You may find it broad, appropriate, constricted, blunted, flat, labile, or anhedonic.

- *Broad:* normal range of moods
- *Appropriate:* appropriate to the situation
- *Constricted:* restricted range of emotional expression
- *Blunted:* even more restricted
- *Flat:* no change of mood, unemotional
- *Labile:* rapid change in mood (crying, then laughing)
- *Anhedonic:* incapable of any pleasurable response, depressed
- *Blunted affect:* **Always** note a blunted affect where you find no change in mood throughout the interview and no change in facial expression. It generally indicates depression.
- *Emotional withdrawal:* **Always** note if the person seems emotionally withdrawn to you. The person would be inexpressive and probably have a blunt affect.
- *Excitement:* **Always** note if the person seems inappropriately excited to you. It means the person is overly enthused or terrified about the given situation.
- *Full range of affect:* This refers to an appropriate affective response to the entire interview. **Always** note inappropriate affect (such as giggling when there is nothing funny happening), as this can be a sign of schizophrenia.

C. Neurovegetative Signs of Depression

In major depression, body functioning often becomes irregular. *Always* inquire about sleep and appetite, and report a loss or gain of more than 5% of body weight. Listen for symptoms such as changes in energy levels, interest, enjoyment of everyday activities, or sexual functioning; constipation; and weight changes (LaBruzza, 1994, p. 115).

- *Initial insomnia:* trouble falling asleep
- *Middle insomnia:* middle-of-the-night wakening

- *Terminal insomnia:* early morning wakening. Depressed individuals will often wake several hours earlier than usual and feel most depressed in the morning.
- *Hypersomnia:* Some depressed individuals, especially those with bipolar disorders, tend to sleep a great deal.

III. Cognitive Functioning

A number of medical and neurological problems, as well as substance abuse, affect one's cognitive functioning. The concern is that many patients who have a disease of the brain may appear with what seems to be emotional and behavioral changes. In taking the history from the client, note previous levels of functioning and any previous emotional problems. If these are appearing in middle or late life, it is quite possible the person has a brain disease.

A. Orientation and Level of Consciousness

Nearly all of the clients who come to you will be alert and aware of their environment and their body. Occasionally, however, you may see individuals who are inattentive, drowsy, or who have a clouded consciousness. If these symptoms are present, use the proper term to indicate the person's level of awareness and briefly describe how the patient exhibits this level. Medication can contribute to these stages as well.

- *Lethargy:* the person has trouble remaining alert and appears to want to drift off to sleep, but can be aroused. The person has trouble concentrating on the interview and seems unable to maintain a coherent train of thought.
- *Obtundation:* the person is difficult to arouse and needs constant stimulation to stay awake. The person may seem confused and unable to participate in the interview.
- *Stupor:* the person is semicomatose, and it takes vigorous stimulation to arouse her; she cannot arouse herself. There is no normal interaction during the interview as a result.
- *Coma:* this is the most severe consciousness problem wherein the person cannot be aroused and does not respond to any stimulation.
- *Oriented x3:* means the person is oriented as to who he is, where he is, and when it is. Even when a person is having difficulty with consciousness, he may be oriented. If orientation problems occur as a result of lack of consciousness, it typically happens that the sense of time is affected first, followed by the sense of place, and finally by the sense of person. To be fully oriented requires an intact memory; thus, disorientation means there are memory deficits.
- *Ask for current date:* reasonably accurate dates are acceptable.
- *Ask where the person is:* you can also ask for a home address, the present city or state, or for directions from here to the person's home or another familiar place. Sometimes people confused about place will behave as if they are at home or in another very familiar setting while in your office.

♦ *Ask who the person is:* ask for personal identifying information (age, birth date, name). Ask if the person recognizes or knows other people who might be present. Does she know her relationships to these other people?

B. Attention and Concentration

Always note inability to pay attention and if the person appears easily distracted.

♦ *Attention:* Can the person remain focused on the interview?

If you feel a need to test this in the person, you can use digit repetition. Say five numbers, and then ask the person to recite them back to you.
Concentration is needed to learn new tasks and for academic success.

♦ *Concentration:* The person can concentrate on one thing for an extended period of time.

You can test the person's concentration by asking the person to perform a complex mental task. (Serial 7s is one way of testing; in this method, you ask the person to add in increments of 7 or subtract from 100 by 7s. Be sure your instructions are on the client's level of education, and do not use this exercise if severe academic problems are present. Be careful not to humiliate clients!)

C. Memory

Memory involves the ability to learn new material, to retain and store information, to acknowledge and register any sensory input, and to retrieve or recall stored material. When there are problems, they usually have to do with three areas:

1. Registration
2. Retention
3. Retrieval

Destruction of significant parts of the brain causes problems with memory. All memory deficits should be noted. The physician or clinician will want to do further tests. If you suspect something, ask others who know the patient about their perceptions of the patient's memory functioning.

♦ *Short-term memory:* refers to immediate recall limited to about seven items and generally lasts for about one minute. Some problems may be due to inattention, so evaluate attention before memory.
♦ *Long-term memory:* rehearsal allows material in short-term memory to convert to long-term memory. Anxiety about the interview or the person's situation or even depression can interfere with this.
♦ *Amnesia:* inability to remember
♦ *Anterograde amnesia:* cannot learn *new* material
♦ *Retrograde amnesia:* cannot recall *recent past* events
♦ *Head injuries:* most common deficits are inability to recall names, recent events, and spoken messages, and forgetfulness or forgetting to do something

important. The person may have trouble telling you what she is experiencing with her memory. Memory loss may be permanent if there was severe or repeated head injury.

- ◆ *Transient global amnesia:* lasts minutes to several hours and is usually seen in older people. The person experiences sudden confusion, loss of memory, and disorientation and cannot recall what happened during the time period in question. Retrograde amnesia will be present. Person will be distraught, asking for reassurance as to where he is and what he is doing. This is caused by an insufficient amount of blood to the brain.

Memory Testing: First, ask the person if she has been having any problems with memory. A family member may be able to shed some light on memory issues if any exist. During the interview, note memory lapses and difficulty recalling what the interviewer has just said. If you notice memory loss, note it so that further testing can be done. All the memory tests described in the following paragraphs would be done only if you had considerable questions about a person's memory.

To Test Immediate Recall: Use a random list of digits, saying them in a normal tone of voice, about one digit per second. Ask the person to repeat them. Start with two digits and keep adding until the person fails. Give the person two times to try this. If the person fails at five digits or less, there is reason for concern about sustained effort, attention span, and immediate memory. Anxiety and depression are the most common reasons people fail this test (LaBruzza, 1994, p. 125). Strokes and other brain injuries can also affect recall.

To Test Recent Memory: Ask the person to recall events that have happened in the last few hours or days before she came to see you. You might ask what she had for lunch or where she parked the car. It is helpful if you can validate the answers with someone close to the client who knows. Another way to test is to ask about something that may have happened or been discussed earlier in the interview. You may get several different versions. In cases of trauma and where the victim feels comfortable with you, the different versions may indicate the person is able to recall more of the details. With some people, you might give three or four unrelated words and ask them to recall these words after a short interval. Begin by saying the words in a normal tone of voice and ask them to repeat the words back to you. Note how many times a client must do this before learning the words. About 3 to 5 minutes later, ask clients to recall the words. With a normal memory, a person should be able to recall them (LaBruzza, 1994, p. 126).

To Test Remote Memory: You can ask clients about personal events in their lives and commonly known public events that happened in years past, such as major news stories. Use material that should be known by a person who is reasonably well informed. If the person does not appear to be able to do this test because of a lack of education, a difference in culture, or mental retardation, decide carefully what you will ask the person (LaBruzza, 1994, p. 128).

Additional information on memory and aging and how to assess memory can be found in Chapter 8 of *Fundamentals for Practice with High Risk Populations* (Summers, 2002).

D. Ability to Abstract and Generalize

Proverbs: Cultural background and intelligence can influence how well a person thinks abstractly or how well the person can deal with similarities. Proverbs are generally used to see how well a person thinks abstractly. You need a general fund of information to be able to use proverbs in this way. Tell the person you are going to say a proverb and you would like the person to tell you in his own words what he thinks the proverb means. Then judge how concrete or abstract the reply is. Repeat the person's response verbatim in your report.

Individuals who are psychotic or on the verge of psychosis will often indicate this in their response to a proverb. Use proverbs that arc free of gender and racial bias. The following are some proverbs you can use (LaBruzza, 1994, p. 129):

- A stitch in time saves nine.
- A rolling stone gathers no moss.
- Don't judge a book by its cover.
- Two wrongs don't make a right.

"A rolling stone gathers no moss" could be explained by a person who thinks concretely as, "If you roll a stone down the hill, it can't collect moss." A more abstract response might be, "If you keep moving, life remains interesting and challenging."

Similarities and Differences: Ask the client to tell you how two objects or two events are different or alike. This will require the client to think somewhat abstractly about categories and relationships. Name two items and ask the client how these differ and how they are similar. The following are some combinations you might use (LaBruzza, 1994, p. 129):

- Apples and oranges
- Trees and flowers
- Houses and cars
- Dogs and cats

E. Information and Intelligence

To get an idea of the person's overall intelligence, ask questions that tap the person's fund of general information. It should be information known by the general public. Again, you must be sensitive to the person's cultural background, level of education, and intelligence. The following are examples of some questions you might ask (LaBruzza, 1994, p. 130):

- Who were the last four presidents?
- Who is the governor of the state?
- How many weeks are there in a year?
- What is the capital of the state (or the country, or France)?
- Who was Mark Twain?

IV. Thought and Perception

When a person's perceptions are disordered, it offers important clues to what the diagnosis might be. Here you want to know how people actually perceive themselves, the world around them, and others in their world. What does the person think, and what thoughts and concepts are most on his mind? Perception is the way in which we form an awareness of our environment. People who have difficulties with perceptions often perceive their world inaccurately (LaBruzza, 1994, p. 131).

A. Disordered Perceptions

Following are some terms that describe various disordered perceptions.

- *Illusions:* the person either misperceives or misinterprets a sensory stimulus. A tree branch brushing the side of the house in the wind sounds like people entering the house, or a dishwasher running sounds like people talking in another room.
- *Hallucinations:* in the absence of external stimuli, the person perceives something. The most common hallucination is hearing voices. Voices generally increase when the person is around white noise. White noise is even background noise, such as the dishwasher running, a roomful of people chattering, or rain drumming on the roof. If you can, find out who is talking, what they are saying, and how the person feels about it. Is there a command for the person to do something? If so, include the command in your report. Some commands are dangerous to the person or to others. **Always** note hallucinatory behavior.
- *Depersonalization:* the person feels estranged or detached from herself
- *Derealization:* the person feels detached from what is going on around her. Be sure to note this. A person who dissociates cannot always be sure that what is happening is real (LaBruzza, 1994, p. 132).

B. Thought Content

The following terms are used to describe thought content.

- *Distortions:* a person distorts a part of reality. A woman with anorexia believes she is fat when she is thin. A person who is well believes his cough indicates tuberculosis. A person whose neighbor does not think to wave assumes the neighbor is angry.
- *Delusions:* an inappropriate idea from which a person cannot be dissuaded using the normal means of argument or evidence. Sometimes it is culturally inappropriate as well. Evidence to the contrary has no effect. For example, a client might insist that she has a case in court that will eventually yield her a great sum of money. No amount of persuasion or documentation can dissuade her from that belief and convince her that this isn't so. **Always** report the content of a delusion. Note if the delusion is incongruent with the client's mood. Delusions indicate psychosis. **Always** note if delusions are present.

People with *paranoid delusions* believe they are being singled out for harassment or are being controlled by forces outside of themselves. They may have an entire system of interconnected ideas developed that support their delusions. Common to schizophrenia are:

- *Thought withdrawal:* belief that one's thoughts are being taken out of one's mind by an outside force
- *Thought insertion:* belief that thoughts are being placed into one's mind by an outside force
- *Thought broadcast:* belief that thoughts are being taken and broadcast so that others know what one is thinking
- *Suspiciousness:* **Always** describe this and the object of the suspicion.
- *Grandiose delusions:* the false belief that one is extremely important or a false belief that one is imbued with special powers. **Always** describe ideas of grandeur and any grandiose behavior.
- *Somatic delusions:* false beliefs about one's physical health
- *Delusional guilt:* falsely believing that one is the reason or cause for terrible things that have happened or will happen
- *Nihilistic delusions:* a false belief in the meaninglessness of life and all events and circumstances, in nothingness; hopelessness; belief in the end of the world
- *Ideas of inference:* refers to the ideas the person holds about what others do to affect him
- *Ideas of reference:* refers to beliefs that people are talking and thinking about one. Messages on TV and radio are meant specifically for this person.
- *Magical thinking:* means belief in astrology or a superstition, or the person thinks he has magical powers in his words, thoughts, or actions. This thinking is found in children who have not developed reality testing. It is part of human development and is not pathological until it becomes extreme, as in obsessive-compulsive disorder or a delusion. **Always** check religious beliefs or cultural background to see how this thinking fits with what is going on in the person's life and these aspects of the person's life (LaBruzza, 1994).
- *Thought content:* **Always** specify unusual or important thought content such as: (a) what the person is suspicious about, (b) what the person feels guilty about, and (c) what the person is preoccupied about.
- *Bizarre behavior:* **Always** note any that you witness or any that is reported to you by reliable others.

C. Thought Processes

You may find the form of the person's thoughts to be spontaneous, logical, goal directed, coherent, impoverished, blocking, nonspontaneous, incoherent, perseverative, circumstantial, tangential, or illogical. You may find it to have loose associations or flight of ideas. You may find that it contains neologisms or is distractible.

- *Flow of ideas:* refers to the quality of the associations the person makes between ideas or between points in the person's discussion. Note the stream of the client's thoughts, the rate of thinking, the coherence, the continuity, and whether the thought process is goal directed (LaBruzza, 1994, p. 134).
- *Spontaneous:* means you do not have to keep asking questions. The person readily volunteers information.
- *Goal directed:* the person answers the main questions about why she came and what she needs, and does not stray to other related topics.
- *Impoverished:* the person uses words but is very skimpy with them. There are too few ideas, and thinking is slow. Often attributable to depression or schizophrenia.
- *Racing thoughts:* the person thinks rapidly. Speech appears pressured. Often attributable to manic or hypomanic state.
- *Blocking:* the person stops, pauses, and starts somewhere else. There is an interruption to the normal flow of speech. The person may appear to forget where she was in the conversation when she resumes talking.
- *Circumstantial:* the person appears to throw in too many irrelevant details. Client has too many ideas associated with one another and too many digressions. Often thought to be a defense against dealing with troubling issues or feelings (LaBruzza, 1994).
- *Perseverative:* the person goes over and over the same point or idea.
- *Flight of ideas:* the person goes from one thought to another in logical sequence but is headed far from the original topic.
- *Loose associations:* the person's points do not hang together logically. Ideas shift in an apparently unrelated way. Characteristic of schizophrenia.
- *Illogical:* what the person is saying does not make sense.
- *Incoherent:* there is no meaning; the speech is disorganized; the person may be schizophrenic.
- *Neologism:* the person makes up new words.
- *Distractible:* person cannot stay focused; may indicate mania.
- *Clang association:* "The sound of a word, rather than its meaning, triggers a new train of thought" (LaBruzza, 1994, p. 136).
- *Tangentiality:* means "veering off" on somewhat related, but irrelevant, topics. May show a difficulty with goal-directed thinking. Common in mania and hypomania (LaBruzza, 1994, p. 136).
- *Overvalued ideas:* the idea might be possible, but it is used or seen by the person to explain more than it could possibly explain.
- *Conceptual disorganization:* **Always** note conceptual disorganization. This refers to an inability to conceptualize the problem clearly and may involve a number of the terms previously noted, such as loose associations, flight of ideas, tangential thinking, or incoherent content.

A note about the word *confused*: Students often say a client is confused when they are describing a person who is having trouble deciding what to do or a person who is feeling very ambivalent about a particular decision. In the mental status examination, however, the word *confused* means that the client was not oriented to time and place and person. In other words, confused clients do not know where they are, cannot understand what is being said to them, or do not recognize familiar people.

When a client is *ambivalent*, use that word; and when a client cannot make up her mind, say just that. Reserve the word *confused* for describing true cognitive confusion.

D. Preoccupations

These are thoughts and issues that appear to be the primary focus of the patient's thinking. There is an "obsessive quality" to the preoccupation (LaBruzza, 1994, p. 136).

- *Somatic preoccupation:* focus on bodily functions, physical health. There is a hypochondriachal quality to the preoccupation. List and describe somatic concerns. Do not assume these are not real problems without proper medical documentation.
- *Obsessions:* persistent thoughts that are intrusive and unwanted and that appear to haunt the person (LaBruzza, 1994, p. 136). The person may hold an idea that is not true in that intensity.
- *Compulsions:* actions that are often the "counterpart of the obsession." These are "persistent, intrusive and unwanted urges" to take some action. If one does not complete the action, there is intense anxiety. These actions can be repetitive and ritualistic, such as checking the stove, counting steps, and straightening picture frames (LaBruzza, 1994, p. 136).
- *Phobias:* these are "irrational, intense, persistent fears" of such items as dogs, heights, elevators, insects, leaving home, closed spaces, and flying (LaBruzza, 1994, p. 136). The person will go to great lengths to avoid the situation or object of the phobia.

V. Suicidality, Homocidality, and Impulse Control

Suicidality and Homocidality: You have a clinical and a legal responsibility to assess whether the person is a danger to herself or to others. A person who is dangerously impulsive or holds thoughts of suicide or homicide needs special observation. When conducting an interview, look for these thoughts. These are called suicidal ideation or homicidal ideation. Discover if there are plans to carry out these ideas or if the client seems to have an undeniable intention. Thoughts present some danger, plans make the situation more dangerous, and the clear intention to go forward with the plans creates an extremely dangerous situation.

The mildest form would be thoughts, followed by actually making plans. If the client tells you she has purchased a gun and learned the intended victim's work schedule, you may assume there is a plan. If the client tells you he has saved 3 months' worth of medication for an overdose, this would appear to be a plan. If the client has a plan and expresses to you her obvious intention to carry out this plan, the situation becomes more serious (LaBruzza, 1994).

Always include the plan, the means, and the timetable in your report. If the client is homicidal, include toward whom the thoughts are directed as well.

Impulse Control: When you assess impulse control, you want to know how the person deals with aggressive urges, sexual urges, and strong desires to carry forward any plan not particularly well considered. Look at ways the client has handled stressful situations in the past. Is there a history of acting on impulse without much thought as to the consequences? Does the person seem unable to tolerate stress? How did this person handle stress in the past? Is there a history of uncontrolled aggressive behavior, either sexual behavior or hostile behavior? Can this client tolerate frustration?

The three behaviors to look for in childhood are setting fires, cruelty to animals, and bedwetting. When these behaviors all occur in childhood, they appear to be significantly associated with cruel adult behavior. In adulthood, you might find behaviors such as punching holes in the wall, smashing furniture, slitting one's own wrists, drinking excessively, or turning to drugs or a drug overdose.

VI. Insight and Judgment

Insight: The person understands that she is "suffering from an illness" or has an emotional or personal problem. Make a note if the client completely denies any problems or denies having any part in a problem that obviously affects the client's relationships with significant others. For instance, some people have extremely acrimonious relationships with their relatives but seem unaware that their hostile responses actually elicit more hostility from these relatives. As another example, a person may come in seeking help for a substance abuse problem and genuinely believe that there is no problem and that his behavior is appropriate. In addition, he may indicate that those who are concerned are actually inappropriately concerned. People hold insight in "varying degrees" and may show only partial understanding of their difficulties (LaBruzza, 1994, p. 137).

Judgment: The person can critically evaluate her situation and make good decisions about a course of action. Look for risky behavior in the past that could have been potentially harmful (practicing unsafe sex, binge-drinking and driving, and so forth). "Assess whether clients are able to understand the potential consequences in their behavior" and can plan preventive measures. You might ask what the client would do if he spotted a fire in a movie theater or what he would do if he found a stamped, sealed, and addressed envelope (LaBruzza, 1994, p. 138).

VII. Reliability (Accuracy of the Client's Report)

You need to state briefly your impression of clients' reliability and accuracy in giving you the details of their situations. If a person is psychotic, the material presented is likely to be extremely unreliable. A person who is suffering from dementia or delirium may be having considerable difficulty remembering what has happened or what is happening now. Some clients deliberately tell falsehoods to qualify for disability or to give false impressions of themselves to the worker (LaBruzza, 1994, p. 139).

VIII. The Environment

Sometimes you will be asked to go to someone's home to do an assessment or to do an interview. People's surroundings often hold clues to the way they are currently structuring their lives.

- ◆ *Inappropriate surroundings:* means the person has arranged furnishings inappropriately. It may be that furniture blocks doors and windows or that the windows are covered oddly, perhaps with tin foil or some other material. There might be strange wires leading nowhere, odd decorations, or strings of odd things hung across a room. You might find household objects being used inappropriately. Sometimes a person believes the people on TV can see into his home or the people on the radio can hear what he says. In such cases, you may find these devices covered or blocked in some way.

Be very careful in making these judgments. At one time a worker decided that windows partially covered with foil-wrapped insulation were a sign of something amiss in his client. It turned out the man was doing that to save energy. In another home, a worker decided the blanket over the TV indicated her client was paranoid. In fact, it turned out the TV was very new and the client was very proud of it; she had put a blanket over it the day before when her young nieces came to visit so the TV would not get scratched. It helps to inquire matter of factly about what you see.

- ◆ *Waste and Trash:* Look at the way the person keeps his home. Are there unusual collections of junk or trash? Are there piles and piles of paper and magazines everywhere, or collections of string, bags, and other objects? Sometimes the home is very cluttered or dirty, with unwashed bed linens and with unwashed dishes stacked all over the kitchen. This tells you something about the person's capacity to attend to the routine details of living, or it may indicate a debilitating mental illness. You might find urine or feces on the floor or walls. You might find the pets in the home neglected, their food bowls full of rotten food. Sometimes the house might be overrun with strays the person has taken in, but is unable to adequately care for.

Note: It is not unusual for a middle-class worker to assume that the manifestations of poverty are the signs of a person who is mentally ill. You must be very careful not to ascribe mental problems to someone who is actually too poor to live by middle-class standards.

Always report environmental cues that seem to support the rest of your mental status examination.

Summary

Every contact you have with clients must be documented, and every documentation of a client contact must contain your impressions of how the client seemed at the time of that contact. In social histories and evaluations, these impressions are lengthy and contain material observed by you during your contact with the client.

The mental status examination is a snapshot of where the client is at a particular time. You are not trying to document how the client will always seem. Tomorrow the client may be different. Your notes can be used to follow clients' progress or regression. Using the material in this chapter will help you to write full, accurate impressions of clients that will help clinicians understand what has been going on with them between sessions and determine the best course to follow with each client.

◆ Exercises: Using the MSE Vocabulary

Instructions: See if you can fill in the blanks for each of these questions. This exercise is simply to acquaint you with words you might encounter in the course of your work.

1. The chart on Mr. Kling reads that he has conceptual disorganization. What was the psychologist referring to? _____.

2. In a staff meeting, the psychologist and the case manager discuss the fact that Mrs. Purdy seems to have racing thoughts. They are talking about what? _____.

3. The neurologist's report comes for Mr. Engler. The diagnosis is Broca's aphasia. What does that mean? _____.

4. When the psychiatrist saw Mrs. Nguyen, he said her mood was euthymic. He meant _____.

5. Mr. Kissel's speech is described as impoverished. That means his speech is _____.

6. Another term for severe restlessness is _____.

7. Another way to describe a broad range of moods is _____.

8. When Dr. McCoy said Mr. Perkins used neologisms, Dr. McCoy was referring to _____.

9. Mrs. Dell has been on antipsychotic mediation for some time, and now she shows signs of tardive dyskenesia. That means she _____.

10. When Mrs. Jones was described by the psychologist as seductive, he meant that Mrs. Jones was _____.

11. The chart says that during the interview with Mr. Landon at the prison, where he was being held after being arrested for drug possession, Mr. Landon's speech was guarded. That means his speech was _____.

12. When the ambulance crew called in about 93-year-old Mr. Keller, they said they were bringing him into the hospital, but he was oriented x3. They meant _____.

13. Mrs. Harris complained of trouble falling asleep. In the chart, this was written as _____.

14. Discussing Mr. Rodriquez's delusions with you, the psychiatrist remarks that Mr. Rodriquez has thought withdrawal. The psychiatrist means _____.

15. The psychologist is describing his interview with Mrs. Carter. "She tends to perseverate," he noted. He means that Mrs. Carter _____.

16. Mr. Trong has been depressed ever since he came to this country from Vietnam. Lately the depression has worsened. Today his therapist calls from the International Center asking if you can arrange hospitalization for Mr. Trong because he is catatonic. Mr. Trong is _____.

17. Miss Aller is homeless and mentally ill. The mission calls to say that Miss Aller believes that her thoughts are being taken out of her head and broadcast so that others know what she is thinking. Another way to write this is _____.

18. When Mr. Cruz talks about the accident, he tells you he feels detached from himself. Another word for that feeling is _____.

19. The chart tells you that after the accident Mr. Cruz had retrograde amnesia for a while. That means he _____.

20. The record that comes from the hospital on Ms. James states that she suffered from terminal insomnia during her stay there. That means that she _____.

21. After the stroke, Mr. Torres was described as having Wernicke's aphasia. That means _____.

22. During the interview, Miss Bell constantly pulled her gloves on and off, on and off, in a ritualistic fashion. One word for this kind of behavior is _____.

23. Miss Bell was asked to interpret several proverbs to test her _____.

24. Mr. Lincoln was seen with his wife for marital difficulties the couple was having. He said that he personally had no problems at home and that if his wife said there were problems at home, these were her problems and she was bringing them on herself. What might we say about Mr. Lincoln's insight? _____.

25. The family doctor of Mrs. Fong calls to arrange for an appointment. She believes Mrs. Fong is depressed and "is showing strong neurovegetative signs of depression." What does the family doctor mean by that? _____.

26. When you interview Mr. Marks, you notice that the *sound* of a word seems to trigger a new line of thought for him. You call this _____.

Chapter 19

Receiving and Releasing Information

Introduction

You have done an assessment of the client who is seeking treatment or services through your case management unit. Before you can adequately plan, it may be a good idea to obtain records or summaries of past treatment or services the client might have received. This information gives you a clearer picture of the client and will help you to plan for that person. Knowing what has been done in the past will prevent your trying programs and services with which the client has had little success.

Sending for Information

During the assessment, have the client sign the appropriate release forms. Then, immediately after the interview, mail or fax those forms to the other agency so the information can be obtained in a timely manner.

If You Release Information

Sometimes clients will bring you a form and ask you to release their records to another agency. It is important to protect clients when releasing information. Even though they tell you it is all right to do so, clients may not fully realize the consequences of giving out information. It is your responsibility to see that clients understand what could happen when information is released.

For example, a woman with mild mental retardation had suffered from depression in the past. She was hired in a position at the police station as a cleaning person. When the police personnel office learned of her involvement with MH/MR, they asked for her records. She was very willing to oblige. Her case manager talked to her, however, and the two of them decided to release only a brief, noncommittal summary with few of the details.

The facts of a client's situation belong to the client. These facts are not yours, even though they are in your possession. Releasing them without written consent is unethical—and also illegal, unless covered by the exceptions we looked at in Chapter 1 on ethics.

Before continuing your work in this chapter, review the discussion on confidentiality in the Client's Rights section of Chapter 1. In addition, review the regulations for the Health Insurance Portability and Accountability Act (HIPAA) in that chapter so that you are entirely familiar with those guidelines. Reviewing these materials will prevent you from erroneously releasing information and placing your agency in legal jeopardy.

You may find, when you are practicing case management, that some places still use a blanket release form. The client signs the blanket form approving release of information to a number of places listed on the form for an unspecified length of time. These forms, while saving the staff time, are no longer legal.

Directions for Using Release Forms

Included in the Appendix of this book are two release forms for your use. The first is a standard release form, and the second is a release form specifying that information regarding the client's HIV/AIDS status may be released. These forms will allow you to obtain the information you need to plan for the client.

General Release Form

Here is information you will need to correctly fill out the general form:

1. RE: refers to the client. Neatly and clearly write in the client's name on that line.
2. DOB: refers to the client's date of birth. Place that date on this line.
3. "I hereby authorize ... " is the client speaking. It is the client who is authorizing that her information can be either released or received by your case management unit. If the client wishes to have you release information for another agency, check the first box. The purpose of the release is generally "developing a service plan" or "goal planning." You might also write for the purpose of "developing a treatment plan."
4. If the client wants you to receive material from another agency where the client received services in the past, check the second box, and then provide

name of the agency to which the form will be sent and from which you will receive the information.

5. The phrase "for the purpose of" refers to why the material is being sought. Generally, filling in the blank with "goal planning" or "treatment planning" or "developing a service plan" will be sufficient. Sometimes a doctor with whom you are working is seeking the information for "ascertaining past medications for the purpose of prescribing." Do not go on a fishing expedition, asking for material that you think would be interesting to read, but which bears little impact on what you are planning for the client.
6. Next write in the date on which the release permission will expire. This date should be 90 days from the date below next to the signatures.
7. Information you are seeking is always best obtained in summaries. You do not want everything because you cannot store it all. Only seek what is relevant. For instance, do not ask for school records if the person is an adult with no school problems. Do not seek all the hospital records if the discharge summary will suffice.

    On the line marked "other," it is perfectly all right to write in "medical records pertaining to ..." This way you will not get all medical record information, including that which you do not need for planning, but only the information pertaining to what is relevant (for example, the most recent thyroid surgery or the two hip replacements).
8. The authorized signature is the signature of an adult or the signature of the parent or guardian if the client is a child. You countersign the form, as well, and date it.
9. Your signature goes on the line next to the authorized signature as the person who will receive the information from the other agency. Date your signature.
10. If your client is not able to write but is able to indicate that he wants his records sent to you, you will need to get two witnesses to sign. By signing, they are saying that they witnessed the client indicating the desire to have the records sent.

Again, as the staff person, you must sign the form and date your signature.

HIV/AIDS–Related Release Form

The HIV/AIDS-related release form is used only when:

- The information to be released contains references to the person's HIV/AIDS status (including testing for HIV that was negative).
- The client has given permission for this information to be released.

The two forms go together if there is any information related to the client's HIV/AIDS status. You may staple them together so that they do not get separated. The expiration date on the general release form will also apply to the attached release.

Most states have laws providing that HIV/AIDS information is to be released only to individuals who "have a need to know." These laws take the position that only those directly involved in the medical and physical care of a person with this disease "need to know." Therapy, therapeutic programs, and other services generally can give quality services without knowing the client's status. Therefore, it is important to use universal precautions with every individual.

If your client does not want HIV/AIDS material released, you must send records with all references to the client's status deleted. Blacking out portions of the record is insufficient, as such copies can give the person's status away; therefore, they are not adequate in preserving the client's confidentiality.

Examples of the Release Forms

General Release Form

A sample release form signed by a woman who has been in a drug and alcohol treatment program in another state is shown in Figure 19.1. The case manager needs to understand what took place there in order to plan adequately for the client.

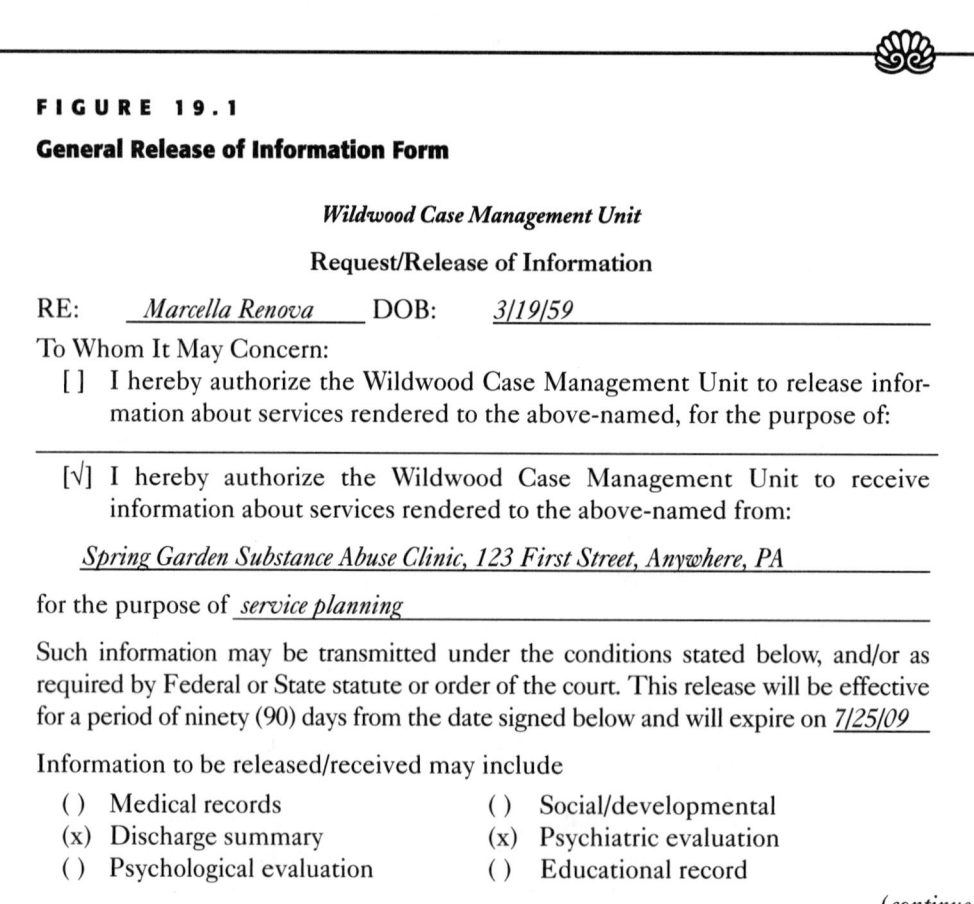

FIGURE 19.1

General Release of Information Form

Wildwood Case Management Unit

Request/Release of Information

RE: _Marcella Renova_   DOB: _3/19/59_

To Whom It May Concern:

[ ] I hereby authorize the Wildwood Case Management Unit to release information about services rendered to the above-named, for the purpose of:

[√] I hereby authorize the Wildwood Case Management Unit to receive information about services rendered to the above-named from:

Spring Garden Substance Abuse Clinic, 123 First Street, Anywhere, PA

for the purpose of _service planning_

Such information may be transmitted under the conditions stated below, and/or as required by Federal or State statute or order of the court. This release will be effective for a period of ninety (90) days from the date signed below and will expire on _7/25/09_

Information to be released/received may include

( ) Medical records   ( ) Social/developmental
(x) Discharge summary   (x) Psychiatric evaluation
( ) Psychological evaluation ( ) Educational record

(continued)

FIGURE 19.1 *(continued)*

    ( ) Vocational evaluation/summary   ( ) Substance abuse treatment history
    ( ) Treatment summary   ( ) Social/developmental history
    ( ) Personal information including Social Security no(s) address(es) and telephone no(s)
    ( ) Other _____

To the agency or professional person receiving this release:

THIS INFORMATION HAS BEEN DISCLOSED TO YOU FROM RECORDS WHOSE CONFIDENTIALITY IS PROTECTED BY STATE LAW. STATE REGULATIONS PROHIBIT YOU FROM MAKING ANY FURTHER DISCLOSURE OF THIS INFORMATION WITHOUT PRIOR WRITTEN CONSENT OF THE PERSON TO WHOM IT PERTAINS.

    THIS CONSENT TO RELEASE OF INFORMATION CAN BE REVOKED AT THE WRITTEN REQUEST OF THE PERSON WHO GAVE THE CONSENT.

I have read this form carefully and I understand what it means.

Marcella Renova   4/25/09   *Kathryn Parsons*   4/25/09
Authorized signature   Date   Staff person signature   Date

I have read this carefully and I understand what it means. As I am not physically able to give my written consent, I am giving my verbal consent to release these records.

_____
Witness signature   Date   Staff person signature   Date

_____
Witness signature   Date

HIV/AIDS–Related Release Form

For our purposes, we will assume that the woman on our general release form, Marcella Renova, has contracted HIV/AIDS. We will need to attach the HIV/AIDS–related form. Figure 19.2 provides a sample of this form.

When the Client Wants You to Release Information

You will receive, from time to time, requests that you or your agency release information on clients you have served. Be sure that the release form is in order and follows the guidelines that you have learned in this chapter and Chapter 1 on ethics. If there is HIV/AIDS material in the file, be sure that the proper forms have been received. If there are no HIV–related release forms, you cannot send the material until all references to the client's HIV status have been eliminated.

FIGURE 19.2

HIV/AIDS–Related Release of Information Form

Wildwood Case Management Unit

Release of HIV/AIDS–Related Information

RE: _Marcella Renova_   DOB: _3/19/59_

To Whom It May Concern:

- [√] I hereby authorize the Wildwood Case Management Unit to release information about services rendered to the above-named, for the purpose of: _service planning._

- [√] Such information to be released includes information regarding my HIV/AIDS status and/or treatment.

To the agency or professional person receiving this release:

THIS INFORMATION HAS BEEN DISCLOSED TO YOU FROM RECORDS WHOSE CONFIDENTIALITY IS PROTECTED BY STATE LAW. STATE REGULATIONS PROHIBIT YOU FROM MAKING ANY FURTHER DISCLOSURE OF THIS INFORMATION WITHOUT PRIOR WRITTEN CONSENT OF THE PERSON TO WHOM IT PERTAINS.

THIS CONSENT TO RELEASE OF INFORMATION CAN BE REVOKED AT THE WRITTEN REQUEST OF THE PERSON WHO GAVE THE CONSENT.

I have read this form carefully and I understand what it means.

Marcella Renova	_4/25/09_	_Kathryn Parsons_	_4/25/09_
Authorized Signature	Date	Staff Person Signature	Date

I have read this carefully and I understand what it means. As I am not physically able to give my written consent, I am giving my verbal consent to release these records.

Witness signature	Date	Staff person signature	Date

Witness signature	Date

When the Material Is Received

When you have received the material from the other agency, you have the elements to construct a fairly accurate clinical picture of the person who has come to you for help. You have the person's initial description of the problem, followed by a more detailed explanation and a thorough social and medical history. You have sought and noted the client's expectations for services and done some preliminary planning with the client. You have at least a general idea of how the *DSM* categories might or might not apply to your client. You have assessed the person's mental status and received information to support or enhance your own conclusions. It is time to structure a service plan for your client.

Summary

At many different times in your career you will be involved in collecting and organizing important information about clients for the purpose of understanding their history and for planning current services. When you request information for your use or the use of your agency, be sure to collect only those summaries and evaluations that are relevant. Do not send for large quantities of material that will be bulky to store and difficult to maintain in the record.

When you are asked to supply information about a client, take care to operate within the guidelines and the law regarding confidentiality. Be particularly careful about what is released when the client is a child, has a mental disability, or is infirm. We are the ones who are charged with maintaining the clients' privacy.

Social service agencies frequently make requests, with clients' permission, for information from other agencies. It will be your role to choose carefully what to request and what to release.

◆ Exercise: Send for Information Related to a Middle-Aged Adult

Instructions: Using the blank form in the Appendix entitled "Request/Release of Information," send for information relevant to planning for one of the cases you are developing. Choose the information for which you are sending carefully, and be able to explain how this information will assist you in planning for your client.

◆ Exercise: Send for Information Related to a Child

Instructions: Using the blank form in the Appendix entitled "Request/Release of Information," send for information relevant to planning for the child's case you are developing. Choose the information for which you are sending carefully, and be able to explain how this information will assist you in planning for your client.

◆ Exercise: Send for Information Related to a Frail, Older Person

Instructions: Using the blank form in the Appendix entitled "Request/Release of Information," send for information relevant to planning for one of the cases you are developing. Choose the information for which you are sending carefully, and be able to explain how this information will assist you in planning for your client.

◆ Exercise: Maintaining Your Charts

Instructions: Place your completed release forms into the appropriate clients' charts. They should be placed under the long assessment forms in the charts. If there is more than one form, staple them together.

Chapter 20

Facilitating a Meaningful Change and Recovery

Introduction

In the last few years, systems of care have moved from viewing clients as helpless and incompetent, hopelessly crippled by their diagnosis or their problems, to recognizing that people, in spite of their disabilities and personal problems, are basically strong and self-interested. Women's services and services for those with developmental disabilities have long viewed their clients in this way, and other service systems now are beginning to see that their clients are valuable partners in their own change and recovery effort. Today life-long chronic disorders and problems are treated as only a part of the individual's life. As these systems undergo transformation to greater individual responsibility, some workers, unwilling to view clients as competent partners, have left social services.

Successful planning, whether constructed at the case management unit or at the agency providing the service, includes specific elements not considered only a few years ago. When these elements are applied, the plan is more likely to succeed, and the client is more likely to recover. Before moving on in the case management process, let us stop and look at those elements and how people make changes and recover.

All good plans addressing client needs and goals have these elements:

- Self-determination, wherein the client takes charge of the decisions and the stated goals
- One or more good relationships that are trustworthy
- Collaboration and a shared decision-making process
- Support and encouragement when needed

- Professionals who understand how people make changes and recover and how the change process works
- Services the client can use to make successful changes, sustain these changes, and recover

These elements, when in place, put into practice the values talked about earlier: independence and hope. People may not "recover" from developmental disorders or from old age, but significant changes can take place in their lives to move them in the direction of hope and independence.

A family member coming for another family member or a person seeking help is coming for one reason: The person is seeking some sort of change. Things as they are now are painful, uncomfortable, perhaps dangerous in some way, and even inexplicable. When the circumstances of the problems people face are too overwhelming or painful, they often seek our help. In seeking help the person wants something to change for the better, and that is where you come in.

After you have taken a history, sent for previous records (if needed), and discussed the person's needs and what help the person is seeking, you and your client begin to develop a plan. This chapter looks at how to make the plan fit the person and specifically address that person's needs and aspirations for a better situation.

How People Do Not Change or Recover

We know now that people do not change or recover if we make decisions for them and set goals we see as important without consulting them. We know that people cannot change if they are denigrated or demeaned. We have seen that people do not change when we act as if they are less competent or less capable than they really are. And we have learned that recovery demands more than making an immediate problem go away. Recovery involves looking well ahead and surveying each person's future with him or her.

What Is Change?

Change has different meanings for different people. It can mean immediate changes to painful circumstances, or it can mean long-term changes that affect the person's future well-being and sense of competence. You may begin by looking first at the near term changes such as abstinence through admission to a rehab program, relief of severe anxiety through the use of medication, or a change in an older person's unsafe living arrangements. But at some point you and your client will address how to prevent the same problems from occurring again and how to develop a worthwhile future.

When change involves giving up a way of being, an old habit, or accepting one's diagnosis, it can be difficult. People do not just change, even when they have suffered a setback or uncomfortable crisis, asked for help, or said they want to change. Fear, uncertainty, stubbornness, denial, lack of confidence or hope, or the inability to envision the future can be significant obstacles to change. Change takes commitment and hard work.

What Is Recovery?

Ideally recovery is what we would like to see for all our clients. Recovery happens when individuals assume control of their lives and work to establish a sense of purpose. When people recover, they are encouraged to look toward a future that is more productive, more meaningful, and less stressful in ways it has not been before. Recovery involves the long-range view, looking at many aspects of a person's life. Recovery involves looking with the client at where she wants to be in a year or in 5 years. How will she get there? What elements does she want in her life? What would she put in her life if she could? What goals would she like to pursue? What issues does she believe need to be cleared up? What treatments and services does she want to use? In answering these questions, we introduce the elements for positive changes and recovery.

Charles Curie, former administrator of the Substance Abuse and Mental Health Services Administration (SAMHSA) in the U.S. Department of Health and Human Services put it this way: "Recovery must be the common, recognized outcome of the services we support." SAMHSA developed the following list of essential elements of recovery for people with substance abuse problems or mental health diagnoses. Today these elements should be observed in creating plans for all our clients.

- *Self-Direction*. Individuals take charge of how they will recover, including making significant choices and decisions.
- *Individualized and Person Centered*. Consideration is given to the very unique attributes each person brings to recovery, including culture, preferences, personal experience, and a collection of strengths and needs.
- *Empowerment*. Clients participate to the fullest extent possible in decisions that will affect them and are given the information they need to participate fully. They speak for themselves and control the elements in their own recovery.
- *Holistic*. Recovery addresses the client's whole life, looking at more than the issues that caused the person to seek help. A client's role in the community, preference for where to live, what work to pursue, and what spiritual needs are not being met, are all considerations.
- *Nonlinear*. Recovery does not happen in predictable steps but involves growth and occasional setbacks.
- *Strengths-Based*. Recovery is based on the strengths clients bring to the process, including their interests, talents, accomplishments, coping skills, and much more.
- *Peer Support*. Mutual support and encouragement are provided by peers who share experiences and information and even advice.
- *Respect*. Clients are accepted and appreciated, their rights are protected, and discrimination and stigma are eliminated wherever possible.
- *Responsibility*. Individuals are personally responsible for their own self-care and path to recovery, relying on their own courage and energy to do so.
- *Hope*. Recovery involves striving for a better future, and clients are encouraged to envision themselves overcoming obstacles and moving forward.

Physical Health Is Part of Wellness

Working within a holistic framework involves looking at all areas of clients' lives. In the past, case managers and other providers focused on the immediate problems and on relieving immediate symptoms. Now case managers, particularly, are looking at all aspects of a person's life. A study by the National Association of State Mental Health Program Directors in 2006 produced some alarming findings. According to the study, "People served by the public mental health system had a higher relative risk of death" (p. 11). The study went on to report, "Deceased mental health clients had died at much younger ages and lost decades of potential life" (p. 11). On average, those with a mental health diagnosis were likely to die 1 to 10 years earlier than a person with no mental health diagnosis. While case managers and other service providers were focused on the mental illness, other health issues had been overlooked. In addition, many who needed health care or even needed to receive disability payments were unable to successfully navigate the system.

This study alerted people in the fields of mental health and other social services to the importance of looking at a person's health as a whole and to the importance of moving people receiving social services toward wellness on many levels.

Self-Determination

Self-determination means that to the extent the individual is able, he or she drives the recovery process. Self-determination involves the client's right to direct his care and to determine the elements that will go into the service plan. In some locations clients are given the resources to pay for the care they deem important to their recovery. For example, Gladys thought she would recover better if she had acupuncture along with her medications and counseling. Arrangements were made to make the resources available for Gladys's acupuncture, and Gladys attributed her seven sessions of acupuncture with augmenting and enhancing her road to recovery.

Within the limits of what is reasonable and the person's capacity for self-determination, clients have the freedom to choose what is best for them and the authority to develop meaningful plans directed toward their own recovery. Their vision of recovery prevails, not the case manager's.

Relationships that Support Recovery

As case managers we form a partnership with clients to work together on the matters they see as important. With a strong relationship based on equal partnership, better outcomes can be expected. If you see clients as helpless and incapable, they will not change or recover. In fact, how you view the client is significant.

A nurse told the story of a patient who was getting better every day after a serious illness. He was in the hospital, but it was planned that he would go home in a few days. As the nurse entered the room to change his dressing, the patient asked her to pour him a glass of water from the carafe sitting within reach on his bedside table to the glass sitting beside it. The nurse chuckled and said, "No I'm not going to pour your water for you. You can do that yourself." And she pointed to the glass and carafe. "But I'm sick," the man moaned. "Yes," the nurse answered, "but I am here to help you go home and be able to take care of yourself. If I do that for you, how will you practice doing it for yourself?"

Had the nurse poured the water, she would have been confirming this patient's helplessness and delaying his becoming self-sufficient. How we view clients can have a profound effect on how they view themselves and what they will be able to accomplish. If we show confidence in clients' ability to grow and recover, they are more likely to grow and recover. If we are doubtful and hover about doing things for them that they can do for themselves, they will remain unchanged and unsure of themselves, and recovery will not be within their reach.

Collaboration

Here are two mistakes some workers might make in trying to help clients make changes:

- ◆ Believing that the worker must have all the answers and must come up with the solution
- ◆ Assuming that clients have no answers of their own or cannot think of solutions on their own

If you think about it, these ideas violate our respect for clients, and neither of these ideas is comfortable for either party.

It is unrealistic to think you should have all the answers for every problem, and it is equally unrealistic to think clients have no valid answers and solutions of their own to offer. To avoid this thinking, form a partnership with clients, a collaborative relationship. As the case manager, you bring a wealth of information about what services and supports are out there for clients to draw on. You have seen what works and where others have tried things that have worked less well. This is valuable information for clients to have. Case managers foster informed consent.

Clients bring valuable information as well. They know themselves, their values, goals, and aspirations, and the things most likely to present obstacles. They can tell you what worked in the past and what did not, and often they can tell you why it didn't work. By combining what each knows best, clients and case managers work together to plan and make decisions.

When you collaborate, talk to the client about what "we" can do or how "we" can look at this differently. Ask the client if he would be willing to consider certain approaches or solutions, and ask what solutions he may have thought of. Give your client an opportunity to express his views or opinions, and suggest ways the two of you can work together to overcome the problems. When you offer information, allow the client to accept what he feels will work and leave the rest.

Peer Support

Some time ago, when people with problems were viewed as incompetent and hapless, asking one of these people to help another was seen as ridiculous. Today peer support has become a significant part of a person's recovery. Peer counselors greatly diminish the feeling of being alone with one's problems.

Sometimes a person will recover if given more sustained time and support, but the case manager does not have the time to devote to this one person. Sometimes a client will benefit from the help of another who has "been there." Peer support by others who have waged a similar struggle and recovered can have an enormous impact on recovery.

One agency director offered this analogy: "A person is in a hole and can't get out. The public walks by, but they don't know what to do so they call the experts. The experts come and bring a ladder, but it isn't enough. Then the peer support counselor comes along and gets in the hole too. The peer shows the person in the hole how to get out, how to use the ladder effectively. That is the beauty of peer support." Today peer counselors are viewed as having something valuable to contribute to the team, and they are used in a wide variety of settings.

Encouragement as Part of Recovery

When Clients Are Discouraged

Part of the case manager's work in the relationship is to provide encouragement to people who may feel very discouraged. Many of the people we see are discouraged as a result of their circumstances, disease, or illness, or because of what has happened to them. Here are some symptoms commonly seen in discouraged people:

- ◆ The situation seems to overwhelm them.
- ◆ They have low regard for their capabilities or put themselves down.
- ◆ They are unwilling or unable to take responsibility.
- ◆ They describe their circumstances or other people as totally domineering and overwhelming.
- ◆ They have no trouble discussing their problems but are unable to focus on solutions to those problems.
- ◆ Their goals seem impossible or unrealistic to them.
- ◆ They set impossible standards for themselves.
- ◆ They sprinkle their conversation with negative global statements such as "*Everybody* hates me" or "*Nobody* ever calls here" or "*Everything* is rotten" or "Bad things *always* happen to me."

How Case Managers Motivate and Encourage

Case managers provide the encouragement clients need to reach beyond their current situations. Case managers encourage their clients to look for and try alternative ways of doing things. Much of this is frightening to people. Change and uncertainty are never easy. Clients, like all of us, resist change. The old ways, however painful or inconvenient, seem preferable to the unknown results of change. The following sections discuss techniques case managers can use to help clients recover.

Begin Where the Client Is

The first step in encouraging others is to accept clients exactly where they are. The worker does not denigrate the client for needing help or coerce the client to be better or work harder. Arnold R. Beisser (1970) talked about Frederick Perls, the father of Gestalt therapy, and what Beisser called Perls's "paradoxical theory of change." Beisser defines the theory this way: "Change occurs when one becomes what he is, not when he tries to become what he is not." Perls believed that forcing people to be different never accomplished real or lasting change. People first have to come to terms with who and where they are at the moment and find some degree of acceptance in that.

If you start immediately telling clients how to do things differently, how their behavior has been the root of the problem, or how erroneous their thinking has been, they will find it important to argue and defend themselves—to explain why they have done those things or thought that way. Valuable time is wasted and rapport lost as clients move into a defensive position rather than a collaborative one with you.

One case manger related that she had begun to work with a client who had battled numerous psychotic episodes. This client had a severe mental disorder that had required emergency hospitalizations in the past, but once she was stabilized on medication and doing well, she would stop the medication and try her best to go on as if she did not have a disorder to address. This is much like the diabetic who knows he is diabetic but goes on drinking or eating cookies anyway in an attempt to ignore his disease. The case manager said it was not until she and the client worked together to help the woman accept the facts of her illness that she began to move beyond denial, took better care of herself, and achieved some of her long-range goals. Until the client accepted her disorder, no change or recovery was possible. As of this writing, this woman is getting married and holds a meaningful job.

As a case manager, you may be the first person to really listen to clients entering the system. Use this opportunity to bring acceptance and understanding to the way things are now. Let clients be exactly where they are at the moment they first see you, without remonstrance from you. Beisser (1970) wrote, "The premise is that one must stand in one place in order to have firm footing to move and that it is difficult or impossible to move without that footing." To really provide useful assistance to clients and encourage them to grow into their true potential, start exactly where they are, not where you think they should be.

See the Client's Strengths

Case managers who encourage their clients will see them as basically capable and wanting to take as much responsibility for their lives as possible. Clients come with varying degrees of independence and abilities. Some can grow into full independence, and others will always need some help. In this wide spectrum of abilities and needs, you will undoubtedly see the strengths of each individual and point those strengths out to the person. Hearing it from you is often all it takes for a person to stop and reconsider. Then together you can work to help the client maximize and take pride in those strengths.

Accurately Assess the Client's Reluctance

Sometimes clients appear overwhelmed and either unable or unwilling to take responsibility. Try to understand accurately how real these obstacles are. For example, an inability to use public transportation may be a small obstacle that is easily overcome for a depressed college graduate but a very real obstacle for an individual with moderate developmental disabilities.

A client may not follow through on projects or goals the two of you set together. The reason may have more to do with the projects than with the client. It may be that the two of you set a goal that is too complicated for now. Perhaps the goal looked safe when the client sat with you in the office, but now it looks terrifying. Explore this with your client. Don't assume that clients who do not follow through are being obstinate or uncooperative.

Appreciate Every Effort

Suppose your client resolves to try something new, and the first efforts are not very successful. To encourage this person to try again, focus on the efforts, not on the results. The attempt to grow or to change is more important than whether or not it worked. Point out that the attempt gave valuable experience or information and that it creates a basis for improving.

Never Lose Sight of Potential

Focus on clients' potential. You know all about their deficits or weaknesses. So do they, but they have far less certainty about their potential for growth and change. Look at clients' strengths, their past experiences, and their accomplishments, however small. Use these to guide you in planning the small steps they can take toward positive change.

Encouragement Guidelines

Here are some rules to follow in encouraging other people:

- ◆ Start right where the client is.
- ◆ Use acceptance and empathy.

- Work at your client's pace.
- Appreciate the significance of all the person's efforts and attempts.
- Recognize the client's strengths verbally with positive feedback.
- Show confidence in the client.
- Keep your sense of humor.

Here are some discouraging things you should not do:

- Never set a goal for the client without the client's participation.
- Never try to force clients to do something they really are not ready to try.
- Never denigrate the client for not moving faster.
- Never demean a client who did not choose your suggestions for handling things.
- Never try to get action by shaming the client or making comparisons to others.

Figure 20.1 summarizes the differences between a human service professional who provides encouragement and one who provides discouragement.

FIGURE 20.1

Encouragement versus Discouragement

The Encourager	The Discourager
1. Says you can	1. Says you can't
2. Helps clients to do their best	2. Wants clients to compete
3. Helps clients look for the best in life	3. Tells clients life is unfair
4. Believes others are capable	4. Believes he or she is more capable than the person being helped
5. Talks directly to people	5. Talks down to people
6. Is supportive of others	6. Is critical of others
7. Is enthusiastic about others	7. Is reluctant and wary of others
8. Is interested in the smallest accomplishments	8. Is interested in the smallest mistakes
9. Helps clients set realistic expectations	9. Has unrealistic expectations for clients and gives up
10. Sees resources and strengths in clients	10. Sees mainly weaknesses and incompetence in clients
11. Lets clients develop their own personal standards	11. Sets personal standards for clients
12. Believes people can improve	12. Believes people never change

Source: Based on D. Dinkmoyer and L. E. Losoncy, *The Encouragement Book: Becoming a Positive Person* (Englewood Cliffs, NJ: Prentice-Hall, 1980).

Stages of Change

Now let's look at how people change. Carlo Diclemente and Mary Valesquez (2002) described five stages of change that individuals pass through as they change and recover. When you meet a client, he or she may be in any one of these stages. Knowing where the person is in the change process helps you to be more effective.

Stage One: Precontemplation

People in this stage are not ready to change, and perhaps they are not even thinking about it. They may not see a need to change, or they may have tried in the past and been unsuccessful. Here you might express your concerns and invite feedback.

Listen to why the person is reluctant to change. Explore obstacles the client sees. Be matter of fact and accepting of where the person is now without passing judgment or arguing.

Stage Two: Contemplation

In this stage a person is willing to explore but not yet willing to commit to change. Talk over the problem with your client. How does she see the problem? What does she think are the causes? What might be some good solutions? What does the client risk if she changes, and what rewards might she reap? Here collaboration is important as you give information and learn from your client.

Here you may experience a person's ambivalence about change, a normal response to thinking seriously about reordering her life. You may encounter people who will never move out of this stage. To support the contemplation, talk through the risks and the benefits involved in change at this point. Collaboration and good listening skills are very important at this stage.

Stage Three: Developing a Plan

At this stage the client is ready to change but needs a plan. You and the client work together to find the best plan of action. He may have tried to change previously and in talking with you finds that he learned some valuable lessons from those experiences. Now is a good time to talk about the options you know about and seek input from the client. If the client indicates he will try something you believe may not work, use an I-message to bring up your own concerns.

Stage Four: Implementing the Plan

In this stage people will actually change their thinking or their behavior or their habits. During this trial run at changing things, it is normal to be uncertain. Some people will miss the way things used to be. Listen to their concerns without judgment. Sometimes a person putting a plan into action will not be entirely committed or may feel awkward and inadequate. Your encouragement and support can facilitate the work your client is doing.

Stage Five: Maintaining the Changes

In this final stage the person is seeking to make the changes a permanent part of her life. People take varying amounts of time to make the changes permanent, and some people never quite accomplish that. What obstacles are in the way of long-term success? Are there still things that will support the original behavior, such as triggers? Does the environment support a change?

Relapse

A client may find that he cannot sustain the new behavior or way of being over a long period of time. A person may return to her addiction, another may stop his medications, another may return to an abusive relationship, while another may resume abusing her children. These relapses usually occur gradually. There is an initial slipup, which is often followed increasingly by the old behaviors. Look at the attempts your client has made rather than focusing on the failure. What was learned? What can be done differently next time? Talk through the relapse using your listening skills to help the person make sense of what happened and why.

In some cases people can learn how to recognize a relapse, self-managing their disorder or addictions. Education about what to do and how to prevent relapse can help. Advance directives can help if the person is likely to have a relapse in her mental disorder. An advance directive allows the client to stipulate how she wants the next relapse handled.

Look together at how the relapse happened: identify what is likely to bring about a relapse, note the early signals of a relapse, prepare a prevention plan, and plan for how a relapse should be handled if it occurs again.

A Case History

Let us follow Claudette who came seeking help for a compulsion to shoplift. After numerous years in therapy and several short stints in the county jail, she still felt the urge to steal. She confided that she thought she had an "addiction" because getting things out of the store without paying for them was a challenge and there was a thrill when this was accomplished successfully. When she came to the agency, she was in danger of losing her children and felt the need to try once again to stop her negative behavior.

Claudette was beyond the precontemplation stage (stage 1). She had thought about changing before she came to the agency (stage 2). When she came in, the case manager took the social history and the two of them talked over the problem at some length. Claudette blamed an older sister and her friends for her "bad habit." The case manager made several suggestions for Claudette to consider, including a 12-step program, but Claudette seemed unsure. The case manager suggested Claudette think about the suggestions and also what she thought would work well and return to talk further.

Claudette made an appointment the next week. She had once again shoplifted, and she was concerned that she would, in time, get caught and lose her children because shoplifting was a violation of her parole. Claudette and the worker devised a plan together (stage 3), which included Claudette attending the 12-step program every evening for the next month and seeking a sponsor there. In addition, Claudette suggested she would not go shopping unless someone was with her who would be distressed if the person found her shoplifting again. A likely person was her aunt, and when contacted, the aunt was willing to accompany Claudette for the next month when she went shopping.

Two weeks later Claudette reported doing well. She had a sponsor and had been to the 12-step program every weeknight since her last visit to the agency (stage 4). Just before the month was completed, however, Claudette called to say she had shoplifted on a Sunday afternoon when her aunt had been busy at church. She was out of milk and had gone to the store, promising herself that she would only buy the milk and return home, but she had also stolen four pairs of children's socks.

Claudette had relapsed. The case manager spent time talking to Claudette about how the relapse happened, what she thought had triggered it, and what she might have done differently. With Claudette's permission, the case manager brought together the people who were most concerned and wanted to help, Claudette's aunt and her sponsor.

Once again a plan was devised, and Claudette actively contributed. This time it was agreed that she would call her sponsor or her aunt if she felt a compulsion to shoplift. She would continue in the 12-step program every weeknight for another month, and she and her case manager would be in contact once a week. With the sponsor acting as a peer counselor, Claudette began to make important changes. At the end of the month she had not shoplifted, and her nights in the 12-step program were reduced to three nights a week (stage 5).

Now the case manager began to work with Claudette about the future she saw as productive and beneficial. Together they looked at the sort of work Claudette might do, the education she would need to do that work, and the need for better parenting skills. Claudette wanted to get off welfare, and she wanted to be involved in other "healthy" activities that would take her away from the compulsion to shoplift. In the next few months she started school and was enrolled in a parenting workshop. After a year there had been no further shoplifting, and Claudette seemed to be on the road to real recovery. Her grades were good, and she confided that most of her time was spent parenting or studying. She and her peer counselor remained friends, and now Claudette was beginning to help another person with a similar problem.

In this case study, the case manager used all the skills he knew would be important. He stayed where Claudette was in the process, even when she relapsed. He collaborated and at times coached her. He worked through the stages with her and accepted her ambivalence. Claudette never had to listen to scolding or denigration, and she never had to use time and energy defending herself to her case manager. Instead the focus remained on where Claudette was at the moment and where she would like to go from there.

Ambivalence and Reluctance

People often move toward recovery at different rates due to their ambivalence. Most people do not readily change without experiencing some ambivalence, some conflict about it, or some degree of pessimism. These thoughts and feelings are a normal part of changing, and case managers need to accept, therefore, that people on their way to making important changes will pass through this stage of uncertainty or ambivalence in varying degrees.

Some people stay with their ambivalence longer than others, and some people never can move beyond it. If you accept this as perfectly normal, you will have less reason to grow exasperated.

Rolling with Resistance

We often think of resistance as something clients do because they are being difficult or uncooperative. It is somehow their fault that they do not follow through with our directives or even plans we worked out with them. We often see this resistance to our planning as a negative part of their problems, a behavioral problem they use that obstructs getting better or changing their lives for the better. Some of that may be true, but we need to back away from these ideas and consider other possibilities.

Sometimes things move too quickly for a client. Change may be coming in unexpected and very uncomfortable ways, and the old, safer ways of being and doing are giving way to the unknown. The client may have excuses, procrastinate, find reasons to avoid you, or just ignore plans you and she made together. It may be that the goals in the action plan you both developed looked good on paper, but your client is finding it enormously difficult to implement the plan the way you both constructed it.

According to Miller and Rollnick (2002), we should see resistance as a "signal to respond differently." In other words, what we worked out with the client or the way we are supporting the client's path to change needs a different approach. Often untrained workers argue with the client, pointing out the work put into the plan for change, the client's initial participation, and why the plan is a good one. Arguing serves to make that person more set in his or her opinions and behavior. When you argue with the client, you are engaging in an adversarial relationship with the very person you want to help. You are laboring under the false belief that by arguing you can make the other person do what you think he or she should do. But that person may have a very different perspective, and plans that seemed reasonable when the two of you sat down together in the office no longer seem reasonable when the client attempts to put the plan into practice.

Rather than arguing, respect the client, accept where the client is at this moment, and try to understand where the client wants to go. Your genuine desire to understand the client's perspective is the foundation for helping the client. To help your client overcome resistance to change, make sure the client understands the following:

- *You want to listen.* Make it clear that you *want* to listen and that you are truly interested in how the client sees the problem.
- *The decision is theirs.* Point out unequivocally that the ultimate decision for what takes place belongs to the client. Neither you nor anyone else intends to force the client to do something he or she is not ready to do or feels uncomfortable about.
- *Ambivalence is normal.* Acknowledge that feeling uncertain, wanting to reexamine things, stop and back up, and all the things people do when they are not sure about changing are normal. Ambivalence comes before real change. The client needs to hear that and know that you accept where he or she is at the moment.

Once the client feels free to talk openly, you are in a position to hear some really valuable information. Then you and the client can begin to look at the problem from another perspective with new ideas on the table.

Sometimes clients don't want to do anything to change the situation just now. Perhaps the plan you had agreed to was too frightening or difficult, so they backed away. Although you may be inclined to feel frustrated and irritated, remember that clients are ultimately responsible for the direction their lives take. Rather than feeling guilty that change did not take place, recognize that you have respected the clients' right to self-determination. When clients with whom you are working seem to be having trouble with plans and solutions you made together, form a partnership to reevaluate the problem and look together for something that might work better; a new path to try; another action to consider.

Summary

Nearly every person who comes to us for help is looking for something better. The request for help, however uncertain the person might be, indicates some sense that things could possibly be better. Change and recovery are difficult processes and proceed at different rates for different people.

Many people look at their mental or emotional illness, their addiction, their current situation, their criminal history, or their self-destructive behaviors and choices and decide to change. Some of them do make changes in the direction of a more stable, healthy life on their own. Some do not. When people reach out for help, it is often case managers who facilitate the move toward the change they are contemplating.

Just because people reach out for our help, however, does not mean that they are entirely prepared to change their situation or their behavior. People come to us who are thinking about possibly changing or who are mandated to come by their employer or the courts. People come to us because they know they should change but really like things the way they are. They are, in a word, ambivalent. There is a conflict for them between what is presently comfortable and what they think they should be doing or even what they want to do, if they thought they could. Some people have lived so long with their illness, situation, or addiction that they feel hopeless. Others just want a little coaching to get on another track in life. Still others come to us for help again and again but never make the change.

Coaching, collaborating, and planning are ongoing processes as people grow and see themselves as doing more, accomplishing more. In the work you do with clients, the first plan may open up to a second more independent plan that paves the way to an even more accomplished plan.

Seeing people as ultimately responsible for the direction their lives take and viewing ourselves as a resource, a coach, and a source of support for change makes our work more effective and gives people more opportunity to recover successfully.

◆ Exercises: Helping People Change

Instructions: Looking at the techniques you learned in Chapter 12 and in this chapter, decide what techniques and skills would be best to use in each of these situations.

1. Kelly has talked and talked about getting a divorce from her husband who abuses her occasionally and has always been remote and uninvolved in their marriage. You feel strongly that she should leave because you see the abuse escalating. What are some things you might do to help Kelly decide what she should do from here?

2. Marlo wants to stop drinking and get her children back. They were removed from her home a year ago after Marlo had her fourth DUI and caused an accident on a city street. She has been in jail and is now in a halfway house while on parole. What are some things you might do to help Marlo decide what to do now?

3. Ben has been sober for 2 years and is now working consistently on a job he likes. He divorced his wife during the time he was in rehab because she could not give up her drinking and seemed to "want to pull me down."

Now she has returned, intoxicated, and begging him to take her back. They talked into the night about "old times" and both of them got drunk. What are some things you could do to help Ben at this juncture?

4. Elmer does not want to be abusive to his wife and wants his marriage to resume. His wife left and is staying in a shelter where she has indicated that she will not come home until Elmer gets some help. Elmer admits to you that abusing his wife was "probably wrong" but seems to resist any ideas about how to go about changing his behavior. What are some things you might do to help Elmer at this point?

5. Elise is using alcohol to self-medicate. She suffers from debilitating depression, but since adolescence she has turned to alcohol and street drugs to alleviate the symptoms of this depression rather than take her medication. Her reasons for doing so are that the medication is too expensive, coming in every time she needs a prescription is "a pain," and she can go to the liquor store and buy cheap liquor without the inconvenience. Lately she seems to be thinking that maybe using alcohol is not the best idea, but she is defensive about why she has used alcohol in the past. What are some things you can do at this point to help Elise?

Chapter 21

Developing a Service Plan at the Case Management Unit

Introduction

Using the information you received (see Chapter 19) and the information you took at the time of your interview with the client, the next step is to develop a service plan. A service plan contains broad general goals for the case management unit to follow with regard to a particular client. Case managers then refer clients to the agency where the actual service will be provided. Generally, the case management unit develops an outline for the provider agency to follow. The provider agency takes these broad, general goals and turns them into very specific and measurable goals with objectives for the client. These will be in effect and constitute the guidelines while the client is receiving service from the agency.

Following is the step-by-step process for developing a service plan. Remember that you will not be giving these services. Instead, you will be determining what the person needs, based on your evaluation or intake assessment, and based on your discussions with the client about services the client feels are important. The services and agencies you choose for your clients will be those that will help clients attain goals that you and they see as important for them.

There are several types of goals for clients. You might develop treatment goals to treat conditions such as mental illness, emotional problems, or drug or alcohol abuse. When a client has treatment goals, the case manager generally refers the client to mental health programs, drug or alcohol rehabilitation, or physical health interventions.

Not all of your clients will need treatment goals. Some clients will have problems involving poverty, home arrangements, and material needs. For these clients you will develop general living goals that will improve their situation, perhaps by providing appropriate in-home care, better transportation, or a more appropriate living arrangement.

Involving the Client and the Family

Only 10 or 20 years ago when clients requested help from an agency they were told by that agency what help they would receive. Often the agency prioritized the client's problems for them. Clients had little or no input into these decisions, and clients who objected or had other ideas were often viewed as difficult and uncooperative. Agencies developed services in part based on the skills and expertise of the employees at those agencies. They might not offer services that were badly needed in their community, and they might offer services that did not meet the needs of any but a select group of people. Clients were expected to fit into the services offered and were often labeled untreatable if they did not.

Today, all that has changed. Several factors have fostered these changes. When the state mental hospitals began to shrink their patient populations, patients were brought back to their communities and back in contact with their families and other support systems. It soon became obvious that many families were unable to cope with the mental illness of their family member without support, and without that support the patients were often abandoned by their families. To a lesser extent this abandonment happened to senior citizens when caretakers were struggling to care for an older person with complex problems. In the field of substance abuse, clients' families often gave up and cut all ties after trying to support their family member to abstinence. Agencies gradually began to recognize the value of including families in planning and implementing treatment. In recent years, children have been receiving services in ever-greater numbers. This has involved families in planning and implementing the treatment or service plans for their children.

Today agencies are expected to engage both the client and the client's family (with permission from the client) when this inclusion is appropriate. Clients and their families assist in developing service or treatment plans. Families receive agency support to remain involved with their family member whenever possible and receive the support they need to remain an intact family. Agencies that work to enable the identified client to live successfully in her community have found that individuals do much better if their families have not cut them off. Children can take better advantage of services if the entire family is considered in the planning. For these reasons, human service professionals are careful to listen to what the client wants to receive from services and to what the family may need to support the client.

An inappropriate use of family involvement would occur if a worker ignored the wishes of an adult seeking services for emotional or situational problems who did not desire family involvement, or if a worker involved family members after a client asked specifically that his family not be involved in any way. In these situations, you follow the wishes of the client and strictly observe confidentiality guidelines.

Using the Assessment

You will receive an evaluation or assessment for each person in your caseload. This will be either the social history or the assessment form. In our hypothetical case management unit, you will have done the assessment or social history yourself, which is often the case. The evaluation tells you what the person's major problems are and what areas of the person's life need attention. Generally these problems are the reason the person is seeking help or is being referred to a therapeutic or supportive program. The assessment alerts you to the expectations and desires of the client as well. All of this will help you to determine what goals you think you should work on with your client. Figure 21.1 lists some common goals to consider for clients. You may think of others.

The goals listed in Figure 21.1 are very broad, long-term, and general. Choose those goals that fit your client's most outstanding needs and give them more specificity. For example, your client might need "to make positive changes regarding stressors and coping mechanisms." You would not word it in just this way. You would give it more specificity by writing something like this:

- Goal: "Job with better work hours" or
- Goal: "Resolution of current marital problems"

When the client is referred to an agency for help in meeting the goals, the agency will set up smaller, more specific goals and develop a specific plan for the client to meet those goals.

FIGURE 21.1

Goals to Consider for Clients

- To obtain (or maintain) housing
- To make positive changes regarding relationships with family members
- To obtain (or maintain) mental health treatment or rehabilitation services
- To obtain (or maintain) physical health treatment or rehabilitation services
- To recognize precipitants to hospitalization and take appropriate action
- To obtain (or maintain) social support
- To obtain (or maintain) recreation and leisure-time activities
- To obtain (or maintain) employment
- To obtain a new role in life
- To continue living independently
- To obtain (or to maintain) food and clothing
- To acquire (or to improve) daily living skills
- To obtain (or to maintain) drug and alcohol treatment or rehabilitation services
- To make positive changes regarding stressors and coping mechanisms
- To obtain legal assistance on legal issues
- To obtain (or maintain) transportation
- To obtain (or maintain) an education program
- To obtain assistance with financial issues
- To develop realistic goals for the future

Creating the Treatment or Service Plan

When you go to the treatment planning conference or a service or disposition planning meeting, you should have a provisional plan for your client. After this meeting, your next step is to create the final service plan for your client. In putting together the provisional plan, write out the goals so you have a clear understanding of what you and the client see as important in this case, and then use the "Treatment or Goal Plan" form found in the Appendix, following these steps:

1. Place the client's name and next of kin on the top line of the form.
2. Check the box for an initial plan, as you have never done one before on this client.
3. Fill in the date the plan was created. Make the review date 3 months from this date, unless in your judgment a review should take place sooner. For instance, if the person is in need of inpatient drug and alcohol services and those services are only expected to last 10 days, check on that service sooner.

NOTE

Not every client who comes for help has a mental health problem. A person who has run out of fuel oil might have a mental health problem, but if the reason that person is seeking help today is to get a voucher from you for more fuel oil, the mental health problem is not relevant. Be careful not to assume that everyone you see must be mentally or emotionally ill. Look at the V codes in the back of the *DSM-IV* for problems people often encounter in life that might become the focus of clinical attention, without meaning that the person is mentally ill. For many people who depend on the social service setting, even these will be irrelevant.

4. Indicate who helped to formulate this plan (the client, daughter, mother, father).
5. Wait until you are in the planning meeting to decide the level of case management, and determine that with others. You may have an idea about the level when you go to this meeting.
6. Print your name as the case manager.
7. The box containing the material on the *DSM-IV* should be left for completion in the planning meeting. Again, you can have a rough idea of what you will suggest for the axes, but wait to make it final until you have heard from others.
8. Sign and date the form at the bottom, placing your name on the line for the case manager. Your instructor will sign and date the supervisor's line.

To fill in the boxes:

1. For each category on the left
   a. Circle or highlight "Strength" if this is an area of strength for the client—that is, if there are no problems for this client in this area or if the client

brings resources to this area. You can make a notation or comment by way of explanation in this box.

b. Circle or highlight "Need" if there is a problem in this area that you intend to address. You can make a notation or comment by way of explanation in this box.

c. *Do not circle either STRENGTH or NEED if the area in the box is not applicable to the client's problem.*

2. Place relevant comments and explanations in the comment box.
3. Write the goals in the boxes underneath the heading "Goal(s)." You can base the goals on the list shown in Figure 21.1, or you can come up with others.
4. In the boxes in the last column, indicate the name of the agency to which you will refer the client to meet the goals. Try to get as much service from one agency as possible. Sending the client to five or six different agencies can be confusing. For clients who have many needs, choose agencies that give more comprehensive services. Providing names of agencies in the community where you plan to practice as the agencies to which your client will be referred for service will help you become familiar with the resources in your area.

An example of a goal plan for a client is presented later in this chapter.

How to Identify the Client's Strengths

Clients have strengths that may be useful in working toward the goals. Be sure to use these strengths in planning for your client. When you are looking for the strengths of the client, here are some factors to check (these apply to both children and adults):

1. Look for supports in the community for the client and the client's family. For example, is the client involved in a church, a club, or a recreational program? Are there any other social services involved? Does the client have a strong circle of friends at work or strong ties to a community?
2. What are the religious or cultural beliefs, practices, or values observed by this person, and how does she use these for support and comfort?
3. When your client interacts with others, such as staff, family, and pets, what interpersonal skills does he appear to have?
4. What special abilities or skills does the client possess?
5. If you gave the client a choice as to what she would prefer to do, what would she be most likely to choose? This is particularly important with children.
6. If the client has contact with his family, what does the family do together? Do they eat together, go to church, meet for special occasions, or watch TV?
7. What hobbies, recreational activities, or talents does the client pursue? What interests this person?
8. What activities, people, or groups give comfort to your client? Does your client have a pet?

9. With whom is the client most likely to want to spend time? This is important with regard to children.
10. Who outside the client's family has shown an interest in this person?

Individualized Planning

All of this has led to individualized planning for clients. Clients no longer have to fit into a certain program or go without treatment. Instead, case managers develop plans for their clients that are specific to that person. No two plans should be exactly alike.

An example of poor planning can be found in the caseload of Alicia, whose clients were all over 70. Alicia was only 24, having recently graduated from school, and to her people over 60 seemed elderly. In planning for her clients, Alicia assumed they were all in the same need of supervision and support. She referred all of them to Homemakers, Inc. for household help. She insisted, when she could, that each of them attend the local senior citizen center. In addition, she tried to line up Meals-on-Wheels for each of her clients.

The clients began to talk among themselves about Alicia's lack of appreciation for what they needed in their lives right then. Marguerita did need Meals-on-Wheels, but only temporarily while her broken arm healed. She found going to the senior center a chore because she wanted to stay home and read and watch her favorite shows on TV with her neighbor. Delbert belonged to a retired businessmen's club and wanted to go there in the afternoon. He found it annoying that Alicia called to check on him when he failed to go to the senior center. Delbert had come in for help with portable oxygen. When Leslie refused to use the Homemaker, Inc. services, Alicia went to Leslie's home to find out why. Alicia appeared astonished that Leslie was able to keep her own home and often entertained family and friends.

Alicia is an example of a case manager who does not view her clients as individual people. She lumped them all together in a category of "elderly people." She devised her service plans based on her assumptions about what elderly people should need.

Understanding Barriers

Barriers are those circumstances that prevent you from understanding the client fully or prevent the client from taking advantage of services and even your support. If you are aware that barriers will diminish the effectiveness of your plan, you can modify the plan accordingly. This helps you to plan in a way that prevents problems later and helps the client to take full advantage of the plan. It is a two-way street.

Barriers prevent workers from fully understanding and helping clients, and they prevent clients from being able to take full advantage of the plans being developed for them. Even when you have identified as many barriers as possible and addressed them, you may refer your client to a place where barriers will appear again. Care in planning is the best way to make sure your client can truly take advantage of the service or treatment.

Following are some common barriers:

- *Language*: The client may not be able to communicate adequately with others because of a difference in primary language. The worker may not be able to communicate with the client because the worker does not speak the client's language.
- *Culture*: The client may be unable to negotiate an unfamiliar culture. The worker may not understand the client's culture or may be inclined to judge the client's culture by the worker's own cultural standards.
- *Disability*: The client may not be able to handle all the details of the plan. The worker may overestimate or underestimate the extent of the client's disability.
- *Lack of resources*: The client may lack the resources to fully participate in the plan, such as lacking transportation or clothing suitable for a job interview. The worker may see the client's poverty as a barrier to the plan or fail to take the lack of resources into account.
- *Mental illness*: The client may be unable to communicate clearly or follow through with the plan. The worker may be afraid of the illness or may fail to understand how the illness affects the client's capabilities.
- *Mental retardation*: The client may be unable to communicate clearly or follow through with the plan. The worker may see the client as a child or may fail to understand how the disability affects the client's capabilities.

Sample Goal Plan

Figure 21.2 shows the goal plan for a 34-year-old man, Larry McCune, who was in a severe car accident 4 years ago. He has come into the case management unit requesting help with symptoms he originally thought would disappear or that he could handle on his own. The police report states that he was driving his car with his family in the car. He approached a busy intersection and failed to stop for a yellow light that turned red while he was in the intersection. He was hit and two people were killed, one of them his 4-year-old daughter.

Larry is well educated, with several degrees, and works as an engineer in a position he enjoys. Since the accident, however, he has been unable to work consistently and has had numerous arguments with his subordinates. His wife left a year ago, taking the remaining child with her, a 9-year-old boy.

Larry is complaining of severe headaches and is not clear if these are from stress or the accident in which he suffered what was diagnosed as a mild head injury. He is asking for help because of recurring nightmares that involve the accident and an intense fear of riding in cars, which recently has spread to using any form of public transportation. He states he feels detached from other people and lately has thought that perhaps his life is really over.

Note that the case manager has put together the plan (see Figure 21.2) so that the client can receive his services almost entirely from one source, in this case the Linden Counseling Center. Personnel at that center will address this client's specific

FIGURE 21.2
Treatment or Goal Plan

Client _Larry T. McCune_ # _03468_ Next of kin _Lydia McCune (Mother)_

Initial plan [√] Updated plan [ ] Date _3/6/09_ Review date _6/6/09_

Developed with _Larry McCune_

Level of case management _Resource Coordination_ Case manager _Kathy Torres_

Provisional DX: Axis I _309.81 PTSD, chronic with delayed onset_ Axis II _V71.09_

Axis III _Headaches following head injury_ Axis IV _Marital breakup_ Axis V _55_

Type	Strength/Need	Goal(s)	Comments	Referral
Income/financial situation	(Strength) Need		Receives income from disability insurance policy	
Housing living arrangement	(Strength) Need		Owns home	
Vocational	(Strength) Need		Would like to return to job, has job to return to	
Educational	(Strength) Need		Has engineering degree	
Transportation	Strength (Need)	To be able to drive independently	Can be addressed in therapy	Linden Counseling Center
Medical	Strength (Need)	To be free of headaches		Michael C. Fillippo, MD Neurologist for neurological evaluation

Activities of daily living	Strength Need		
Legal	Strength Need		
Recreation & leisure time	Strength Need		
Mental health	Strength Need	To reduce or eliminate symptoms of PTSD	Linden Counseling Center
Substance abuse	Strength Need		
Family relationships	Strength (Need)	To re-establish ties with 9 year old son	Linden Counseling Center
Social supports	(Strength) Need		Continues to receive support from friends at work and from mother
Other	Strength Need		

Kathy Torres   3/6/09   *Marshall Potts*   3/6/09
Case manager signature   Date   Supervisor's signature   Date

needs. A neurological assessment will be done by a neurologist, whose findings will ultimately be taken into account at the Linden Counseling Center in working with Mr. McCune.

Summary

For every client we see, we must create a service or treatment plan that specifically addresses that client's needs. In addition, this plan must specifically address the direction the client states she wants to go. No two plans should be exactly alike because clients can have the same symptoms or conditions but for different reasons, and they also can have the same problems but react to them differently. Couple that with other individual concerns that each client brings and the need for an individualized plan becomes obvious.

Case managers, for their part, need to know about a variety of services ranging from formal agencies to folk supports and support groups in their communities. The variety allows workers to easily put together unique plans that address each client's individual needs.

When creating plans, always involve the client and, when appropriate, the client's family. Plans without client input are not acceptable. As clients discuss their problems and the issues they feel should be addressed, you can formulate general goals for them that will become your plan. Once you have some ideas about goals, ask clients if you may share your ideas with them, and always ask for their opinions or additions. Following the guidelines in this chapter makes it more likely that the plans you develop will have a lasting and beneficial effect.

◆ Exercises: Broad Goal Planning

Exercise I Planning for a Middle-Aged Adult

Instructions: Using one of the blank "Treatment or Goal Plan" forms found in the back of your book, develop a plan that addresses the immediate or most important needs of the client you are following. Look at both strengths and weaknesses.

This will be the tentative plan that you will take to the planning meeting. Make certain that you have addressed those areas of your client's life that are most troublesome right now to the client. If one of your clients is facing a poverty situation, do not assign a *DSM* diagnosis. Remember, these are not the goals that will be developed at the provider agency. Your client is not there yet because you have not written a referral for that agency yet. Before you can do that, you must have the broad, general goals that should be pursued at this time with your client.

Exercise II Planning for a Child

Instructions: Using one of the blank "Treatment or Goal Plan" forms found in the back of your book, develop a plan that addresses the immediate or most important needs of the child you are following. Look at the strengths and weaknesses of both the child and the child's family.

This will be the tentative plan that you will take to the planning meeting. Make certain that you have addressed those areas of the child's life that are most troublesome right now to the child and his family with regard to this child.

Exercise III Planning for an Infirm, Older Person

Instructions: Using one of the blank "Treatment or Goal Plan" forms found in the back of your book, develop a plan that addresses the immediate or most important needs of the older person you are following. Look at both strengths, including natural supports the person might be able to call on, and weaknesses.

This will be the tentative plan that you will take to the planning meeting. Make certain that you have addressed those areas of your client's life that are most troublesome to the client right now.

Exercise IV Maintaining Your Charts

Instructions: The "Treatment or Goal Plan" form should be placed under your release forms. This is a tentative form and does not need signatures. You will clean up and revise your recommendations in the planning conference, and then put the revised form in the chart in place of this original.

Be sure that every chart you are following has a plan in it. Charts without plans are often the reason funding and accreditation sources withdraw support.

Exercise V Checking Services

Instructions: If you have a question about a service in your community that you believe might provide the services your hypothetical client needs, call that agency for information. Most agencies have brochures or other informational literature they will send to you.

Chapter 22

Preparing for a Service Planning Conference or Disposition Planning Meeting

Introduction

After you have completed your assessment on each new client and done a tentative plan with the client, your agency might hold a meeting in which more specific plans are made for the client's care or services. In some agencies this is done informally. In small agencies, particularly, individual case managers may make those decisions by themselves, referring the clients to other services in systems that will have more formal case management.

In some places, children who come into the system are presented by their case manager to a "children's panel" consisting of child psychologists, child psychiatrists, social workers, pediatricians, and others who serve children. Many places are adopting this same format for serving clients from different populations; in this situation, the case manager presents the case to representatives of any number of agencies serving or specializing in that population. Together the group decides what combination of services would best suit clients in their current situation and gives a diagnosis, if appropriate.

If a person has both a substance abuse (SA) problem and a mental health problem and the agencies that address these two problems are not combined, representatives from each of the agencies working with the client should meet together to decide what should be done. In the past a client could be turned down for mental health services because he was drinking and turned down for SA services because he was suicidal. That kind of turf exclusion at the expense of the client is no longer tolerated by funding sources that expect the client to be served.

In these meetings, decisions regarding the service your client will receive are made with others who have experience and come, perhaps, from different disciplines. When the meeting is over, a formal plan will be drawn up.

What You Will Need to Bring to the Meeting

You should consider bringing three items to these planning meetings.

1. *Tentative service plan.* You have already developed a tentative service plan with the client. Bring this tentative plan to the service planning conference.
2. *Human service directory.* As you work within the same social service system, you will come to know, without consulting a directory, which agencies are reliable and which services are used most often by your agency in referring clients. As you begin your career, you need to know what human service organizations are available in your community. If there is a directory, bring that to the meeting so that you can work with your peers to find the best placement for your client. A good place to look is the local phone book, where social services are usually listed together. You might copy these pages and bring them to the meeting.
3. *DSM Handbook.* The *DSM* is a large volume containing considerable information. If you are working in an area that is likely to use the *DSM* to give diagnoses, you might consider purchasing the *DSM Handbook*, which contains only the most basic information and is easier to carry with you when you go to meetings of this sort. Bring your *DSM Handbook* to assist in making the provisional diagnosis.

Goals for the Meeting

Goal One: Diagnosis

If the client being discussed is seeking mental health/mental retardation or substance abuse services, you will need to give a provisional diagnosis at this meeting. Older people who appear to have some type of dementia also receive diagnoses. Diagnoses in these service delivery systems are usually required for payment purposes and can be changed after the client is in the system and has been thoroughly observed. Children with mental retardation, clinical disorders, or learning disorders also require diagnoses from the *DSM*, as would someone suffering a significant emotional response after an assault.

Goal Two: Level of Case Management

In addition to the provisional diagnosis, you may assign the level of case management if your agency uses different levels. For our purposes, we will use these four levels.

1. *Administrative case management*: Clients are placed in a pool with other clients who require little service or follow-up beyond the original referral. The client tends to function independently.
2. *Resource coordination*: Clients are often in need of services and assistance on issues such as housing, medication, or therapy, but they generally do well with the services offered and do not pose a risk to themselves or others.
3. *Intensive case management*: Clients are at high risk for rehospitalization or for behavior that poses a danger to themselves or other people.
4. *Targeted case management*: Clients of varying needs are given to a case manager who carries a smaller caseload as a result; the client has the same case manager through stable times and times of crisis, giving the person continuity of care.

Goal Three: Services

In every case management situation, the most important part of the intake process is to make decisions about the service the client will receive. Your assessment prepares you to make those decisions wisely. Remember that you do not give the service. Your task is to look at the material in your assessment interview, such as:

- The strengths and weaknesses of the client
- What the client said she wants or expects
- What services this person could use well or fit into well
- What the major problems or presenting problems were (presenting problems are those that brought the person into the agency in the first place)
- Goals you have for the client and the client's stated goals
- Any other pertinent circumstance or information about the client that you feel is relevant

Using the material you have assembled, you (and presumably a team) will develop in this meeting a plan for services, and for treatment if needed, that matches the client's problems and expectations.

Preparing to Present Your Case

In the planning meeting, you will give the pertinent details that will help the group make decisions about where the client will be referred and the type of treatment the client will need. Your presentation is a short, oral summary of your case to the group. It should be given in an orderly manner.

Before the meeting, review the details of the case. Bring the intake and assessment material with you, and refer to it if you do not know the answer to a question. In general, however, you should be able to answer most questions without reference to the material.

The elements of your presentation will include the following information:

1. Why the client came to the agency. What were the presenting problems?
2. How the client presented in the assessment interview.

3. What the client indicated are his goals and expectations.
4. Additional relevant information that would have bearing on the disposition of this case.
5. Your impressions and recommendations.

These elements are described in more detail in the following text.

1. *Why the client came to the agency. What were the presenting problems?* Discuss why the client came to the agency. What were the outstanding problems she talked about during the phone intake and at the assessment interview? Mention any other outstanding problems that you feel should be addressed.
2. *How the client presented in the assessment interview.* Talk about any unusual or bizarre behavior. Describe any hallucinations or delusions the client might have had. Most clients will not have any of these. Be sure to talk about the client's affect, motivation, and insight.
3. *What the client indicated are his goals and expectations.* What did the client say he wants to have happen as a result of seeking services? Tell why the person sought help, and what the client expects the outcome will be. Even though you will formulate the final specific goal plan for this person, be sure to indicate the client's input here. What did the client want? What were the client's stated goals? What was the client's priority? Have a tentative goal plan ready that addresses these, but expect others to see and suggest additional goals or to suggest changes.
4. *Additional relevant information that would have bearing on the disposition of this case.* If there is other information that the team should have in order to make a decision, be sure to discuss that. In addition, describe any unusual characteristics that might give a clearer picture of the client. Perhaps it is something the client said; provide the client's wording if possible. Perhaps the client has worked for several years at the Humane Society and has four dogs he rescued. During the interview, he talks about his dogs and shows you pictures of them. This fact may not directly influence the treatment plan created to deal with his depression, but it will give the team a clearer picture of the client and the client's interests and the goals the client might have talked about either short term or long term.
5. *Your impressions and recommendations.* What is your impression of this person, and what do you recommend that might address the problems the client felt were most pressing?

Making the Presentation

By following the format discussed here, you will make a good presentation. Be prepared to talk about the case to the team for about 3 to 5 minutes. You should not have to read through notes or shuffle papers. Simply describe your client. After you are finished, the team will ask you questions about your client. You should be able to answer these without reference to your notes, but that may not always be so. If you do not have the information, turn to your notes when you need to.

Sample Presentation

Following is the presentation on Larry McCune by a case manager in the planning conference:

> Mr. McCune is a 34-year-old male, an engineer. He came seeking help for symptoms resulting from a severe traffic accident about 4 years ago. He said he was driving and was in the intersection when the light turned red. He was hit and his 4-year-old daughter died in the accident. His marriage broke up about a year ago, and the remaining child, a 9-year-old boy, is currently with the wife.
>
> Mr. McCune complained of severe headaches, and he says he has nightmares that involve the accident. He also said he thought he had a phobia (his word) about riding in cars and, more recently, in other forms of transportation. He said he doesn't feel able to work consistently and talked about being irritable, especially at work.
>
> During the interview, Mr. McCune had a flat affect and sometimes he was tearful when he discussed the loss of his daughter and later when he was describing the divorce. He seemed to me to have some slowed motor responses. He sat quietly during the interview. He looked sad, and there was no animation in his speech. There were times he appeared not to be focused on the interview.
>
> He is asking for help that will allow him to return to work. He says the two biggest obstacles to that are his problems with transportation and also his irritability with coworkers. I talked to him about the need to find out the origin of the headaches and he agreed with that.
>
> Right now he lives alone. He has stopped attending church, and he said he has few friends. He accepted all my suggestions without much discussion. He seemed pretty passive.
>
> I see this man as depressed and anxious in the sense that he seems to have developed a strong fear about using a car or other transportation. The other impression I had was that he is dealing with a lot of guilt, which he agrees needs to be addressed too. I am recommending that he be evaluated for any residual neurological problems resulting from the accident, just to check on the headaches, and I would like to have him evaluated for depression and possible antidepressant medication. He asked specifically for counseling, and I recommend that. I think he could benefit from that. Mr. McCune might actually benefit from a grief support group in time. His goal for coming, he told me, is to get back to feeling better and being able to work consistently. Does anyone have any questions?

In this presentation, the case manager has briefly addressed all five parts of the presentation. Others at the meeting might want additional information. For example, someone might ask this case manager about the client's relationship with the wife and son. Here is how the case manager might answer that question:

> We really only talked about that a little bit. He pays support but not consistently. He said his ex-wife is working. He did say he sees his son, but I understood that this is not like a regular visitation schedule or anything. He doesn't describe the relationship with his ex-wife as extremely hostile. My understanding was that she left because she couldn't take his irritability and not going to work regularly.

In the Appendix at the back of this book is a form titled "Planning Conference Notes." You may use this form to make sure you have notes on the five points you want to cover in a planning conference on your client. You would not give this form to anyone, but it helps you to make sure that all the points are covered and gives you a place for the notes.

Collaboration

Treatment or service planning, when it is done with a team, is a collaborative activity. Some case managers become defensive as others suggest changes or additions to the tentative plan. One case manager was "upset" when the tentative diagnosis she had in mind was questioned by the psychiatrist. Feeling that a change in the diagnosis would reflect on her and imply incompetence, she resisted any change and became angry.

Another case manager was sure that the man whose situation he was presenting was not experiencing medical problems as a result of his drinking. This case manager became sarcastic in the planning meeting when others asked that a medical examination be part of the plan. "I think I've seen enough alcoholics to know when someone needs medical care and when they don't," he sneered at the others on the team.

In a third situation, a woman presented a case of a client suffering from severe anxiety. The case manager thought the problem was a generalized anxiety disorder. Another case manager questioned the diagnosis, stating that it seemed more like post-traumatic stress disorder. The client's symptoms and complaints needed further evaluation by the team, and a discussion ensued. The case manager was asked questions as the team attempted to assemble more details in order to make the diagnosis. The case manager answered these questions, but she did so in a petulant manner and later reported that her "feelings were hurt" because "people I thought were my friends just ganged up on me in there."

It is important to ask questions of your colleagues in a collaborative and respectful manner. Do not grill the people presenting cases. Do not be dismissive of their interpretations of the situations or demean the conclusions the presenters have made. After all, the presenter is the person who actually saw the client, and her observations are extremely relevant to the decisions made on the client's behalf.

Follow-Up to Meeting

After the treatment planning conference or disposition meeting, you will write up a formal service plan for your client using the "Treatment or Goal Plan" form. When your goal plan is completed, you will:

1. *Meet with the client and discuss the plan.* Your first contact note should be written on your first meeting with the client after developing the goals and referral options and having those confirmed in the treatment planning conference or disposition meeting. In this meeting, you will go over the plan with the client, or the client's parents in the case of a child, and note the client's response and any changes you make to the plan as a result. When you and the client feel comfortable with what is planned, you can move on to referring the client to the place where he will receive the treatment or service. In Mr. McCune's case, he will probably be seen by a neurologist for evaluation of his headaches, by a psychiatrist for evaluation of his depression and possible medication, and by a counselor at a counseling service.
2. *Make referrals* for your client to the agencies that will actually carry out the services.

Summary

After you have met with a client and heard the client's concerns and issues, and after you and the client have developed a plan that appears to meet those needs and seems satisfactory to both of you, often you will be asked to sit down with others to go over the client's situation and the plan for that client. This meeting is meant to offer support in the belief that several people looking at a client's case together can refine the plan somewhat. For that reason, keep in mind that the meeting is a collaborative one. You can expect to answer questions and hear ideas about your client, and you will be expected to ask questions and offer suggestions to others.

Once you have completed this meeting you will:

- Write a formal service plan and have your supervisor (in this text, your instructor) sign it
- Meet with the client to review the final plan
- Write a contact note about the meeting with the client for the client's file
- Refer your client to the people and agencies indicated in the plan

◆ **Exercises: Planning**

Exercise I Developing a Service Directory

Instructions: Before you go to a planning meeting, you need to know what services are available in your community. Gather information on various social service agencies. Some regional phone books contain special pages of social services. Some counties publish a directory you may be able to purchase. The library may have lists of agencies you can copy, or a local agency may have compiled a directory.

Be sure the directory you compile or obtain is relevant to the area in which you intend to work following completion of your courses. In this way, you will begin now to become familiar with the services that are available.

◆ **Exercise II A Simulated Planning Meeting**

Instructions: To simulate a planning meeting, form groups of no more than five students (otherwise it will take too long for everyone to present a case). Present one of the cases you have developed to the group, following the instructions for presentation provided in this chapter. Be sure to bring the information on the client and the material you will need to plan services and give a diagnosis.

You can have your instructor act as the senior specialist who can confirm with you the proper diagnosis, or you and the team can arrive at your own decision.

Sign the revised planning form, and have your instructor also sign it, as your supervisor.

Chapter 23

Making the Referral and Assembling the Record

Introduction

After the service planning conference or disposition meeting, you rewrote the old, tentative service plan to develop a formal service plan for your client, and you had your instructor, who is acting as the supervisor in this case, sign it. You then discussed this final plan with your client, and now you will refer the client to the agency or agencies that will carry out the treatment or service.

Use the "Referral Notification Form" in the Appendix to make referrals to these other agencies. Referrals are generally faxed or sent electronically to the agency to save time, although they can be sent by mail.

1. All referrals are coming from the case management unit for which you work, in this case the Wildwood Case Management Unit.
2. Write the name of the agency to which you are referring the client after the word "To."
3. Note the date the referral was made.
4. Write the client's name, address, and phone number after "Re" in the box.
5. Write the goals the referral is to address in list form.
6. The "Target Date" is the date you expect the goals to be met.
7. After "Review Date," place the date on which you intend to review this case plan to see if the plan is working.
8. Write your name in the blank for case manager.

Determining Dates

Two dates must be determined: the target date and the review date.

The Target Date

When you set a target date, you are stating clearly to the providers how long you expect it will take for the service to obtain the goals you and your client have worked out for your client. You are, however, clarifying something else. You are informing the provider how long you will allow the service to be given without getting the desired result. If the target date is reached and the goal has not been accomplished, it is time to stop this intervention and seek a more useful approach.

When setting a target date, decide how long you are willing to continue to try this approach without seeing any result. Beyond that date, you will not continue funding, and at that point you will evaluate other options for the client.

Physicians routinely expect to see results from medications they prescribe for their clients in a specified amount of time. They know that if the medication has had little or no effect in a specified number of weeks, it is time to switch to another medication. Neither you nor the physician in this example can afford to administer a particular treatment plan for as long as it takes, no matter how long that might be.

The target date is influenced by two factors:

1. *Funding.* The amount of money available to spend on the service will influence how long the client can stay in the service. If you are using public funds or insurance, there may be a cap on the amount of money you can pay for a particular service.
2. *Goal.* The goal is a factor in the length of time needed. Some goals are short term, such as a 6-day detoxification program, whereas others are a substitute for or to prevent inpatient hospitalization and may require weeks or months of service.

The Review Date

The review date is the date you expect to review this specific service in the plan to see if the plan is actually working. In most cases, plans are reviewed at least every 90 days. Therefore, a person in a partial hospitalization program for 6 months would be reviewed in 3 months. As noted, however, some services are short term. In the case of a 6-day detoxification service, you might make a quick review on the 3rd day.

The purpose of the review date is to make sure that the client is getting what the client needs and what the referral stipulated the client would receive and to be sure that if the plan is not working, no further money will be spent on trying to make it succeed. In most cases the plan will be revised to better achieve the client's goals, and in some cases the goals may be reevaluated.

Sample Referral Notification Form

Figure 23.1 contains a simplified version of what you are likely to see in a referral form in actual practice. Many provider agencies have their own referral forms they want the case management unit to use when making a referral to that provider agency. These forms ask for more information about the client, usually in a detailed summary. We will use a simplified referral form for our purposes.

The referral in Figure 23.1 is for Paul Bittinger, a person with chronic schizophrenia. He has been in and out of hospitals for acute episodes of hallucinations during which he believes the voices he hears are giving him the power to walk on water. These voices, and his subsequent delusion that he is omnipotent and can walk on the surface of a nearby river, have caused him to jump in the river at times when it was high or there were huge, swiftly moving ice chunks. In an effort to help him manage his own illness and medications better, the case manager is referring him to a partial hospitalization program.

The Face Sheet

Your clients are now in your agency's system, and a record is assembled from the various forms and contacts you have had with these clients and those concerned with them. All charts on clients who have entered the system have a face sheet. (See the sample of a completed face sheet in Figure 23.2.) This sheet lies on top of all the other information and contains essential information for anyone who might need access to it quickly.

You will find a blank face sheet in the Appendix. To fill out the face sheet:

1. Place the name of the client, the agency number you have assigned the client, and the client's address and phone numbers at the top of the form. (For our purposes here, give the client any agency number you wish. It should be at least four digits.)
2. If the person is a child, someone with a severe mental handicap, or an elderly person in need of a guardian, put the guardian's information in the next section. Most clients will not need a guardian, in which case you can leave this area blank or write N/A (not applicable) in the space.
3. Nearly everyone has someone they wish to have notified in case of an emergency. It may not be a blood relative; a friend or a neighbor is acceptable. The person the client indicates he feels closest to should go in the section under next of kin. Indicate the relationship of that person to the client (for example, mother, sister, or friend) in parentheses.
4. Below the top box, from "Date of First Contact" on down, fill in only the information that applies. Not all clients will be on medication or have a physician involved in their case. Where information does not apply, use N/A to indicate that.

FIGURE 23.1
Referral Notification Form

Wildwood Case Management Unit

Referral Notification Form

Client *Paul J. Bittinger* # *12365*

Address _____

Home phone _____ Work phone _____ Date of referral *9/12/09*

Axis I *295.10 Schizophrenia, disorganized type*

Axis II *V71.09*

Axis III *Hypothyroidism*

Axis IV *Recent arrest for disturbing the peace*

Axis V *50*

Provider *Grandon River Hospitalization Program*

Type of service *Partial hospitalization*

For the purpose of _____

Learning to manage medications

Learning to manage the symptoms of his illness

_____

_____

_____

Review date *10/15/09*   Target date *12/15/09*

Referring case manager *Brenda Walker-Poloski*

a. The top row of boxes is fairly self-explanatory. The date of the first contact is listed followed by who took the contact. The client's date of birth and gender complete this row.
b. In the second row of boxes, give the client's marital status, the last grade completed or diploma received, the current employment if the client is working, and veteran status.
c. The next row deals with issues related to pregnancy so that medications and treatments do not jeopardize the mother or the child.
d. In the fourth row, the first box requires information on current medical conditions and who is treating the client for those. The box next to that requires medications prescribed for that condition and the person doing the prescribing. In most cases it would be the same physician.

FIGURE 23.2
Face Sheet

Wildwood Case Management Unit
Face Sheet

Name _Lucinda Harris_   Agency # _02487_

Address _1235 Pleasant St.; Anytown, PA 01234_

Home phone _555-555-5555_   Work phone _555-555-5555_

Guardian _____

Address _____

Home phone _____   Work phone _____

Next of kin _Jamal Harris (Husband)_

(If different from guardian)

Address _____

Home phone _____   Work phone _____

Date first contact 8/19/06	Taken by Peter Van Voories	DOB 4/8/74	Gender Female
Marital status Married	Education level Associate's Degree	Employment status Secretary Emco, Corp	Veteran status N/A
Currently pregnant N/A	Rec. prenatal care N/A	Given birth last 28 days? N/A	Pregnancy complications N/A
Current medical conditions Fibromyalgia Treated by Carl M. Anchor, MD	Current medications Advil 400 mg TID Prescribed by Carl M. Anchor, MD	Legal status/ incarcerations N/A	Substance abuse problems N/A Treated by
Reason for visit Depression, loss of energy, loss of interest in life, poor job performance	Referred to 1 Linden Counseling Center 2 3 Being seen by Michael Cedaneo	Psychotropic medications Wellbutrin 100 mg BID Prescribed by Carlos Cremara, MD	May not call these numbers [ ] home [ ] work
Dx. 296.33 Major Depressive Disorder, recurrent	Psychiatric evaluation done Carlos Cremara, MD 8/24/06	Psychological evaluation done	Court ordered? No

Assigned case manager _Melinda Lefevre_   First review date _2/19/09_

e. The last two boxes on the fourth row are asking for legal status and for any substance abuse problems, both of which can affect planning and decisions about goals.

f. In the fifth row of boxes, the reason the client contacted the agency is noted, followed by the referral that was made in the client's behalf. If the client has been prescribed psychotropic medications—that is, medications that treat mental and emotional symptoms—those medications are entered in the next box along with the name of the prescribing physician. Finally, there is a place to note whether the client will allow calls to be made to the phone numbers she gave.

g. In the last row of boxes, the diagnosis is noted. Psychiatric and psychological evaluations are noted, along with the name of the person who conducted each of these and the date. There is also a place to note whether the client was ordered by the court to seek services.

h. On the last line, you sign your face sheet and place the date for the first review on the sheet.

When you place the face sheet in the front of the chart, you have an organized collection of documents. Using a manila file folder, place the other forms on your client in the following order, with the face sheet on the top and the referrals on the bottom:

1. Face sheet
2. Inquiry and referral form
3. Verification letter
4. Assessment form and/or social history
5. Release of information forms
6. Service plan
7. Referrals

Now you can add to the chart all further contacts, letters, and monitoring activities that take place for this person.

Summary

With the referral of your client to the agencies and people who will provide service and treatment, your client has become a formal client of your agency. When you make the referral, plan the target date and the review date carefully. The target date is the date beyond which you would not want to continue the service if there has been no improvement. The review date is the date you plan to check to see how well the service is going for the client. When you review the plan, be prepared to modify the service if that seems useful. At the target date, the client still may not have reached the goal, but there may be improvement. Again, this would be a time to modify the plan.

Once the client has a plan and is a part of your case management caseload, the client becomes a formal client of the agency. A file or record must be kept on the contacts and changes that occur while the client is being served by your agency. Set up a file on the client, using a manila folder, and place a completed face sheet on the top of your documents.

◆ Exercises: Assembling the Record

Instructions: Complete the following exercises.

1. Look at the completed forms on the clients you have developed. Fill out referral forms for each agency to which you intend to send your clients for services. In each client's chart, clip these together and place them at the back of the chart. Use a separate referral form for each agency.
2. Next, develop a face sheet for the front of each chart.
3. Now assemble each chart as indicated in this chapter, using a manila file folder and placing the forms on your client in the following order, with the face sheet on the top and the referrals on the bottom:
    a. Face sheet
    b. Inquiry and referral form
    c. Verification letter
    d. Assessment form and/or social history
    e. Release of information forms
    f. Service plan
    g. Referrals

Once you have written them, your case notes will follow the referrals when they are put into the chart. Be sure the client's name and agency number are on the folder.

Chapter 24

Documentation and Recording

Introduction

Once a person is in the case management unit's system and is receiving services from a provider, it is your responsibility to keep a record of all contacts relevant to this case. These contacts will be with the client or with those connected to the client in some way, such as providers of service, family, and counselors. You will document these contacts on the form titled "Contact Notes" (see the Appendix).

While you are a person's case manager, you will see the client for many reasons. Sometimes clients will come to your office because something upsetting has happened in their life or because they need a prescription. At other times, clients will call on the phone because of a problem or need. You might see clients at provider agencies where they are receiving services when you make site visits. Every contact of this sort is documented.

Keeping accurate records and documenting all contacts with or related to clients is needed primarily for legal and administrative purposes. Legally you need to be able to show that the service for which you are being paid is being given to the client. Administratively you need a record that documents the activities on behalf of the client and all contacts related to the client so that case managers are not relying on memory to reconstruct what has happened before.

These notes should focus on your client, and not on you. The treatment plan begins to go out of date soon after it is written due to the changes in programs and clients' lives. The purpose of your notes is to keep the record current.

Writing Contact Notes

Your contact notes in the chart should *always* include the following:

1. The focus of the interview
2. Your assessment based on a concise summary of behavior, appearance, affect
3. Any resolution that takes place
4. The reason for the next contact or follow-up that will occur

Figures 24.1 and 24.2 illustrate contact notes. Figure 24.1 identifies the four parts of a contact note. See if you can identify the four parts in the example shown in Figure 24.2.

FIGURE 24.1

Sample Contact Note Broken into Four Parts

Focus of the Interview

Linda came into the office today to discuss her medication.

Your Assessment

She appeared somewhat disheveled and tearful and indicated her belief that the medicine is "not strong enough."

The Resolution

An appointment was set up for her to see Dr. Wentworth on July 2. She was advised to remain in her program where her depression can be closely monitored.

Reason for the Next Contact

Client will return July 2 after her visit with the doctor to let CM know what was done about her medications.

FIGURE 24.2

Contact Note: Can You Identify the Four Parts?

Mark called today asking for a voucher for public transportation in order to get to Polyclinic Medical Center for kidney dialysis. Suggested he go by county transportation for more direct service. Mark seemed bright and pleased with the results of dialysis. He will call next week to confirm that county transportation has begun to pick him up.

A case note of this type is never more than six or seven sentences. Write concisely to facilitate others having access to the information. No one can sit down and read through lengthy, descriptive narratives. Your notes must be clear, and they must be concise.

Labeling the Contact

In the left-hand margin for every case note, place (1) the date and (2) the type of contact in parentheses (Collateral Contact, Office Visit, Phone, Site Visit, Group, Home Visit). The types of contact are as follows:

- *Collateral Contact:* A collateral contact is with someone other than the client such as the client's mother, minister, or nurse. Be careful in all collateral contacts that you have the client's permission to make that contact and, if the client is a child, that you have the parent's permission to talk with this person.
- *Office Visit:* The client was seen in the office.
- *Phone:* The client called you on the phone or you called the client.
- *Site Visit:* You went to the site where services are being given to your client and evaluated those services or discussed problems that have arisen.
- *Group:* You saw the client in a group, and you are noting what took place during that contact. Sometimes clients are seen in groups to use time more efficiently.
- *Home Visit:* The client was seen at home.

Here are examples of several contacts that are labeled:

- 4/3/08 (Office Visit)
- 9/8/08 (Phone)
- 12/6/08 (Group)

Documenting Service Monitoring

In addition to your direct contact with the client, document your efforts to monitor the delivery of service to your client. Those notes should be set up and labeled in the same way. For example, if you went to the provider agency and talked to the client and the client's therapist there, it would be labeled like this: 2/14/08 (Site Visit). If you went to a provider agency to attend a treatment planning meeting that focused on your client's treatment or services from the program, your contact note would be labeled the same way: 2/19/08 (Site Visit). Be sure to name the agency in your notes.

Following is an example of notes from a site visit:

1/6/08 (Site Visit) Met with client and social worker at Riverview Center to monitor client's progress toward job readiness. Client seemed eager to begin job search and somewhat annoyed at the length of time the job-readiness classes are taking. It was agreed that client will begin his job search with support next week, while completing the remaining segments of the training. Client will notify CM in 2 weeks regarding outcome of job search.

All your contact notes must reflect the fact that you have made efforts to monitor the services delivered to your client. If you spoke to a contact person at another agency by phone regarding your client's progress or services, or you talked to a child's parent or teacher, you would also identify this as a collateral contact:

2/24/08 (Collateral Contact) James's teacher, Mrs. Pike, called today to say that James is doing much better in school. She reported that he seems better able to focus on classroom assignments. Further, she has had two meetings with James's parents, and they have begun to inquire about homework and enforce the need to complete it each night. Overall Mrs. Pike is feeling better about James finishing fifth grade this year with his other classmates. She stated she will call again if there are signs of problems.

Documentation: The Finishing Touches

There are a number of ways to make your case notes sound professional. The following sections contain some tips for writing better notes.

Avoid Hostility

Do not use your notes to release hostility. When we are angry with someone, it is easy to sound sarcastic, facetious, or even annoyed with the person. Make sure your notes do not reflect any negative feelings you might have about another person.

Document Your Interactions with the Client

Your interaction with the client may be the most important thing that occurred. This could be a verbal exchange or some other form of interaction. Document what happened and what you observed. Always use quotation marks to indicate a word-for-word verbal exchange.

Document Significant Aspects of the Contact

Some aspects of the contact with a client are extremely significant. These are clues to the client's state of mind or situation. When you think it is significant, document these aspects of the client's behavior:

- Appearance
- Dress
- Facial expressions
- Mannerisms
- Responses to others or to activities
- Participation concerning interaction with you or participation in the services referred to
- Attitudes concerning interaction with you or participation in the services referred to
- Cognitive problems

Here is a sample statement in a contact note that documents significant aspects of an interaction with a client:

> Mrs. Peters seemed unable to understand exactly when we would be meeting again or what services would be provided in the meantime. She appeared confused and was somewhat unresponsive to her daughter and son-in-law who tried to clarify these for her.

Be Clear and Precise

One factor that can make your notes more professional is your precision and clarity. Many people write vague notes or notes that give only general descriptions. Be clear about what you are documenting. Do not use vague terms or indefinite statements. For example:

Poor: *Alice was friendly today.*
Better: *Alice initiated the conversation, joking about her Christmas shopping.*

Poor: *Bill was upset today.*
Better: *Bill was concerned about the possibility that he could lose his job.*

Poor: *Marcella got along well in the program today.*
Better: *Marcella's affect was improved today, and she participated in preparing lunch for the group and in both group sessions.*

Use Quotations

What the client has said to you may be extremely important. You may feel that this information should go into the record. The rule is to place *only* the client's exact words in quotation marks. If you paraphrase what the client has said, do not use quotation marks. Do not use them for any reason other than indicating a client's exact words.

Avoid Contradictions

Your progress note must not contradict other previous notes without explanation. If the plan is changed, that must be documented. If the client regresses or improves considerably, this should be documented. There should not be gaps that lead the reader to conclude that something happened that has not been documented.

Use Language Clients Can Understand

You have learned a rather extensive vocabulary that is used by professionals in the field. To the client, these words can sound like jargon. Sometimes new workers use a lot of jargon in an attempt to sound knowledgeable. Avoid jargon. Write your notes in language the client or the child's family can understand.

Accurately Describe Disabilities

When writing about a person with a disability, make sure to use language that accurately reflects the person's life circumstances and does not label the person in pejorative ways. Here are some guidelines from the Three Rivers Center for Independent Living in Pittsburgh:*

- *Person first:* Identify the person first, rather than the disability. Use *person with disability* or *a person who is deaf* rather than *disabled person or deaf person*.
- *Disability:* The terms *afflicted with, suffering from, cripple,* and *victim* are all unacceptable. They emotionalize and sensationalize, often to induce pity. The term *handicapped* is based on the image of a person with a disability on the street with a cap in his hand, begging for money. Except when citing laws, regulations, or environmental conditions (such as the stairs are a handicap to her), always use *disability* rather than *handicap.*
- *Wheelchair:* People are not confined to their wheelchairs; they use them for mobility. Say she *uses a wheelchair,* not that she is *wheelchair-bound* or *confined to a wheelchair.*
- *Blind:* This term refers to total loss of vision. *Partial vision, partial sight,* or *visual impairment* are more accurate terms in some cases.
- *Deaf:* This term refers to total loss of hearing. *Partial hearing, hard of hearing,* or *hearing impairment* are more accurate terms in some cases.
- *Nonverbal:* A *person who cannot speak* is preferred over terms like *mute, deaf-mute,* or *deaf-dumb.* These terms imply that people who are deaf are also unintelligent. The inability to speak does not indicate intelligence or lack of intelligence.

---

*Adapted with permission from the Three Rivers Center for Independent Living, 7110 Penn Avenue, Pittsburgh, PA 15208-2334.

- *Congenital disability:* This is a disability that has existed since birth. Do not use the term *birth defect*. *Defect* is derogatory and is not a synonym for disability.
- *Learning disability:* This term refers to a disorder affecting the understanding or use of spoken and/or written language.
- *Mental disorder:* This term describes any of the recognized forms of mental illness or other emotional disorders. Terms such as *neurotic, psychotic,* or *schizophrenic* are pejorative labels.
- Be careful about using phrases such as *he overcame his disability* or *in spite of her handicap*. These terms inaccurately reflect the barriers people with disabilities face. They do not succeed in spite of their disabilities as much as they *succeed in spite of an inaccessible environment* or *a discriminatory society*. They do not overcome their disabilities so much as they *overcome prejudice*.

Government Requirements

You must follow state and the federal government requirements for documentation to be reimbursed for your services to the client. These may vary from state to state and from one type of service to another. These funding sources treat the record the same way blank checks are treated: Correction fluid, erasures, and blank spaces are not acceptable.

Here are some general rules for documentation that are often required by state and federal governments:

1. Use black ink. Blue ink does not copy well.
2. Never use either a pencil or correction fluid.
3. All notes must be legible.
4. The client must be identified by name on each page. Sometimes you can use an agency number instead. For children, a date of birth on each page is often required. Do not use nicknames or initials.
5. When recording, place the actual date of the contact note in the margin.
6. Sign (do not initial) every note.
7. After your signature, add the date the note was written. It should be on or as close to the date of service as possible.
8. If the client is in ongoing service, every note must end with the next scheduled service date. In some places, case managers are required to note the actual date and time of the next appointment and also the plan of action. For example, "John will return on March 6, 2008, for an appointment at which time we will discuss what he has done about housing."
9. To correct a mistake in a note:
    a. Draw a line through the error—whether it is a letter, word, phrase, or entire paragraph.
    b. Write the word *error* above the line.
    c. Write the correction next to the word *error*.

d. Sign or initial the line.
e. Date your signature or initials.
10. If any blank lines are left on a page once you have completed your notes, draw diagonal lines through the blank spaces.

Do Not Be Judgmental

Do not write notes that sound as if you are sitting in judgment of the client. You may be inclined to judge some aspect of your client's life or behavior in negative terms, but that is not helpful. When negative judgments are obvious in your case notes, they leave a legacy that can follow the client. Avoid judgmental words in your notes. Figure 24.3 contains a list of words that tend to sound judgmental and a substitute word that is more objective for each. Become familiar with these.

FIGURE 24.3
How to Avoid Sounding Judgmental

Poor Words for Documentation (Judgmental)	Better Words for Documentation (More Objective)
dirty	unclean habits, poor hygiene
nasty	unpleasant
lazy	inactive
stubborn	resistive
nervous	anxious
wild	restless
bad-mouthing	argumentative
sarcastic	critical
mean	unpleasant, insulting others
troublesome	uncooperative
whining	complained of
glum	sullen
just sat there	passive
jittery	restless
foolish	used poor judgment
slow	had trouble completing
pushy	persistent
aggravating	irritated others

Distinguish Between Facts and Impressions

A fact is something you observed, whereas an impression is a clue you picked up from the client. Use words such as the following to introduce your impressions:

- Client seemed...
- Client appeared...
- Staff felt...

For example:

Poor: *Mary acted pleasant but was putting on a front.*
Better: *Mary was pleasant, but CM felt she was sensing some anger over losing her job.*

Poor: *Manuel wasn't telling the truth when he said he was comfortable with the new group.*
Better: *Manuel said he was happy in the new group, but he appeared uncomfortable in the first session.*

Give a Balanced Picture of Your Client

Do not paint your client as entirely positive or entirely negative. Clients have strengths and weaknesses, and they have assets and problems. Give a balanced picture of the client, noting strengths and weaknesses, positive gains and negative problems. As noted previously, your notes should not be simply a collection of problems.

Provide Evidence of Agreement

There should be evidence in the written record that you and the program to which the client was referred agree on the plan for the client and that you have had interaction with each other regarding the plan. This interaction and agreement can be documented by reporting on team or staff meetings you attended at the other facility or meetings called specifically to discuss the client's goal plan or treatment. This does not mean that the client is excluded from participation in developing the specific plan for himself at the provider agency. You should also see evidence that the client was a participant in developing his plan, and if that is not clear, you should inquire about how the client took part.

Making Changes to the Plan

Sometimes even the best plans must be changed for any number of reasons: the client gets sick, the provider is closed for snow or overcrowding, the client has a death in the family, the plan is too difficult or is not addressing the real issue. If there is a lack of progress toward the original goals:

1. Note the lack of progress in the notes.
2. Note the recommended changes to the treatment plan in the notes.
3. Revise the treatment plan.

See the Appendix for samples of contact notes.

Summary

The ability to write good contact notes is important. These notes constitute the written record about the service the client receives from you. In addition, they serve to document changes in the client, the client's life, and the service plan. Keep your notes brief. Too much information is difficult to read quickly and is easily taken out of context by lawyers or others seeking to distort the client's care. On the other hand, do not make the notes so brief that they ignore significant information.

Become familiar with the government guidelines as well. The government views the record as a blank check and wants to be able to see clearly when corrections and revisions have been made to the notes. Memorize the common government guidelines for making corrections so that your notes are not subject to government censure.

◆ Exercises: Recording Your Meeting with the Client

Instructions: Your contact note will be written about your first meeting with the client after the treatment planning conference or disposition meeting and after developing the final plan and referral options. In this meeting, you go over the plan with the client, guardian, or the client's parents, in the case of a child, and note the client's response to your proposed plan. Also note any changes you make as a result of this interview.

Write a note for the record of the client whom you are following. This note will indicate that you met with the client and discussed the service plan. Use the four elements for writing notes. This first note is generally a little longer than the others—perhaps 6 to 12 sentences in all. Here is an example of such a note:

> 3/24/08 (Office Visit) John came into the agency today to discuss his service plan. He continues to appear anxious and asked repeatedly for directions to the Susquehanna Counseling offices where he will be receiving services. CM went over the plan for 10 sessions of counseling at Susquehanna Center with John who agreed to this plan. He will begin at Susquehanna Counseling on Monday March 30, 2008, where he will have his appointment with the intake staff and meet his therapist. John will call in one week to let CM know how that meeting went and what specific plans he and the therapist developed for him. *Carly Jameson*

Practice writing your own contact note in the space provided here. When you complete the note satisfactorily, rewrite it into the chart, using the form in the Appendix marked "Contact Notes."

◆ **Exercises: Recording Client Contacts**

Recording a Client Contact–Part I

Instructions: Read the following material, and then write a paragraph of no more than six sentences that covers the following:

1. The focus of the interview
2. Your assessment based on a concise summary of behavior, appearance, affect
3. Any resolution that takes place
4. The reason for the next contact or the follow-up that will occur

Mrs. Pell is seen in the emergency room, after which you are called by the ER physician. He tells you that her friend brought her in and that she arrived complaining of chest pains and shortness of breath. She was extremely anxious, and during her physical examination, she confided in him that she is suffering physical abuse at home and is afraid. He is uncomfortable with discharging her from the ER until you have seen her. She is about 26 years old, intelligent, and a bit unkempt. You notice old bruises on her arms.

YOU: How are you?

MRS. P: I guess Dr. Ingram told you—a little scared.

YOU [SITTING DOWN BESIDE HER]: He said that you were facing some problems at home.

MRS. P: I am [avoids looking at you].

YOU: Can you tell me a little bit about that?

MRS. P: [nods]

YOU: Where would you like to start?

MRS. P [SPEAKING JUST ABOVE A WHISPER]: Well, I, I can't seem to get along with my husband. We've had some really bad fights lately. Really bad. I seem to be on the losing end of those fights.

YOU: So things are pretty rough at home right now.

MRS. P: Well, we seem to fight all the time. [tears well up] I love him. I really do, but he doesn't believe me! He accuses me of seeing other men or being attracted to other men, and when I deny that he blows up.

YOU: Do you feel like you could talk a little more about some of those fights?

MRS. P [NODS AND REACHES FOR A TISSUE]: Yeah. I'm going to have to. I just don't know how to begin. It's gone on so long.

YOU: Maybe you'd like to start with what's been going on recently.

MRS. P: Well, recently things have gotten so much worse. I feel as though it's something I'm doing. I think my husband has a short fuse. He had a head injury as a child, and he blames his temper and his moods on that.

YOU: So he can be pretty moody.

MRS. P: Oh yes! And I get the brunt of it. I try to remember that and be careful—not upset him. I just feel like I'm walking on eggshells all the time lately. He just goes off at me at the least little thing. I try to please him. I tell myself that I know what it is he likes and what he dislikes, but no matter how hard I try, there is a fight because I didn't do something or I did it but I didn't do it right.

YOU [GENTLY]: Can you give me some examples?

MRS. P: Well, 2 days ago I forgot to get a roast at the store. I made a meat loaf for dinner instead. He wanted roast, and he just went off when he got home. He wouldn't eat, threw the dishes on the floor, and turned over the table and then held my head under the tap in the kitchen sink. I could hardly breathe. He told me he'd let me up when I agreed to fix exactly what he asked for from now on.

YOU: That must have been so frightening.

MRS. P [NODDING]: Yes. I just don't have a choice with him. I have been thinking for years—well, we've been married 6 years—that I could help him with this. I even thought I could become so important to him that he would never hurt me. But in all this time things have gotten worse.

YOU: So, in other words, no matter how hard you try, things don't improve and have actually gotten worse.

MRS. P: Much worse. This is the first time I started to think maybe I should leave him, although that is scary too. Who knows what he will do then?

YOU: So leaving has some good points and some bad points.

MRS. P: Well, if he would leave me alone, then I think it might be pretty good. I'm just afraid he would come after me.

YOU: It sounds like you would be interested in a safe place to go for a while.

MRS. P: [nods]

YOU: I notice your friend brought you in. Are there people you can turn to?

MRS. P: My friend only suspects what goes on. We never talk about it directly, but I'm pretty sure she knows. She told me one time I didn't have to stay in a bad marriage, and she looked at me kind of funny when she said it. I just think she has her suspicions.

YOU: So you really don't feel comfortable opening up to her about this.

MRS. P: I don't feel comfortable opening up to anyone. My family told me not to marry him. He was a loner. He didn't like to be around them, and they thought he would keep me from seeing them. They were right, but for all these years I've pretended they were wrong.

YOU: You felt bad that their predictions turned out to be so true.

MRS. P: That's right. He doesn't like them. About a year after we were married, he told me I couldn't see them again, and I've been sneaking around ever since. I make excuses to them—why we're not there at Christmas or why he didn't come along. They probably know.

YOU: It sounds like your world is getting tighter and tighter.

MRS. P: Well, as I try to do everything he demands, it is. I have no friend except Suzanne [nods toward the waiting room], and I spend a lot of my time doing everything for him.

YOU: Do you work outside the home?

MRS. P: Well, see, I used to, but he put a stop to that. He said the company I worked for was putting ideas in my head after the second promotion I got there. I think he was jealous, but he made me quit and said no wife of his was going to have a better job than he has!

YOU: It sounds like you are under a lot of stress. Can you tell me a little bit about what Dr. Ingram said about your stress?

MRS. P: Yeah. He said he thinks there is nothing seriously wrong. But he could see these bruises, and he asked about them and then he called you. He was very nice, and he said I needed to look at the way things were going so I didn't keep having these episodes. [blurts out] I wish I didn't have to go home!

YOU: You don't have to. I can easily arrange for you to go into a shelter, and that would give you time to think some of this through.

MRS. P: If I did that, I could never go home again. He's likely to kill me for seeing the people here. He doesn't like it when I see people he doesn't know. If I actually left and stayed somewhere for a while, he'd never forgive me.

YOU: So in many ways he means a lot to you.

MRS. P: He's all I have. I, I, I've just started to think maybe I should leave. I'm just so afraid to. Afraid of what he'd do and afraid to be on my own. [looks pensive] He won't find out from the hospital that I saw you?

YOU: He shouldn't. I'll speak to them out there before I leave. But the hospital and my agency have very strict confidentiality guidelines, and your time with me is absolutely confidential.

MRS. P: I better get out of here. I'm afraid he'll find out I was here and—thanks. Really, this has made me feel better.

YOU: I think you should go, too, if you are concerned. Let me ask you one thing, just because I am concerned about your situation at this point. How do you think I can continue to help you?

MRS. P [PULLING HER CLOTHES ON, LOOKS OVER AT YOU STARTLED]: You want to stay in touch?

YOU: I'd like that. My agency stays in touch with any number of women in your situation, and we have a support group for women and a hot line if you need us quickly. Is there some way you think we could help you?

MRS. P [BRIGHTENING]: I didn't think about staying in touch with you. I could do that. I could even come in. Suzanne is bringing me here on Tuesday morning for an EKG. Could I see you then?

YOU: I would be happy to see you then. When is your appointment?

MRS. P: I have to be here at 10:30. You could meet me in the waiting room out there at 10:20 and go up with me. We could talk more about what I should do—sort it out.

YOU: I'll be there. Could you think a little bit about our shelter in the meantime, and some of the other services I described? See if you think there is something you might want to do if things get too bad.

MRS. P: They just might. I, well, it can't continue like this. I've told him I love him. He doesn't hear me. Sometimes I think he'll kill me someday, and I say to myself, "What are you waiting for? Run. Get out of here." But I have no place to go, and like I told you, I can't turn to my family. Oh, they'd help me in a minute, but he'd look there first, and they are no match for his anger. [Mrs. P has her coat on and her hand on the door handle.]

YOU: I will be here Tuesday morning. If you need me in the meantime, or the agency, call us [handing her a business card]. Tuesday we'll talk some more and see if there are some other things we might be doing to help you with this.

MRS. P [SMILES, EXTENDS HER HAND]: Thanks! [calling over her shoulder] I promise to call if I need anything!

Write your contact note here:

Recording a Client Contact—Part II

Instructions: Read the following material, and then write a paragraph of no more than six sentences that covers the following:

1. The focus of the interview
2. Your assessment based on a concise summary of behavior, appearance, and affect
3. Any resolution that takes place
4. The reason for the next contact or the follow-up that will occur

Mr. Dudley comes to your office in a rumpled plaid shirt. He has oily hair. He appears to have neglected his appearance since he stopped drinking, which is not typical. He has been in an outpatient alcohol treatment program for 4 weeks. He sits in the chair beside your desk and appears sad and ready to weep.

YOU: How are you?

MR. D: Not so hot.

YOU: Can you tell me a little bit about what's going on?

MR. D: I quit the treatment program.

YOU: Tell me something about what happened.

MR. D: Well, I got tired of going. I figured I could do this myself.

YOU: So you wanted to try not to drink on your own.

MR. D: Yeah. I thought most of the people in that program were whiners and complainers—all the time whining about how hard life had been, and I got tired of listening to it.

YOU: So you went out on your own.

MR. D: Yes.

YOU: How did that work?

MR. D: Not so hot.

YOU: Could you tell me a bit more about that?

MR. D: What does it look like? I started drinking again. There isn't a whole lot more to tell.

YOU: So, in other words, you left the program and immediately started to drink?

MR. D: Well, no. I was sober for about 4 days. Went to work and everything. Stuff was happening at work. Some guys got laid off, and I thought I might be next.

YOU: It sounds like you got off to a good start on your own, but then things began to happen at your work and you decided to drink.

MR. D [HESITANTLY]: Well, yeah.

YOU: And the drinking helped you deal better with the possibility that you might be laid off.

MR. D: Well, yes, it did. I was upset. I thought I might be next. I don't know. It all happened so fast. I just thought I'd stop with the fellows for one drink on the way home from work, and one thing led to another, and I've been drinking ...

YOU: For several days?

MR. D: Yeah, I can't stop.

YOU: Tell me a little more about what's going on with your job.

MR. D: The first day I called in sick, but today I didn't do anything. I came here because I'm afraid I'm heading right back where I was before.

YOU: Sounds like you really want to stop this binge.

MR. D: I do. I didn't know where else to go.

YOU: It looks to me like you could use a detox unit. What do you think of that as a place to start?

MR. D: I could use getting away from bars and getting cleaned out. I would really like to start over—try again.

YOU: Well you had 4 days where you did fine. We can begin by getting you into detox, and from there we can talk about a plan for when you are sober. What do you think of going into detox?

MR. D: Yeah. Well, I suppose the missus and the boss would appreciate that.

YOU: What about you?

MR. D: That's why I came here. I can't stop drinking. I'm a loser.

YOU: You must be feeling pretty bad about yourself.

MR. D: Well, I screwed up again. Wouldn't you?

YOU: It's hard to feel like a loser. We can't address that while you are drunk, but after you sober up I will be happy to talk to you about making some changes. There are some things you did that tell me that you can handle things. First you had those 4 days on your own where you didn't drink at all, and then when you started to drink you knew where to go for help in stopping the binge you were headed on.

MR. D: Haven't we been through all this before?

YOU: I don't think we have. We only started this 5 weeks ago. It might be helpful for you to know that people often have relapses as they are moving toward healthier choices. It might be that you learned something valuable here. That's just my opinion. What do you think?

MR. D: I hadn't thought of it as a learning experience or anything. Hmm. I don't know. I just wouldn't have thought of it that way.

YOU: I would like to see you go to the detox unit for 7 days, and then we could sit down and look at this together.

MR. D: Yeah, I will.

YOU: Good. I'm not willing to talk to you about changes when you've been drinking. I'll call First Step Detox, and then I will see you there during your stay so that we can plan what happens next.

MR. D: Thanks.

Write your contact note here:

_____

◆ Exercises: Using Government Guidelines to Correct Errors

Instructions: Using the section in this chapter on the common requirements of government funding sources, correct (or change) the following case notes.

Case Note 1: Winnie was at the hospital for tests on 3/17/07. Those tests were done to determine whether she has a tumor on her thyroid gland. Homemaker assistance has been arranged.

(The date for the tests is wrong. It should read 2/13/07. Correct the note accordingly in the space provided.)

Case Note 2: Carmela is attending the partial hospitalization program 3 days a week. Today she appeared brighter and more talkative. Our interview focused on her need to find a more independent living arrangement. Partial staff will assist her in looking at supported living programs in the community.

(Carmela is actually attending the partial program 5 days a week. Correct the note accordingly in the space provided.)

◆ Exercises: Spotting Recording Errors

Instructions: Tell what is wrong or left out of each contact note and rewrite an improved contact note in the space provided.

Case 1: Jim came into the office today looking depressed. He said he wants another job. He sat slumped over in a chair and was unkempt. The worker wrote:

> 1/17/08 (Office Visit): Jim came into the office today to see about getting a different job. He is not working at present. Will call Goodwill to see if they can place him temporarily at the bakery where he was before.

Case 2: Alice has been asking to be relocated to another group home since December when another client, Cheryl, moved in. Alice and Cheryl have fought ever since. The staff is not sure which client should move, and they have communicated their concerns to the case manager. The worker wrote:

> 3/8/08 (Phone): Alice is carrying on again about her housemates. She is trying to get a better housing assignment. Will call the house where she is staying and see if something can be done.

Case 3: Kitsu is attending an intensive outpatient rehabilitation program for his drinking. He sees his case manager at the site about once every month. Recently it was decided that Kitsu is not making the progress he was expected to make. Part of this is due to his job, which he says prevents him from coming to outpatient meetings regularly. To accommodate his night schedule at work, his services will now be given in the early evening before he goes into work. The worker wrote:

> 8/6/08 (Site Visit): Met with Kitsu and his therapist at the rehab program. Therapist is concerned about Kitsu's lack of attendance. Changes will be made in his program to facilitate attendance.

Chapter 25

Monitoring the Services or Treatment

Introduction

Monitoring your cases on your caseload is important for several reasons. First, it is generally required that you document that you have monitored your cases in order for your agency to be reimbursed for your time. Why, though, do funding sources insist on monitoring? These organizations recognize that with careful monitoring the client is more likely to receive the service you are requesting. In other words, monitoring allows you to check to see that the services being given to your client at the provider agency are addressing the goals you and the client developed. In addition, when done on a regular basis, monitoring allows you to spot and address problems early. Done in this way, a case manager may be able to take steps to prevent costly hospitalization or relapse.

    Case managers bring new clients into the agency, assess their needs, listen to their desires and expectations, develop plans to address clients' most outstanding goals and needs, and make referrals of clients to the agencies that can best respond to the clients' plans. That is the first half of what a case manager does. The second half is to monitor clients regularly (in some cases, frequently) to make certain there is movement toward the desired goals you and the client developed for the client. During this process, the case manager may make suggestions for midcourse corrections, encourage the client to participate in revising the plan, and discuss with providers any changes in focus or goals.

What Is Monitoring?

Monitoring is an ongoing review of clients' participation in the services to which they were referred. This review must be documented in the client's file and will be part of the case notes of each file. Reviews are carried out by doing the following:

1. Talking to clients regularly to see if they feel they are making progress and to learn whether they are satisfied with the services. If a client points out needed revisions in the plan, this must be in your notes, as well as what was done in response.
2. Contacting people in the agencies or programs that are primarily responsible for your clients meeting their goals in their service plans. In talking with such a person, find out what this person thinks of the client's progress toward completion of her goals. Should the service be continued or discontinued? Should the service be modified in any way?
3. Contacting other people, agencies, and services involved with the client. For instance, if the client is a child, contact the parents. If the child is in school, contact the teacher to learn whether there have been noticeable changes.

Remember that all monitoring is subject to the rules of confidentiality and the Health Insurance Portability and Accountability Act (HIPAA) standards. These will be clear to you at the agency where you work. For now, however: Do not question individuals or organizations about your client unless you have the express permission of the client or the client's parent or guardian.

Purpose of Monitoring

Let's study the purpose of monitoring more closely. Many of the clients with whom we deal are receiving services paid for by public funds. These funds are limited and must be spent wisely. As the case manager, you are responsible for deciding what services a client will receive, based on the goals you have developed with the client. Then you must estimate how long it will take to reach these goals.

You might have a client with developmental disabilities who needs to develop a marketable skill. You refer the client to Goodwill Industries. You authorize services there for one year. This means that you have allowed for payment to be made to Goodwill Industries for one year of job training for this particular client. The expectation is that at the end of the year, the client will have a marketable skill.

You would then go to Goodwill Industries at regular intervals to see whether the goal is being approached. Is the client moving toward a marketable skill? Are there obstacles and problems you did not foresee or that are new in the client's life? Rather than referring the client to Goodwill Industries and leaving him there for the year without ever checking up on how well things are going, you visit with him at the site, talk to him and to his supervisor, and get a feel for how well the plan is working.

Angelica provides another example. She needed a supportive environment in order to be able to live with minimal supervision in the community. She had been hospitalized four times for severe depression, and it was only during the last hospitalization that the medical staff was able to combine medications for her in such a way that she really felt free of her depression symptoms. The severity of her depression and the number of acute episodes had prevented her from working or from living on her own successfully. Now, as the depression cleared, the staff was looking for a program in which Angelica could begin to work toward an independent living arrangement and other goals Angelica saw for herself.

The case manager in a mental health case management unit placed her in a small program called the Yellow House, so named for the color of the house. There, three women lived for a period of 90 days, preparing to move out on their own. The time in the house was spent in normal activities such as cleaning, cooking meals, decorating for the holidays, and going to the movies. During the day, the residents engaged in activities to help them secure a job and a place to live.

Case management chose the Yellow House program specifically for Angelica, believing this was the best place for her to receive the support she needed to move toward independence. Her improvements and her accomplishments were reported to the case manager, and as Angelica began to make plans to move to her own apartment, the case manager collaborated in the planning, coming to the Yellow House for meetings with Angelica and the staff.

Let us look at another example. Suppose you have a client who came into your transitional housing program after suffering years of marital difficulties and homelessness. You would develop a service plan for this client that addresses his most urgent needs. Perhaps you and he decide that one of his needs is for a community college degree in order to be self-sufficient. In addition, he may need professional help in parenting his children, who appear to be out of his control. His children may need academic and recreational programs as well, and there may be a medical problem requiring attention. After you develop the plan with him, you would refer him to the appropriate services. In this case, your program would not pay the actual costs of each of these services. A Pell grant and other financial aid will pay for college; the children's programs are supported by community funds and are free to the participants; and the parenting help is obtained through the public child protection agency's parenting classes.

Nevertheless, your agency is receiving public money to develop good service plans for clients like this one to help them move from dependence to independence. The funding source expects you to develop plans that are usually successful. Too many poor plans and resulting failures might cause you to lose your funding. The plan you devise, therefore, must be in the best interests of the client. Thus, for these reasons, you would carefully monitor your client's participation in the services and his progress toward the goals. Very often, in a situation like this, you would talk more directly with the client about his progress or obstacles rather than talking to the providers of the service. For instance, it would be an invasion of his privacy to go to the community college to check on his grades, but you would want to keep in touch with him so you would know about problems that might arise and might cause him to fail if they are not addressed. From time to time, you would ask him about his parenting course and how his studies are progressing.

Collaboration

Collaborating with other agencies is not always as simple as it seems. There are times when people at other agencies begin to think they know the client better than the case manager does, and they may develop goals and objectives without collaboration with the case manager. Sometimes they discharge clients or switch them to other services within their agency without telling the case manager.

You may also run into situations in which an agency is willing to take any client referred to them, but gives very poor care or minimal service. Generally agencies are motivated to do this to collect the funds that come with the client for the client's care. Although the agency appears to be an ideal place to put clients for whom there is no other service, this may not be in the best interests of the client.

In these situations, it is tempting to become angry with the agency or with specific individuals working there. Anger and unpleasant disputes can permanently spoil relations between entire groups of professional people, curtailing the system's effectiveness and creating a hardship for clients. There are other, better ways to handle disagreements.

Try going to the other professionals and expressing your concern. If that does not work or the same difficulties continue to occur with other clients, ask your supervisor to talk to their supervisors, or ask the head of your agency to work with the head of the other agencies, to create a positive agreement on how these issues will be handled in the future.

For your part, make every effort to be responsive to the concerns of the provider agency. Be available for planning meetings and reviews. Support decisions the agency wants to make that really are in the best interests of the client. In this way, all the professionals involved with the client present a united approach to the client's problems. If your client is creating a problem at the provider agency, help the agency develop a plan to deal with it, talk to your client if that will help, and invite the staff there to join you in looking for the causes of the problem.

Do not blame the staff in the provider agency—not to them personally or behind their backs. Refrain from gossiping about how poor the program is or the limited abilities of staff members. Instead, use the communication skills you have perfected to raise your concerns and listen to the responses. By following these guidelines, you will serve your clients better and maintain the smooth operation of the delivery system.

Leave the Office

Too many case managers want to monitor their clients' progress from the comfort of their offices. They find it to be too much trouble to drive around town, find parking, go out in all kinds of weather, or visit in homes located in areas that make them uncomfortable. Talking to providers and clients on the phone and insisting that clients and their families always come to you appears both arrogant and somewhat lazy.

When your client is admitted to the hospital, visit her there. When your client begins a job-readiness training program, drop in to check with him there. When your client is in a program to gain independent living, stop by to see how she is doing. If the neighborhood makes you uncomfortable, go in pairs to see clients.

Clients live and work and strive toward their goals in a community. Only by visiting them in the settings in which they are living and functioning can you get a true picture of who they are and their real obstacles or accomplishments. The telephone is certainly useful as a support to your monitoring efforts, but relying on that exclusively cuts off important information and opportunities to strengthen rapport.

Responding to a Crisis

From time to time your clients may experience an unsettling life event or escalation of their condition. For all of us there are events that throw us off balance for a while, and for our clients this is true as well. However, if a person is already handling problems or an illness, these events can precipitate a serious breakdown in functioning. A person in such a situation may not use good judgment, may become overwhelmed and immobilized, or may disregard personal safety in an attempt to feel better.

Wherever possible, foresee and plan for destabilizing events. For example, if a client's mother is dying of cancer and you know she will die, begin to work with the client about handling this event, and be prepared to give additional support when it happens.

We can't, however, foresee everything. A client loses his job, another person is evicted, the state closes a group home for corruption by the workers there and your client is suddenly without housing. People who have lived together for years now find themselves being separated and going to strange new environments. A client's liver fails, and there is emergency hospitalization. A client's wife and children leave; a client calls seeking shelter after a domestic dispute.

Life events and problems can throw people off balance, and so can illness and emotional issues. The desire or intention to commit suicide is one such emergency. Another might occur when a client becomes so ill she must be placed in a safer environment because she is suffering from delusions that endanger her or others around her. Another might be clients who have become so ill from their addictions that their condition is life threatening.

Here are four steps for handling crisis events effectively.

1. *Respond immediately.* The faster you are able to make contact with your client, the more likely it is that you can stop the crisis from escalating. Your presence alone can have a calming effect, particularly if your client knows you.
2. *Construct the best course of action under the present circumstances.* Consult your client if possible, but be ready to act. A person may have to be hospitalized for her own protection or to address a serious medical condition. Another may have to go to another home where he knows no one. Your being there for these changes and supporting your client can make the interventions more effective. When Jason's mother died, his case manager went through the entire funeral with him, including the planning at the funeral home. When Meg was

hospitalized following liver failure, her case manager went immediately to the emergency room and spent that evening with Meg. After that the case manager visited daily to give support even when she could not stay long.
3. *Listen to your client.* By now you are probably a very good listener. What did the relapse or the move or the abuse mean to them? Let clients talk to you about this event or change in their life and help them to put it all in perspective. This is part of accepting what is and being able to look at the event in a more practical and realistic light.
4. *Help your client to begin to look ahead.* What do they want to see in their future following this? Where would they want to be a year from now? What is their thinking about where they should go from here? In this phase encourage your clients to brainstorm, look at all the options, talk about possibilities, discuss real obstacles and new considerations. In this way you are supporting a return to the clients' taking back control of their lives.

Crises are difficult for everyone in the sense that they require an immediate response and concentrated effort. On the other hand, we don't want to lose sight of the fact that our clients can grow as a result of these crises, and our participation can facilitate that growth.

Follow-Up

Follow-up is a term used to mean the case manager went back to check on things after a contact with the client. It may be a call to see if the new medication is working, a home visit after a suicide attempt, or a visit to a partial hospitalization program after the client begins a program there. Slightly different from the usual monitoring, follow-up refers to going back to make sure things are going well for the client after a considerable change or emergency. Follow-up occurs when the situation was unstable in the first place and the case manager is seeking to stabilize things for the client.

Generally case managers follow up for two reasons. First, they want to be sure that the changes or the introduction of new services they made with the client are actually working for the client. Second, they want to be sure that the client is doing well since the last contact when changes were made. In these situations, the sooner follow-up is made, the more likely it is that problems can be avoided and relapses prevented.

Summary

Some agencies do a considerable amount of case management. Such agencies are responsible for large numbers of clients who fall within a certain category of need or difficulty. In these agencies, case management is broad and encompasses many services rendered to many clients. Usually county agencies, mandated to exist in each county by state law, operate in this way. Services for aging, for mental health and mental retardation, and for children and youth are other examples of this type of large case management organization.

In such large agencies, every case that is accepted into the system is managed by the central office. Sometimes an agency will elect to provide the services as well, using its own staff, rather than send the client to another service provider. In those situations, the case managers and those who provide the services work for the same organization. For instance, a county Office of Aging might contract out to another organization the management of its senior citizen centers, or it might decide to employ the managers and run the centers itself. This decision is usually based on cost effectiveness or on the availability of services in a community.

Other agencies do very limited case management or only manage cases within their own organization, monitoring for success and failure of their own services. Often these are agencies that receive limited public money and must account for it carefully. An example might be a small partial hospitalization program for people with chronic mental illness. This program might be receiving referrals from a number of sources, some of them private physicians and some of them public agencies for mental health. Within the partial hospitalization program, clients might be assigned a person who functions as the case manager. This person would see that the plan is implemented and followed and would make corrections to the plan as needed. Agencies like this are generally accountable to a case management organization elsewhere that authorizes payment of the bill for that service and monitors clients' progress toward their goals.

In another instance, a small agency may make only a few referrals to other services and must make sure the client is receiving the correct service and moving toward the goals within its own program. A client of a domestic violence program, for example, might be referred to legal assistance, a job-readiness program, and public housing. A worker might act as the case manager, developing an individualized plan, implementing it, and monitoring the plan. The worker would be an employee of the domestic violence agency, which would not only provide helpful referrals but also provide services to help the client handle the transition and possible posttraumatic stress disorder. The case manager might also be the leader of a support group that this particular client would attend. This is not an unusual arrangement in small, very focused agencies.

The funding source, the client, and the client's family all expect you to collaborate to improve some aspect of the person's life. They expect you to put into place new circumstances and skills to prevent future problems, and to catch wasteful or inappropriate planning before too much time and money have been invested. Skillful monitoring can help you accomplish all of this.

Chapter 26

Developing Goals and Objectives at the Provider Agency

Introduction

Now let's look at the provider agency to which you have referred your client for service. Your client has arrived there, and the people at the provider agency have read over the general goals you wrote on your referral sheet. Now they will sit down and develop with the client very specific goals and objectives to address the larger goals you put on the referral form.

In this chapter, you will step out of your role as case manager at the case management unit and step into the role of the person primarily responsible for implementing the client's service plan at the provider agency. In the agency where the service is actually given (the provider agency), goals and objectives are written very specifically and in greater detail. Here the broad general goal supplied by case management is broken down into more specific goals and objectives. This enables the staff at the agency to know exactly what they are planning for the client.

When the referred client arrives at the treatment or service agency, that agency's staff takes their turn looking at the case manager's stated goals worked out with the client. They then decide with the client just how to meet those goals in the time allotted. Completion of the more specific goals is expected to take place during the time for which the case manager has authorized payment of services for the client. Sometimes the client cannot meet the goals in that time or needs more time because of other issues that have surfaced or new problems that have occurred. For example, a client who has periodic difficulty with asthma was hospitalized on a pulmonary unit for a week and missed several weeks of services, necessitating an extension to the agreement. In another case, a client did not do well in the program where she went 4 days a week to learn more about independent living. Although she appeared to make progress, her progress was slower than anticipated, so the case manager extended the authorization for 6 more weeks. In these cases, the case manager authorized additional time for the client in that agency.

Much of the material in this chapter is based on the work of Arnold R. Goldman (1990), from his newsletter *Practical Communications*.

Client Participation/Collaboration

We would not make goals for clients without collaborating with them. If you are working with a child, you want to note that the parent or parents were involved in the decisions. For an adult, you need to include the fact that the adult has participated in determining his own goals. If the person is unable to participate at the time due to his mental or physical condition, try to learn who the person would want to participate in the planning on his behalf. For example, Ardith assisted her mother in developing a plan with the worker because her mother was in the beginning stages of Alzheimer's disease.

Assessment and evaluation forms usually have places to record clients' answers when you ask them what they see as the main issues to be resolved and what they expect of services. Each of these forms addresses this issue in a different way, but look at this material when developing client goals. The information you collect from the client should indicate that you and the client developed the goals and objectives together. Someone reading your plans should see it clearly indicated that the client participated and agreed with the direction the goals tend to lead.

Expect Positive Outcomes

Goals are actually the outcomes you expect to occur as a result of the treatment, service, or intervention you have chosen. Goals are written, therefore, in the positive—what *will* happen, rather than what will *not* happen or what *might* happen.

NOTE

- The goal is the result of the treatment or intervention.
- The client is the subject of the goal. (The therapist, case manager, or treatment team is never the subject.)
- There is only one condition for the goal.
- The goal is written in one sentence.
- Goals are written in the positive.

To write a positive goal, state what will happen as a result of the intervention or service being provided. Use the word *will* in constructing your goals. Following are some examples:

Poor: *Johnny's grandfather will get along better with Johnny.* (Johnny's grandfather is not the identified client. Instead, make Johnny the focus of the goal.)
Better: *Johnny will work cooperatively with his grandfather.*

Poor: *To help Anne relate better to others.* (This makes the therapy team the object of the goal. Instead the therapy team needs to talk about what intervention will be used to support this goal in another place and write the goal making Anne the focus of the goal.)
Better: *Anne will work with the other workers without arguing.*

Poor: *Alice will communicate verbally and attend AA meetings.* (Here there are two goals that are unrelated in the same sentence.)
Better: *Alice will communicate verbally. Alice will attend AA meetings.* (Two separate goals.)

Poor: *Horace will attend work consistently. He will accomplish this by August 6, 2008.* (Two sentences are cumbersome.)
Better: *By August 6, 2008, Horace will attend work consistently.*

Poor: *Alice will no longer frequent bars.* (Here the goal tells what Alice will not do.)
Better: *Alice will attend AA meetings 4 times a week.* (Here the goal tells what Alice will do.)

Poor: *Paul will go to public housing and hopefully find housing there.* (Here the goal sounds doubtful and contains an editorial note that has no place in the goal.)
Better: *Paul will obtain housing for his family.*

Writing the Goals

Most clients will identify more than one goal. Be careful that the person does not have so many goals that they are impossible to complete or overwhelming to the person. First write the goals for the client. In broad general terms, state what it is you intend to bring about. For example:

- *Phyllis will be able to play cooperatively with the other children.*
- *John will be able to abstain from drinking.*
- *Gladys will be able to prepare her own meals.*
- *Harriet will obtain reliable housing.*
- *Paul will complete job-readiness training.*
- *Michael will complete the outpatient drug treatment program.*
- *Agnes will have regular medical checkups for her asthma.*

Objectives

Goals are often quite similar for similar populations. Many clients seek help for similar reasons and, therefore, may have similar goals. *What individualizes a client's plan are the goal objectives*, often called "treatment objectives." Every goal has objectives. The objectives either are concrete, observable, and measurable manifestations of a treatment goal (Figure 26.1) or the individual steps to achieving the treatment goal (Figure 26.2). The figures provide some examples of these two types of objectives for three different clients.

Combining Goals and Treatment Objectives

Think of goals and objectives as being part of a continuum ranging from abstract to concrete. Figure 26.3 shows where goals and objectives would fall along such a continuum.

FIGURE 26.1

Examples of Treatment Goals and Objectives

Written with Objectives You Expect to Achieve on the Way to Achieving the Goal

Client: Billy
Goal: *Billy will play cooperatively with other children as manifested by:*

Objectives (concrete, observable, measurable manifestations):

- *Billy will talk to at least three other children every day without hitting.*
- *Billy will eat lunch with the other children at least 4 days a week.*
- *Billy will help other children carry out a classroom chore without yelling.*

Client: Karen
Goal: *Karen will take steps to curb her alcohol intake as evidenced by:*

Objectives (concrete, observable, measurable manifestations):

- *Karen will attend AA meetings.*
- *Karen will work collaboratively with her AA sponsor.*
- *Karen will attend her church on Sunday mornings.*
- *Karen will not miss work for the next month.*

Client: Katherine
Goal: *Katherine will use her local senior center to meet new friends as demonstrated by:*

Objectives (concrete, observable, measurable manifestations):

- *Katherine will go to the senior center twice a week.*
- *Katherine will attend at least one special event at her senior center during the month.*
- *Katherine will participate in one activity each time she is at the center.*

FIGURE 26.2

Examples of Treatment Goals and Objectives

Written with Objectives as Individual Steps to the Goal

Client: Billy
Goal: *Billy will play cooperatively with other children as manifested by:*

Individual Steps:

- *Billy will observe the activities without hitting other children.*
- *Billy will participate in part of at least one activity daily without hitting other children.*
- *Billy will complete one activity daily without hitting.*
- *Billy will participate in more than one activity without hitting.*
- *Billy will participate in an entire day of camp without hitting other children.*

Client: Karen
Goal: *Karen will take steps to curb her alcohol intake as evidenced by:*

Individual Steps:

- *Karen will determine where AA meetings are held.*
- *Karen will choose the site most convenient for her.*
- *Karen will attend one AA meeting as an observer.*
- *Karen will participate in an AA meeting.*
- *Karen will attend two AA meetings a week.*

Client: Katherine
Goal: *Katherine will use her local senior center to meet new friends as demonstrated by:*

Individual Steps:

- *Katherine will call her local senior center for hours.*
- *Katherine will choose the dates and times she prefers to go to the center.*
- *Katherine will arrange for transportation with the case manager's help.*
- *Katherine will attend the senior center twice a week.*

To check on whether you have written a goal or an objective, apply the "See Billy" test. Read what you have written, and ask yourself if you actually will be able to see or hear the client doing that. If you cannot, you have a goal; but if you can, you have an objective. You can see or hear the client achieve the objectives. Here are some things you could not hear or see, and so you would not use these as objectives:

1. *The client will gain insight into his problems with his mother.*
2. *The client will understand the importance of AA.*
3. *The client will work well with other children at school.*

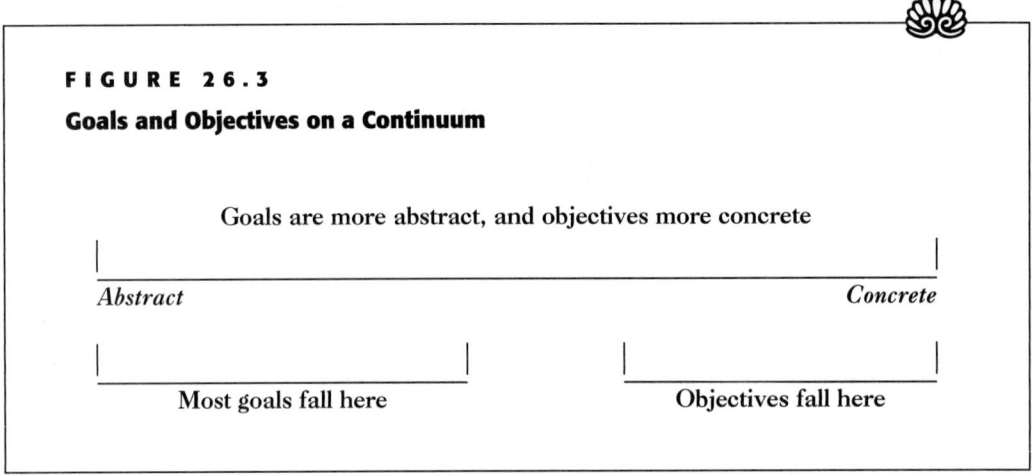

FIGURE 26.3

Goals and Objectives on a Continuum

Goals are more abstract, and objectives more concrete

Abstract — Concrete

Most goals fall here — Objectives fall here

These would work better as goals. Objectives in these areas might be written as follows:

1. You might know the client gained insight by what he talks about. So you might write a treatment objective that reads: *The client is able to talk about the problems he and his mother have.*
2. You could see the client's understanding of the importance of AA by the way the client attends meetings. So you might write a treatment objective that reads: *The client will attend AA meetings twice a week.*
3. You could hear that the client worked well at school. So you might write a treatment goal that reads: *The client will receive positive reports from his teacher that he cooperated with the other children on classroom projects.*

Finishing Touches

Following is information on other things to consider when writing goals.

Proper Endings

End every goal statement with one of these phrases:

- "as manifested by..."
- "as evidenced by..."
- "as demonstrated by..."
- "as indicated by..."

Then write the objective after that phrase. For example:

Goal A: Anita will understand the importance of AA *as evidenced by* . . .
Objective 1: Attendance at AA meetings twice a week for 6 weeks.

Numbering System

Develop a numbering system for easy identification so you can tell which objectives go with which goals. For example, you could use this system: Goals: A, B, C, D, and so on; Objectives: 1, 2, 3, 4, and so on. Thus, A1 would represent goal A, objective 1. In this way, you do not have to write out everything in your notes; you have an easy reference system with which to refer to goals and objectives. For instance, in the example of Anita, you might want to note progress in Anita's consistent attendance at AA meetings. You would say that Anita is meeting A1 by having attended AA meetings twice weekly for 2 weeks.

Every goal must have at least two objectives. It can have more than one objective, as you see fit.

Target Dates

Give each objective a target date. Remember to set the date for the amount of time you are willing to try this particular intervention without getting the desired result. In this way, as the worker, you will be able to monitor whether the client is progressing. With no target date, it is easy to leave people in programs and treatment for unnecessarily long periods of time. Even if the client has not reached the goal by the target date, you can assess any progress that has been made and determine whether the program is working and needs a new target date or whether the program is not working and other interventions need to be tried or other arrangements need to be made for the client.

If the client meets the goal or the objective before the target date, simply record this in the progress notes. Also note the new goals and objectives and the new target dates for these as the client continues along an improving continuum.

When a client has a chronic mental illness, some form of mental retardation, or problems related to aging, a provider of service may be asked to provide an intervention to simply prevent the client's condition or circumstances from growing worse. In this case, you set the target date according to the date at which you would expect to see deterioration if your intervention was not working. When you reach the target date, if the patient's behavior or situation has remained stable, you can extend your target date. Review the intervention and the person's stability at each target date before extending it, and note your review and extension in the chart.

Treatment Interventions

If you give the client an assignment or some task to do that will help her complete one of the objectives, this is a treatment intervention. It is not a goal or objective. It is a treatment intervention because it is what you (the worker) are doing to help the client complete an objective and work toward her ultimate goal. As an example, you might ask Clara, whose goal is to become a better parent, to read some testimonials of people who found a particular parenting workshop to be very helpful. Or if Clara attended a parent training workshop and you were the trainer, your training of Clara would be a treatment intervention.

Notice that a *treatment objective* gives some anticipated change in the client's behavior (for example, client will attend a parenting workshop twice a week), whereas an *intervention* tells what you, the worker, will use to bring about this change (for example, worker will give client testimonials to read). Another intervention by the worker, in Clara's case, might be for the worker to contact and get Clara into the parenting workshop. When case managers support their clients by offering information, finding good programs, making effective arrangements, or setting up services, the case managers are practicing treatment interventions.

Long Term and Short Term

Sometimes you are asked to state what your targets are for the long term and for the short term. This may happen if you are in a meeting regarding the client or receive a letter from the client's insurance company. Simply state your goals as your long-term targets and your objectives as your short-term targets. Figure 26.4 provides examples of goals and objectives for two clients.

When case managers make a referral to another program, the program generally sets the objectives with the client. Goals are developed in broad general terms at the case management unit with the client, and the service provider develops the more specific goals and objectives—or the staff of a service provider can take the broad general goals from case management and develop objectives for them with the client. For example, a person referred to a partial hospitalization program would be referred there because of the need to attain a particular goal, such as learning to control anger. The objectives would be designed by the staff there. A person referred to AA would work out the objectives with his case manager because there is no paid staff at AA. Exactly who designs goals and objectives will depend on the program chosen for the client and the extent to which that program has in-house case management services. However the goals are developed and with whom, this is always done with the client's input and collaboration.

Summary

Goals and objectives developed at the provider agency give more specificity to the plan you and your client have agreed upon. Remember to write each goal with only one result, to write the goals in the positive, and to provide objectives that are observable and measurable. Include clients and their families, when that is useful, in planning these goals. This helps you to maintain goals for clients that they believe are obtainable. It is not helpful to clients, nor does it garner their cooperation, if goals and objectives are made up by workers and imposed on them.

Be flexible in reworking goals that the client has not been able to accomplish. Keep the goals small enough to be attainable. In this way, the client has more successes than failures.

FIGURE 26.4

Examples of Goals and Objectives for Two Clients

Client 1: Sherry is a young girl who is participating in a therapeutic camp program. Here are her goals and objectives as a camper in this program:

Goal A Sherry will play cooperatively with the other children as evidenced by:

1. Sherry will be able to engage in one group activity daily without yelling and pushing the other campers by the end of camp.
2. Sherry will be able to follow her team leader in games each day by the end of camp.

Goal B Sherry will demonstrate her understanding of leadership as evidenced by:

1. Sherry will lead one activity with her team every week from the third week of camp to the end.
2. Sherry will talk in group about what it takes to be a good leader.
3. Sherry will assist younger children in a team activity at least once during the camp session.

Goal C Sherry will express anger verbally as evidenced by:

1. Sherry will tell another about her anger at least twice during the camp session.

Client 2: Chapter 23 contains a referral notification form for a client named Paul J. Bittinger. Paul has been diagnosed with schizophrenia and has been referred to the Grandon River Hospitalization Program where there are mental health technicians as well as psychologists, social workers, and psychiatrists. Here are his goals and objectives at this provider agency.

Goal A Paul will learn how to manage his medication by February 15, 2008, as evidenced by:

1. Paul will attend Medication Management group twice a week.
2. By January 15, 2008, Paul will ask for his medication without prompting.
3. By February 15, 2008, Paul will take his medications during the day without assistance.
4. By February 15, 2008, Paul will be able to discuss in Medication Management group the importance of his medications to managing his illness.

Goal B Paul will be better able to manage the symptoms of his illness by March 15, 2008, as evidenced by:

1. By January 15, 2008, Paul will be able to discuss in group his behaviors that contribute to an exacerbation of his symptoms.
2. By February 15, 2008, Paul will smoke only one cigarette during the day.
3. By February 15, 2008, Paul will have only one drink with caffeine a day.
4. By February 15, 2008, Paul will sleep 8 hours each night.

The treatment intervention on the part of the worker at the provider agency would be the private sessions he has with Paul in which they discuss what kinds of behavior exacerbates Paul's illness, useful behavior changes Paul might make, and his personal concerns about making those changes. It would include activities such as the worker giving Paul literature to read, making a chart for Paul to note the number of cigarettes he smokes each day, or giving him the number for Crisis Intervention to call if he feels he needs help when the program is closed.

Goal development is sometimes difficult as you look for just the right exercise or activity for clients to use to get to their goals. With practice, however, you will begin to write goals easily, and thereby provide your clients with the means to move forward.

◆ Exercises: Developing Goals and Objectives

Exercise I

Instructions: Use the following vignette to develop a detailed treatment plan for the client.

Helen is 89 years old. She has lived independently in her own home until now. Last week she fell off a chair in her home while reaching up to clean out the top shelves in one of her closets. She sat with her arm aching all night until morning when she called her daughter to take her to the hospital. There an x-ray was done, and the arm was set. The hospital staff sent her home; and her daughter, who works, called the Office of Aging to help her plan so that her mother could remain at home. The Office of Aging set the main goal, "To continue living in her own home with assistance" and referred the case to your agency to provide the service. Helen is unable to make meals or bathe herself, and the pain medication is making her dizzy. The Office of Aging has called your agency, which provides homemaker and in-home care, to provide the actual service to Helen. As the case manager for the agency, you go out and evaluate Helen's situation.

1. The broad goal is *to keep Helen in her own home.* List two very specific goals your agency will work on with Helen. Next, place the objectives for each goal under that goal. Remember the phrase "as evidenced by. . . ."

Goal A:

   Objective 1:

   Objective 2:

Goal B:

   Objective 1:

   Objective 2:

2. Identify Helen's strengths, and show how these strengths will help her meet the goals.

Helen's strengths:

Explain how these will help her meet the goals:

3. Helen broke her arm on November 9th. What are your target dates for your goals?

4. Describe an intervention you will use with Helen to help her meet her goals.

Exercise II

Instructions: Use the following vignette to develop a detailed treatment plan for the client.

Art has been chronically ill with schizophrenia for many years. It started when he was in college, and he has been unable to hold a job. His family has just moved to your area. Art's sister, with whom he lives, has gone into the mental health center seeking services for her brother. Art's parents are deceased. The sister states the move has upset Art, and he appears ready to have another acute episode. She is also concerned that he is not taking his medication as he should, further jeopardizing his health. The sister hoped the case manager could find a place to send Art for treatment following the move. In college Art majored in engineering, and he is quite good at math. Art has been referred to the partial hospitalization program. There you are responsible for devising goals and objectives for Art.

1. The broad goal is *to help Art adjust to the move*. List two very specific goals your agency will work on with Art. Next, place the objectives for each goal under that goal. Remember the phrase "as evidenced by. . . ."

Goal A:

   Objective 1:

   Objective 2:

Goal B:

   Objective 1:

   Objective 2:

2. Identify Art's strengths, and show how these strengths will help him meet the goals.

   Art's strengths:

   Explain how these will help him meet the goals:

3. Art and his sister went to mental health case management on January 12th. What are your target dates for your goals?

4. Describe an intervention you will use with Art to help him meet his goals.

Exercise III

Instructions: Use the following vignette to develop a detailed treatment plan for the client.

Lester has been in prison and has recently been released on parole. He has family in the area, but he distanced himself from them after high school. They did visit him while in prison. Lester has been referred to your agency, which works with ex-convicts to help them turn their lives around. Lester has indicated that his juvenile crime spree was "crazy" and that he would like to become a useful citizen. As the case manager, you interviewed Lester and learned that he would like to become a chef. He tells you that he had some cooking classes in the prison and that he worked mainly in the kitchen there and enjoyed the work. He feels, however, that he could have learned more and taken on more responsibility. At present Lester is staying in a halfway house and is charged with getting a job and a place to stay.

1. The broad goal is *to help Lester get acclimated to the community*. List two very specific goals your agency will work on with Lester. Next, place the objectives for each goal under that goal. Remember the phrase "as evidenced by. . . ."

Goal A:

    Objective 1:

    Objective 2:

Goal B:

    Objective 1:

    Objective 2:

2. Identify Lester's strengths, and show how these strengths will help him meet the goals.

    Lester's strengths:

    Explain how these will help him meet the goals:

3. Lester came into your office on May 6th. What are your target dates for your goals?

4. Describe an intervention you will use with Lester to help him meet his goals.

Exercise IV

Instructions: Use the following vignette to develop a detailed treatment plan for the client.

You are a case manager in an alternative school for teenagers who have behavioral and emotional problems, and Rick is referred to you. Rick's mother is addicted to cocaine, and his father is not in the picture. Only recently Rick was moved to his grandmother's home. His grandmother seems to be very intent on helping Rick. She works as a domestic in a large office building downtown and is not home before 9:00 p.m. You are concerned that Rick is home alone after school, and you are also concerned about his getting his homework done. In addition, Rick has been having problems with other teens: hitting and punching, name-calling, and cutting up in class, all behaviors that need to be curbed if Rick is going to get anything out of the alternative school.

1. The broad goal is *to help Rick succeed at the alternative school*. List two very specific goals your agency will work on with Rick. Next, place the objectives for each goal under that goal. Remember the phrase "as evidenced by. . . ."

   Goal A:

       Objective 1:

       Objective 2:

   Goal B:

       Objective 1:

       Objective 2:

2. Identify Rick's strengths, and show how these strengths will help him meet the goals.

   Rick's strengths:

   Explain how these will help him meet the goals:

3. Rick came into your office on December 10th. What are your target dates for your goals?

4. Describe an intervention you will use with Rick to help him meet his goals.

Exercise V

Instructions: Use the following vignette to develop a detailed treatment plan for the client.

Twelve-year-old Christina has come to the attention of your agency because her parents have abused her physically. The case was reported to Child Welfare, where you work, by a teacher at Christina's school. The teacher noticed that Christina always seemed to have bruises, and when she asked Christina about these, Christina was reluctant to discuss them. You have met the parents and talked at length with Christina. All three say they want the family reunited in time. For the time being Christina is being placed with an aunt who offered to provide foster care for Christina. Christina is a good student, particularly in math and science. She is extremely shy and quiet and has few friends. You are not sure whether this is because she was forbidden to bring friends home or whether she has always been this way.

1. The broad goal is *to help Christina and Christina's family reunite successfully.* List three very specific goals your agency will work on with Christina and her family. Next, place the objectives for each goal under that goal. Remember the phrase "as evidenced by. . . ."

Goal A:

    Objective 1:

    Objective 2:

Goal B:

    Objective 1:

    Objective 2:

Goal C:

    Objective 1:

    Objective 2:

2. Identify Christina's strengths and any strengths you see within her family, and show how these strengths will help Christina and the family meet their goals.

Christina's and Christina's family's strengths:

Explain how these will help them meet their goals:

3. Christina came into your office on April 4th. What are your target dates for your goals?

4. Describe an intervention you will use with Christina and her family to help them meet their goals.

Chapter 27

Terminating the Case

Introduction

We have looked at how clients enter the human service system and how their services and treatment are determined and monitored. There is usually a point at which clients leave the system, moving on in their lives. Here are some of the reasons a case may be terminated.

1. *The client and the case manager agree the client is ready to move on.* This is the ideal. The service or treatment has been successful and is no longer needed. Many clients do leave for this reason, feeling that their original issues and problems are less significant than they once were or that these problems have been resolved.
2. *The client dies or moves away.* When clients die or move to another jurisdiction, their cases are closed. If they formally request that their records be sent to the new jurisdiction, this should be done immediately to facilitate a smooth transition to the new program.
3. *The funding source will no longer finance services.* Managed care has introduced limitations on care that you and the client may find unrealistic. It is important to work with the client to find alternatives to your service. Support groups or specialized programs funded by other sources may not give the level of service you have provided, but they may help the client make the adjustment. It is not ethical to drop a client with no plan or referral when the insurance runs out.
4. *The client no longer wants the services.* Clients may be dissatisfied with the services being offered and request that their cases be terminated. In situations

like this, sit down with the dissatisfied clients and learn why they are not pleased with the service. This may provide you with valuable information about how you or a provider agency are perceived by clients, and it may facilitate clients' leaving with the feeling that they can come back if they need to do so.

5. *You cannot find the client.* Sometimes individuals indicate they are not interested in our services by disappearing. It may be a person you feel is really in need of support, medication, or treatment of some sort; but often clients feel case management is either intrusive or a nuisance, and just disappear. You may make attempts to find such people, and you may even track some of them down, but clients have every right to refuse services. When you encounter this situation, make sure that both your contact notes and the termination summary reflect your attempts to contact the client who has disappeared.

Not all clients will leave case management. A child with autism may need services all his life. A woman with severe developmental disabilities may require case management during her entire lifetime in order for her to live in her community successfully.

A Successful Termination

Cases should not be closed without the client, or the client's family, if they are involved, knowing that this is about to occur and why. A letter by itself cannot convey warmth and concern for the client and often comes across as bureaucratic and unfeeling. A phone call is not much better. You might convey warmth, but there is no meaningful exchange or documentation.

All clients whose cases are being closed, except those who have moved away or died, should receive two things from the case management unit:

1. An opportunity to meet with you to discuss the termination
2. Follow-up by letter outlining the main points in your final interview and inviting the client to return if the need arises

The Final Interview

Leaving anything can be difficult, and leaving services can be particularly difficult for clients who have grown fond of the people at the agency or who feel uncertain about how they will handle life on their own. Sometimes terminations are milestones. The clients have reached a new level of independence, emotional health, or sobriety. But the accomplishment still can be tinged with misgivings. Try to recognize the underlying feelings your client is experiencing in the final interview and respond empathically.

Use the interview to summarize the reasons for the termination. If there are accomplishments, review how far the client has come since first seeking help some time before. For clients who have requested termination of their cases themselves, ask them to tell you more about their reasons for making the request and be open to their suggestions for change. Invite questions. Clients often want to know where they should turn should former problems resurface. Give clients information they can use, particularly information that will help them prevent a relapse or regression.

There should be a sense of reassurance during the interview that clients are not being cut off or dumped and that they are welcome to return should they need services again. You may not need to say all of that explicitly. Nevertheless, clients may feel dumped or dropped and be unable to express that to you. Speak to these concerns in the final interview.

The Letter

The letter is a follow-up to the final interview. It should summarize the main points of the interview, recapping briefly what was discussed. There should be a brief statement about why the termination took place so the client has documentation of it. In addition, questions that seemed particularly important to the client during the interview should be answered again in the letter, especially if the client needs addresses, names of resources, and other supportive information. Figure 27.1 provides a sample termination letter.

FIGURE 27.1

Sample Termination Letter

Dear Mrs. Warren,

It was good to talk to you the other day and to hear about your plans to move. As we discussed in our meeting, we will be terminating your case here because of your move to another state. We will forward those records you asked for to the new case management unit when you are settled.

We have given you a prescription for medications for one month that can be filled at a pharmacy where you will be living. If you have been unable to see a doctor before the prescription expires, call us and we will issue a prescription for one more month of your current medication.

The case management unit where you will be living is at 3132 Green. The unit's phone number is (555) 555-5555.

If there is any way we can be helpful in the future, please don't hesitate to get in touch with us again. It was a pleasure working with you, and we wish you all the best in your new home.

Sincerely,

Case manager

Documentation

Like all contacts with the client, this last contact and letter should be documented in the client's chart. In the note, the focus of the interview would be the termination of the case. You would note the highlights of the discussion, any follow-up arrangements that were made for the client, and the client's response to the interview.

The Discharge Summary

In most cases, your agency will ask for a termination summary or discharge summary. This is not the same thing as the final case note discussed earlier. Although you include the information from that contact note in the discharge summary, you are actually summarizing the most important information about what took place while the client was working with you. It is wise to think of your summary as a document that may go to other professionals who will see the client in the future. What you include in your summary should be helpful to a new person developing a strategy to help the client. For this reason, your summary should discuss what was tried, what worked, and what was less successful and why. Figure 27.2 provides a sample discharge or termination summary.

Your discharge summary is also a public relations tool for your agency. This is a major way that other programs and professionals can learn about the quality of the care given in your case management unit. The summary provides a view of the excellence of your services. Sloppy summaries containing little useful information or those that indicate little organized effort on the client's behalf can make your agency look unprofessional. Your agency may have a standard format for discharge summaries that you can use as a guide to writing good discharge summaries. If not, you can use the "Discharge Summary" form provided in the Appendix at the end of this book.

Here are important items to include in the discharge summary:

1. Diagnoses
2. Any medication that was prescribed by physicians who were working with the case management unit and whether it has been discontinued. (Make sure to note the name of the medication, the dosage, the frequency, and any adverse reactions.)
3. The reason for discharge
4. The major presenting problem that brought the client to you
5. Your goals and objectives for the client
6. The extent to which the client participated in formulating these goals and objectives
7. Progress that was made or goals that were accomplished
8. Problems that were identified but were not addressed
9. How the client appeared to be at intake and how the client appeared to be at termination
10. Attempts to locate the client if she has disappeared

FIGURE 27.2

Sample Discharge or Termination Summary

Wildwood Case Management Unit

Discharge Summary

Name *Juan Gonzales*　　　　　　　　Date of birth *1/17/1958*

Date of admission *11/24/09*　　　　Date of discharge *3/5/10*

Diagnosis on Admission

Axis I *309.81 Acute Post Traumatic Stress Disorder, Acute*

Axis II *V71.09*

Axis III *Asthma following smoke inhalation during fire*

Axis IV *House fire and death of his wife and 2-year-old daughter*

Axis V *GAF 62*

Medication:

Welbutrin 100 Mgs TID

Reason for discharge:

Client is moving to Cambridge to be near relatives

Presenting problem:

Juan Gonzales is a 48-year-old male, a draftsman with a large engineering company, who came to the case management unit suffering from anxiety and depression following a house fire 4 months before in which he lost his wife and 2-year-old daughter. He was referred by his family physician after his physician had seen the client on several occasions. At the time Juan came to the agency, he was complaining of depression, feeling tired and "numb," and feeling intense anxiety about the status of other loved ones, particularly his surviving child. He reported recurrent, intrusive memories about the fire and an unsuccessful struggle to diminish these memories. His affect was flat. He stated that others in his life were concerned about his irritability. At work he was unable to concentrate and felt intense irritability with coworkers.

Goals:

The case manager and Mr. Gonzales developed two goals. The objectives were developed with Mr. Gonzales by his therapist, Kelly Marcuson.

GOAL I　To feel less depressed by 1/24/10 as demonstrated by:
　　A. Attending 10 session of psychotherapy with Dr. Kelly Marcuson
　　B. Meeting with Dr. Pederos to evaluate his need for medication
　　C. Attending at least one session of the Market Square Presbyterian Church's grief support group

(continued)

FIGURE 27.2 *(continued)*

GOAL II To be able to work consistently by 1/25/10 as demonstrated by:
  A. Obtaining information from Dr. Pederos as to how much he is able to work at present
  B. Meet with his employer and discuss his recent absences
  C. Discussing with his employer a schedule for his gradual return to work full time
  D. Keeping the devised schedule for at least one month

These were the two most important concerns when Mr. Gonzales came to the case management unit, and he participated in developing the goals and objectives.

Progress:

At intake Mr. Gonzales was unable to attend work regularly, was experiencing intrusive memories of the fire, and had a flat affect. At discharge he appeared more animated and expressed hope that being near his family would offer support to both him and his son. He was referred to Family and Children's Services where he saw Kelly Marcuson.

Mr. Gonzales attended nine sessions with Kelly Marcuson, psychologist, from November 2009 through March 25, 2010. He reported the sessions were helpful in relieving some of his more acute symptom and in helping him to "sort out what happened to all of us." In November 2009 he was evaluated by Dr. Marcella King, who prescribed Wellbutrin, 100 mgs. TID, which he tolerates well. He remains on this medication at discharge. He reports the memories of the fire are less intrusive, and he is more animated in contacts with CM.

The client followed up with a meeting with his employer and began to attend work 3 days a week. At discharge he was attending work full time but still concerned about some lack of concentration and some irritability with coworkers.

In addition, client attended the grief support group at a local church where he met two individuals who became close friends. He credits them with helping him to think more about the effect the fire had on his son. His one regret in leaving is that he will be leaving this support group.

Client is leaving the area to move closer to relatives in the Cambridge area. He is seeking employment with the Massachusetts Department of Highways as a draftsman and has taken a civil service examination, on which he obtained a high score.

Additional issues:

Not addressed in our time with Mr. Gonzales were his concerns for his surviving 7-year-old son, now in second grade. He indicated a willingness to discuss his son's problems in school that started after the fire. Client intends to seek help for his son in Cambridge.

Impressions and recommendations:

Juan Gonzales is a 48-year-old man, widowed as the result of a house fire, and currently caring for his 7-year-old son. He sought help for debilitating symptoms of Post Traumatic Stress Disorder, primarily depression and anxiety and an inability to work consistently. At discharge his symptoms are less acute and he remains

(continued)

FIGURE 27.2 *(continued)*

on 100 mgs. of Wellbutrin TID, which he tolerates well. He met both goals. His depression is diminished and he has returned to working consistently.

The reason for termination was a move to be closer to relatives in the Cambridge area. Recommend he seek further assistance with remaining symptoms and also seek assistance for his son.

Will need a medication reevaluation and continuation of his Wellbutrin until that evaluation.

Prepared by
Angela Carter, Case Manager

Summary

Termination should be approached as skillfully as all other aspects of case management. When cases are closed well, both clients and agencies benefit. Clients feel reassured and supported as they take leave of your services. In the community, the perception of your agency as a caring and professional place is strengthened.

◆ Exercises: Termination of a Middle-Aged Adult

Instructions:

1. Record in your contact notes a termination interview, indicating the reason for termination and any follow-up arrangements you made for the client after he leaves your services. Refer to the goals for such an interview in this chapter.
2. Write your client a letter as a follow-up to this interview, summarizing for the client the discussion and resolutions that took place in your last contact.
3. Prepare a discharge summary on your client. It will be the last item in the client's chart. Use the guidelines for a discharge summary found in this chapter.

◆ **Exercises: Termination of a Child**

Instructions:

1. Record in your contact notes a termination interview, indicating the reason for termination and any follow-up arrangements you made for the client after she leaves your services. Be sure your termination interview includes the parents, and indicate if the child was present. Refer to the goals for such an interview in this chapter.
2. Write your child's parents a letter as a follow-up to this interview, summarizing for them the discussion and resolutions that took place in your last contact.
3. Prepare a discharge summary on this child. It will be the last item in the client's chart. Use the guidelines for a discharge summary found in this chapter.

◆ **Exercises: Termination of a Frail, Older Person**

Instructions:

1. Record in your contact notes a termination interview, indicating the reason for termination and any follow-up arrangements you made for the client after he leaves your services. Indicate if others were present, such as relatives or a worker from a new service where your client will be going. Document where you conducted the interview. Refer to the goals for such an interview in this chapter.
2. Write your client a letter as a follow-up to this interview, summarizing for the client the discussion and resolutions that took place in your last contact. If you have the client's permission to do so, indicate that you are sending a copy of your letter to the person who was present for the termination interview.
3. Prepare a discharge summary on your client. It will be the last item in the client's chart. Use the guidelines for a discharge summary found in this chapter.

Chapter 28

Taking Care of Yourself

Introduction

We have looked carefully at how people are helped by people like you. We haven't talked, however, about how important your health and well-being are in this important process. Before you close this book and set forth to help others, let's take a minute to talk about you and what you can do to bring the best of yourself to work every day. When workers fail to think about caring for themselves, it is usually because they tend to believe that helping others involves giving of themselves completely. Thinking about our own welfare can be viewed as selfish, but taking care of ourselves is just as important as all the other tasks explored in previous chapters. Social service workers tend to neglect themselves or fatigue themselves in five ways, often to the point of burnout. Let's explore each one.

See Yourself as an Effective Tool

In many other professions and occupations people need tools and equipment to do the job. In social services you are your own best tool. Your feelings on a particular day, your attitudes toward certain clients, and your energy and commitment are all significant contributors to the outcome of your work. To be effective, you need to see your own wellness as an important contribution to the lives of the people you are seeking to help.

One of the errors workers in this field make is to assume that any attention paid to their own well-being is attention being directed away from clients. Workers who need to feel selfless feel guilty about caring for themselves. They consistently neglect their own needs so that they will not experience themselves as uncaring or self-centered. The failure lies in their inability to see the connection between their readiness to do the work at hand and the good outcomes of their work. The first step, therefore, is to recognize the importance of taking care of yourself. In many ways you are key to what happens in other people's lives.

While Attempting to Understand Others, Don't Fail to Understand Yourself

Focusing on the problems of other people makes it easier to ignore problems we might need to address ourselves. To be effective when working with other people, you will need a level of self-awareness. Here are some possible ways you can increase your self-awareness and your self-acceptance.

- *Accept your strengths and weaknesses.* Not one of us is perfect. We all have foibles, and we all have wonderful attributes. To help others, it works best to know what these are for you. Where are your strengths and weaknesses? Are these a little bit comical, or do they need to be modified in some way? Look at yourself as a normal, fallible human being just like everyone else. Become realistic about who you are.
- *Be flexible. Don't demand perfection.* Flexible people who can accept their own imperfections and the mistakes and imperfections of others are a great deal more helpful than workers who insist that they and their clients be perfect. Because perfection is unattainable, seeking it is a fruitless and frustrating exercise, and that frustration and that unrealistic notion that perfection can be attained can serve to drive a wedge between you and the people you want to help.
- *Understand why you feel strongly about certain behaviors and conditions.* It is neither good nor bad to feel a certain way, but you may have strong feelings that you find on closer examination are not very useful or realistic. Some of your reactions may seem irrational when looked at more carefully.
- *Before you even get started in the field, know why you chose to work with other people.* There are a host of reasons for choosing social services, from wanting to genuinely contribute something to wanting to control other people. You become more effective when you can pinpoint what it is about helping other people that brings you satisfaction.
- *Look ahead and choose a direction.* There are people who have no direction in their lives. They get so far and there they are stuck for the rest of their lives. Choose your own direction and work toward it. One worker, who was an excellent case manager, took geology courses in the evenings and ended up working as a geologist after 15 years in case management and case management supervision. Another case manager took history courses and became a history professor after 12 years in case management. Another

looked for opportunities to do education about and with the population with whom she worked. In time she moved into a position involving education and research. And, of course, many case managers seek further education to improve their skills in working with other people. Without direction and goals it is easy to drift and gather a sense of purposelessness.

- ◆ *Resolve your personal problems.* We all have issues we would like to clear up, and sometimes life's problems and issues impinge heavily on what we want to do and where we really want to be. Some people ignore these problems, and some of the people who do ignore them think, unrealistically, that because they help others with problems and issues they can't have a problem themselves. But life isn't smooth sailing for anyone. From time to time things will happen or something will bother us that really needs to be addressed. Address these problems in your own life when they occur.

Consistently Underestimating Clients Wears Workers Out

Underestimating the competence, wisdom, and power of our clients is one of the major ways social service workers can burn out and become ineffective. In 1968 Stephen Karpman developed a set of roles and interrelationships he called the Karpman Drama Triangle. Since 1968 this triangle has been applied to a host of situations to show dysfunctional relationships and how they could be improved. In applying this model to formal helping relationships, we can see how they too can become dysfunctional and contribute to a worker's burnout and fatigue.

According to Karpman, people in dysfunctional relationships play three roles in relation to each other: rescuer, victim, and persecutor. During the course of the impossible relationship, individuals involved with each other can play all the roles. Karpman's triangle is illustrated in Figure 28.1.

Here is how it works: A person or group of people seek to do everything they can for a person or group of people. These are the rescuers. Those being helped come to resent the interference or the view of themselves as helpless. They are the victims. Finally, the victims' resentment leads them to sabotage the helping relationship. They show a lack of appreciation, fail to cooperate, and demonstrate a lack of commitment. They have become the persecutors now of the people who were their would-be rescuers. And so it can go: Rescuers "victimize" their clients with too much unhealthy involvement, and clients feel victimized and retaliate, becoming persecutors. The rescuers feel victimized after all they did for this person and tend to persecute the person in return, retaliating with persecution of their own. As you can see, this is extremely unhealthy and counterproductive.

Applied to social services, it works like this: Social service workers are expected to give of themselves. In our society helping other people and giving of ourselves is a

FIGURE 28.1

Karpman's Triangle Illustrating Rescuer, Victim, and Persecutor Roles

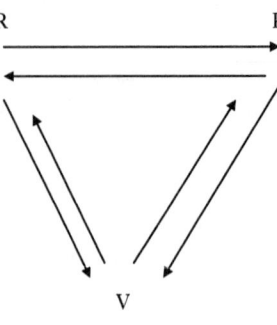

socially supported role. Society likes to have people who can take care of others, and often society expects selfless giving, even toward people who can do more for themselves or who don't want our help. When workers buy into this perspective, giving clients more responsibility can be viewed as a negative act, uncaring and selfish. Workers who subscribe to the idea that all clients are helpless and incapable will do work the clients could learn to do for themselves. The harder these workers give to their clients, the more exhausted they become. And in some cases a client may find it in his or her best interest to appear helpless in order to get the worker to take over and handle things the client does not feel like doing.

Furthermore, a worker who is overly helpful and overinvolved in a client's life can come to be resented by that client. Doing everything for people is not always what they want in the long run. They may grow tired of seeing themselves as needy and helpless and refuse to follow through with plans they made with you. When you are working as hard as you can for a client and that person doesn't follow through or fails to keep appointments, or drops away from contact with you, it is frustrating. Invariably you ask yourself why you are working this hard for someone who doesn't appreciate it and who either relapses or stops cooperating.

To demonstrate how the Karpman triangle is unproductive in helping others, let us look at the case of Henrico and Martha. Martha was an alcoholic by her own admission, and she came to Henrico from a rehabilitation unit where she had detoxed after 3 years of drinking. At the time she became a part of Henrico's caseload, she had no job, had been on welfare, and was without shelter. Martha was in the victim role. Henrico went to work, assuming the rescuer role with energy. First he found an apartment for Martha in an apartment complex where the county had several units for cases like Martha's. Martha seemed very surprised at how quickly Henrico found her a place, and she was grateful. In addition, Henrico took her in the car to see where the AA meeting would be held. Then he took her for a hamburger at MacDonald's and drove her to the AA meeting. From then on Henrico either drove Martha to her AA meetings or called before the meetings to be sure she was going. He did not quite trust her to consistently attend. Henrico went to the welfare office with Martha and expedited her getting her check quickly, intervening when there was a problem with the application.

Martha was also involved in outpatient treatment. Henrico checked often to see whether she was there and talked with Martha to see if she was going and if she had any problems with the program. When Martha said she needed furniture for her apartment, Henrico went to the second-hand furniture store and picked out some things for Martha himself. When these were delivered, Martha again expressed appreciation and Henrico felt good about himself and how well things were going. Martha was regularly attending AA and her outpatient treatment program and was settled in an apartment with furniture, indicating she intended to stay.

Now Henrico took the next step and began to suggest things Martha might do when her treatment program ended. He brought her an application from the local state university and brochures from the state employment bureau. Where would she like to start? he asked. He would make the appointment and go with her. She just needed to decide which of these she would like to pursue. For the first time Martha seemed noncommittal. She would have to think about it, she told Henrico. Maybe she wouldn't choose either of these options. Several days later she complained to Henrico on the way to AA that she no longer liked her apartment because the neighbors were "spooky." This led to Henrico visiting the apartment complex management and trying to arrange better housing for Martha. Martha let him do all this and did not express as much gratitude as she always had before.

A week later when Henrico went to pick up Martha for her AA meeting she wasn't there. Fearful she had begun to drink again and distressed that she would stand him up "after all I have done," Henrico set out to find Martha. He never did find her, so he parked at her apartment and waited for her to return home. Martha didn't come back until 10:30 that night and told Henrico she had been visiting her aunt. Henrico was suspicious. Martha hadn't ever mentioned an aunt, but he couldn't smell alcohol on her breath so he went home. From then on Martha was not there when Henrico came for her. Sometimes she went to AA and sometimes she did not. She never definitively said whether she wanted a job or to take some college courses, and she left messages about her lousy apartment.

Henrico felt angry and frustrated. Things with Martha had been going well. He thought she had turned her life around. Fruitlessly he called her, left messages, and tried to entice her to come in with predictions about how good her life would be if she would choose one of the options he had arranged for her. Martha did not come in and stopped returning his calls. Then one night Henrico encountered her as he waited at her treatment program; she was rude and said she had no time to talk to him. Martha had grown tired of Henrico's constant interference and his treatment of her as if she were a child. She didn't tell him this directly. Instead she stopped cooperating. Martha had gone from the victim role to the persecutor role, and Henrico was her victim. Henrico felt betrayed and perplexed.

Finally Henrico withdrew his attention from Martha, focusing it on other clients, but he was bitter. She had potential, a "golden opportunity to do something with her life." He was frustrated over the time he had given her and the fact that she wasn't more grateful and cooperative. And then one afternoon Martha called. She had dropped out of AA and treatment and she needed Henrico's help to get back into treatment. Henrico brushed her off. "You didn't take my help when I offered it to you. Why would I offer you any assistance now?" he said angrily. When Martha asked again, Henrico replied, "Look I'm busy right now. You can come in, but I can't guarantee I will see you." From then on he was curt with Martha and refused to be particularly helpful. He was now the persecutor and Martha was again a victim.

Over and over in the helping profession workers engage in this triangle and exhaust themselves doing so. By doing too much, these workers wear out and lose energy to keep up such intense investment in all their clients. Clients come to feel irritated with what seems to be interference and a lack of respect for what they can do for themselves. When these clients drop away from their workers, the workers feel betrayed and let their clients know this by being cool or outright rude when they do have contact.

Giving clients the right to make their own decisions, including decisions that result in mistakes, works better for everyone concerned. Moving clients toward health and recovery by encouraging independence is much more effective.

Develop Healthy Relationships Away from the Agency

Rescuing and taking care of others can become a total way of life for some people. Perhaps it is a need to be seen as benevolent, or better able than others to "fix people," that leads some in the social service field to gravitate toward relationships with people who need help.

This can happen in a number of ways. Perhaps the worker chooses friends who need constant counseling and reassurance. A friend in a bad relationship, for instance, calls often about the latest bad news in her relationship and seeks advice. Another person may come to expect favors. Sometimes workers become involved with people who are entirely unsuitable for a long-term relationship. These workers are inclined to believe that they can change the person, bring about positive changes in the person's life, or give that person the support needed to help the person turn his or her life around. For example, one worker, Elaine, became involved in a relationship with a man who had an addiction problem with cocaine. Elaine was certain the man would stop using cocaine because of their relationship. In Elaine's mind, the man valued her so much he was willing to give up the cocaine, and she, because of her work, would give him the necessary support to do it. It never worked out that way. Seven years later Elaine was disillusioned and angry, and nothing had changed except for occasional temporary periods of abstinence.

Markus was attracted to a woman with a criminal background. He thought he had the skills to entirely turn this woman's life around. He believed he could make her over into a respected and productive member of the community, and he was flattered when at first this woman seemed honored to be dating a professional. However, after a brief period of good behavior during which she got off probation and enrolled in college courses, the woman again resorted to shoplifting and writing bad checks. Markus felt demoralized, exhausted, and less confident about his ability to do his work well.

It is one thing to give of ourselves to others as part of our work. At work there are parameters and guidelines. It is quite another to be faced with the same problems when we come home at night. Problems at home are draining and distracting, but from time to time we all have them. Deliberately choosing to work with people who are needy and draining is not wise. Allowing friendships with people who constantly need something drains away energy you need to do your work well.

Develop Other Stimulating and Rewarding Interests

For some workers, helping others is all they know how to do. They talk, eat, and sleep their job. They carry it home at night; they fret about it over the weekend. They go the extra mile all the time. The major reality in their lives is their work. These workers have lost sight of the rest of life.

What hobbies would you like to pursue? What subject have you always wanted to know more about? What talents do you have that you are not using? Miranda took cooking lessons occasionally and loved trying the recipes out at home. In fact, she became very interested in Polynesian cooking and began to widen her circle of friends as she invited others over for dinners. Pete took up fitness. Jorge went back to school in accounting. Andrea started training dogs for people on the weekends. Pete joined a choir. Leonard took a trip to Norway to see where his ancestors had come from. Adam and his friends started a bowling team.

It is a large, interesting world we live in. There are many places to go and things to do. Don't limit yourself to just your job. Look at yourself as a whole person with many talents and interests and pursue them. It gives you much needed respite from the daily work of helping others.

Summary

Remember the five ways social service workers can wear themselves out, and protect yourself from these pitfalls. As you enter the field of human services, don't impose limits on what you can do. Look way out to the horizon and ask yourself where you would like to be, what you would like to be doing, what you would like to know more about in 5 or 10 or 15 years down the road. By taking the focus off your work and your clients during your down time, you give yourself a much needed rest. The more you care for and nurture yourself, the more energy you will have to care for those on your caseload.

Appendix A

Wildwood Case Management Unit Forms

Arrangement of the Client's Chart

1. **A Clean File Folder** Place client's name and number on the tab of the folder, last name first.
2. **Face Sheet**
3. **Phone Inquiry Sheet**
4. **Verification Letter**
5. **Social History** Your instructor may ask you to provide either a social history or an assessment form, or both, for practice purposes. Be sure you show collaboration with client on goals and expectations.
6. **Assessment Form** Your instructor may ask you to provide either a social history or an assessment form, or both, for practice purposes. Be sure you show collaboration with client on goals and expectations.
7. **Release of Information Form(s)**
8. **Notes for Service Planning Conference** These may be handwritten notes you made for yourself.
9. **Service Plan**
10. **Referral Form(s)**
11. **Provider Agency Goals and Objectives** This should be on a letterhead from the provider agency, informing you of the goals for the client in response to your referral. Students usually make up a letterhead for the provider agency on their computers.
12. **Contact Notes** Be sure these reflect monitoring.
13. **Termination Letter**
14. **Discharge Summary**

Wildwood Case Management Unit
Face Sheet

Name _____ Agency # _____

Address _____

Home Phone _____ Work Phone _____

Guardian _____

Address _____

Home Phone _____ Work Phone _____

Next of Kin _____
If different from Guardian

Address _____

Home Phone _____ Work Phone _____

Date first contact	Taken by	DOB	Gender
Marital Status	Education Level	Employment Status	Veteran Status
Currently Pregnant	Rec. Prenatal Care 28 days?	Given birth last Complications	Pregnancy
Current Medical Conditions Treated by	Current Medications Prescribed by	Legal status/ Incarcerations	Substance Abuse Problems Treated by
Reason for visit	Referred to 1 2 3 Being seen by	Psychotropic Medications Prescribed by	May not call these numbers [ ] home [ ] work
Dx.	Psychiatric Evaluation Done	Psychological Evaluation Don	Court Ordered?

Assigned Case Manager _____ First Review Date _____

424 Appendix A

Wildwood Case Management Unit
New Referral or Inquiry

CLIENT _____ SEX _____ DOB _____

ADDRESS _____

_____ ZIP _____

HOME TELEPHONE _____ WK TELEPHONE _____

PARENT OR SPOUSE _____

EMPLOYER _____

SCHOOL _____

REFERRED BY _____

CHIEF COMPLAINT &/OR DESCRIPTION OF PROBLEM _____

_____

_____

_____

_____

_____

_____

_____

_____

_____

_____

_____

PREVIOUS EVALUATION, SERVICES, OR TREATMENT

_____

_____

_____

_____

TAKEN BY _____ DATE _____

DISPOSITION FOR INTAKE _____

VERIFICATION SENT _____

Wildwood Case Management Unit Forms

Wildwood Case Management Unit
4600 Wildwood Drive
Harrisburg, PA 17110
255-5555

Verification of Appointment

Date _____

Dear

This letter is to inform or remind you that you have an appointment scheduled:

Date: _____

Time: _____

Staff: _____

Location: _____

Please contact me if you have any questions or if you need to reschedule.

Sincerely,

Case Manager

Wildwood Case Management Unit
Request/Release of Information

RE: _____ DOB: _____

To Whom It May Concern:

[ ] I hereby authorize the Wildwood Case Management Unit to release information about services rendered to the above-named, for the purpose of:

_____

[ ] I hereby authorize the Wildwood Case Management Unit to receive information about services rendered to the above-named from:

_____

for the purpose of_____

Such information may be transmitted under the conditions stated below, and/or as required by Federal or State statute or order of the court. This release will be effective for a period of ninety (90) days from the date signed below and will expire on

Information to be released/received may include

( ) Medical records   ( ) Social/developmental
( ) Discharge summary   ( ) Psychiatric evaluation
( ) Psychological evaluation   ( ) Educational record
( ) Vocational evaluation/summary ( ) Substance abuse treatment history
( ) Treatment summary   ( ) Social/developmental history
( ) Personal information including Social Security no(s) address(es) and telephone no(s)
( ) Other_____

To the agency or professional person receiving this release:

THIS INFORMATION HAS BEEN DISCLOSED TO YOU FROM RECORDS WHOSE CONFIDENTIALITY IS PROTECTED BY STATE LAW. STATE REGULATIONS PROHIBIT YOU FROM MAKING ANY FURTHER DISCLOSURE OF THIS INFORMATION WITHOUT PRIOR WRITTEN CONSENT OF THE PERSON TO WHOM IT PERTAINS.
   THIS CONSENT TO RELEASE OF INFORMATION CAN BE REVOKED AT THE WRITTEN REQUEST OF THE PERSON WHO GAVE THE CONSENT.

I have read this form carefully and I understand what it means.

_____ _____
Authorized signature   Date   Staff person signature   Date

I have read this carefully and I understand what it means. As I am not physically able to give my written consent, I am giving my verbal consent to release these records.

_____ _____
Witness signature   Date   Staff person signature   Date

_____
Witness signature   Date

Wildwood Case Management Unit
Release of HIV/AIDS–Related Information

RE: _____ DOB: _____

To Whom It May Concern:

[ ] I hereby authorize the Wildwood Case Management Unit to release information about services rendered to the above-named, for the purpose of:

_____

[ ] Such information to be released includes information regarding my HIV/AIDS status and/or treatment.

To the agency or professional person receiving this release:

THIS INFORMATION HAS BEEN DISCLOSED TO YOU FROM RECORDS WHOSE CONFIDENTIALITY IS PROTECTED BY STATE LAW. STATE REGULATIONS PROHIBIT YOU FROM MAKING ANY FURTHER DISCLOSURE OF THIS INFORMATION WITHOUT PRIOR WRITTEN CONSENT OF THE PERSON TO WHOM IT PERTAINS.
    THIS CONSENT TO RELEASE OF INFORMATION CAN BE REVOKED AT THE WRITTEN REQUEST OF THE PERSON WHO GAVE THE CONSENT.

I have read this form carefully and I understand what it means.

_____	_____	_____	_____
Authorized signature	Date	Staff person signature	Date

I have read this carefully and I understand what it means. As I am not physically able to give my written consent, I am giving my verbal consent to release these records.

_____	_____	_____	_____
Witness signature	Date	Staff person signature	Date

_____	_____
Witness signature	Date

Wildwood Case Management Unit
Intake Assessment Form

Client Name _____ # _____
D.O.B. _____ Unit # _____
Date of assessment _____

1. PRESENTING PROBLEM (Functional impairment, symptoms, background)

_____
_____
_____
_____
_____
_____
_____
_____
_____
_____
_____
_____

2. CURRENT CLIENT INVOLVEMENT WITH OTHER AGENCIES

Agency/Person	Phone	Service	Date

3. ASSESSMENT OF LIFE CIRCUMSTANCES OR CHANGES IN THE FOLLOWING AREAS

Family

_____
_____
_____

Social

_____
_____
_____

Support

_____
_____
_____

Legal
_____
_____
_____

Education
_____
_____
_____

Occupation
_____
_____
_____

Finances
_____
_____
_____

Psychosocial & environmental problems
_____
_____
_____

4. CURRENT MEDICAL CONDITIONS

Condition	Physician	Treatment

5. PREGNANT ( ) YES   ( ) NO

Receiving prenatal care? ( ) YES   ( ) NO

6. PRIMARY CARE PHYSICIAN
_____
_____
_____

7. CURRENT MEDICATIONS

Name/Dosage   Prescribed by   Condition

_____
_____
_____
_____

Side effects

_____
_____
_____

Medication allergies

_____
_____
_____

8. RELATIONSHIP RISK FACTORS

Is client safe at home? ( ) YES   ( ) NO

Does client feel threatened in any way? ( ) YES   ( ) NO

If *YES* describe

_____
_____
_____
_____

Has client been abused in any way? ( ) YES   ( ) NO

If *YES* check all that apply

( ) Physical   ( ) Emotional   ( ) Sexual

Relationship of perpetrator to client

_____

Any legal action taken?

_____
_____
_____
_____

Does client have a safety plan? ( ) YES   ( ) NO

Needs shelter ( ) YES   ( ) NO

Needs protection from abuse order ( ) YES   ( ) NO

9. SUICIDE/HOMICIDE EVALUATION

Client's self-rating of suicide risk _____

Client's self-rating of becoming violent_____

Client's self-rating of homicide risk _____

(1 – none   2 – slight   3 – moderate   4 – extreme/immediate)

10. MENTAL STATUS EXAM

Appearance
( ) age appropriate   ( ) well groomed   ( ) disheveled/unkempt   ( ) bizarre   ( ) other

Orientation
( ) person   ( ) place   ( ) time   ( ) situation

Behavior/Eye Contact
( ) good   ( ) limited   ( ) avoidant   ( ) none   ( ) relaxed/calm   ( ) restless   ( ) rigid
( ) agitated   ( ) slumped posture   ( ) tense   ( ) tics   ( ) tremors

Motor Activity
( ) mannerisms   ( ) motor retardation   ( ) catatonic behavior

Manner
( ) appropriate   ( ) trusting   ( ) cooperative   ( ) inappropriate   ( ) withdrawn   ( ) seductive
( ) playful   ( ) evasive   ( ) guarded   ( ) sullen   ( ) passive   ( ) defensive   ( ) hostile
( ) manic   ( ) demanding   ( ) inappropriate boundaries

Speech
( ) normal   ( ) incoherent   ( ) pressured   ( ) too detailed   ( ) slurred   ( ) slowed
( ) impoverished   ( ) halting   ( ) neologisms   ( ) neurological language disturbances

Mood
( ) appropriate   ( ) depressed   ( ) irritable   ( ) anxious   ( ) euphoric   ( ) fatigued
( ) angry   ( ) expansive

Affect
( ) broad   ( ) tearful   ( ) blunted   ( ) constricted   ( ) flat   ( ) labile   ( ) excited
( ) anhedonic

Sleep
( ) good   ( ) fair   ( ) poor   ( ) increased   ( ) decreased   ( ) initial insomnia
( ) middle insomnia   ( ) terminal insomnia

Appetite
( ) good   ( ) fair   ( ) poor   ( ) increased   ( ) decreased   ( ) weight gain   ( ) weight loss

Thought process
( ) logical and well organized   ( ) illogical   ( ) flight of ideas   ( ) circumstantial
( ) loose associations   ( ) rambling   ( ) obsessive   ( ) blocking   ( ) tangential
( ) spontaneous   ( ) perseverative   ( ) distractible

Thought content
( ) delusions   ( ) paranoid delusions   ( ) distortions   ( ) thought withdrawal
( ) thought insertion   ( ) thought broadcast   ( ) magical thinking   ( ) somatic delusions
( ) ideas of reference   ( ) delusional guilt   ( ) grandiose delusions   ( ) nihilistic delusions
( ) ideas of inference

Perception/hallucinations
( ) illusions   ( ) hallucinations   ( ) depersonalization   ( ) derealization

Suicide risk
( ) none   ( ) slight   ( ) moderate   ( ) significant   ( ) extreme   ( ) no plan   ( ) plan (describe)
_____
_____
_____

Violence risk
( ) none   ( ) slight   ( ) moderate   ( ) significant   ( ) extreme   ( ) no plan   ( ) plan (describe)
_____
_____
_____

Judgment
( ) intact   ( ) age appropriate   ( ) impulsive   ( ) immature   ( ) impaired   ( ) mild
( ) moderate   ( ) severe

Insight
( ) intact   ( ) limited   ( ) very limited   ( ) fair   ( ) none   ( ) aware of current disorder
( ) understands personal role in problems

Sensorium
( ) alert   ( ) drowsy   ( ) stupor   ( ) obtundation   ( ) coma

Memory
( ) intact   ( ) impaired   ( ) immediate recall   ( ) remote   ( ) amnesia
type of amnesia

Intelligence
( ) average   ( ) above average   ( ) below average   ( ) unable to establish

Interviewer summary of findings (add details where appropriate)
_____
_____
_____
_____
_____
_____
_____
_____
_____
_____
_____
_____

12. SUBSTANCE USE/ABUSE

Type	Amount used	How taken	Duration	Frequency	Date of last use
Tobacco					
Alcohol					
Illicit Drugs					
Prescription Drugs					
OTC Drugs					
Other					

Experiencing:
- Withdrawal ( ) YES ( ) NO
- Blackouts ( ) YES ( ) NO
- Hallucinations ( ) YES ( ) NO
- Vomiting ( ) YES ( ) NO
- Severe Depression ( ) YES ( ) NO
- DTs and Shaking ( ) YES ( ) NO
- Seizures ( ) YES ( ) NO
- Other ( ) YES ( ) NO
- Describe

_____
_____

Patterns of use
- Uses more under stress ( ) YES ( ) NO
- Continues use when others have stopped ( ) YES ( ) NO
- Has lied about consumption ( ) YES ( ) NO
- Has tried to avoid others while using ( ) YES ( ) NO
- Has been drunk/high for several days at a time ( ) YES ( ) NO
- Neglects obligations when using ( ) YES ( ) NO
- Usually uses more than intended ( ) YES ( ) NO
- Needs to increase use to become intoxicated ( ) YES ( ) NO
- Has tried to hide consumption ( ) YES ( ) NO
- Sometimes uses before noon ( ) YES ( ) NO
- Cannot limit use once begun ( ) YES ( ) NO
- Failed to keep promises to reduce use ( ) YES ( ) NO

Describe attempts to stop
_____
_____
_____

Describe circumstances that usually lead to relapse
_____
_____
_____

Is client involved in AA/NA? ( ) YES ( ) NO

13. CLIENT REQUESTS, GOALS, EXPECTATIONS

_____
_____
_____
_____

14. CLINICAL SUMMARY (Pull together information you have collected and summarize, identifying possible relationships, conditions and causes that may have lead to current situation.)

_____
_____
_____
_____
_____
_____

15. IMPRESSIONS

_____
_____
_____
_____

16. RECOMMENDATIONS

_____
_____
_____
_____

17. DIAGNOSTIC IMPRESSION

Axis I   _____
Axis II _____
Axis III _____
Axis IV _____
Axis V   _____

Case manager signature   Date

Peer Support Services Referral Form

Peer support is a therapeutic system based on self-help founded on the principles of respect, shared responsibilities, and mutual agreements between peers.

GENERAL DEMOGRAPHICS:	
Name _____	Date _____
Agency Number _____	SSN _____
Date of Birth _____	Gender: ☐ Male ☐ Female
Address _____	Phone Number _____
_____	Phone Number _____
Case Manager _____	

CURRENT LIVING STATUS ☐ Lives independently ☐ Lives with Family ☐ Lives with others
  ☐ Other

HEALTH Serious health condition _____ Physician's name _____ Phone _____

CRITERIA
Individual must meet all of the following criteria in order to be eligible for Peer Support Services

( ) 18 years of age or older with one or more serious challenges to recovery

( ) Has a moderate to severe functional impairment that interferes with or limits role performance in at least one of the following areas

( ) Educational ( ) Social ( ) Vocational ( ) Self-maintenance

( ) Individual agrees to Peer Support Services

REASON FOR REFERRAL
_____
_____
_____

REFERRAL SOURCE
_____ Phone _____
Peer signature _____ Date _____
☐ Accepted ☐ Not accepted Reason _____
_____

Wildwood Case Management Unit
Peer Support Mutual Agreements, Outcome Report, and Renewal

Peer Name _____	Agency Number _____
Certified Peer Specialist _____	_____
Date of Original Agreement _____	Review Due by _____
Review Completed _____	Next Review Date _____

Domain: ☐ Educational ☐ Social ☐ Vocational ☐ Self-maintenance

Overall goal for a _____ month period _____

_____

Objectives (Action steps toward goal)

Action	Target Date	Person Responsible

Certified Peer Specialists Role _____

_____

Progress Made/Obstacles encountered

_____

_____

_____

Domain: ☐ Educational ☐ Social ☐ Vocational ☐ Self-maintenance

Overall goal for a _____ month period _____

_____

Objectives (Action steps toward goal)

Action	Target Date	Person Responsible

Certified Peer Specialists Role _____

_____

Progress Made/Obstacles encountered

_____

_____

_____

Domain: ☐ Educational ☐ Social ☐ Vocational ☐ Self-maintenance

Overall goal for a _____ month period _____

_____

Objectives (Action steps toward goal)

Action	Target Date	Person Responsible

Certified Peer Specialists Role _____

_____

Progress Made/Obstacles encountered

_____

_____

_____

Domain: ☐ Educational ☐ Social ☐ Vocational ☐ Self-maintenance

Overall goal for a _____ month period _____

_____

Objectives (Action steps toward goal)

Action	Target Date	Person Responsible

Certified Peer Specialists Role _____

_____

Progress Made/Obstacles encountered

_____
_____
_____

Domain: ☐ Educational ☐ Social ☐ Vocational ☐ Self-maintenance

Overall goal for a _____ month period _____

_____

Objectives (Action steps toward goal)

Action	Target Date	Person Responsible

Certified Peer Specialists Role _____

_____

Progress Made/Obstacles encountered

_____
_____
_____

Signatures and Agreement with Plan and Review/New Goals Developed

Plan _____ Date _____ Review _____ Date _____
    Consumer _____
    Certified Peer Specialist _____
    Practitioner/case manager _____

Plan _____ Date _____ Review _____ Date _____
    Consumer _____
    Certified Peer Specialist _____
    Practitioner/case manager _____

Plan _____ Date _____ Review _____ Date _____
    Consumer _____
    Certified Peer Specialist _____
    Practitioner/case manager _____

Plan _____ Date _____ Review _____ Date _____
    Consumer _____
    Certified Peer Specialist _____
    Practitioner/case manager _____

Plan _____ Date _____ Review _____ Date _____
    Consumer _____
    Certified Peer Specialist _____
    Practitioner/case manager _____

Plan _____ Date _____ Review _____ Date _____
    Consumer _____
    Certified Peer Specialist _____
    Practitioner/case manager _____

Plan _____ Date _____ Review _____ Date _____
    Consumer _____
    Certified Peer Specialist _____
    Practitioner/case manager _____

Wildwood Case Management Unit
Planning Conference Notes

Client _____ Date of conference _____

PRESENTING PROBLEM

_____
_____
_____
_____
_____

HOW CLIENT PRESENTED IN INTERVIEW

_____
_____
_____
_____
_____

CLIENT'S EXPRESSED GOALS, EXPECTATIONS, REQUESTED SERVICES

_____
_____
_____
_____
_____

ADDITIONAL RELEVANT INFORMATION

_____
_____
_____
_____

IMPRESSIONS AND RECOMMENDATIONS

_____
_____
_____
_____
_____

Treatment or Goal Plan

CLIENT _____ # _____ Next of Kin _____ Review Date _____
Initial plan [ ]   Updated plan [ ]   Date _____
Developed with _____
Level of case management _____   Case Manager _____

Provisional DX: Axis I _____ Axis II _____
Axis III _____ Axis IV _____ Axis V _____
Secondary diagnosis: Axis I _____ Axis II _____

TYPE	STRENGTH/NEED	GOAL(S)	COMMENTS	REFERRAL
INCOME/FINANCIAL SITUATION	STRENGTH/ NEED			
HOUSING/LIVING ARRANGEMENT	STRENGTH/ NEED			
VOCATIONAL	STRENGTH/ NEED			
EDUCATIONAL	STRENGTH/ NEED			
TRANSPORTATION	STRENGTH/ NEED			
MEDICAL	STRENGTH/ NEED			

TYPE	STRENGTH/NEED	GOAL(S)	COMMENTS	REFERRAL
ACTIVITIES OF DAILY LIVING	STRENGTH/ NEED			
LEGAL	STRENGTH/ NEED			
RECREATION & LEISURE TIME	STRENGTH/ NEED			
MENTAL HEALTH	STRENGTH/ NEED			
SUBSTANCE ABUSE	STRENGTH/ NEED			
FAMILY RELATIONSHIPS	STRENGTH/ NEED			
SOCIAL SUPPORTS	STRENGTH/ NEED			
OTHER	STRENGTH/ NEED			

Case Manager Signature   Date   Supervisor's Signature   Date

Wildwood Case Management Unit
Referral Notification Form

Client _____ # _____

Address _____

Home phone _____ Work phone _____ Date of referral _____

_____

Axis I _____
Axis II _____
Axis III _____
Axis IV _____
Axis V _____

_____

Provider _____

Type of service _____

For the purpose of _____

_____

_____

_____

_____

_____

_____

_____

_____

Review Date _____ Target date _____

Referring Case Manager _____

_____

Wildwood Case Management Unit
Contact Notes

Client _____ Agency# _____

Wildwood Case Management Unit
Contact Notes: Children's Case Management Services

Client _____ DOB _____ Agency # _____

Wildwood Case Management Unit
Discharge Summary

Name _____ Date of birth _____

Date of admission _____ Date of discharge _____

DIAGNOSIS ON ADMISSION:

Axis I _____

Axis II _____

Axis III _____

Axis IV _____

Axis V _____

MEDICATION:

REASON FOR DISCHARGE:

PRESENTING PROBLEM:

GOALS:

PROGRESS:

ADDITIONAL ISSUES NOT ADDRESSED:

IMPRESSIONS AND RECOMMENDATIONS:

PREPARED BY
_____
CASE MANAGER

Appendix B

Work Samples

Examples of Progress Notes or Contact Notes

1/5/09 (Office Visit) Clementine came in today to discuss her medications. After her last hospitalization she has been concerned about running out of medications. She was given a county prescription signed by Dr. Horace Merkle. Clementine seemed bright and eager to return to work. She will call next week after her first day at work.

4/9/09 (Phone Contact) Larry called today stating he was intoxicated and requesting CM's help. He stated he had been drinking for 2 days since his boss where he works gave him a bad evaluation he feels he did not deserve. Larry states that since rehab he has worked hard to reverse his work record at the plant. He sounded depressed and was tearful at times. CM will visit the home this afternoon.

4/9/09 (Home Visit) CM went to Larry's residence today after he called sounding intoxicated and requesting assistance. He and his wife were home and both expressed anger over the evaluation Larry received and concern over the fact that it led to renewed drinking on Larry's part. CM learned that Larry has not gone to AA meetings or outpatient treatment since he was discharged from inpatient rehabilitation. CM offered 3 days of inpatient detox followed by a meeting to decide what would be the best course of action regarding Larry's job. Larry agreed to this plan and arrangements were made at Madison Detoxification Center. Client seemed relieved to have a plan and resigned to the need for further treatment. Larry will come into the office when discharged.

4/13/09 (Office Visit) Larry and his wife came to the office today to decide how Larry should work on both his employment situation and his treatment. After listening to Larry's concerns with his present position and his concerns about relapse, he and CM worked out a plan for Larry to meet with his boss to better understand how he can improve in his present position. In addition, Larry was referred at his request to Madison's outpatient rehabilitation program.

Larry appeared more confident today and seemed eager to develop a plan. Larry will call after he makes an appointment to meet with his boss.

8/3/09 (Site Visit) CM visited Marvel at the sheltered workshop where she works. Marvel sat in on a meeting with CM and her worker at the workshop. She seemed to enjoy her work at the workshop and to relate well to her worker, Karen Pillsbury. Karen stated that Marvel works hard and is careful about her work. During the visit Marvel took CM to see her workstation and introduced CM to her friends. CM requested that both Marvel and her worker call if they need anything. It was agreed that this placement is working well for Marvel and that she seems to have developed more of a social life as a result. CM will make another follow-up visit in 3 months.

Dating Your Forms

Students often ask about dates for their forms. Below is an outline for dating forms.

Type of Form	Example	Description
Initial Referral or Inquiry Form	The form was filled out March 6, 2007. The disposition is for March 12, the verification letter went out on March 6 after the client called in.	Give the date the form is filled out/the inquiry was received. Disposition would have the date the client is coming in to be seen the first time. Date this within 2 weeks of the date of inquiry. Verification sent should have the date it went out and that should be within the first few days after the inquiry.
Verification Letter	March 12	The date it is sent should be the same date you said it was sent on your Inquiry form.
Release of Information Form	The client comes in March 12 so a few days later you send for information.	These are sent after meeting with the client the first time and the client signed the forms on the date of the first interview. You presumably signed it on that date as well.
Treatment or Goal Plan	The planning conference was March 16th, so date the plan for March 16th or later. Most review dates are 6 months later, but you might want yours sooner.	Give the date the plan was developed after the first interview and the Treatment Planning Conference. Review date is the general date the agency will remind you to check on this plan again. Make that 6 months later.
Referral Form	The plan is in order and you refer the client out on a date soon after the 16th. Decide how long you want the treatment to continue and give that as the target date. Make your review date halfway between March 16th and the target date.	The top date is the date you are filling out the referral form after the service plan is decided. The target date can be as far ahead as you feel is reasonable for the goals to be achieved. The review date is a date for you to check on this particular service to see how well it is going, generally about halfway to the target date.
Contact Notes	Give the notes dates that follow March 16th.	These dates can begin with the second contact with the client to go over the plan developed. Your initial inquiry is on the Inquiry Form. and your First Interview is documented in the social history and the assessment form.

Termination	Give the date well after the March 16th date so that the person has had time to go through the treatment and services you authorized.	Date of the final interview would be well after you opened the case.
		The letter sent after that interview should be dated for a day or two after the final interview.

Sample Cases with Service Plans

Beverly

Beverly is a second-grade teacher whose children had become increasingly unruly. The principal reported that on a recent visit to the classroom, children were jumping on the desks and chasing each other around the room. Beverly had been a good teacher for several years, and the situation in her classroom had not existed in former years. To the principal, Beverly looked exhausted and unable to organize her thoughts. She appeared unconcerned about the children's misbehavior and equally unable to handle it. The principal suggested a leave of absence, and a substitute took over Beverly's classroom. Beverly came into your office seeking help with a problem with marijuana. She reported that she started smoking marijuana at age 14 and had been smoking it all her life. She noticed, however, as the years went by that she became less and less motivated to do anything. On the other hand, she doesn't feel she can get through the day without using marijuana.

Here is Beverly's service plan:

1. Weekly individual and group counseling to gain an understanding of the addiction process, identify supports for marijuana use, and develop appropriate coping skills to deal with relapse situations.
2. Weekly drug tests.
3. Attendance at least three 12-step meetings weekly.

Hal

Hal has been working for a trucking company for years as a loader on the dock. He is divorced and has minimal contact with his three children. At a party about 4 years ago someone gave him some meth to try. From then on he occasionally found more meth and was able to take it, gradually increasing his use of the drug. Hal is brought in by a coworker who tells you that Hal "hasn't been right for months." The coworker went to Hal's home after Hal missed a week of work and failed to call in to the company. The company tried unsuccessfully to reach Hal, and when they couldn't, the coworker went to Hal's home and found Hal had chills and was vomiting. When the coworker suggested that Hal go to the emergency room, Hal said he wanted to go to a substance abuse clinic instead. The coworker reports that Hal has been losing weight, "but there's so much to do at work I just noticed it—didn't say nothing though." He goes on to tell you that Hal stopped "hanging around with us after work and, you know, his work got behind. We covered for him some, and then he disappeared last week." Hal seems to be confused and is showing signs of moderate confusion.

Here is Hal's service plan:

1. Enter detox for 3 to 5 days stat.
2. Complete inpatient drug and alcohol treatment with group counseling, lectures on addiction process, recovery tools, and relapse process.
3. Attend 12-step meetings.
4. Possible halfway house referral.

Marrietta

Marrietta was in an abusive relationship over an 11-year period. Recently she was hospitalized with severe injuries following another domestic dispute in her home with her husband. Husband has been jailed and cannot make bail. Marrietta will not be discharged from the hospital for another 3 or 4 days. The worker from a domestic violence program comes to the hospital to meet with Marrietta to plan what will happen following her discharge from the hospital. Marrietta is adamant that she does not want to return to her home and the relationship with her husband. However, she fears that if she leaves she will be in even greater danger. She asks the worker to help her leave the relationship and help her remain safe. She is against getting a Protection from Abuse Order as she feels this will make her husband even angrier when he comes out of jail.

Here is Marrietta's service plan:

1. Discharge to her sister's home temporarily.
2. Complete 12 sessions in support group for survivors of domestic violence.
3. Evaluation of housing situation to determine whether shelter or new housing is required.
4. Legal support from attorney and worker in the program.

Angelina

Angelina is an 82-year-old grandmother of eight and a mother of four children. A widow, she has been living alone successfully for a number of years, but recently she has seemed confused and agitated. She is irritated with her children who try to help her, and her daughter reports that she has gone into the home and found her mother "almost normal" one time and regressed several hours later. The daughter has accompanied her mother to your office and gives the following history: Her mother has been active in her community and lived alone since her husband died 10 years ago. She is currently on medications for high blood pressure, but other than that she has no other health problems. In the office she appears to be sweating profusely and seems agitated and irritable.

Here is Angelina's service plan:

Angelina's Strengths	Angelina's Needs	Angelina's Service Plan
• Financial stability	• Medical reevaluation	• Joseph Eberly Medical Center for complete gerontology workup
• Owns home	• Psychiatric evaluation	• Hargrave home health services for in-home care
• Drives and has friends who drive for her	• Neurological evaluation	• CM to work out visitation among family members for next 2 weeks
• Moderately good health	• Temporary assistance in her home	• Plan to be reviewed in 2 weeks
• Can manage activities of daily living		
• Belongs to a number of organizations and her church		
• No substance abuse problems		
• Strong family relationships		
• Good friends		

Appendix C

Grading the Final Files

If you are turning in a file to your instructor on a hypothetical client, use this rubric to check yourself to be sure your work is in order.

The File	Is the file in order? Is the name on the tab? Is there a number on the tab? Is the folder clean?
Face Sheet	Does the personal information match? Are the appropriate boxes filled in? Is it signed?
New Referral and Inquiry	Is parent or spouse circled? Is N/A in appropriate places? Does the chief complaint adequately capture the reason the client called today? Is the narrative organized? Does it state how the client seemed? Do referrals go to the places mentioned in the file?
Verification Letter	Is the letter dated? Is there a name after Dear . . . ? Is the letter signed? Is the signature between Sincerely and Case manager?
Brief Social History	Is presenting problem fully and concisely described? Is pertinent background to the presenting problem provided? Are case manager's impressions and recommendations included? Are subheadings used?

Assessment Form	Are interviewer comment spaces used appropriately? Is the form in order and stapled? Does the assessment fit the presenting problem?
Release of Information	Were appropriate documents sent for and recorded? Is the form filled out correctly? Is the authorized signature the correct one? Are there witness signatures?
Service or Treatment Plan	Are goals in the goals column, comments in the comments column, and so forth? Is the diagnosis correct? Are all five axes filled out? Were services consolidated in one or two places?
Referrals	Are they grammatically correct? Is the type of service the right one for this case? Are all five axes filled out? Are review and the target dates entered correctly?
Goals and Objectives	Are the goals and objectives doable for this client? Are they written properly? That is, are goals lettered and objectives numbered? Do goals and objectives meet the "See Billy Test"? Are the goals and objectives written up in a letter on a letterhead from the other agency? Did the other agency person sign the letter?
Case Notes	Is every case note dated? Is every case note labeled? Is every case note signed? Is there evidence that the case manager collaborated with the client? Is there evidence of client agreement? Does each note have all four parts? Are there at least 12 notes? Is information about how the client seemed, not just how the client says he feels, included in each note?
Termination Letter	Does the letter match the case note for the final interview? Were client's questions answered? Does the letter summarize major points discussed in the termination meeting? Is the client invited to contact the agency again in the future should the need arise?
Termination or Discharge Summary	Are all the headings addressed? Are the impressions and recommendations well written? Do impressions and recommendations match where the client is now?
General	Is written work free of spelling errors? Is written work free of grammatical errors? Are headings in bold? Are similar items stapled together (pages in the social history; all the release forms)? Do all the dates fall as they should? Is there a believable chronological progression? Is colored paper used for any of the forms?

	Is professional language used throughout (not "some guy," but "some man"; not "all shook up," but "anxious or agitated")? Are descriptions specific rather than generalities (not "gives mother a hard time," but "does not conform to rules mother has set for her"; not "she's been drinking," but "she began to drink heavily on Saturday and was still drinking this morning")? Are all diagnoses numerical and also written out? Is everything signed and dated where required? Is handwriting legible?

References

American Psychiatric Association. (1982). *Desk reference to the diagnostic criteria from DSM-III*. Washington, DC: Author.

American Psychiatric Association. (1987). *Diagnostic and statistical manual of mental disorders: DSM-III-R* (3rd ed., rev.). Washington, DC: Author.

American Psychiatric Association. (1994). *Diagnostic and statistical manual of mental disorders: DSM-IV* (4th ed.). Washington, DC: Author.

American Psychiatric Association. (2000). *Diagnostic and statistical manual of mental disorders: DSM-IV-TR* (4th ed., text rev.). Washington, DC: Author.

Bednar, R. L., Bednar, S. C., Lambert, M. J., & Waite, D. R. (1991). In G. Corey, M. S. Corey, & P. Callanan (Eds.), *Issues and ethics in the helping professions*. Pacific Grove, CA: Brooks/Cole.

Beisser, A. (1970). In Fagan & Shepherd, *Gestalt therapy now*. Harper Colophon.

Burns, D. D. (1980). *Feeling good: The new mood therapy*. New York: William Morrow.

Caudill, O. B. (1996, October). Warning signs. *The California Psychologist*.

Codes of ethics for the helping professions, 2nd ed. (2004). Belmont, CA: Brooks/Cole.

Diclemente, C. C., & Valesquez, M. M. (2002). Motivational interviewing and the stages of change. In W. R. Miller & S. Rollnick, *Motivational interviewing* (pp. 201–216). New York: Guilford Press.

Dinkmoyer, D., & Losoncy, L. E. (1980). *The encouragement book: Becoming a positive person*. Englewood Cliffs, NJ: Prentice-Hall.

Goldman, A. R. (1990). Special focus on basic rules of writing treatment goals and objectives. *Accreditation and Certification, 4*(3), 1–9.

Gordon, T. (1970). *Parent effectiveness training: The tested way to raise responsible children*. New York: David Mackay.

Gudykunst, W. B., & Kim, Y. Y. (1997). *Communicating with strangers: An approach to intercultural communication* (3rd ed.). New York: McGraw-Hill.

Jackson, S. W. (1992). The listening healer in the history of psychological healing. *American Journal of Psychiatry, 149*(12), 1623–1632.

Johnson, L. C., & Yanca, S. J. (2007). *Social work practice: A generalist approach* (9th ed.). Boston: Allyn & Bacon.

Karpman, S. (1968). Fairy tales and script drama analysis. *Transactional Analysis Bulletin, 7*(26), 39–43.

LaBruzza, A. L. (1994). *Using DSM-IV: A clinician's guide to psychiatric diagnosis*. Northvale, NJ: Jason Aronson.

Lukas, S. (1993). *Where to start and what to ask: An assessment handbook*. New York: Norton.

Miley, K. K., O'melia, M., & Dubois, B. (2007). *Generalist social work practice: An empowering approach* (5th ed.). Boston, MA: Allyn & Bacon.

Miller, R. M., & Rollnick, S. (2002). *Motivational interviewing: Preparing people for change*. New York: Guilford Press.

National Association of State Mental Health Program Directors. (2006). *Technical report on mortality and morbidity.* Washington, DC: Author.

Siegel, M. (1979). In G. Corey, M. S. Corey, & P. Callanan (Eds.), *Issues and ethics in the helping professions.* Pacific Grove, CA: Brooks/Cole.

Stadler, H. A. (1990). Confidentiality. In B. Herlihy & L. B. Golden (Eds.), *AACD ethical standards casebook* (4th ed., p. 102). Alexandria, VA: American Association for Counseling and Development.

Stephan, W. (1985). Intragroup relations. In G. Lindzey & E. Aronson (Eds.), *Handbook of social psychology* (Vol. 2, 3rd ed.). New York: Random House.

Summers, N. (2002). *Fundamentals for practice with high risk populations.* Pacific Grove, CA: Brooks/Cole.

Tarasoff v. Regents of University of California, 551 P.2d 334 (Cal. Sup. Ct. 1976).

Three Rivers Center for Independent Living. (n.d.). *Language references.* Pittsburgh, PA.

Weiner, I. B. (1975). *Principles of psychotherapy.* New York: Wiley.

Index

A

Accessing the file, 17
Adversarial, 217, 222
Advice, 217–218
Advocacy, 49
Agencies, 44, 346, 386, 388
  provider, 55–57, 386, 391
Ambivalence, 214, 216, 218, 219, 333, 334, 335
American Psychiatric Association, 276
Anger, 144, 197
  common reasons for, 197–198
  disarming, 144, 201–203
  managing angry outburst, 205–206
  not taking personally, 199–200
  why disarm, 198–199
Appearance, 293, 295, 362
Assessment, 42–43, 168, 291, 313, 339, 349,
  forms, 249, 266–267, 349, 362
  See also Impressions and Recommendations
Attitudes, 105
  basic, 106–108
  changing, 99–100
  client attitude, 293, 295

B

Barriers, 342
Basic helping attitudes, 106–108
  genuineness and, 167
  warmth and, 160
Behavior, 296
Beisser, Arnold R., 158, 327
Boundaries, 105, 114, 115–116
Brainstorming, 217
Burns, David, 201

C

Case management, 337, 408
  levels of, 350–351
Case management unit, 337, 391, 398
Case manager, 391
  as effective tool, 415
  impaired, 28–29
  owns the problem, 127
  as resource, 127
  self-care, 417–421
  traps, 219
CASSP *see* Child and Adolescent Service Program
Change, stages of, 330–331
Change talk, 212
Charity Organization Society, 40
Charts, 359
  See also record
Children's panel, 349
Clark, Elizabeth, 62
Client, 398
  arguing with
  as separate person, 112–113
  discouraged, 109
  expectations, 246–247
  family of, 338
  first meeting, 244
  gift giving by, 3–4
  mistakes, 18
  physical health, 324
  progress, 250
  protecting, 25
  reflects on you, 113
  relationships with, 4–5, 209
  reluctance, 328
  rights, 9, 10
  self-esteem, 26–27
  stealing from, 26–27
  strengths, 39, 41, 43, 341–342
  trapping, 216–217
  vulnerable, 24

Cognitive functioning, 294, 300
Collaboration, 145–146, 186, 199, 202, 209, 210, 217, 219, 221, 222, 321, 325–326, 330, 335, 354, 389, 392
Communication, 89–92, 92, 152
  barriers to, 136, 152
  see also responses
  roadblocks to, 136
  scripts, 90–91
  skills that facilitate, 211–216
  useful, 140–146
  with new clients, 141
Confidence, 215
Confidentiality, 384
Conflict, 99
Confrontation, 181, 217
  collaterals and, 189
  discrepancies and, 182
  See also I-messages
  overbearing, 189, 191
  reasons to use, 183
  rules for, 184–188
  when to use, 182
Contact notes, 365, 366–367
  labeling, 367
Countertransference, 4, 115
Crisis, 387
Cultural competence, 83–102
  we-versus-them attitude, 86
  with strangers, 86–87
Cultural relativism, 99
Culture, 98–99
Cultures, 84–85, 102
  anxiety about, 87
  collectivistic, 92–94, 96–97
  dimensions of, 92–93
  horizontal, 94
  individualistic, 92–94, 96–97
  vertical, 94

D

Developmental transitions, 74, 106
Diagnostic and Statistical Manual
  Of Mental Disorders,
  273–275, 282, 286
  axes, 279
  axis I, 279–280, 282, 283, 286
  axis II, 280–281, 282, 283, 286
  axis III, 281–282
  axis IV, 282–283
  axis V, 283
  background, 275–298
  cautions, 274
  coding with, 284
  See also diagnosis
  DSM III, 277, 278
  DSM IV, 278
  DSM IV TR, 278, 340
  Handbook, 350
  how to use, 278–279
  language, 274, 277
  NOS *see* diagnosis
  V codes, 283
Diagnosis, 321, 274–275,
  349, 350, 354
  deferred, 286
  making, 279
  modifiers, 284–285
  monothetic, 278
  multi-axial, 279–280
  not otherwise specified, 286
  polythetic, 278
  provisional, 285
  subtypes, 284
  unspecified, 286
Diagnostic labeling, 21–22
Disabilites, 370
Discharge summary, 410–413
Discouragement, 326
Discrepancies, 212–213
Dix, Dorothea, 275
Documentation, 365, 410
  balanced, 373
  finishing touches for, 368–369
  government requirements for,
    371, 372
  service monitoring, 367–368
  see also disabilites
Dual relationships, 2–4, 30

E

Ecological model, 69–77
  See also developmental
    Transitions
Emotions, 294, 299–300
Empathy, 107–108, 152, 328

Encouragement, 327
  guidelines for, 328–329
  and recovery, 326
Environment, 294, 309,
Ethical principles, 1
  to colleagues, 28–29
  competence and, 27–28
  responsibilities for, 23–24
  to the profession, 28–29
  violations of
Ethnocentrism, 98
Everyday Lives, 62
Exploitation, 309

F

Face sheet, 359, 362
Feedback, 146
Final interview, 408–409
First Interview
  note-taking during, 245
  preparing for, 242
  your office for, 243–244
  your role in, 241–242
  wrapping up, 247
Folk supports, 346
Follow-up, 388

G

Global assessment of
  functioning, 283
Goals, 337, 339, 385, 386, 398
  finishing touches for, 396
  numbering system for, 397
  objectives for, 391, 394
  writing, 393
Goal plan, 343–346
Greisinger, Wilhelm, 276

H

Health Insurance Portability and
  Accountability Act, 15–16,
  17, 384
Homocidality, 294, 307–308
Human service directory, 350

I

I-messages, 142–143, 183–184, 190
Impressions and recommenda-
  tions, 257, 264, 265
Impulse control, 294, 307–398
Information, 245, 246, 313–314
  forms for, 314–317
  HIV/AIDs and, 315–316
  long term, 398

  short term, 398
  receiving, 318
  releasing, 11, 13–14, 15,
    16, 19, 313–314, 317
  sending for, 313
Informed consent, 10
Initial inquiries, 231
  guidelines for, 232
  form for, 232, 234–236, 237
Insight, 294
Intake, 249, 274, 275, 337
  brief, 262
  limited time for, 258, 262
Intelligence, 303
Intention to harm, 19
International Classification of
  Diseases, 278, 280
Interventions, 75–76, 77, 216,
  397–398
Involuntary commitment, 22

J

Jackson, Stanley W., 151
Judgment, 294
Judgmental, 108, 136

K

Kraeplin, Emil, 276

L

LaBruzza, Anthony, 275, 293
Linking, 48–49
Listening, 151–152, 160, 173

M

Managed care, 57–58
Mandated reporting, 21
Memory, 301
Mental Status Exam, 291, 257, 310
Meyer, Adolph, 276
Miller, R. M., 212, 218, 333
Monitoring, 49, 384, 385, 386
  purpose of, 384
Mood *see* emotions
Motivating clients, 9
Motivational interviewing, 210

N

National Association of Social
  Workers, 62
National Association of State Men-
  tal Health Directors, 324
Neurovegetative signs, 299

O

Observations, 292
One Flew Over the Cuckoo's Nest, 276
Outcomes, 392–393

P

Peer Support, 45, 326
Perception, 294
Perls, Fritz, 158, 327
Permission to share ideas, 188–189
Person in environment *see* ecological model
Person-in-situation *see* ecological model
Planning, 41, 44, –47, 321, 322
    changes to, 373
    continued, 47–48
    individualized, 40, 41, 42, 44, 323, 342, 346
    see also interventions
Praise, 146
Prejudice, 99
Presenting problem, 250, 251, 252, 293
President's New Freedom Commission on Mental Health, 62
Privacy, 14–15, 16, 126
Privileged communication, 18
Psychoanalysis, 276
Psychological testing, 291
Psychotropic medications, 362

Q

Questions, 142, 167, 173
    closed, 142, 168
    formula for, 171–172
    open, 142, 168–170, 250
    prying, 167
    tips for, 171
    uncomfortable, 170–171
    when important, 168
    why, 170
Quotations, 369

R

Record, 357, 365
Recovery, 322
    Support for, 324–326
Recovery Model, 59, 63, 391
Referrals, 30, 355, 357, 362, 385
Reflective listening, 152, 153, 167, 211, 220, 221
Resiliency Model, 59, 61
Resistance, 333
Resource coordination, 53
Resources, 44–45
    generic, 44–45
    community, 45
    informal, 47–48
Responses
    empathic, 152, 153
    good, 135
    poor, 135
    solutions and, 159
    to content, 152, 156–157
    to feelings, 152–156
Review date, 357, 358, 362
Rollnick, S., 212, 219

S

Schizophrenia, 295, 297, 298, 299, 305, 306
Self-determination, 17–18, 58–60, 61–62, 126, 212, 321, 324
Self-direction, 323
Service plan *see* treatment plan
Services, 313, 351
Siegal, M, 14
Social history, 247, 250, 251, 258, 339
    brief, 262
    details of, 257
    layout, 250
    on computer, 267
    who took, 258
Speech, 298
Stadler, H., 14
Stephan. W., 99–100
Stereotypes, 98, 102, 114, 115
Subcultures, 85
Substance Abuse and Mental Health Services Administration, 59
Summarizing, 218–219
Supervision, 12, 20, 25–26
Suicidality, 294, 307
Suicide, 387
Szasz, Thomas, 277

T

Tarasoff, 19
Tardive dyskenesia, 297
Target date, 357, 358, 362, 397
Termination, 407
    See also Discharge summary
    letter, 409
    reasons for, 407
    successful, 408
Third ear, 107
Thomas, Gordon, 136, 183
Thought, 294, 304–307
Transference, 4, 114
Treatment, 407
    Least restrictive, 22–23
    See also services
Treatment plan, 55, 58, 338, 346, 354, 362, 365
    creating, 340
Treatment Planning Conference, 340, 354, 357
    goals, 350
    preparing to present in, 351–352
    presenting in, 352
    follow-up to, 354–355
    what to bring, 350

U

Universal precautions, 316
U.S. Department of Health and Human Services, 59

V

Value conflicts, 5–8
    avoiding, 8
Values, 137, 171
Verification of appointment, 236
Veterans, 276, 282

W

Who owns the problem, 123, 126–128,